MW01073540

HOLMAN
New Testament Commentary

HOLMAN *New Testament* Commentary

I & II Corinthians

GENERAL EDITOR
Max Anders

AUTHOR
Richard L. Pratt, Jr.

**HOLMAN
REFERENCE**

Nashville, Tennessee

Holman New Testament Commentary
© 2000 Broadman & Holman Publishers
Nashville, Tennessee
All rights reserved

ISBN 0–80540—207–1

Unless otherwise stated all Scripture citation is from the HOLY BIBLE, NEW INTERNATIONAL VERSION®. Copyright © 1973, 1978, 1984 by International Bible Society. Used by permission of Zondervan Publishing House. All Rights Reserved. The "NIV" and "New International Version" trademarks are registered in the United States Patent and Trademark Office by International Bible Society. Use of either trademark requires the permission of International Bible Society.

1,2 Corinthians / Pratt, Richard
    p.   cm. — (Holman New Testament commentary)
Includes bibliographical references.
ISBN 0–80540-207–1 (alk. paper)
    1. Bible. N.T. 1,2 Corinthians—Commentaries.   2. Bible. N.T. 1,2 Corinthians—
    Commentaries. I. Title.   II. Title: 1,2 Corinthians.   III. Series
226.6'07—dc21   98–39365
                                                                           CIP

6 7 8 9   08 07 06 05
EB

Dedicated to

Ra McLaughlin

whose friendship and

help with this

commentary

has meant so much

to me.

Richard Pratt

July 2000

Contents

Contents

Editorial Preface

Today's church hungers for Bible teaching, and Bible teachers hunger for resources to guide them in teaching God's Word. The Holman New Testament Commentary provides the church with the food to feed the spiritually hungry in an easily digestible format. The result: new spiritual vitality that the church can readily use.

Bible teaching should result in new interest in the Scriptures, expanded Bible knowledge, discovery of specific scriptural principles, relevant applications, and exciting living. The unique format of the Holman New Testament Commentary includes sections to achieve these results for every New Testament book.

Opening quotations from some of the church's best writers lead to an introductory illustration and discussion that draw individuals and study groups into the Word of God. "In a Nutshell" summarizes the content and teaching of the chapter. Verse-by-verse commentary answers the church's questions rather than raising issues scholars usually admit they cannot adequately solve. Bible principles and specific contemporary applications encourage students to move from Bible to contemporary times. A specific modern illustration then ties application vividly to present life. A brief prayer aids the student to commit his or her daily life to the principles and applications found in the Bible chapter being studied. For those still hungry for more, "Deeper Discoveries" take the student into a more personal, deeper study of the words, phrases, and themes of God's Word. Finally, a teaching outline provides transitional statements and conclusions along with an outline to assist the teacher in group Bible studies.

It is the editors' prayer that this new resource for local church Bible teaching will enrich the ministry of group, as well as individual, Bible study, and that it will lead God's people to truly be people of the Book, living out what God calls us to be.

Holman Old Testament Commentary Contributors

Vol. 1, Genesis
ISBN 0-8054-9461-8
Kenneth O. Gangel and
Stephen J. Bramer

Vol. 2, Exodus, Leviticus, Numbers
ISBN 0-8054-9462-6
Glen Martin

Vol. 3, Deuteronomy
ISBN 0-8054-9463-4
Doug McIntosh

Vol. 4, Joshua
ISBN 0-8054-9464-2
Kenneth O. Gangel

Vol. 5, Judges, Ruth
ISBN 0-8054-9465-0
W. Gary Phillips

Vol. 6, 1 & 2 Samuel
ISBN 0-8054-9466-9
Stephen Andrews

Vol. 7, 1 & 2 Kings
ISBN 0-8054-9467-7
Gary Inrig

Vol. 8, 1 & 2 Chronicles
ISBN 0-8054-9468-5
Winfried Corduan

Vol. 9, Ezra, Nehemiah, Esther
ISBN 0-8054-9469-3
Knute Larson and Kathy Dahlen

Vol. 10, Job
ISBN 0-8054-9470-7
Steven J. Lawson

Vol. 11, Psalms 1–75
ISBN 0-8054-9471-5
Steven J. Lawson

Vol. 12, Psalms 76–150
ISBN 0-8054-9481-2
Steven J. Lawson

Vol. 13, Proverbs
ISBN 0-8054-9472-3
Max Anders

Vol. 14, Ecclesiastes, Song of Songs
ISBN 0-8054-9482-0
David George Moore and Daniel L. Akin

Vol. 15, Isaiah
ISBN 0-8054-9473-1
Trent C. Butler

Vol. 16, Jeremiah, Lamentations
ISBN 0-8054-9474-X
Fred M. Wood and Ross McLaren

Vol. 17, Ezekiel
ISBN 0-8054-9475-8
Mark F. Rooker

Vol. 18, Daniel
ISBN 0-8054-9476-6
Kenneth O. Gangel

Vol. 19, Hosea, Joel, Amos, Obadiah, Jonah, Micah
ISBN 0-8054-9477-4
Trent C. Butler

Vol. 20, Nahum, Habakkuk, Zephaniah, Haggai, Zechariah, Malachi
ISBN 0-8054-9478-2
Stephen R. Miller

Holman New Testament
Commentary Contributors

Vol. 1, Matthew
ISBN 0-8054-0201-2
Stuart K. Weber

Vol. 2, Mark
ISBN 0-8054-0202-0
Rodney L. Cooper

Vol. 3, Luke
ISBN 0-8054-0203-9
Trent C. Butler

Vol. 4, John
ISBN 0-8054-0204-7
Kenneth O. Gangel

Vol. 5, Acts
ISBN 0-8054-0205-5
Kenneth O. Gangel

Vol. 6, Romans
ISBN 0-8054-0206-3
Kenneth Boa and William Kruidenier

Vol. 7, 1 & 2 Corinthians
ISBN 0-8054-0207-1
Richard L. Pratt Jr.

Vol. 8, Galatians, Ephesians, Philippians, Colossians
ISBN 0-8054-0208-X
Max Anders

Vol. 9, 1 & 2 Thessalonians, 1 & 2 Timothy, Titus, Philemon
ISBN 0-8054-0209-8
Knute Larson

Vol. 10, Hebrews, James
ISBN 0-8054-0211-X
Thomas D. Lea

Vol. 11, 1 & 2 Peter, 1, 2, 3 John, Jude
ISBN 0-8054-0210-1
David Walls & Max Anders

Vol. 12, Revelation
ISBN 0-8054-0212-8
Kendell H. Easley

Holman New Testament Commentary

Twelve volumes designed for Bible study and teaching to enrich the local church and God's people.

Series Editor	Max Anders
Managing Editors	Trent C. Butler & Steve Bond
Project Editor	Lloyd W. Mullens
Marketing Manager	Greg Webster
Product Manager	David Shepherd
Page Composition	TF Designs, Mt. Juliet, TN

Introduction to

1 Corinthians

LETTER PROFILE

- The letter was probably written about A.D. 54–56 from Ephesus during Paul's third missionary journey.
- Paul wrote to the church in the city of Corinth, the capital city of the Roman province of Achaia. Paul had planted this church during his second missionary journey only a few years earlier.
- The original audience in Corinth contained members from all levels of society, but consisted mostly of people who were neither rich, wise, nor of noble birth.
- The original audience had sat under the ministry of Paul, Apollos, and Peter.
- Subsequent to the ministries of Paul, Apollos, and Peter, the Corinthian church had begun to place improper value on worldly wisdom, including probably Greek philosophy.
- The letter is occasional, written both in response to reports Paul received about conditions in the Corinthian church, and in response to a letter Paul received from the Corinthian church.
- Paul wrote the letter to correct the problems he saw in the Corinthian church, although he also included praise for certain things the church was doing well.
- Literary form: epistle
- Doctrinal themes:
  - ➤ the nature of the church, and its implications,
  - ➤ the nature of believers' union with Christ, and its implications,
  - ➤ God's wisdom,
  - ➤ proper worship,
  - ➤ the Lord's Supper,
  - ➤ spiritual gifts, and
  - ➤ resurrection of the dead.

- Practical themes:
  - ➢ the importance of unity in the church,
  - ➢ proper valuations and roles of church leaders,
  - ➢ the importance of church discipline,
  - ➢ lawsuits,
  - ➢ prostitution,
  - ➢ marriage and divorce in light of famines,
  - ➢ Christian freedom and responsibility,
  - ➢ interaction with the secular world,
  - ➢ proper roles and honor in worship,
  - ➢ love, and
  - ➢ ministering to the physical needs of others.

AUTHOR PROFILE

- The apostle Paul wrote this letter.
- He was not one of the original twelve apostles.
- He had formerly been named Saul (Acts 13:9).
- He had formerly been a zealous Pharisee (Phil. 3:5).
- He had formerly persecuted the church (Acts 8:3; Gal. 1:14,23).
- He had been converted and appointed to his apostleship by direct encounter with the risen Christ on the road to Damascus (Acts 9:3–19).
- He was one of the church's earliest missionaries, and was especially commissioned to evangelize the Gentiles (Acts 9:15; Gal. 2:9).
- He planted churches all over the Mediterranean world.
- He authored more New Testament books than any other writer: Romans; 1 and 2 Corinthians; Galatians; Ephesians; Philippians; Colossians; 1 and 2 Thessalonians; 1 and 2 Timothy; Titus; Philemon.

1 Corinthians 1:1–17

Greetings and an Earnest Appeal

I. INTRODUCTION
"Hello Dear, We've Got a Big Problem"

II. COMMENTARY
A verse-by-verse explanation of this section.

III. CONCLUSION
In the Name of the Gospel

An overview of the principles and applications from this section.

IV. LIFE APPLICATION
Home Run

Melding the section to life.

V. PRAYER
Tying the section to life with God.

VI. DEEPER DISCOVERIES
Historical, geographical, and grammatical enrichment of the commentary.

VII. TEACHING OUTLINE
Suggested step-by-step group study of this section.

VIII. ISSUES FOR DISCUSSION
Zeroing the section in on daily life.

Quote

"*The* church of the apostolic days embraced all nations, and kindreds, and peoples, and tongues. There is no evidence in the New Testament for the diversification of distinct denominations, and anything tending to such diversification was condemned. The emphasis falls upon the oneness of faith and the oneness of the fellowship of the saints."

John Murray

1 Corinthians 1:1–17

IN A NUTSHELL

In these verses the apostle Paul gave sincere greetings to the believers in Corinth whom he loved dearly. But his heart was so heavily burdened by reports of troubles in the church that he appealed to them to change their ways.

Greetings and an Earnest Appeal

I. INTRODUCTION

"Hello Dear, We've Got a Big Problem"

*I*t had been another one of those days at the office. Ron hadn't stopped for a moment, not even for lunch. He'd been running all over town, trying to deal with this project and that project. At last, it was four o'clock— time to start thinking of home. *What's going on there? How are the kids? What's for supper? Maybe I should pick up something on the way home,* he thought to himself as he reached for the phone.

"Hello?" Mary answered.

"Hi! It's me. How have you been today?"

"Uh . . ." Mary hesitated.

At that moment Ron could hear a lot of noise in the background: hammers pounding, shouts of workers, radios . . . and was that a fire truck? . . . the police?

"Hello Dear, " Mary began again. "Um . . . We've got a big problem."

When we have not talked with someone we love for a while, we just hate to bring up problems right away. It is much nicer to enjoy one another first, and then bring up difficulties later. But sometimes troubles tower so tall that we have to bring them up in the very first moments.

Today the church has many problems. Some of them are small, and we can afford to take them in stride as we focus on other things. But the church also has some very large problems which it needs to address directly and immediately. One of these is disunity. We have thousands of denominations, and great disunity exists even within many of those denominations. In individual churches, we see strife over building programs and mission statements. People divide over minor theological issues, and even over personal incompatibility. Sometimes church politics cause factions within our ranks.

These are exactly the kinds of problems Paul encountered in Corinth. But unlike us, Paul saw the disunity caused by these problems as a terrible disaster. He was so worried about the divisions in Corinth that he barely got through saying "hello" before he launched into a rebuke against this gospel-opposing behavior.

Paul opened his letter to the Corinthians by declaring, "Hello, we've got a big problem."

II. COMMENTARY

Greetings and an Earnest Appeal

> **MAIN IDEA:** *Christians have been so blessed by God that divisions over trivial matters have no place among us.*

A Introduction (1:1–9)

> **SUPPORTING IDEA:** *God's gift of salvation had brought the Corinthians into a relationship with other believers; they were members of one body.*

1:1. Paul wrote with the authority of **an apostle** (one commissioned and sent) **of Christ Jesus**. He had been called **by the will of God**, so his words were to be received as God's own commands (Matt. 10:40; 1 Cor. 14:37). **Sosthenes**, a Jewish believer and resident of Corinth (Acts 18:17), may have served as Paul's secretary for this letter (1 Cor. 16:21).

1:2. Paul sent this letter to believers **in Corinth**, a Greek seaport and center of international commerce. The apostle's description of these Christians revealed his deep concern for them. First, he called them **the church of God**. The readers were not merely individuals. They constituted a church community that belonged to God. Only God's desires held sway over the life of this church. Second, the believers in this church had been **sanctified**, or set apart from the world, by virtue of their faith in Christ. Third, the Corinthian believers were called to pursue pure and holy lives. Fourth, they were called to holiness together with all believers everywhere. Holiness was not to be pursued simply by individuals, but by the entire church.

This opening address set the stage for Paul's central concern in this section: God's gift of salvation had brought the Corinthians into a relationship with other believers; they were members of one body (1 Cor. 10:17; 12:12–27).

1:3. Paul issued a standard greeting among Christians in his day. He expressed his hope that God would continue to bless his readers through Christ with his enabling **grace** and the experience of **peace**.

1:4. Before wrestling with a long list of problems in the Corinthian church, Paul mentioned several positive feelings and hopes. He affirmed that he was **always** sure to **thank God** for his readers, and explained why.

Paul first explained that the cause of his gratitude was the **grace**, or unmerited favor, the Corinthians had received **in Christ Jesus**. Some interpreters have also suggested that **grace** refers to the Corinthians' charismatic gifts. The phrase **in Christ** appears often in Paul's writings. It refers to his teaching that all who trust in Christ have been joined to him, participating in his death and resurrection. Those united to Christ die to the judgment of death and come alive to countless blessings of new life, sharing in Christ's inheritance (Rom 6:1–7; Gal 3:28–29; Eph. 1:3–14). By being united to Christ, believers draw their life from him (Gal. 2:20; cf. John 15:1–8; 17:22–23), and Christ represents them as righteous before the Father (Rom. 5:15–19; 1 Cor. 15:22).

1:5. Paul specified a number of blessings which the Corinthians had received. Their lives had been enriched with **speaking** and **knowledge**. Chapters 12–14 explain that Paul's readers greatly prized their spiritual gifts of revelation and knowledge. Although the apostle warned against the abuses of these gifts (1 Cor. 8:1–13; 13:1–2), he was also pleased that God had granted them these blessings.

1:6. Paul acknowledged the great privileges that God afforded the church at Corinth. Then he foreshadowed the argument he would pursue later in this chapter. He pointed out that the Corinthians' gifts confirmed the **testimony**, or witness, which he himself had given them. Paul's preaching of the gospel had been the conduit of their gifts of revelation and knowledge. As a result, the presence of spiritual gifts in the church **confirmed** the efficacy and truth of Paul's gospel message. This brief aside was important because the Corinthians took great pride in human wisdom. Yet, the gospel that had enriched their lives with these gifts was not based on human wisdom and pride, but on humility and spiritual wisdom.

1:7. Although the Corinthians longed for Christ to return in glory, their spiritual gifts equipped them to live lives of faith in the meantime. As Paul wrote in Ephesians 1:14, the Holy Spirit "is a deposit guaranteeing our inheritance until the redemption of those who are God's possession." The Spirit supplies believers with a host of blessings as they long for Christ's return.

Paul mentioned the return of Christ here to remind the Corinthians of the true nature of their condition. Many people in the Corinthian church thought they were more blessed with gifts than they actually were. For example, Paul wrote, "Already you have all you want! Already you have become rich! You have become kings—and that without us! How I wish that you really had become kings so that we might be kings with you!" (1 Cor. 4:8). He also had to remind them that their gifts were only temporary, partial manifestations of the blessings they would receive at Christ's return (1 Cor. 13:8–13). Paul probably mentioned Christ's return to remind them that they needed to stop being satisfied with the progress they had made. They needed to apply themselves to waiting **eagerly** for Christ's return.

1:8. The gifts of the Spirit displayed in Corinth gave Paul great confidence that God would keep them safe until the end of this age. **The day of our Lord Jesus Christ** is the fulfillment of Old Testament prophecies concerning the great "day of the LORD" (Amos 5:18–20; Joel 2:31). That day will bring judgment against the enemies of God and wondrous reward for God's people (Joel 3:14–21; 2 Pet. 3:10–13). Although Paul later warned the Corinthians that flagrant apostasy could prove their faith in vain (1 Cor. 9:27; 10:1–12), he fully expected them to be **blameless**, without guilt.

1:9. Paul's confidence in the Corinthians' future rested not on them, but on God's faithfulness both to them (1 Cor. 10:13) and to his Son (cf. John 10:29; Eph. 1:18; Heb. 2:13). God had called them **into fellowship with his Son** (cf. 1 Cor. 1:4), and **God . . . is faithful.** He will keep all who believe safe until the end. Paul did not place his confidence in the church as the Corinthians did, but in the church's God.

Paul pointed out that God had called the Corinthian church together into **fellowship with his Son.** He did this not only to assure them of their salvation, but also to remind them that the fellowship they shared with one another was in Christ. When they disrupted their fellowship with one another, they disrupted their **fellowship** with Christ.

After his brief greeting, Paul immediately turned his attention to one of the dominant problems in the Corinthian church. Instead of serving one another in harmony, Paul's readers had divided into factions, each of which thought itself superior in wisdom to the other segments of the church. This section first describes the problem, and then introduces two responses to it.

🅱 Paul's Appeal in Response to Church Divisions (1:10–12)

SUPPORTING IDEA: *Paul appealed to the Corinthians to heal the divisions that had developed in the church.*

1:10. The apostle began with a respectful but forceful appeal. In this verse and the next, he called his readers **brothers** to remind them of his intense familial affection for them.

Paul also revealed the intensity of his concern by appealing to his readers **in the name of our Lord Jesus Christ.** By so doing, Paul reminded them that the authority of Christ himself stood behind his exhortations.

The appeal divides into three parts. He asked the Corinthians to **agree with one another,** to eliminate **divisions,** and to **be perfectly united in mind and thought.** Each part says basically the same thing: the Corinthians needed to eliminate the divisions in their church. They needed to become like-minded with one another.

Paul did not desire unity at the expense of truth (see 11:18–19). Paul himself stood against others in the church when the central truths of the gospel were at stake (Gal. 2:5,11; 5:12). Here, he expressed plainly that Christian unity requires like-mindedness. The verses that follow reveal the beliefs which should have formed the center of agreement among the Corinthians.

On the other hand, Paul did not mean that unity implied uniformity on all matters. As he pointed out in several places, there is much room for disagreement and diverse opinions over secondary issues in the Christian church (Rom. 14:1–14; 2 Cor. 8:10).

1:11. Paul revealed the source of his concern for the unity of the Corinthian believers, whom he again called **brothers**. He had received information from members of **Chloe's household**. Scholars disagree about whether Chloe was a member of the Corinthian church. In any case, members of her household had informed Paul about some serious problems in the church. Paul had learned that there were **quarrels** within the church.

1:12. Paul got right to the heart of these quarrels: the church had divided into personality factions. It is possible that the use of the singular "I" as opposed to the plural "we" in this context indicates that these groups were not organized, solidified factions. The problem may have been much more individualistic.

Whatever the case, Paul identified four factious loyalties in the church at Corinth. First, some declared themselves followers of **Paul**. As much as this group may have fed the apostle's ego, he rejected its practice as inappropriate. Second, some followed **Apollos**, a teacher who came to Corinth after Paul (Acts 18:24–19:1). He was the subject of concern several times in this epistle (3:4–9,22; 4:6). Apparently, his following was substantial. Third, others followed **Cephas** (the apostle Peter) believing he had the greatest insights of all.

Finally, one group claimed to **follow Christ**. Although this claim sounds positive on the surface, it is likely that Paul included this group in his list because even they thought themselves superior to others because they refused to identify with a human leader. Boasting in Christ would have been fine (1 Cor. 1:31), but boasting in oneself for following Christ was sin (1 Cor. 1:29–30; 4:7). All of these groups or individuals took pride in the fact that they followed one leader or another.

It appears that a good number of the Corinthians also rejected Paul's authority to speak to matters of theological substance. This may help explain Paul's defense of his apostleship and authority in this letter (1 Cor. 1:1,17; 4:9; 9:1–2; 11:1; 14:37–38).

Ⅽ Divisions Are Contrary to Paul's Ministry (1:13–17)

SUPPORTING IDEA: *Paul declared that divisions in the church are contrary to the unity that exists in Christ's body.*

1:13. The apostle responded to the strife within the church by asking three questions to which he expected negative responses. First, he asked, **Is Christ divided?** The kinds of divisions in the Corinthian church could be justified only if Christ's own resurrected body had been dismembered.

Elsewhere, Paul described the church as the body of Christ, the community of those joined to him and to one another by faith (Rom. 12:3–5; Eph. 3:6). If Christ had been dismembered after his resurrection, the divisions within the church might have been theoretically acceptable. But since Christ remained whole, the church needed to do so as well.

Second, because some members of the Corinthian church identified themselves as the followers of Paul (1 Cor. 1:12), Paul asked if he himself had been **crucified** for the believers in Corinth. By this question he made it clear that to identify oneself as a follower of Paul was to insult the saving work of Christ. Paul was the servant and apostle of Corinth, but he was not their Savior.

Third, Paul asked if the Corinthians had been **baptized into the name of Paul**. The New Testament makes it plain that Christian baptism was performed in the name of the Trinity (Matt. 28:19). This formula was often abbreviated as baptism "in the name of Jesus" (Acts 2:38; 19:5). Even so, nowhere in the New Testament were believers baptized in the name of an apostle or church leader. The loyalties of believers in all ages must be directed toward Christ alone.

1:14–15. Paul breathed a sigh of relief that he had not baptized many people in Corinth. In his evangelistic work there, he had baptized **Crispus** (see Acts 18:8) **and Gaius** (see Rom. 16:23), but no others. These words do not suggest that Paul did not consider baptism important. Elsewhere Paul stressed the importance of baptism. It is the sign and seal of faith in Christ, demonstrating union with the Savior in his death and resurrection (Rom. 6:4). For this reason, evangelism normally included baptism. Even so, in this particular circumstance where believers aligned themselves against others as followers of Paul, he was relieved that he had not provided them with support for their divisive spirit by baptizing many of them.

1:16. Paul qualified his statement that he had only baptized Crispus and Gaius. In the process of writing these verses, he recalled that he had also baptized **the household of Stephanas** (see 1 Cor. 16:15). Stephanas himself may have reminded Paul of these baptisms as Paul dictated, since Stephanas was apparently with him (1 Cor. 16:17). Beyond this, however, the apostle confessed that he could not remember if he had baptized anyone else. This qualification indicates how intent the apostle was on not providing his opponents any grounds for objections to his argument.

1:17. This verse serves as a hinge in Paul's discussion. It closes his preceding discussion of baptism and transitions to his next topic. The conclusion to the previous matter amounts to an explanation that Christ did not send him **to baptize, but to preach the gospel.** It would appear that Paul followed the example of Jesus in this matter. Christ preached, and delegated baptism primarily to his disciples (John 4:1–2). Paul followed the same practice; he proclaimed the gospel and left baptism primarily to his converts, who supervised the ongoing life of the church.

The expression "preach the gospel" moved Paul's thoughts in a different but related direction. What was the nature of the gospel he preached? It was devoid of **words of human wisdom.** This phrase may be translated more literally, "wisdom of words." The idea is that his preaching did not rely on cleverness or eloquence. Paul distinguished himself from the Greek orators of his day who sought to persuade with impressive rhetoric and style. Paul insisted that his own preaching was simple and straightforward. He avoided great oratory because he did not want to distract from the message itself. His style of preaching was self-effacing, pointing to the source of salvation, Christ.

Paul was concerned that **the cross of Christ** not be emptied of its power when presented in preaching. The gospel message contradicts human wisdom, so that it cannot be mixed with the power of human wisdom and manipulative persuasion. For this reason, those in Corinth who tried to defend their faith and practices through human wisdom actually opposed the way of the gospel. The **power** of the **cross** was the "power of God for the salvation of everyone who believes" (Rom. 1:16). Salvation comes only from the atonement of Christ, purchased by his suffering on the cross. The recognition and reception of that power was Paul's chief concern as he proclaimed the gospel.

MAIN IDEA REVIEW: *Christians have been so blessed by God that divisions over trivial matters have no place among us.*

III. CONCLUSION

In the Name of the Gospel

It is hard to imagine, but Christians can actually find themselves doing things in the name of the gospel that are absolutely contrary to the gospel. Many Corinthian believers had fallen into such a predicament. They had aligned themselves against one another, using human wisdom and persuasive powers to support their divisive ways. Paul's response to this situation cut straight to the heart of the matter. To divide the church on the basis of human wisdom is to oppose the gospel of Christ. The true gospel does not rely on human wisdom, but on the power of God received through faith in the death and resurrection of Christ.

PRINCIPLES

- The church consists of all those who have been sanctified in Jesus Christ.

- Jesus Christ and God the Father will make sure that believers will persevere in salvation.
- The church owes loyalty to Jesus Christ.
- Divisions in the church are contrary to the gospel.

APPLICATIONS

- We should rejoice in the many blessings we receive from God in Christ.
- We must hold fast to the testimony of Jesus Christ.
- Because God is faithful, we should be confident that true believers persevere in salvation.
- We must not divide the church along lines of loyalty to human leaders.

IV. LIFE APPLICATION

Home Run

I saw something on a special news bulletin recently that caught me off guard. Mark McGwire, the first baseman for the St. Louis Cardinals, set a new major league baseball record for the most home runs in a single season. On the opposing team, the Chicago Cubs, was Sammy Sosa, a player who had almost as many home runs as Mark McGwire, and who was also a contender to break the same record. The two teams were opponents, and they both had leaders in home runs on their teams.

But when McGwire hit his record-breaking home run and ran the bases, everyone he passed on the other team either shook his hand and patted him on the back, or actually hugged him. If the teams had acted like the Corinthians, they would have used McGwire's new record as an occasion for division, not as a cause for mutual celebration.

Our lives and churches parallel the Corinthians in many ways. First, the church today is blessed in countless ways just as the Corinthians were. Second, the modern church is bonded together by the blessings we have received in Christ. Most of us do not value our brothers and sisters because we forget that we all need Christ and the power of his death and resurrection.

Because of the importance of this bond, we need to evaluate carefully the divisions that occur in our churches. Are we separating ourselves from those who deny the gospel of Christ? Or are we dividing and quarreling because of human pride? By keeping Christ central, we can avoid many of the factions that develop around persons and doctrinal issues. We can also stem the personal abuse that takes place and draw ourselves back to treating others as we would treat Christ himself.

V. PRAYER

Lord Jesus, you have given your followers so many mercies. We all depend solely on you for our life now and our eternal life to come. When we are tempted to quarrel with one another, do not allow us to fall prey to human wisdom and pride. Help us to stand for the truth of the gospel, but make us humble because of our total dependence on you. Amen.

VI. DEEPER DISCOVERIES

A. Corinth (1:2)

Corinth had a sordid history. Strabo claimed the city had one thousand temple prostitutes servicing the temple of Aphrodite on the Acrocorinth. Archaeologists have discovered many clay models of human genitalia offered to Asclepius, the god of healing, presumably to petition him to heal venereal disease. But that perverse city was destroyed by Rome in 146 B.C.

The Corinth Paul knew had been rebuilt on the site of the ancient city by the Roman emperor Julius Caesar in 44 B.C. It was populated largely by freemen whose status was barely above that of slave. It was a center for international trade, attracting people from all over the world. It followed Roman laws and culture and Greek philosophy and art.

Corinth's religious composition varied greatly, including worship of the Roman and Greek gods, the mystery cults from Asia and Egypt, and Judaism. Because of its commercial strength, the city possessed wealth. These riches brought all kinds of people to populate the area: the educated and sophisticated; people seeking their fortunes; prostitutes and criminals. The Corinthian church itself contained people who had been sexually immoral, idolaters, adulterers, male prostitutes, homosexuals offenders, thieves, greedy, drunkards, slanderers, and swindlers (see 6:9–11). Not many were "wise by human standards," "influential," or "of noble birth" (1:26). Rather, they were "foolish," "weak," and "despised" (1:27–28), and some were certainly "slaves" (7:21–22; 12:13).

B. Sanctified, Holy (1:2)

Given the nature of Corinth and its people, and of the Corinthian church itself, it is no wonder that Paul reminded the church that it had been "sanctified" or set apart as God's people, and was "called to be holy" (1:2). "Holy" referred to the fact that the church was to remain dedicated to God as his people, and that it was to be pure. It may have been a remembrance of the church's formerly deplorable members that caused Paul to be so thankful for the "grace" given to the Corinthian church (1:4), and for their spiritual gifting which "confirmed" that they had believed the gospel (1:5–6). Paul reminded them that Christ would keep them strong until the end because their past lifestyles tugged strongly at them through the influence of the Corinthian society and culture (1:8; cf. 12:2).

C. In Christ (1:2,4)

Central to Paul's thinking in all his letters was the concept of being "in Christ" (1:2,4). He used this exact phrase seventy-three times and frequently employed related phrases and concepts. This complex idea incorporates both a legal and an experiential aspect. On the one hand, "in Christ" refers to the fact that believers are covered by Christ's imputed righteousness (Rom. 5:15–19; Gal. 2:17). Because Christ has died for them and imputed his righteousness to them, believers stand before God's judgment throne with Christ's own status. They are accounted righteous because Christ stands in their place as their representative.

On the other hand, "in Christ" is also much like John's term "abide" (John 15:1–7, NASB), meaning that Christ lives within believers, and they live in him (Rom. 6:23; Gal. 3:28). It refers to an intimate union that affects believers on the level of their very being.

VII. TEACHING OUTLINE

A. INTRODUCTION

1. Lead Story: "Hello Dear, We've Got a Big Problem"
2. Context: Paul had received news that the church in Corinth had a big problem. It had fallen into divisions because its members boasted in their leaders. He loved the Corinthians and was thankful for their salvation and gifts. But he was upset that they had taken sides against one another. He began his letter by reminding the Corinthians of the nature of the church and the gospel, and he followed this with a brief section of thanks that contained similar ideas. He then addressed the Corinthians' problems of divisions.
3. Transition: Like the Corinthians, modern believers have big problems with divisions. We divide over church polity, theology, tradition, worship style, and even race and social standing. Paul's teaching should help us remember the true nature of our calling and encourage us to work for unity and fellowship.

B. COMMENTARY

1. Introduction (1:1–9)
   a. The church has been called to unity in Christ (1:1–3)

      b. The blessings of God should help us establish unity in the church (1:4–9)

  2. Paul's Appeal in Response to Church Divisions (1:10–12)

      a. Christ commands us to be unified (1:10)

      b. Divisions and quarrels attack Christ (1:11–12)

  3. Divisions Are Contrary to Paul's Ministry (1:13–17)

      a. Earthly allegiances are treason against Christ (1:13–16)

      b. Only quarrels defending the gospel may be tolerated (1:17)

      c. The gospel demands unity (1:17)

C. CONCLUSION: HOME RUN

VIII. ISSUES FOR DISCUSSION

1. How often did Paul mention Christ in this section? What does this tell you about his purpose and argument?
2. What various blessings did Paul say the Corinthians had received?
3. Why was Paul so upset about the divisions in Corinth?
4. Can you think of any divisions in your own church that need to be addressed? Have you contributed to these problems in any way? What steps can you take to prevent or correct divisions in your own church?

1 Corinthians 1:18–2:5

The Wisdom of the Gospel

I. INTRODUCTION
Wise Guy or Wise Man?

II. COMMENTARY
A verse-by-verse explanation of this section.

III. CONCLUSION
God's Wisdom, Not the World's

An overview of the principles and applications from this section.

IV. LIFE APPLICATION
Propping Up the Table

Melding the section to life.

V. PRAYER
Tying the section to life with God.

VI. DEEPER DISCOVERIES
Historical, geographical, and grammatical enrichment of the commentary.

VII. TEACHING OUTLINE
Suggested step-by-step group study of the section.

VIII. ISSUES FOR DISCUSSION
Zeroing the section in on daily life.

1 Corinthians 1:18–2:5

Quote

"God's wisdom is ... that perfection of God whereby he applies his knowledge to the attainment of his ends in a way which glorifies him most."

Louis Berkhof

IN A NUTSHELL

The Corinthians had misunderstood the nature of wisdom. From Paul's perspective, the wisdom of the world opposes God's wisdom revealed in Christ. The former is based on human arrogance and leads to destruction; the latter is based on the gospel of Christ and leads to eternal life.

The Wisdom of the Gospel

I. INTRODUCTION

Wise Guy or Wise Man?

*E*very time they did anything, he had something smart to say. The Sunday school class went on an all-day picnic at the national park. It could have been a great time, but Jimmy seemed interested only in picking everything apart. "Well, *that* was really a lot of fun." "So this is supposed to be *good* food?" "I don't see why everybody's so excited about coming here." Jimmy just loved quoting statistics, giving trivial facts, and scrutinizing everything with the biggest words he could muster. Jimmy was not a happy fellow, and he meant for everyone else to be unhappy, too.

After a day of this, the driver could not take it any more. "Jimmy," he shouted, "we all know you think you're the only one on this bus with any sense and you may be the smartest guy here. But let me tell you something, you're not a wise man—you're just a wise guy."

What's the difference between a wise person and a wise guy? I suppose we could list a dozen things or so. But one thing is true in every case. Wise people know how to use their intelligence to serve others and to help those around them. Wise guys are out for themselves. They use their intelligence to destroy.

In this passage, Paul addressed those in the church at Corinth who claimed to be wise. They used their "wisdom" to divide the church and to promote themselves. These people took pride in the human "wisdom" of the world. They had not trusted worldly, human wisdom for their salvation initially, but they had begun to emphasize such wisdom over the gospel itself. In their pursuit of wisdom, they became arrogant wise guys.

Paul showed these people that their so-called wisdom was worthless. It could not save anyone; it could not further the cause of Christ. All it did was destroy. The wisdom the Corinthians were so proud of actually opposed the gospel. As far as Paul was concerned, these people were not truly wise—they were only wise guys.

II. COMMENTARY

The Wisdom of the Gospel

MAIN IDEA: *The Corinthian emphasis on human wisdom and the divisions this caused were contrary to the gospel of Christ.*

In the last verse of the preceding section, Paul had touched on the fact that he had not allowed human eloquence and wisdom to obscure the power of the cross (1:17). In this section, he expanded on this theme by explaining why this approach to preaching was so important. Paul perceived arrogance and pride in human wisdom as a source of division in the Corinthian church, but this privileging of human wisdom would never do in the Christian faith.

Paul focused this passage on three major issues. First, the gospel itself utterly contradicts the worldly wisdom the Corinthians admired so much. Second, the Corinthians' own original experience of receiving the gospel by grace contradicted their pride. Third, Paul's message was entirely devoid of human wisdom.

A Worldly Wisdom and the Wisdom of the Gospel (1:18–25)

SUPPORTING IDEA: *Paul established that the worldly human wisdom cherished by unbelievers opposes the wisdom of God revealed in the gospel. By basing their divisions on human wisdom, the Corinthian Christians revealed that they had forgotten this basic truth.*

1:18. Paul began by explaining his straightforward manner of preaching in terms of the ways believers and unbelievers view the gospel. On the one hand, **those who are perishing** (unbelievers) live according to the standards of sinful human wisdom, and therefore wrongly conclude that the **message of the cross is foolishness.**

On the other hand, the Holy Spirit changes the perspectives of those **who are being saved.** Those who follow Christ rightly perceive that the Cross is not foolishness, but **the power of God** bringing salvation from sin and death. Paul pressed this radical antithesis between the outlook of believers and unbelievers in order to remind the Corinthians that the way of Christ does not rely on sinful human wisdom. By this means, he pointed out that they thought and acted like unbelievers when they were arrogantly and pridefully divided.

1:19. To support his claim, the apostle appealed to Isaiah 29:14, where the prophet rebuked Israel for challenging God by relying on **the wisdom of the wise** and **the intelligence of the intelligent.** In times of trouble, the Israelites to whom Isaiah spoke relied on their own wisdom instead of God's wisdom. James described this kind of wisdom as "earthly" wisdom (Jas. 3:15).

Isaiah warned Judah that God would destroy human wisdom. He would do things to frustrate the intelligent, philosophical, and religious outlook that humans raised against his revelation. Paul used this Old Testament quotation to show the Corinthians that a fundamental antithesis exists between the true wisdom of God and the wisdom of the world.

1:20. Paul continued to point out God's opposition to worldly wisdom in several questions, the first two of which alluded to the Book of Isaiah. **Where is the wise man?** Isaiah spoke similar words in Isaiah 19:12 to mock the Egyptian wise men who could not comprehend the ways of God. **Where is the scholar?** Isaiah also ridiculed the Assyrians for their arrogance in assuming they would be victorious over the God of Israel (Isa. 33:18). **Where is the philosopher of this age?** Here Paul focused more on the situation at hand. He associated the wisdom of words with those whose boasting God opposes.

Paul ended with a question to which he expected a positive response. He asked if God had not **made foolish the wisdom of the world.** God had certainly done so in the days of Isaiah by defeating the Egyptians and the Assyrians. But Paul's idea was greater than this. God had also demonstrated the folly of human wisdom in Christ in that human wisdom would never lead anyone to think that God would allow his Son to be crucified to save man. By acting in a way that human wisdom would label "foolish," God frustrated human wisdom.

1:21. Paul explained that the world's wisdom was unable to find ultimate reality, namely God himself. As hard as they tried to raise themselves to heights of wisdom, the greatest religious leaders and philosophers of the world **did not know** God.

Paul did not mean that unbelievers were unable to know truths about God. God has revealed himself to all people in the general revelation of creation (Rom. 1:18–20). Moreover, many unbelieving Jews understand much in the Scriptures. Instead, Paul was saying that the religious leaders and philosophers had not come to know God intimately, in a saving way, through their human wisdom.

In opposition to the efforts of sinful humanity, **God was pleased** to choose another way of salvation for **those who believe.** In the world's terms, the way of salvation through the gospel is viewed as **the foolishness of what was preached.** Here Paul contended that God's sovereign pleasure was to choose something that the wise of this world would consider foolish—the crucified Savior. By ordaining this seemingly foolish means of salvation, God made the world's so-called wisdom to be foolishness.

1:22. Paul expanded his assertion by pointing out particular ways in which the world's wisdom had been foiled by the preaching of Christ. First, he described the standards of human wisdom which Jews and Gentiles endorsed: **Jews demand miraculous signs.** The gospels record that the Jews repeatedly requested signs from Jesus to prove he was from God (Matt. 12:38–39; John 2:18; 6:30). Yet, even the miracles he performed did not satisfy them because he would not perform at their bidding. They reasoned that the true Messiah would provide whatever proof the Jews required. For this reason, many Jews rejected Jesus.

Paul also pointed out that **Greeks look for wisdom.** By and large, the Greeks (many Corinthian believers were Greek) did not demand miracles to corroborate the gospel. Instead, they exalted the standards of their pagan philosophies and poets. Ancient Greece was well known as the seat of many influential philosophers. The Greeks took great pride in their philosophical sophistication. Their loyalties were not primarily to the empirical, but to that which was rational according to their own fallen standards. Many Greeks also rejected the gospel because it did not meet their standards of human wisdom.

1:23. In contrast to the standards of judgment used by Jews and Greeks, the apostle said he simply preached **Christ crucified.** Paul constantly used the word *cross* to represent the redemptive work of Christ. He was under direction from God not to reduce the Christian message to something acceptable to Jews or Greeks. In fact, the gospel of the cross was a **stumbling block** to Jewish listeners and **foolishness** to Gentiles.

The Jews understood the cross of Christ as a demonstration that Christ was cursed of God (see Deut. 21:23), not blessed as they expected the Messiah to be.

Many Gentiles, in turn, could hardly have imagined a more ridiculous religion than one that proclaimed salvation through the death of one man on a Roman cross. A God who could not overcome his human enemies and who died at their hands like a common thief was not a God one should reasonably trust for salvation.

1:24. Although most Jews and Gentiles rejected the true gospel because it did not meet their standards of judgment, one group of people joyfully accepted the gospel of the cross: those **whom God** had **called** to himself by the power of his Spirit. When God's grace touched their lives, their old standards of judgment fell away. They saw with new eyes and understood that the gospel of the crucified Christ was **the power of God** that could rescue them from the dominion of sin and from divine judgment.

1:25. Paul closed this paragraph by explaining how a person could accept the way of salvation in Christ as wise when most people considered it foolish. Believers have come to recognize something about the gospel of the crucified Christ: it is **wiser than man's wisdom.** In other words, the message of Christ peers into reality in ways that far exceed any human wisdom.

Moreover, the gospel is **stronger than man's strength.** People cannot rescue themselves from bondage to sin or its punishment by their own power. Human wisdom is unable to conquer "the wages of sin" (Rom. 6:23), that is, death. Even so, the good news of Christ rescues and delivers. It overcomes even death (2 Tim. 1:10). Those who believe the gospel know the reality of its wisdom and power. For this reason, they exalt nothing above Christ and his saving work.

B Worldly Wisdom and the Experience of the Gospel (1:26–31)

SUPPORTING IDEA: *The apostle invited the Corinthians to remember their condition when God first called them. From a worldly point of view, they had been utterly foolish to believe in Christ as the way of salvation.*

1:26. The Corinthians needed to remember something about their status in the world when they **were called.** Showing his affection for them by calling them **brothers,** Paul reminded the Corinthians of several facts.

When they had first received the gospel, most of them were not **wise by human standards.** They were neither **influential** nor **of noble birth.** When they were called, they had no basis from which to assert superiority over one another or to boast because they had no wisdom, no status, and no power. Yet, when God called them, they believed the simple gospel. Unfortunately, many of the Corinthians had forgotten this experience and had appealed to human wisdom to exalt themselves and to divide from one another.

1:27–28a. The Corinthian experience of the gospel made God's outlook on the world's wisdom clear. **God chose** as his people those whom the world did not respect. Most Corinthian believers represented the **foolish, weak, lowly,** and **things that are not** (i.e., count for nothing) in the eyes **of the world.** Paul described the Corinthians as **things** in order to indicate how little the world thought of their condition.

Even so, there was a divine purpose in all of this. God planned **to shame** those whom the world considered **wise** and **strong.** Although the Corinthians appeared foolish and weak to the unbelieving world when they trusted in Christ, they were not foolish for believing the gospel. Instead, the world was shown to be foolish and weak.

Paul did not use these unflattering descriptions of the Corinthians to belittle them, but to remind them that they had no basis for boasting. When the Corinthians first experienced the gospel in their lives, they did not feel superior to one another and they were not divided. From God's perspective, nothing had changed between that time and the time Paul wrote—they still had no reason to boast, to divide, or to quarrel. Paul reminded them of this so they would abandon those things that caused them to treat one another disdainfully (1 Cor. 1:10–12).

1:28b–29. God selected lowly people for a remarkable reason: to **nullify the things that are** (i.e., amount to a lot). In other words, God filled the church at Corinth with people who amounted to very little by human standards in order to demonstrate that these standards were wrong. The goal of this demonstration was plain. God wanted to make certain **that no one** might **boast before him.**

The wise, powerful, and sophisticated of the world tend to boast that they become Christians because they deserve to be the people of God. The elect become elite in their own minds. In the same way, the Corinthians' boast of being "of Paul" or "of Apollos"—the source of the divisions in the church—demonstrated forgetfulness that their salvation never depended upon their own merit. But the lowly of the earth understand that they have nothing in themselves of which to boast. They know they do not deserve to be in Christ's kingdom. Therefore, God chooses these kinds of people **so that no one may boast before him.**

1:30. To dispel any pride remaining in the Corinthians, Paul reminded them why they believed the gospel. It was not because they were wise or powerful enough to receive salvation. It was **because of** God that they were **in Christ Jesus.** God himself is the ultimate force behind the salvation of those who believe. Although salvation is "by grace through faith," even faith itself is "a gift from God" (Eph. 2:8–9). No credit belongs to the humans who have come to Christ. All credit belongs to God.

Paul described salvation in poignant terms. He said that believers are **in Christ.** This phrase describes the saving relationship that all believers have with Christ. Believers are joined to him in baptism and become members of his body. For this reason, the judgment that Christ bore on the cross applies to all who are in him. Moreover, believers share in his resurrection life both now and in the final resurrection of their bodies (Rom. 6:3–8). Paul emphasized this unity in Christ to reconcile the divided factions of the Corinthian church.

Because of believers' union with Christ, Christ has become **wisdom from God** to them. This union with Christ should make believers value Christ as the greatest wisdom of all. The Corinthians needed to stop following the wisdom of the world and to recognize that Christ embodies divine wisdom.

Finally, the apostle delineated the nature of this wisdom that believers identify with Christ. He is **our righteousness, holiness and redemption.** Christ bore the sins of his people on the cross so they might receive his right standing before God (Rom. 10:4; Phil. 3:9). In Paul's vocabulary "holiness" or "sanctification" often describes the purity which should characterize the daily lifestyles of believers (Rom. 6:19,22; 1 Thess. 4:3–4,7; 1 Tim. 2:15). The Corinthians had seen their practical lives changed by the power of the gospel of Christ. He had become the source of their holiness.

Christ also purchased believers with the price of his own blood (Rom. 3:24–25). All believers have been "bought at a price" (1 Cor. 6:20). Paul reminded the Corinthians that Christ had become the most important thing in their lives. They owed to him every dimension of their salvation.

1:31. The purpose of Christ's exclusive role as the wisdom of God bringing salvation is that all boasting will be done to the glory of God. Paul paraphrased Jeremiah 9:24. The prophet Jeremiah warned Judah not to boast in their own wisdom and ability. They were to put their confidence in the Lord to deliver them from trouble.

Paul recalled this verse to apply this Old Testament principle to his readers. Those who understand rightly will not be so foolish as to boast in themselves or in any other human being. They will take confidence only in the Lord. Paul hoped that when the Corinthians ceased to boast in themselves, they would be reconciled to one another.

C Worldly Wisdom and the Preaching of the Gospel (2:1–5)

SUPPORTING IDEA: *Paul argued that he had not presented the gospel according to the world's wisdom. Instead of employing logic and rhetoric, he had focused his attention on the central message of Christ's death.*

2:1. Paul called the Corinthians **brothers** and reminded them that he had first come to them preaching without **eloquence or superior wisdom**. Earlier he had asserted that God had not sent him to preach "with words of human wisdom" (1:17). Here he affirmed that he had fulfilled this divine design.

Contrary to those who had divided the Corinthian church on the basis of human arrogance and eloquence, Paul had simply announced the **testimony about God.** He had testified to what God had done in Christ. In his view, to preach the gospel was to make plain what God had done in sending his Son into the world. If Paul had presented the gospel eloquently and with sophistication, converts might have been swayed by his rhetoric and sophistry and not by the Holy Spirit.

2:2. Paul explained how he avoided human wisdom and sophistication as he preached in Corinth. He had determined to **know nothing . . . except Jesus Christ.** He had decided to make Jesus the center of his teaching while at Corinth. He chose not to involve himself in the practices of sophistry so prevalent in the cities of Greece. He emphasized the simplicity of his message by adding **and him crucified.** The crucifixion as the way of salvation was the most offensive dimension of the gospel, and it opposed the human arrogance of Jews and Gentiles. But it was nevertheless the power of God for salvation.

Paul personalized his recollection for the Corinthians by the phrase **while I was with you**. The Corinthian church could not deny that they had come to Christ through a gospel that did not employ human wisdom.

2:3. Paul continued to focus on the manner of his prior ministry in Corinth. He had come with **weakness, fear**, and **much trembling**. In all likelihood, the **weakness** of which he spoke was his physical ailments. Paul had suffered physical abuse because of his faith in Christ (2 Cor. 12:7). He had also had difficulties with his sight (Gal. 6:11), and perhaps other illnesses (2 Cor. 12:7–10). The apostle had not come to Corinth asserting himself with human strength as the factions in the Corinthian church had begun to do. He had come as a weak person—and in his weakness he had brought the wisdom of God.

2:4. Paul's proclamation of the gospel at Corinth had accorded with his physical and emotional state. He had not preached **with wise and persuasive words**. It was common in Greek cities of that day for philosophers and pagan religious leaders to gather followers through powerful rhetoric. Paul's human weakness made it evident that he had relied on the **demonstration of the Spirit's power**. The term *demonstration* was a technical legal term describing irrefutable evidence offered in court (cf. Acts 25:7). Paul's preaching had the support of the Holy Spirit's transforming power in the Corinthians' lives. When the Corinthians believed in Christ, they received many powerful demonstrations of the Spirit's work among them (see 2:13–15; 12:7). Even though Paul's preaching lacked sophistication and human wisdom, the fact that the Spirit manifested himself through his preaching proved that it did not lack power.

2:5. Why did Paul come to Corinth in this manner? He came with the message of the cross, in human weakness and relying on the Spirit so the Corinthians' **faith might not rest on men's wisdom**. Greek culture tended to rely on the worldly wisdom of its philosophers and rhetoricians. At this time, the Corinthian believers had begun to return to this cultural standard by exerting themselves in the church through human wisdom. In response, Paul pointed out that one of his central goals in his earlier preaching had been that they would build their lives on a new foundation, not on **men's wisdom, but on God's power**. The power of the gospel, brought through the ministry of the Holy Spirit, was the foundation of the Corinthians' Christian faith.

MAIN IDEA REVIEW: *The Corinthian emphasis on human wisdom and the divisions this caused were contrary to the gospel of Christ.*

III. CONCLUSION

God's Wisdom, Not the World's

The Corinthians had fallen into the trap of being wise guys rather than wise people. They relied on arrogant sophistry to compete with fellow believers in their church. Paul made it plain that this practice contradicted the gospel. The wisdom of God, upon which the Corinthians had placed their hopes, opposed the human wisdom that had crept into the church and begun to destroy it.

PRINCIPLES

- Christianity is fundamentally opposed to the world's beliefs, values, and standards.
- God chooses people whom the world considers weak and foolish.
- The gospel is divinely powerful to convert the lost without resorting to arguments from worldly wisdom.

APPLICATIONS

- No matter what the world says about our Christian beliefs, we can rest assured that the gospel is true.
- We should adjust our standards and values to match God's, not the world's.
- We should proclaim the gospel in a simple and straightforward manner, trusting God's power to convert the lost.

IV. LIFE APPLICATION

Propping Up the Table

I once broke a small table in my parents' bedroom. I sat on it when no one was looking and broke off one of the legs. I was so afraid of what my folks would say that I propped up the table with the broken leg. But when I came back a few minutes later, the table was leaning. So, I put several long sticks from my tinker-toy set underneath it to keep it standing. It looked good to me, but when my father came in that evening and put his things on the table, it came crashing to the floor. All of my props were not able to hold up the table.

This passage tells us that relying on human wisdom will never hold up the table of our lives. When things go bad, we begin to prop up our lives with human wisdom. We even try to prop up our church with human wisdom. Some of us seek our own ways rather than the glory of Christ by using our intelligence and skills of persuasion. Others of us submit ourselves blindly to gifted and talented leaders in the church who lead us in ways that please them.

But Paul made it plain in this passage that relying on human ingenuity and wisdom is like propping up a table in a way that will eventually send it crashing to the floor. In the body of Christ we are to rely solely on Christ's wisdom as revealed in the gospel. God's wisdom in sending Christ to bring salvation through his death displays the folly of relying on human wisdom. Just like the Corinthians, we did not begin this way in our faith. Nor did we receive Christ because someone was clever or eloquent. We need to get back to the sure foundation of our faith: the wisdom of exalting Christ above all others.

Paul outlined three ways for us to do this. First, we must remember that the world rejects the truth of the gospel and that worldly "wisdom" is error. Second, we can resist arrogance by remembering who and what we were before God saved us. Third, we can act humbly by emulating Paul's simplicity in his preaching.

V. PRAYER

Lord Jesus, you have shown us that your wisdom is contrary to the wisdom of the world. Forgive us, Lord, when we harm ourselves and your church by following the standards of this world. Give us hearts that affirm the great divide between your wisdom and the foolishness of a sinful world. Amen.

VI. DEEPER DISCOVERIES

A. Power (1:18,24; 2:4–5)

Paul used the word *power* in a variety of ways. In 1:18, he described the "message of the cross" as the "power of God." In 1:24, the "power" is Christ himself. In 2:4 it is what Paul demonstrated when preaching, and in 2:5 it is that on which faith depends.

Primarily, the Greek word for power, *dynamis* means "strength, force, might," and related to this it may also mean "ability or capability." *Dynamis* also has a variety of secondary meanings, including "meaning," "supernatural spirit," "wealth or resources," and "deed of power, miracle or wonder." This last definition seems to be the one Paul used most consistently throughout this passage.

The gospel is the power (strength) of God because God converts people to Christ through the simple means of preaching. Christ himself is God's power because he embodies God's strength and he manifests God's deeds of power, particularly in his death and resurrection.

B. Wisdom (1:19)

In the Old Testament, wisdom often incorporated ideas of prudence and practicality relating to the mastery of life and its problems. It also referred to learned skill or experience and to ethical behavior. In both Greek and Hebrew thought, wisdom could indicate not only intellectual perspective or content, but also action and mode of life. Proverbs even personifies wisdom (Prov. 1:20–33; 8:1–36) and attributes to it a role in the creation of the cosmos (Prov. 3:19). This gives precedent to Paul's insistence that Jesus himself is the wisdom of God.

Throughout Paul's writings, "wisdom" seems to denote true insight and understanding, and carries nuances of typical Old Testament usage (1:21,25), particularly in his references to power (1:24; 2:5) and Christ (1:24,30).

C. Scholar (1:20)

Grammateus, the word translated "scholar," is frequently also translated "scribe." It often refers to an expert in Jewish law. Paul may have intended this verse to challenge those who would interpret the Scriptures in a way contrary to the gospel. Such people, primarily Jews, opposed him in nearly every city in which he preached the gospel.

D. Boast (1:29,31)

Unlike our modern term "boast," the Greek word *kauchaomai* was used positively as well as negatively. For example, men could boast appropriately when taking pride in God (Rom. 2:17; Gal. 6:14), or in something truly meritorious that they or others had done (Gal. 6:4; Phil. 1:26). But when they wrongly took pride in themselves, their boasting was wrong (1 Cor. 3:21; 9:16). At times, boasting was neutral, seeming to refer to relating favorable truths (2 Cor. 12:1). Clearly, the boasting that Paul saw in Corinth was sinful.

VII. TEACHING OUTLINE

A. INTRODUCTION

1. Lead Story: Wise Guy or Wise Man?

2. Context: The Corinthians thought they were wise because they had come to value human wisdom. But Paul knew that the human wisdom they valued contradicted the gospel. As a result, the Corinthians were not wise but foolish.

3. Transition: Modern Christians sometimes make the same mistake as the Corinthians. We think we are wise because we know what the world says we should know, and because we think the way the world has taught us to think. But if the wisdom we embrace differs from God's, we are not really wise but are as foolish as the Corinthians.

B. COMMENTARY

1. Worldly Wisdom and the Wisdom of the Gospel (1:18–25)
   a. Human wisdom thinks the cross is foolish (1:18,21–23)
   b. The work of Christ is wise and powerful (1:21,24–25)
   c. Human wisdom cannot produce the power of the gospel (1:19–20,25)
2. Worldly Wisdom and the Experience of the Gospel (1:26–31)
   a. How the Corinthians received the gospel (1:26–28)
   b. How God used the gospel with the Corinthians (1:27–30)
   c. The Corinthians' salvation left them with no claim to superiority (1:27–29,31)
3. Worldly Wisdom and the Preaching of the Gospel (2:1–5)
   a. Paul did not preach with human wisdom (2:1,3–4)
   b. Paul preached the gospel in plain terms (2:1–2,4)
   c. The Corinthians were converted by the simple gospel (2:4–5)
   d. Power lies in God's wisdom, not man's (2:4)
   e. People must trust in the power of God (2:5)

C. CONCLUSION: PROPPING UP THE TABLE

VIII. ISSUES FOR DISCUSSION

1. What makes the message of the gospel foolish in the world's eyes?
2. Why did God ordain a gospel that the world would find foolish?
3. If everyone thinks the gospel is foolish or a stumbling block, how does anyone come to faith?
4. How do you think this portion of Paul's letter relates to the sections that immediately precede and follow it? What is the flow of Paul's argument?

1 Corinthians 2:6–16

Wisdom of the Christian Message

I. INTRODUCTION
Wisdom—for the Mature Only

II. COMMENTARY
A verse-by-verse explanation of this section.

III. CONCLUSION
Forsake the World's Wisdom

An overview of the principles and applications from this section.

IV. LIFE APPLICATION
Wrong Turn

Melding the section to life.

V. PRAYER
Tying the section to life with God.

VI. DEEPER DISCOVERIES
Historical, geographical, and grammatical enrichment of the commentary.

VII. TEACHING OUTLINE
Suggested step-by-step group study of the section.

VIII. ISSUES FOR DISCUSSION
Zeroing the section in on daily life.

Quote

"All the wisdom of man consists in this alone, the knowledge and worship of God . . . Here is that which all philosophers have sought throughout their whole life; and yet, they have not been able to investigate, to grasp, and to attain to it, because they either retained a religion that was corrupt, or took it away altogether."

Lactantius

1 Corinthians 2:6–16

IN A NUTSHELL

In this passage Paul continued his discussion of God's wisdom. He reminded the Corinthians that true wisdom comes not from the sinful world, but from Christ and his Spirit alone.

Wisdom of the
Christian Message

I. INTRODUCTION

Wisdom—for the Mature Only

*E*very parent faces this protest at one time or another. "It's not fair! Everybody's doing it! Why can't I? It's just not fair!"

Now, good parents try to explain their decisions. You know how it goes, "Sweetheart, it's for your own good . . ."

But despite our best efforts to explain, sometimes our children just cannot understand the wisdom of our decisions.

Many times it takes years, even decades, before our children can see the wisdom of a decision we made for them years ago. Often it is not because they are rebellious; they are simply too immature to grasp it. Wisdom is only for the mature.

Maturity has many downsides—aches and pains, bills and pressures—but one of the great benefits of maturity is that it often opens our eyes to wisdom. We are able to see things clearly that we could never have seen in our youth.

What is true about maturity in the natural realm is also true in the spiritual realm. In this passage, the apostle Paul spoke about a wisdom that is only for those who are spiritually mature. It is a wisdom that comes from God and opposes the foolishness of a sinful world. Sadly, it is a wisdom that many in Corinth lacked, and a wisdom that many in the modern church still lack. Like the Corinthians, many of us today think we can be wise without being mature. Or, we consider ourselves more mature than we really are. We think we can make biblical decisions, but we do not realize that we lack the spiritual maturity we need to recognize the biblical alternatives.

II. COMMENTARY

Wisdom of the Christian Message

MAIN IDEA: *The radical contrast Paul set up between human wisdom and his Christian message could have led to the misconception that the Christian faith is foolishness. So, Paul carefully explained that the gospel is a very special kind of wisdom that can be discerned only by those who are spiritually mature.*

Wisdom for the Mature (2:6–10a)

SUPPORTING IDEA: *Paul distinguished his message as wisdom for the mature in order to rebuke the Corinthians for seeking wisdom elsewhere. By prizing human wisdom, the Corinthians thought in the world's terms, opposing the very gospel they professed to believe. Paul hoped to turn them back to the deep wisdom of the gospel so they would be reconciled to one another.*

2:6. Paul asserted that he proclaimed **a message of wisdom among the mature.** In his view, those who have the seasoned outlooks of adulthood see that the gospel is indeed wisdom. This does not mean, however, that one must be a physical adult to believe the wisdom of the gospel, or that all physical adults have this wisdom. Rather, Paul had spiritual maturity in mind. The contrast is between Christian wisdom and the wisdom of the world. Christian wisdom is the gospel, while the so-called **wisdom of this age or of the rulers of this age** is the worldviews, sophistry, and belief systems which fail to recognize the gospel.

Thus, all who believe the gospel and recognize it as true wisdom qualify as "mature," while those who follow the immature standards of this present evil age do not (Gal. 1:4).

Paul mentioned the **rulers** (political leaders and the powerful) because they seemed so successful and wise. Yet, because they rejected the gospel of Christ, they were actually foolish. When Christ returns, all of their accomplishments will come to **nothing.** Powerful people seem to have all they desire, but they will suffer the judgment of God one day because they have rejected the true wisdom of God in Christ.

This verse reinforces the idea of 1 Corinthians 1:24–25 that God's wisdom far surpasses the world's wisdom. The metaphor of maturity points out that the world's wisdom is so defective that it is similar to the simplistic thoughts of children (cf. 13:11). By this argument, Paul let the Corinthian church know that their pursuit of human wisdom made them look like immature children who did not recognize what truth and wisdom were. By their boasting and dividing according to the folly of the world, they lived and thought like immature children.

2:7. Paul first described the wisdom of the gospel as **God's secret wisdom . . . that has been hidden.** The wisdom of Christ's crucifixion was first revealed when Jesus ministered on the earth, but it had been hidden in the secret counsels of God **before time began.** This eternal wisdom was also **destined for our glory,** unlike the wisdom of this age which is earthly, temporal, and brings destruction. The wisdom of the gospel is divine, eternal; and it brings the glory of eternal life to those who believe.

2:8. To contrast earthly and divine wisdom even further, Paul noted that none of the powerful of the world (**the rulers of this age**), such as Pilate and Herod (Acts 4:27–28), **understood** God's true wisdom. On the surface it may have seemed that earth's leaders had discovered the wisdom of God. They were successful in earthly terms. Yet, their wisdom led them to crucify **the Lord of glory.** Their antagonism toward Christ made it clear that they had no wisdom at all. By pointing out this folly, the apostle showed that the pretense of human wisdom has no place in the Christian community.

Paul dealt the Corinthians' pride a severe blow by telling them that their pursuit of human wisdom placed them in the same company as the people who **crucified the Lord** they claimed to worship. Further, by mentioning that Christ is **the Lord of glory,** who possesses glory himself and is able to give it to those who believe in him, Paul made sure the Corinthians realized that the glory they sought could never come through association with particular church leaders. The Corinthians needed to repent of their human wisdom and to return to the pure gospel. They could only receive glory through Christ.

2:9–10a. Paul here contrasted the belief that the rulers of this world understood wisdom with the reality that they did not understand. To draw out this contrast, he alluded to Isaiah 64:4, and added elements from Isaiah 52:15; 65:17 and Jeremiah 3:16. He pointed out how the prophets occasionally indicated that God's wise plan remained hidden from all but those who loved him. The ordinary ways of understanding (**eye, ear, mind**) cannot perceive the mysteries of God. The rulers of the world may be adept at these means of perception, but these senses cannot discern the wisdom of God. God must reveal wisdom in a special way.

To drive home his main point, Paul applied the prophetic word directly to the Corinthians. Although the world cannot perceive the wisdom of God, **God has revealed it.** It has come in a supernatural way directly from God. Moreover, this word came not to the world but **to us**—to Paul and other followers of Christ.

Many in Corinth relied on pretentious human reason in their struggles within the church, so Paul reminded them that they did not perceive the gospel of Christ by human ingenuity. It was foolish for the Corinthian believers to turn to human insight when they had discovered the ways of Christ through divine revelation **by his Spirit.** Paul affirmed as before that the wisdom of God comes through the ministry of the Holy Spirit in the church (1:4–5; 2:4).

B The Spirit of Wisdom (2:10b–12)

SUPPORTING IDEA: *Paul explained how the Holy Spirit imparts true wisdom to the mature. Through this argument, Paul undermined the Corinthians' claim to spirituality—another source of their wrongful pride and divisions. True spirituality would not have led to their human wisdom. To be truly spiritual, they would have to turn from human wisdom to the pure wisdom of the gospel.*

2:10b. Paul began with a bold statement, proclaiming that the **Spirit searches** not only **all things** of this world, but also fathoms **the deep things of God.** Nothing is hidden from the Spirit of God; he shares in the divine attribute of omniscience. Although an infinite number of things about God will always remain hidden from the human mind, even these hidden thoughts of God are evident to the Holy Spirit. For this reason, he is the reliable source of all human insight into the wisdom of God. None of this insight comes through the human wisdom of which the Corinthians boasted and over which they divided, so their divisions and quarrels were unjustified.

2:11. To lend support to his assertion, Paul drew upon an analogy between the human spirit and the Holy Spirit. He began by acknowledging that many things about a person's thoughts remain hidden to other people. Yet, the person's own **spirit** knows these thoughts. No one can get inside the minds of other people as deeply as they can understand themselves.

The comparison with the Holy Spirit is evident. We are not able to peer into the mind of God from the outside by human wisdom. In this sense, **no one knows the thoughts of God.** At the same time, however, **the Spirit of God** knows and can reveal the wisdom of God to us. The Corinthians, of course, took credit for their understanding of the gospel and other spiritual things, thinking they had attained them through human wisdom. By correcting this error, Paul removed the basis for the quarrels and divisions that existed among them.

2:12. The importance of Paul's analogy becomes clear in his affirmation that he and the Corinthian believers had not come to Christ under the influence of **the spirit of the world.** No mere earthly wisdom brought the Corinthians to the gospel of Christ. **The Spirit who is from God** did this for them. The Spirit of God comes upon all who believe in Christ (Rom. 8:9) and reveals to them the mind of God.

For what purpose does the Spirit of God come to those who believe? He comes in order that they **may understand what God has freely given.** Christians cannot understand the wonder of all they have received from God by observing things with their natural eyes. God freely gives the salvation that culminates in their blessings with Christ in the new heavens and new earth.

The Holy Spirit enables them to see the wonder of this gift as well as the wisdom that leads to it.

Ⓒ Spiritual and Unspiritual People (2:13–16)

SUPPORTING IDEA: *Having explained that wisdom is for the mature and comes from the Spirit of God, Paul turned his attention to the kind of people who are able to receive the revelation of truth by God's Spirit. The truth of Christ revealed by the Spirit of God comes only to those who depend on the teaching of the Spirit. Because wisdom comes only by dependence on the Spirit, those who do not have the Spirit cannot judge the wisdom of those who do. More importantly for Paul's argument, even those who have the Spirit can resist his illumination and disqualify their own judgments. Thus, even though the believers in Corinth had the Spirit, those among them who pursued human wisdom instead of God's wisdom had no authority to quarrel or to divide the church.*

2:13. The message that Paul and the other apostles spoke was not an ordinary, natural message. **Human wisdom** (i.e., eloquent human reasoning) could not find the words to express it. Instead, it came through **words taught by the Spirit** who expresses **spiritual truths in spiritual words.** This final phrase may also be translated "interpreting spiritual truths to spiritual men" or "combining spiritual *thoughts* with spiritual *words.*" Paul's main idea is evident. The Holy Spirit gives a revelation that is very special and cannot be discerned or communicated by ordinary means.

The word *spiritual* appears frequently in this context. It is important to remember that Paul did not use the term *spiritual* as contemporary English often does. Paul used this word to indicate that something or someone "has to do with the Holy Spirit." In this passage he pointed out that the Christian gospel which he had brought to the Corinthians was from the Holy Spirit and taught by the Holy Spirit alone. It could not be learned or communicated by human wisdom, as the Corinthians would have preferred.

2:14. The Spirit's role in bringing the message of the gospel raised an important issue for Paul. People **without the Spirit** are not able to **accept the things that come from the Spirit.** Only those who are under the influence of the Holy Spirit can receive Christian instruction with open hearts. The Christian message appears to be **foolishness** to people without the Spirit. They **cannot understand** the teachings of the Spirit.

Of course, Paul did not mean that unbelievers have absolutely no understanding of the Christian gospel and instruction. It is evident that unbelievers can exceed the abilities of believers in many ways. In fact, Jesus' parable of the sower and the seeds indicates that unspiritual people can even grasp the gospel of Christ to varying degrees (Matt. 13:3–7). Indeed, Paul himself occasionally affirmed that unbelievers understand some truths (Rom. 2:14–15).

Paul meant that unbelievers cannot lay hold of or deeply appropriate the Christian message. People without the Spirit are impaired in their ability to understand and accept the instructions of the Spirit because their orientation in life is so contrary to the Spirit.

The teachings of the Spirit are foolish and cannot be understood **because they are spiritually discerned**. People without the Spirit cannot grasp the revelation of God's wisdom because they hold to wrong standards of judgment. They employ the standards of human wisdom to judge the truth claims of Christ. The revelation of the Spirit, however, is properly evaluated only by the Spirit's work in the heart and mind of a person.

Paul laid out this perspective on unbelievers to prepare his Corinthian readers for a point he was about to make. They had the Spirit in their lives because they were believers, but they still had to evaluate whether or not they depended on the Spirit. They had to reassess their own habit of turning from the Spirit to the false wisdom of the world.

2:15. In contrast to unspiritual people, the **spiritual man** is able to make proper judgments. Spiritual people are those under the influence of the Holy Spirit's power. They can see matters rightly. Paul said that spiritual people make **judgments about all things** (all kinds of things). The insight afforded by the Spirit of God equips spiritual people with wisdom in all areas of life.

Moreover, the insights of those taught by the Spirit are beyond **any man's judgment**. In other words, the wisdom of the world is not able to critique or scrutinize the revelation and wisdom of God. Paul realized that the world often criticizes believers. He also knew that Christians often deserve severe criticism when they fail to live consistently with the revelation of the Spirit. Yet, as believers walk according to the teachings of the Spirit, they hold fast to outlooks and practices far superior to the ways of the world.

Paul knew the Corinthians were spiritual in the sense that they believed the gospel and had the Holy Spirit. But he would soon criticize them for acting as if these things were not true (3:1). Their ability to have wisdom depended upon submission to the Holy Spirit's revelation. By this argument, Paul prepared to disarm those who would resist correction, and defended his own authority to speak to their problems. He also destroyed the foundation for the arguments of those who caused divisions and quarrels, those who prized human wisdom. Their preference for human wisdom over God's wisdom disqualified them from judging rightly.

2:16. To support his belief that the revelation of the Holy Spirit is beyond criticism from those who rely on the world's wisdom, the apostle turned to Isaiah 40:13. In a context exalting the supremacy of God over all humans (Isa. 40:1–31), Isaiah insisted that God's mind is beyond human instruction. No mere human can **instruct him**.

This principle was relevant to the apostle's outlook because he and other people taught by the Spirit had **the mind of Christ**. The Holy Spirit knows the mind of God and reveals it to his people through the teaching of the apostles. As believers' minds are influenced by the Spirit, they themselves take on the **mind of Christ**. They think as he thinks; they evaluate life as he evaluates it. Consequently, insofar as believers follow the teaching of the Spirit, they are beyond the criticisms and instruction of human wisdom. Those taught by the Spirit do not follow their own faulty reasoning; they learn from the Spirit, who judges all human wisdom.

> **MAIN IDEA REVIEW:** *The radical contrast Paul set up between human wisdom and his Christian message could have led to the misconception that the Christian faith is foolishness. So, Paul carefully explained that the gospel is a very special kind of wisdom can be discerned only by those who are spiritually mature.*

III. CONCLUSION

Forsake the World's Wisdom

Many people in the church at Corinth prized the Paul ridiculed this outlook as that of the immature. Tr from the Spirit, who knows the mind of God. Mo depend on the Spirit and his revelation discern this the criticisms of worldly thinking. Arrogant huma offer the Corinthians. They should have forsaken caused their church.

PRINCIPLES

- The wise in the world failed to so they crucified him.
- We are dependent on God's Sp
- Pride and arrogance often

APPLICATIONS

- We should not be afr defend the truth of t'
- We should not plac wisdom as reveale
- We should lean o
- In church mat should remain

IV. LIFE APPLICATION

Wrong Turn

Have you ever made a wrong turn that took you a long distance out of your way? Whenever I take a long trip in my car, I usually make a wrong turn at some point along the way. I just hate it when going left instead of right takes me miles in the wrong direction.

That is the way it is with the spiritual choices Christians make as well. We all make them; mistakes in life are inevitable. But it is much better when we do not take wrong directions that make huge differences.

In this passage Paul spoke of one of those critical wrong turns that have a tremendous impact on our lives. His words challenge us to ask ourselves if we are firmly committed to God's wisdom revealed in Christ, or if we compromise with the wisdom of the world.

We should consider this passage carefully, making certain that we base our life choices on God's true wisdom. If we fail to do so, our best intentions will take us far away from the right path. As Francis Bacon wrote, "The lame man who keeps the right road outstrips the runner who takes a wrong one. Nay, it is obvious that when a man runs the wrong way, the more active and swift he is the further he will go astray."

In this passage Paul vindicated the wisdom of the gospel. He contested that the gospel is superior, mature, spiritual wisdom, and that the world's wisdom is inferior, immature, and unspiritual. This outlook has many practical implications for believers today. We will mention two important ways it applies to our lives.

First, we need to admit that Paul's outlook is so radical that it is difficult to maintain on a daily basis. We live in a world where the truth of Christian faith is questioned and mocked every day. Television, books, magazines, ordinary conversations—you name it—we find that people whom we respect for their learning and skills scoff at the claims of Christ. As a result, we begin to think that Christian perspectives are inferior, immature, and unspiritual.

Sometimes this misapprehension is evident in the quarrels and divisions of our churches just as it was in Corinth. Quarrels fueled by human arrogance appear in the church today. But more often, we exhibit this loss of confidence by compromising with the world. For instance, dishonesty in the workplace is considered par for the course. "Greed is good" becomes our motto as well.

This radical outlook also leads many Christians to look for ways to make the gospel of Christ more acceptable to the unbelieving world. We accommodate ourselves to the world, and we give up on important Christian beliefs such as the resurrection of Christ and the authority of Scripture. We can resist these tendencies only by reaffirming Paul's outlook: Christian

V. PRAYER

Lord Jesus, you have given us the Spirit to teach us a wisdom that is better than the world's wisdom. Have mercy on us and give us the ability to seek the Spirit's wisdom in all of our ways. Give us the wisdom that comes from you as we deal with the world and with our brothers and sisters in Christ. Amen.

VI. DEEPER DISCOVERIES

A. Secret (2:7)

The Greek word translated "secret" in the NIV may also be translated "in a mystery" or "secret and hidden." In Paul's writings and in the New Testament in general, *mysterion* seems generally to refer to things which are beyond human ability to determine.

"Secret" also does not refer to something that should not be told to others. In fact, when it refers to the gospel (God's wisdom), it must be told to others: "Pray also for me, that whenever I open my mouth, words may be given me so that I will fearlessly make known the mystery (*mysterion*) of the gospel" (Eph. 6:19).

B. Freely Given (2:12)

What does it mean that the things God gives us are "freely given"? The Greek verb for this idea (*charizomai*) generally conveys the thought of giving without regard to merit. *Charizomai* also means "forgive" (Luke 7:42; Col. 3:13).

C. Spiritual (2:13–15)

Paul contrasted the man "without the Spirit" (*psychikos*) with the "spiritual (*pneumatikos*) man." Generally, Paul contrasted *pneuma* (spirit) with *sarx* (flesh), not with *psyche* (soul, nature). In fact, only in 1 Corinthians did he draw this contrast. Some interpreters speculate that this was due to a special understanding the Corinthians had regarding these terms in tandem. Very frequently, *psyche* and *pneuma* are used synonymously, and neither term normally carries a negative connotation. The most prudent course is to understand that *psyche,* when contrasted with *pneuma* in 1 Corinthians, identifies the corruptible, fallen condition, and that *pneuma* identifies the condition of salvation.

VII. TEACHING OUTLINE

A. INTRODUCTION

1. Lead Story: Wisdom—for the Mature Only

2. Context: Paul wrote this portion of his letter to address the Corinthians' notion that they had acquired a superior wisdom by their own efforts. Each faction seemed to think that it had a superior wisdom to that of the others. This led to boasting and division. In reality, the only true wisdom came from the Holy Spirit as a gift, and it was something they all possessed.

3. Transition: Like the Corinthians, many of us think we can be wise without being mature. Or, we consider ourselves more mature than we really are. We think that we can make biblical decisions, but we do not realize that we lack the spiritual maturity necessary to recognize the biblical alternatives.

B. COMMENTARY

1. Wisdom for the Mature (2:6–10a)
   a. The wisdom of the gospel is mature wisdom (2:6)
   b. The wisdom of the gospel is not the wisdom of the world (2:6,8)
   c. The wisdom of the gospel is God's secret wisdom (2:7,9–10a)
2. The Spirit of Wisdom (2:10b–12)
   a. Only the Holy Spirit searches out God's wisdom (2:10b–11)
   b. The Holy Spirit teaches God's wisdom to believers (2:10b,12)
3. Spiritual and Unspiritual People (2:13–16)
   a. Through the Holy Spirit, believers understand God's wisdom (2:13)
   b. The Holy Spirit and proper judgment (2:14–16)

C. CONCLUSION: WRONG TURN

VIII. ISSUES FOR DISCUSSION

1. What are the things that God has freely given us? Which of these things can we figure out on our own, and which of these do we need the Holy Spirit in order to understand?
2. If people without the Spirit do not accept the things that come from the Spirit of God, how can they be saved? Does not the gospel come from the Spirit of God?
3. Do you have the mind of Christ? How do you know? How does this affect the way you think?
4. How should this passage of Scripture have helped solve the Corinthians' problems of divisions?

1 Corinthians 3:1–23

Divisions and Personalities in the Church

I. **INTRODUCTION**
Celebrities or Leaders

II. **COMMENTARY**
A verse-by-verse explanation of this section.

III. **CONCLUSION**
The Folly of Church Celebrities

An overview of the principles and applications from this section.

IV. **LIFE APPLICATION**
We Deserve Better

Melding the section to life.

V. **PRAYER**
Tying the section to life with God.

VI. **DEEPER DISCOVERIES**
Historical, geographical, and grammatical enrichment of the commentary.

VII. **TEACHING OUTLINE**
Suggested step-by-step group study of the section.

VIII. **ISSUES FOR DISCUSSION**
Zeroing the section in on daily life.

1 Corinthians 3:1–23

Quote

"*T*hose that extol men above measure, strip them of their true dignity. For the grand distinction of them all is . . . that they gain disciples to Christ, not to themselves."

John Calvin

I N   A   N U T S H E L L

*H*uman leaders in the church are ordained by God and serve a vital role. But human leaders also present dangers. It is easy for sincere believers to give their loyalties to human leaders above loyalty to Christ.

Divisions and Personalities in the Church

I. INTRODUCTION

Celebrities or Leaders

"*S*he'll make a great leader," the teenage boy assured his friends on election day. "She's got all it takes: looks, brains, popularity, and a great smile."

"Yeah," Sally said as she handed back the mock election ballot. "She's got all it takes to be a celebrity, but I'm not so sure she's a leader."

More and more we seem to forget that celebrities—people whom we celebrate—are not necessarily good leaders. They may not have what it takes to lead others.

One of the things that separates good leaders from celebrities is that celebrities often believe their press. They think more of themselves than they should. Leaders, however, know their limits and understand that they are not all that others think they are or want them to be.

At Corinth, Paul faced a problem with celebrities. The Christians at Corinth were dividing the church by pledging their loyalties to different celebrities. Each group claimed to be better than the others, and a party spirit began to grow in the church. One of the celebrities was Paul himself. Some believers at Corinth actually claimed to be his followers.

Paul, however, was a good leader; he knew better than to believe those who wanted to make him a celebrity. He insisted that believers should follow only one person: Christ himself.

II. COMMENTARY

Divisions and Personalities in the Church

> **MAIN IDEA:** *Having shown that the gospel of Christ opposed the arrogant wisdom of this age, Paul warned against the celebrities whom worldly wisdom had created in Corinth.*

A The Worldly Practice of Divisions (3:1–4)

> **SUPPORTING IDEA:** *The apostle complained that the Corinthian believers did not behave like people taught by the Holy Spirit. Although they were believers, they acted like unbelievers by quarreling and being jealous.*

3:1. Paul began this portion of his letter with a conciliatory address: **brothers.** In Paul's epistles, as elsewhere in Greek writings, this terminology included the women of the congregation. The term *brother* expressed Paul's sense of the familial unity that all Christians should enjoy with one another. He was about to rebuke the Corinthians, but he wanted them to know that his words were motivated by strong affection for them. This address also reminded the Corinthians that they were all brethren of one another, and that they should have been united rather than divided.

In this passage Paul remembered the time when he had first brought the Corinthians the gospel. Then, he had not treated them **as spiritual but as worldly** because they were **mere infants in Christ.** When men and women first become believers, they begin lifelong journeys toward spiritual maturity (Eph. 4:14–17; Heb. 5:11–14). New believers often think and live much as they did before they believed in Christ. In this sense they are **worldly.** The Holy Spirit had indwelt the Corinthian believers, but the Spirit's sanctifying work had not progressed very far when Paul had first ministered to them. At that time the Corinthians could not receive much in the way of the Spirit's matters because they were spiritual **infants in Christ.**

3:2–3a. Continuing the analogy, Paul said that earlier he had given the Corinthians **milk, not solid food.** Just as newborn infants choke on solid food, the Corinthians were unable to take the solid food of Christian teaching. The Corinthian believers had first received only the simple, introductory teachings of the Christian faith because they had not been **ready** for deeper, more difficult matters. This had been an understandable and appropriate condition for them at the time.

The difficulty for Paul was that the Corinthians were **still not ready.** Though they should have abandoned worldly practices long ago, they remained immature in their faith. As a result, they were **still worldly,** acting like unbelievers. While unbelievers have the excuse that they lack the Holy Spirit, the Corinthians behaved like unbelievers even though they possessed the Holy Spirit.

3:3b. Paul proved his accusation that the Corinthians were worldly and immature. He offered as evidence their **jealousy and quarreling**. The Corinthians had divided themselves into quarreling parties, employing the pretenses of human arrogance and worldly wisdom to fight one another. This behavior revealed that they lived by the principles of the world rather than by the teaching of the Spirit. They acted **like mere men**, not like people in Christ who had the Holy Spirit.

By referring to **quarreling**, Paul began to bring his argument full circle, reminding the Corinthians that so far he had aimed his whole discourse at correcting the false views that had caused their divisions (cf. 1:11).

3:4. To specify his complaint even further, the apostle quoted the claims of factions within the church: **I follow Paul . . . I follow Apollos.** Apparently, these words struck deeply into Paul's heart—he had already recalled them in this letter and would do so again later (3:22; 4:6). Earlier, Paul argued that such divisions were unthinkable for a variety of reasons (1:13–17). Here he described them as worldly.

By resorting to such contentious practices as church celebrities, the Corinthians behaved just like the unbelievers around them. In Christ they were called to fellowship. By quarreling and dividing, they lived as **mere men** who did not have the Spirit or the gospel. They were striving against the goals of the gospel and of Christ.

B The Proper Role of Church Leaders (3:5–15)

> **SUPPORTING IDEA:** *The Corinthians displayed their immaturity by forming loyalties to certain human leaders in the church. Paul attacked this practice by reminding them of the true nature of Christian leadership. He described leadership by using two metaphors, portraying the church as a plant in need of cultivation and as a building in need of builders.*

3:5. Paul began his discussion of church leadership by asserting that both he and **Apollos** were **servants.** Jesus said something similar when he insisted that the greatest in his kingdom must be the least (Luke 22:26). Unlike worldly leaders who seek positions of power so they may be served, Christian leaders are the servants of all. As God's servants, church leaders carry out their responsibilities **as the Lord has assigned.** Worldly leaders seek to force their own ways on others. Christian leaders should seek only to serve the will of God.

By identifying himself and Apollos as servants, Paul reminded his readers that Christ was the true Lord. To celebrate a servant rather than the Lord would be foolishness. The Corinthians should not have taken pride in their human leaders because such leaders had no authority or power of their own. The powerful gospel and preaching which had converted the Corinthians belonged to God alone.

3:6. Employing an agricultural metaphor, Paul explained that he had **planted the seed** by bringing the gospel to Corinth. Apollos, in turn, **watered** the seed that Paul had planted. Apollos evidently taught the Corinthians after Paul did. Neither Paul nor Apollos was more important to the church at Corinth. Without a sower, there would have been nothing to water. Without someone to tend the growing seed, it may as well not have been planted.

Paul also designated God's role in the process. Paul and Apollos simply served the Lord, who **made it grow.** Their human leadership accomplished nothing apart from the Spirit's power. Further, they only planted and watered because God told them to do so. The blessings of salvation on the church at Corinth came through the power and will of God.

Because the church's blessings could not be attributed to its leaders, the Corinthians had no basis for preserving loyalty to any particular leader, and therefore no basis for their divisions. The good they received through Paul and Apollos should have made them loyal to God, not to his appointed servants.

3:7. On the basis of this analogy, Paul concluded that neither the sower nor the one watering was **anything**—both were incidental instruments used by God, **who makes things grow.** The importance that the Corinthians placed on human leaders proved their failure to understand that God deserves all the credit for the blessings believers receive.

3:8. To carry the analogy one step further, Paul argued that the planter and the one watering have **one purpose**—seeing the church grow and bear fruit. The tasks of Paul and Apollos were not at odds, nor were Paul and Apollos themselves. They would never have argued over credit for the work done in Corinth because each expected to be rewarded **according to his own labor.** Paul and Apollos were unified. They did not oppose one another as the Corinthians had boasted, but all served the same Lord. The Corinthians' divisions presumably had been based on perceived conflicts between the leaders. Since no such conflicts existed, there existed no basis for the Corinthians' divisions and quarrels.

3:9. To support his claims, Paul stated that he and Apollos were **God's fellow workers.** The preceding context suggests that Paul meant that he and Apollos were fellow workers *for* God. They formed a team, working together in God's service. Each one needed the other in order to fulfill the goal, and the goal was of divine design. The Corinthian church, therefore, was **God's field**, not theirs. God was the church's ultimate leader, and its allegiance belonged to him alone.

Paul closed this verse by calling the Corinthians **God's building**, speaking of the church as God's possession under God's leadership. Both metaphors illustrated the fact that God was building a unified church—one building, one field—not a fragmented, divided church. By quarreling and dividing, the Corinthians struggled to destroy what God was building.

3:10. Paul developed more fully the architectural analogy. He presented himself as **an expert builder** who had **laid a foundation. Someone else** was **building on it.** Paul took no pride in his initiating role, but admitted that he only served to lay a foundation through **the grace** God had **given** to him.

Paul balanced his claims for himself and Apollos by adding a note of humility for each. He admitted that he did not deserve his leadership role in the church. Only by God's grace was Paul Christ's servant in this way (Gal. 1:15; 2 Tim. 1:9). Some argue that "grace" here refers to the spiritual gift of apostleship, not to God's unmerited favor. In either case, the result is the same for Paul's argument: Paul served the church only through God's gracious gift.

To extend a note of humility to Apollos and others who also worked in the Corinthian church, Paul added another thought: anyone building on Paul's foundation was to be careful how he built. This warning also rebuked the Corinthian leaders who built upon Paul's foundation when he and Apollos were absent. By allowing such dissension to exist, they did not build wisely.

3:11. Why should the builders of the church have been careful? Paul answered first by reminding the Corinthians that their foundation had already been laid. Paul had set the foundation of the church at Corinth when he had initially brought them the gospel of Christ. No builder of the church should try to lay **any foundation other than . . . Jesus Christ.**

Paul implied what he had already stated plainly: some leaders of the Corinthian church had begun to replace the church's true foundation. They were not careful to build on the gospel of the crucified Christ, but they tried to found the church on human wisdom and pretense. Any church leader who substitutes human imaginations for the true gospel of Christ has set aside the only acceptable foundation for the church.

3:12–13. Builders must also show caution because God will reward church leaders according to the work they accomplish. Because Paul spoke of **any man**, his words apply to every believer. But they form a direct warning to church leadership.

Church leaders can build upon the foundation of Christ's gospel in two different ways. On the one hand, they can use **gold, silver,** and **costly stones.** These materials will withstand **the fire** of God's scrutiny that **will test the quality of each man's work.** On the other hand, they can build with **wood, hay or straw.** Such materials will not withstand the fire of divine judgment.

Paul said that **the Day** (the day of final judgment) would **bring . . . to light** the nature of each leader's work so that **his work** would **be shown** for what it was. So, all Christian leaders should pay careful attention to what they bring to the church. Although the true nature of their work may remain hidden for a while, it will be revealed one day for all to see.

By this argument, Paul called the leaders and participants of the Corinthian divisions to account. He asserted that the trouble they caused would detract from their eternal rewards. He also encouraged them to reaffirm the gospel so they would gain greater rewards on the day of judgment.

3:14–15. Paul further explained the two possible outcomes for church leaders. If a leader's work **survives** the fire of God's judgment, **he will receive his reward.** God promises great rewards to those who serve him faithfully (Matt. 10:41–42; Rev. 11:18). But if a leader's work **is burned up** by divine judgment, the true believer **himself will be saved, but only as one escaping through the flames** of a burning house. Judgment on church leaders is more severe than on ordinary believers (Jas. 3:1). For this reason, leaders must lead the people of God very carefully.

Ⓒ The True Nature of the Church (3:16–23)

> **SUPPORTING IDEA:** *Divisive loyalties to human leaders are not only contrary to the nature of leadership in the church, but also to the nature of the church. In this section, Paul demonstrated that the church of Christ is too wonderful to be caught up in following human celebrities.*

3:16–17. Paul pointed first to the sanctity of the church. He wanted the Corinthians to understand how special they were in God's eyes, and how their status as the temple of God required a particular kind of leadership. Leaders must not serve the church with human wisdom, but with divine wisdom from the Spirit, because the church is holy before God.

Paul expected an affirmative answer to his question: **Don't you know?** Believers should recognize that they **are God's temple and that God's Spirit lives** in them. Just as the name of God dwelt in Solomon's temple (1 Kgs. 8:29; 2 Chr. 6:2), the Holy Spirit lives in the New Testament temple which is the body of believers gathering in the name of Jesus (Matt. 18:20).

The sanctity of the Holy Spirit's dwelling requires that church leaders be very careful. In fact, **if anyone destroys God's temple,** harming the church by leading through arrogance and human pretense, **God will destroy him.** Why is this judgment so severe? Because the temple of God **is sacred.** The Corinthian leaders needed to preserve the unity of the temple, not destroy it with divisions. If they divided the fellowship, they attacked God's holy temple, his body (Col. 1:18,24) and his bride (Eph. 5:23–27), thereby provoking God's wrath.

3:18–20. The Corinthian believers had fooled themselves into thinking they were doing the right thing by dividing the church and exalting human wisdom to support their contentions with others. In their culture such behavior seemed reasonable. But Paul insisted to the contrary. The **wise by the standards of this age** should take heed. Instead of pursuing the standards of the world, every believer must become a **fool** in the world's estimation by following the wisdom that comes from the Spirit of God. In this way, the Corinthians would actually **become wise**.

Paul explained that in **God's sight** the **wisdom** held so strongly by **this world** is actually **foolishness**. To prove this, he quoted Job 5:13 in which Eliphaz said that God was like a hunter, catching Job as he caught the wise in their craftiness. Job was caught in the trap of depending on his own reasoning rather than accepting the wisdom of God (Job 42:3).

Second, Paul paraphrased Psalm 94:11 which mocks those who think they are safe when they rebel against God, but whose thoughts **are futile**. People who exalt human wisdom in rebellion against God will find that God overcomes and destroys their efforts. Paul was warning the Corinthians that their reliance on pretentious human wisdom would bring them under God's judgment.

3:21a. The apostle drew a final conclusion: the Corinthians were to cease **boasting about men**. Paul had warned them earlier to boast in the Lord (1:31). Here he focused on the negative side of the issue. The Corinthians needed to forsake the wisdom of this age that led them into exaltation of themselves and other human leaders. They needed to see their boasting for what it was—not boasting in higher theology or wisdom, not boasting in greater righteousness, but boasting in mere men.

3:21b–23. Paul gave one final reason for this rejection of human pride. He began with a comprehensive statement: **all things are yours**. The language of this expression derives from Stoic philosophy. It originally described wisdom as mastery over all that one encounters in life. Paul used this Stoic saying to encourage the Corinthians to gain a proper, Christ-centered perspective on their lives. If they became people of spiritual wisdom, they would see that everything had been given to them in Christ.

All things are Christ's inheritance, and Christ shares that inheritance with all believers (Eph. 1:10–14). The gifts that the Corinthians received in Christ were boundless, and they included the blessing of the leadership of **Paul**, **Apollos**, and **Cephas**. These men were gifts from God to the church, and should not have become sources for division. Moreover, the **world**, **life**, **death**, **present**, and **future** also belonged to the Corinthians. Christ controls all these things, and he will place them all under the feet of his faithful ones. Because all believers share these blessings equally, including the leadership of these people, the Corinthians had no basis for their divisions.

Beyond this, all believers **are of Christ**. No matter what happens, believers can rest assured of their eternal destiny because they belong to Christ (Rom. 14:8). Finally, **Christ is of God**; the Son belongs to the Father who rules over all. The blessings of believers in Christ are secure because Christ's place with the Father is secure.

MAIN IDEA REVIEW: *Having shown that the gospel of Christ opposed the arrogant wisdom of this age, Paul warned against the celebrities whom worldly wisdom had created in Corinth.*

III. CONCLUSION

The Folly of Church Celebrities

In this passage, Paul forcefully argued against divisions based on the exaltation of human leaders. He declared that Christians should recognize the folly of making celebrities of church leaders. Leaders must work for the unity and peace of God's temple and Christ's body, the church. They must never try to detract from our loyalty to Christ and his kingdom. Leaders are servants who must exalt Christ as their Lord and as the Lord of the church.

PRINCIPLES

- Divisions in the church are contrary to the gospel.
- Believers are of great value, and they deserve to be treated well by other believers.
- God loves his church and dwells in its midst—it is his holy temple.
- Believers possess everything in Christ.

APPLICATIONS

- We must be loyal to Christ, not to human leaders.
- Church leaders should exalt the gospel in the eyes of their people so Jesus Christ is always the primary focus of the church's loyalty.
- We must treat other believers with dignity and respect, not looking down on them or acting toward them with arrogance.
- We must reconcile unrighteous divisions in our churches.

IV. LIFE APPLICATION

We Deserve Better

"I just don't deserve any better." That is what many women who suffer from physical abuse by their spouses believe about themselves. They think they are unworthy of good treatment. One of the first things counselors must do is convince these women that they are far too valuable to submit to physical abuse.

Christians sometimes think that realizing their worth and value as the temple of God and the heirs of Christ's kingdom always leads to sin. Not so. Paul told us that the church is far too valuable to be abused by self-serving human leaders. We need to look closely at the honor that belongs to the church. When we do, we will see that human leaders are servants of the one Leader who alone is worthy of our total loyalty: Christ.

V. PRAYER

Lord Jesus, so often we find ourselves more devoted to human leaders than to you. Help us see our leaders for what they are. Give us strong convictions of who we are as well. Grant that we and our leaders may always look to you as the only head of the church. Amen.

VI. DEEPER DISCOVERIES

A. Worldly (3:1,3)

In these two verses, Paul used two different words for "worldly": *sarkikos* and *sarkinos*. *Sarkinos* seems to denote physical flesh in almost all of its biblical occurrences (2 Chr. 32:8; Rom. 7:14; Heb. 7:16), even though it is sometimes used metaphorically. First Corinthians 3:1 seems to be the only occurrence that may potentially vary from this meaning.

Sarkikos, in half of its biblical occurrences, describes that which is material, though not made of actual flesh. In two of the three remaining usages, it identifies that which opposes the Holy Spirit, that which is of the nature of the fallen world. The only fairly ambiguous uses of *sarkikos* come in 1 Corinthians 3:3.

To make matters more difficult, in the verses at hand, Paul used *sarkikos* and *sarkinos* as if they were synonymous. In verse 1, he described the Corinthians as being "worldly" (*sarkinos*), but in verse 3 he said they were "still" (*eti*) worldly (*sarkikos*), even though this was the first time he employed any form of *sarkikos* in the letter. The uses of *sarkikos* in 1 Corinthians 3:3 probably are best seen as references to that which opposes the Holy Spirit, and thus parallel the uses of *sarkikos* in 2 Corinthians 1:12 and 1 Peter 2:11.

B. Rewarded, Reward (3:8,14)

The Bible frequently speaks of heavenly rewards that we will receive in accordance with our works on earth (Matt. 5:12; John 4:36; Rev. 11:18). While the Bible makes clear that we receive blessings only "in Christ," on the basis of his merit, it also says that we will be rewarded according to our works (Rev. 22:11–12). These two ideas are hard to reconcile.

We must affirm, on the one hand, that the rewards we will receive belong rightly to Christ alone. On the other hand, we must affirm that he will share them with us according to our works. At the same time, we need to avoid the error of saying that we earn our rewards by our own merit.

C. The Day (3:13)

The Day of the Lord is a central concept in Scripture. It is when God comes as a warrior to defeat all of his enemies in a single day. He judges the nations, and fully restores his people to the Promised Land so that they will never lose their covenant blessings again (Isa. 2:11–12; Ezek. 13:5; Amos 5:20; Mal. 4:5). The New Testament echoes this expectation (1 Thess. 5:2; 2 Pet. 3:10).

VII. TEACHING OUTLINE

A. INTRODUCTION

1. Lead Story: Celebrities or Leaders
2. Context: The Corinthians had developed strong loyalties to different leaders in the church. They had lost sight of the fact that Jesus is the church's only figurehead. They had forgotten that the leaders to whom they claimed allegiance were merely Christ's servants. As a result, they developed partisan attitudes toward one another. These attitudes damaged the church.
3. Transition: We in the modern church often fall into the same thinking that trapped the Corinthians. When we discover a leader or a teacher whom we respect, we develop loyalties to them, to their thinking, and to the way they do things. Sometimes we do this even when what these leaders teach and do is not biblical. Many troubles in the modern church develop over egos and personalities in church leadership.

B. COMMENTARY

1. The Worldly Practice of Divisions (3:1–4)
    a. Divisions demonstrate spiritual immaturity (3:1–2)
    b. Divisions cause believers to act like unbelievers (3:3–4)
2. The Proper Role of Church Leaders (3:5–15)
    a. The church is like a plant that needs watering (3:5–9)
    b. The church is like a building that needs builders (3:10–15)
3. The True Nature of the Church (3:16–23)

a. The church is God's temple (3:16–17)
b. God's wisdom is superior to the world's wisdom (3:18–23)

C. CONCLUSION: WE DESERVE BETTER

VIII. ISSUES FOR DISCUSSION

1. What does it mean to be a worldly Christian? What did the Corinthians do to make Paul call them worldly? Why is this unacceptable for true believers?
2. What is the role of Christian leaders? Do they accomplish their tasks by natural abilities? How much credit for church growth can leaders accept?
3. If Christian leaders serve Christ perfectly, will they ever be at odds? Do Christian leaders ever serve Christ perfectly? Why or why not? If Christian leaders served Christ perfectly, would this eliminate jealousy, quarreling, and divisions?

1 Corinthians 4:1–21

Following the Apostles

I. **INTRODUCTION**
"I'm Your Father, That's Why"

II. **COMMENTARY**
A verse-by-verse explanation of this section.

III. **CONCLUSION**
A Father's Love
An overview of the principles and applications from this section.

IV. **LIFE APPLICATION**
"Who Does He Think He Is?"
Melding the section to life.

V. **PRAYER**
Tying the section to life with God.

VI. **DEEPER DISCOVERIES**
Historical, geographical, and grammatical enrichment of the commentary.

VII. **TEACHING OUTLINE**
Suggested step-by-step group study of the section.

VIII. **ISSUES FOR DISCUSSION**
Zeroing the section in on daily life.

Quote

"*Though he cannot hold strictly to the ways of others or match the ability of those he imitates, a prudent man must always tread the path of great men and imitate those who have excelled . . . at least he will achieve some semblance of it.*"

Niccolo Machiavelli

1 Corinthians 4:1–21

IN A NUTSHELL

In this chapter Paul closed his instructions on divisions within the church. He did so by affirming his authority as an apostle. The Corinthians may have had loyalties to other Christian leaders, but they should have listened to Paul with even greater regard because he was their spiritual father.

Following the Apostles

I. INTRODUCTION

"I'm Your Father, That's Why"

I do not know any statement a father can make that is more frustrating for a child than this: "I'm your father, that's why." Dads have a habit of saying these words when their children keep asking, "Why? . . . Why? . . . But why?" When we just cannot think of anything else to say, we pull rank: "I'm your father, that's why."

The hilarious thing about this response is that we hated it as children. It makes absolutely no sense at all to a child's way of thinking, especially in the teenage years. But as soon as we become parents ourselves, those words make so much sense that we can hardly keep from saying them to our own children.

Why do they make so much sense to us as parents? I think we all know why. Let us be frank. It is because we see how much we do for our children. We understand the sacrifices we make, the countless hours at work, long nights by the sickbed, food and clothing. In many ways our children owe their lives to us. So, we think to ourselves, *The least they can do is to have some respect for our opinions and comply with a few simple wishes.*

There is a lot of truth in these parental feelings. Children should appreciate what their parents do for them. As Paul tried to turn the Corinthians away from their quarrels and divisions, he appealed to them as their spiritual father. Many people had helped the church at Corinth, but only one person had brought them to life in Christ—Paul himself. So he asked them to remember that they were his spiritual children and to listen carefully to what he had to say.

II. COMMENTARY

Following the Apostles

MAIN IDEA: *In the preceding chapter Paul explained the proper roles of Christian leaders. In this chapter he drew out some implications for the ways the Corinthians should respond to him as an apostle of Christ.*

🅰 Obligations of Leaders (4:1–5)

SUPPORTING IDEA: *Before he addressed the Corinthian congregation's responsibilities toward him as an apostle, Paul focused on the obligations of Christian leaders. He explained their roles in the church in the light of his discussion in the previous chapter.*

4:1. The apostle concluded that the Corinthians should view him and other Christian leaders in two ways. First, Christian leaders should be viewed as **servants of Christ**. The term translated "servant" often denoted a domestic servant. Such persons served others in a variety of ways, but always exalted those whom they served. Paul and other leaders were servants of Christ who did his bidding with humility.

Second, Paul said that Christian leaders were stewards (**those entrusted**). Stewards were high-ranking servants entrusted with the oversight of households. They were especially responsible for the management and distribution of household resources. Paul used this office as an analogy for church leadership because both stewarded **the secret things.** The term *mysteries* describes the redemptive grace of God kept secret for a long time, but finally revealed in Christ. God commissions church leaders to bring this great treasure of revelation to the church.

4:2. What is required of stewards? Above all, they **must prove faithful.** The Corinthians valued eloquence and pretentious human wisdom. Paul rejected this standard for evaluating leaders. He and all leaders should be evaluated only by the standard of fidelity to Christ—their trustworthiness in handling the mysteries entrusted to them.

4:3. Paul opposed the standards of leadership the Corinthian church had endorsed. In response to their thoughts, Paul said he did not care if the Corinthians or **any human court** (literally, "day") **judged** him. Only God could know how faithful Paul had been to the mysteries God had revealed to him; therefore, only God could properly evaluate Paul's performance. In fact, he reserved such a special place for Christ that he said, **I do not even judge myself.** Of course, he did not mean that he never evaluated his own life. He meant that he would not supplant Christ as his judge. Paul did not reject legitimate human criticisms with these words. Rather, he reminded his readers that there was only one authoritative judge and that the time for judgment had not yet come.

4:4. Paul admitted that his **conscience** was **clear,** but this did not support his own innocence. It did not matter if Paul thought he was blameless, just as it did not matter if the Corinthians thought he was blameworthy, because **it is the Lord who judges.** He did not reject the appropriate use of discernment between good and evil people. In fact, he went on to judge one of the Corinthians in the very next chapter (5:3) and to instruct the Corinthians to judge between matters within the church (5:12; 6:2). Rather, as the next verse makes clear, he spoke of the ultimate judgment of a person's life—the judgment of one's eternal destiny.

4:5. Paul drew a conclusion from the foregoing argument. Because God restrains final judgment until the day of the Lord, Christians should **judge nothing before the appointed time.** Instead, they should **wait** for the day when Christ will expose **what is hidden,** even **the motives of men's hearts.** In many passages, Paul affirmed his belief that Jesus' return will be accompanied by a great judgment for all people. Not only will God judge actions, but he will also judge intentions and motives (Heb. 4:12). As a result, at this final judgment everyone will **receive his praise from God** (see Rom. 2:29). God will honor those who prove faithful to Christ.

Paul mentioned these facts about future judgment so the Corinthians would stop judging him. It seems evident from Paul's objections to the Corinthians' behavior that they stood against Paul, judging him to be foolish and weak. For example, in their divisions, the Corinthians not only supported Apollos or Peter but opposed Paul. As the rest of the chapter would show, they evidently thought him low and foolish, preferring human wisdom to the wisdom he preached. Paul wanted them to stop judging him and to accept his authority as he addressed their problems.

B The Responsibility of Followers (4:6–7)

SUPPORTING IDEA: *Paul explained why he had spoken of himself and Apollos in this manner. He wanted the Corinthians to react appropriately to human leadership in the church, not by taking pride in some association with a leader, but by humbly serving others.*

4:6. Paul began by explaining to his **brothers** why he had applied to himself and Apollos the principles of service to God and of belonging to Christ. Both he and Apollos had become occasions for pride among the Corinthians. Paul offered his outlook on leadership so they might **not go beyond what is written.** The expression "what is written" usually refers to the Old Testament (Matt. 2:5; 2 Cor. 4:13). Here the apostle indicated his own loyalty to the Old Testament and his interest in seeing the Corinthians live up to its guiding principles.

Paul had already alluded to the Old Testament several times in the preceding context (1 Cor. 1:19, 3:19). It is likely that he had these passages in mind as he wrote this instruction. If the Corinthians would live under the authority of the Scriptures, they would **not take pride in one man over against another,** damaging the fellowship by causing divisions.

4:7. Paul gave another reason for rejecting pride by asking several questions. Who makes one person (**you** is singular here) in the church **different from anyone else?** The expected answer was "no one" and "nothing."

Although the parties within the Corinthian church exalted themselves over one another, they really and obviously were not better than one another.

To prove his point Paul asked if they had anything that they had **not receive[d]**. The Corinthians had many good gifts in their church, but these gifts all came from the Holy Spirit. They had no basis for pride in their spiritual abilities because these were simply free gifts from God. To drive the point home, Paul asked why the Corinthians boasted as though they had not received what they possessed. Those who recognize that they have nothing apart from God's grace never raise themselves over others as the Corinthian factions were doing.

 Sarcasm (4:8–13)

> **SUPPORTING IDEA:** *Paul was so confident of his criticisms against the pride of the Corinthians that he began to ridicule their practices.*

4:8. Having reminded his readers that they had nothing in and of themselves, Paul accused them further. First, they behaved as if they **already** had **all** they wanted. The Corinthian believers involved in prideful factions behaved as if their gifts and wisdom were perfect and complete, though these were really temporary and incomplete (13:9–12).

Second, Paul chided them for acting as if they had **already . . . become rich.** The word *rich* probably has multiple meanings here. It may refer to the wealth of blessings that believers will receive at Christ's return when they begin to reign with him. It may also refer to actual wealth that some Corinthians had amassed since their conversions—the rich easily fail to see their spiritual poverty (Matt. 19:24). Or, "rich" may refer to the mature possession (1 Cor. 13:9–12) of spiritual gifts (cf. 1 Cor. 1:5–7).

Paul thought that those who divided the church through pretension and arrogance behaved, on the one hand, like self-assured rich people lacking humility, and, on the other, like Christians who had already received all their future blessings and took great pride in them.

Third, Paul accused them of behaving as if they had already **become kings.** Christians hope for the day when believers will reign with Christ over the new earth, but the divisive members of the church acted as if they had already reached this destiny. They behaved as if they had no flaws, no weaknesses, and no need to grow (1 Cor. 13:11–12). Paul admitted his wish that this were true. If it were, then he and the other apostles would be **kings** with the Corinthians because all Christians will begin their reigns simultaneously. Since the Corinthians clearly would not have considered Paul a king, they had no business acting like kings themselves.

Paul pointed out the Corinthians' specific boasts so they would see themselves as he saw them. He wanted them to realize they had no basis for their high opinions of themselves. He also wanted them to abandon their arrogance, to be reconciled to one another, and to respect his authority.

4:9. Paul next explained why he wished he already reigned as a king with the Corinthians. He and other **apostles** suffered severely for the gospel. They were like those led in public **procession** to the **arena** to die. What more humiliating description of his service could Paul offer? He felt that he had been made **a spectacle to the whole universe.** Everyone, both **angels** and **men,** watched with glee at his painful suffering and humiliation. That the apostles suffered so greatly further emphasized to the Corinthians their error of thinking that they had already become kings.

4:10. To bring out the irony he saw in the Corinthians' pride, Paul contrasted his experience of suffering with their attitudes. He had been a **fool, weak,** and **dishonored,** but they behaved as the **wise, strong,** and **honored.** From the Corinthians' perspective, and from the world's, the Corinthians really were wise, strong, and honored, while Paul was foolish, weak, and dishonored. But God did not share such worldly perspectives. The Corinthians' wisdom, strength, and honor stood only according to worldly principles that God did not recognize. If the Corinthians wanted true strength, wisdom, and honor, they would have to seek it by being weak, foolish, and dishonored like Paul.

This verse turned the tables on the Corinthians' self-esteem. They needed to repent of the things in which they took pride, while those things they despised in Paul made him more worthy of their respect. They had no basis for their pride, and thus no basis for their divisions. In order to gain the things they thought they already had, they would have to become the kind of people who would have no reason to divide into factions.

4:11–13. Paul digressed to describe his apostolic experience even further. He and other apostles suffered terrible times to that **very hour** and **moment.** The list of experiences in 4:11 is striking: **hungry and thirsty, in rags, brutally treated,** and **homeless.** In 4:12–13 Paul indicated that he and other apostles **work[ed]** with their **own hands, endure[d]** when **persecuted,** and **answer[ed] kindly** when **slandered.** Paul then summarized his condition as **the scum of the earth** and **the refuse of the world.** The apostles did not err like the Corinthians. They did not behave as those who had already received their rewards.

This section points out that the apostles themselves—the very people over whom the Corinthians divided—did not live up to the Corinthians' boasts. Did the Corinthians feel superior because they followed Peter? Peter was persecuted, and he rejoiced in his suffering (Acts 5:41). Did they follow Jesus? His suffering exceeded that of every apostle. They could not rightly claim to follow these leaders and also claim to be above suffering and persecution.

ⅅ Paul's Purpose as a Spiritual Father (4:14–17)

SUPPORTING IDEA: *Paul mentioned his own suffering for Christ to make the Corinthians aware of how inappropriate their pride and self-assurance were.*

4:14. It would have been easy to misunderstand Paul's intentions here. He did not engage in sarcasm and mention his trials as an apostle **to shame** the Corinthians. Sensitive readers at Corinth were put to shame by the contrast between Paul's humility and their own pride. Yet, Paul's goal was not to shame them, but **to warn** or admonish them. That is, though he intended to shame them to some degree, their shame was not his ultimate goal. He employed shame as a tool for admonishing them, for inspiring them to reject their pride and repair their divisions. Paul wanted to help the Corinthian church imitate his own life, and thereby to help them avoid the consequences of the sin in their church. Love, not anger, motivated Paul to do this. He cared for the Corinthians as his **dear children**, and this affection guided his words.

4:15. Paul was justified in calling himself the father of the Corinthians. They may have had **ten thousand guardians**, various leaders and teachers in the church. Nevertheless, they had only one spiritual **father**. Paul became their father when he first brought them to faith in Christ through the preaching of **the gospel**. By this metaphor, Paul reminded them of several things.

First, he had authority over them, just as a father has authority over his children. Many Corinthians had rejected Paul's authority, but the fact that he had brought them to faith established that God approved of Paul's ministry, even if many Corinthians no longer did. Second, he reminded them of the example he provided for them, as a father provides for his children—a point he raised explicitly in verse 16. Third, he implied their obligation to obey him. Because he had brought them the gospel, they owed him their lives.

4:16. On the basis of his fatherly role in the Corinthian church, Paul urged his readers **to imitate** him, just as children are instructed to follow the example of their fathers. He told others to imitate him as well (Gal. 4:12; 2 Thess. 3:7). Here, he encouraged the Corinthians to forsake their pride and to gain the same kind of humility he demonstrated.

4:17. As a practical expression of his fatherly love, Paul planned to send **Timothy**, perhaps along with this letter. Paul loved Timothy as his dear **son** and trusted him in the work of ministry (Acts 17:15; 1 Thess. 3:1–3). So, Paul commended Timothy to the Corinthian believers as a man who was **faithful in the Lord**. Timothy had proven himself to be a loyal follower of Christ and a reliable leader of the church.

Paul assured his readers that Timothy could be trusted to **remind** them of Paul's **way of life in Christ Jesus**. That is, Timothy would tell them more of the sufferings and faithful service Paul had rendered as an apostle and of Paul's way of life when he had been in Corinth previously, both of which Paul would have the Corinthians imitate. Timothy's efforts would be reliable because he agreed with what Paul taught **in every church**—he would not vary from the apostle's true teachings. Paul sent Timothy as an act of love in the hope that the younger minister would be able to facilitate the restoration of the Corinthian fellowship.

E Paul's Upcoming Visit (4:18–21)

> **SUPPORTING IDEA:** *Paul rounded off his discussion of the divisions in the Corinthian church by reaffirming his intention to visit. He warned those who had opposed him that his visit would prove who was right.*

4:18–19a. Paul worried that some of his readers had become **arrogant**, thinking he would never return to Corinth. In Paul's absence, these members of the church had become bold in their stances. They had probably grown confident in their opposition to Paul, assuming he would never return to challenge them.

Even so, Paul warned them that he would **come . . . very soon.** Paul frequently revealed his keen desire to visit the churches of Christ throughout the world (Rom. 1:10; 1 Thess. 2:18). This should have encouraged his opposition to rethink their attitudes and to correct their behavior, or else to prepare themselves to deal with one imbued not with mere words, but with power (1 Cor. 5:4). Although some people in the church did not believe it, Paul was determined to come to Corinth.

Still, he admitted that his desire was not ultimately the determining factor in his travel plans. He qualified his intention by saying, **If the Lord is willing.** Paul planned to spend the winter in Corinth after traveling through Macedonia (1 Cor. 16:5–7).

4:19b–20. Paul explained that upon his arrival he would find out two things. He would investigate **how these arrogant people** were **talking.** He would find out for himself exactly what they were saying and **what power** they had. He wanted to see if these proud leaders who opposed him had the gifts and demonstrations of the Holy Spirit to back up their theological claims. He wanted to demonstrate to them that their "gospel" lacked the power to mend lives and create unity. Paul mentioned the power of God on a number of occasions, having in mind God's works in the church (1:18; 6:14; 15:43).

The apostle then gave the reason for his focus on the power of the Spirit in his opponents. The **kingdom of God** does not consist of **talk.** It consists of **power.** Put simply, Paul said, "Talk is cheap." Anyone can use words to persuade the naíve, but Paul would expose his opponents by showing that their ministries failed to display the work of the Holy Spirit.

4:21. Paul had spoken rather forcefully to the Corinthians. He closed this section with a pointed question: In coming to visit and test his readers, how should he treat them? Should he come like Jesus cleansing the temple (Mark 11:15), **with a whip** to drive out his opponents who refused to change their ways? Or, should he come to them with **love and with a gentle spirit,** they having heeded his warnings and changed their ways?

If the Corinthians continued to follow human pride by dividing the church into factions, Paul would rebuke them harshly on his arrival. If they recommitted themselves to the true humility that comes from the gospel, he would come peacefully. Paul offered this choice in the hope they would choose the latter.

> **MAIN IDEA REVIEW:** *In the preceding chapter Paul explained the proper roles of Christian leaders. In this chapter he drew out some implications for the ways the Corinthians should respond to him as an apostle of Christ.*

III. CONCLUSION

A Father's Love

Paul realized that the first chapters of this epistle challenged the Corinthians in ways that were difficult to accept. Yet, he appealed to them to remember both his fatherly love for them and their need to honor him as their spiritual father. His teachings were not Paul's self-aggrandizement. They were difficult teachings, but they should have been accepted as Paul's good intent toward the Corinthian believers.

PRINCIPLES

- Christ alone is the ultimate judge of all people.
- When Christian leaders teach the Word faithfully, their teaching honors Christ.
- Neither a clear conscience nor sincerity is the standard of righteousness; the Scripture is.
- Christians will never reach perfection or completion in this life.
- Christian leaders must be humble servants.

APPLICATIONS

- We should not judge our leaders or other believers in inappropriate ways.

- When our leaders teach Scripture faithfully, we should submit to their teaching as the Word of Christ.
- We must accept the Scriptures as our standard of righteousness, correcting and informing our consciences accordingly.
- We should follow Jesus' example in blessing those who do us wrong.

IV. LIFE APPLICATION

"Who Does He Think He Is?"

Have you ever had a near stranger offer you serious criticism? It happens to most of us at one time or another. And what goes through our heads? "Who is this person? Why does she feel the right to criticize me?" "You don't even know who I am!"

Those thoughts are appropriate when a stranger judges us sternly, but we all know how different it is when a dear friend or loved one offers us criticism. It may hurt for a while, but in the back of our minds we remember something very important. "I know she cares about me." "He has demonstrated love for me many times." "I can take this from her."

Paul hoped that the Corinthians remembered these kinds of things about him. He had made a great sacrifice to bring them the gospel. He demonstrated love for them time and again. He hoped they would take his criticism to heart because he loved them dearly.

V. PRAYER

Lord Jesus, we who are leaders cry out to be leaders like Paul was. We who are followers cry out for leaders who seek to imitate Paul's devotion to the cause of Christ, even to the point of suffering. We will give you great praise as you work in our hearts and lives. Amen.

VI. DEEPER DISCOVERIES

A. Judge (4:3–5)

The words Paul used for "judge," *anakrino* (4:3–4) and *krino* (4:5), have broad ranges of meaning. It is probably best not to make too much of their differences in the context of 1 Corinthians 4:3–5 because Paul appears to have used them synonymously here. If he intended any difference between them, *anakrino* may have meant "examine" and *krino* "render judgment," but this is speculative because Paul also used *anakrino* in 1 Corinthians to mean "discern" (2:14–15) and "convict or call to account" (14:24).

B. Become Kings (4:8)

Basileuo, translated "become kings," may also mean "reign." The Bible's hope is not that we will become kings, but rather that one Davidic king will reign over the restored community of the people of God (Ezek. 37:22; Luke 1:33). The New Testament also makes clear that believers will share in Christ's reign (2 Tim. 2:12; Rev. 20:6), but even in this, Christ's reign is preeminent. Thus, it seems better to translate *basileuo* as "reign" rather than "become king" in this particular instance.

C. Kingdom of God (4:20)

"The kingdom of God" is also known as "the kingdom of heaven," "the kingdom of Christ," and "the kingdom of the Lord." It seems first to have taken the form "the kingdom of the LORD" in the post-exilic restoration literature of Chronicles, and to have been used as a term for the restored community of the people of God under David (1 Chr. 28:5; 2 Chr. 13:8). The New Testament authors greatly expanded the term's use, making it a central motif in their theology. In fact, the gospel itself is frequently called "the gospel of the kingdom" or the "good news of the kingdom" (Matt. 4:23; Mark 1:15).

In bringing the kingdom of God, Jesus began to fulfill the restoration promises of the Old Testament. He inaugurated the kingdom during his first coming, it continues now in his physical absence, and awaits its final consummation at his return.

VII. TEACHING OUTLINE

A. INTRODUCTION

1. Lead Story: "I'm Your Father, That's Why"
2. Context: The Corinthians were immature in their faith, and they demonstrated their immaturity by boasting in the gifts God had graciously given them. They thought they had received their spiritual gifts in full, and they looked down at Paul because he apparently lacked glory equal to theirs. Paul argued that his example ought to have proven to the Corinthians that they were not really glorious either. As a loving father, he pointed them to the truth and rebuked their foolishness.
3. Transition: The modern church has much in common with the Corinthian church. Many of us are immature in faith. Even so, most of us think we are relatively mature. We also have the idea that, if we are good, God should take care of us by making our lives easy. We need to learn, as Paul taught, that our lives will not be easy until Jesus returns. In the meantime, we need to submit to Scripture as it

teaches us to recognize our true state, to have humility, and to find strength in Christ.

B. COMMENTARY

1. Obligations of Leaders (4:1–5)
    a. Leaders should teach the Word of God (4:1–2)
    b. Leaders are obligated to the Lord (4:3–4)
    c. Leaders should leave judgment to Christ (4:5)
    d. Christ reserves judgment until his return (4:5)
2. The Responsibility of Followers (4:6–7)
    a. Followers should submit to Scripture (4:6)
    b. Followers should recognize that their gifts come from God (4:7)
3. Sarcasm (4:8–13)
    a. We have not yet begun to reign (4:8–9)
    b. None of us will begin to reign without the others (4:8)
    c. If our apostolic leaders are not wise, none of us are (4:10–13)
4. Paul's Purpose as a Spiritual Father (4:14–17)
    a. Paul wrote these instructions because he loved the Corinthians (4:14–15)
    b. Paul wanted the Corinthians to imitate him (4:16)
    c. Paul sent Timothy so the Corinthians would imitate him (4:17)
5. Paul's Upcoming Visit (4:18–21)
    a. Paul's opponents thought themselves better than him (4:18)
    b. Paul planned to visit soon (4:18–19)
    c. Paul would confront his opponents (4:19–21)

C. CONCLUSION: "WHO DOES HE THINK HE IS?"

VIII. ISSUES FOR DISCUSSION

1. What obligations do Christian leaders face? To whom are they accountable? Can modern Christian leaders claim the same autonomy and authority that Paul claimed? What type of authority do your church leaders claim?
2. Under what conditions may Christians judge one another? What types of judgments may they render? How will Christians participate, if at all, in the final judgment?
3. How does this chapter function as a conclusion to the first three chapters?
4. Why do you suppose Paul spent four chapters on this subject?

1 Corinthians 5:1–13

A Situation of Immorality

Quote

"*B*ut I, miserable young man . . . had entreated chastity of Thee, and said, 'Grant me chastity and continency, but not yet.'"

St.   Augustine

1 Corinthians 5:1–13

IN A NUTSHELL

*T*he apostle Paul addressed a case of sexual immorality in the church at Corinth. He did not approve of the immorality, but he was not so astounded that immorality was occurring. His greater dismay was that the church actually took pride in tolerating it.

A Situation of Immorality

I. INTRODUCTION

Sometimes We Should Be Shocked

*W*e all do things that are wrong, sometimes seriously wrong, but that shouldn't shock us. After all, we are sinners, waiting for our final redemption in Christ. But sometimes we should be shocked by the way we react to the sins we have committed. I have a pastor friend who once told me, "What Christians do seldom shocks me. I've seen it all. What shocks me is how they sometimes react to what they have done."

Pastors often have church members who come to them with heavy burdens of guilt. "I did it . . . and I'm so ashamed," they tell us. One of the privileges of pastors is to lead sincere believers to Christ for forgiveness and healing. This scenario is so common that pastors are seldom surprised.

Occasionally, pastors run into more difficulty. "I did it, but I don't think it's wrong," these people say. These people sometimes surprise their pastors, and often take a lot of convincing before they are ready to turn from sin.

On rare occasions, pastors are shocked to hear the words, "I did it and I'm proud of it!" Despite the harm it has caused their families, friends, and church, some people actually delight in their sinful actions. They take pride in their waywardness. In these situations, even experienced pastors can be shocked.

In this chapter Paul dealt with a sin that shocked him. He was concerned that sexual immorality had taken place in the church, but this had not surprised him. He was shocked, however, when he realized that the Corinthians were proud of it!

II. COMMENTARY

A Situation of Immorality

MAIN IDEA: *Paul received a report that the Corinthian church was taking pride in the fact that incest was occurring among them, and he responded to that report.*

🅐 Report and Instructions (5:1–5)

SUPPORTING IDEA: *Paul addressed the situation in Corinth, identifying the problem and ordering action.*

5:1. By saying, **It is actually reported**, Paul indicated his astonishment at the situation he was about to address. The original language of this passage conveys the idea that the news shocked and horrified Paul. He was appalled to hear that the church tolerated **sexual immorality** which even **pagans** found morally repulsive: **a man** had **his father's wife**. In the context of sexual immorality, the verb "to have" did not refer to occasional sexual liaisons, but to a continuing sexual relationship. The man may actually have lived with his father's wife as if she were his own wife.

Paul described the woman not as the man's "mother," but as **his father's wife**. This terminology probably identifies her as the man's stepmother rather than his biological mother. Paul did not indicate whether the man's father still lived, but if the father was alive the immorality was all the more severe.

5:2. Paul continued to express his astonishment by focusing on the Corinthians' reaction: they were **proud** of their tolerance. They actually took pride in their willingness to accept the unrepentant, immoral man. By taking pride in such a blatantly sinful thing, they exposed the error of their pride.

Instead of proudly accepting the man, the church should have been **filled with grief**. Paul wanted his readers to experience great sorrow over their fellow believer's sin because that immorality was destructive both to the sinner and to the church. Sorrow over the sins of others appears as a proper response on a number of occasions in Scripture (Gen. 6:5–6; Ezra 10:1; Rom. 9:2–3).

The Corinthians were blind to the imminent destruction this immorality threatened to bring upon the church and their friend. This lack of concern for the church seems to have permeated the Corinthians, and it appears as a unifying theme throughout the entire letter.

Paul also demanded that the Corinthians take proper corrective action. Without having to be told, his readers should have **put out** the immoral man from their **fellowship**. Excommunication was the only proper response to such a flagrant and severe sin. In the Old Testament, such sin was punishable by the deaths of the sinners (Lev. 20:11) and the exile of the entire nation from the land (Lev. 18:28).

5:3. Evidently, some Corinthian believers hesitated to discipline their wayward brother so long as Paul was absent. To counter this strategy, Paul argued that he was present with them **in spirit**. He had already made his preliminary judgment. If the charges were true as reported, he supported removing the man from Christian fellowship. Paul's words sound harsh to our modern ears (cf. 1 Tim.5:20), but they are in line with the teachings of Jesus (Matt. 18:15–17).

Moreover, Paul's outlook was quite balanced, as demonstrated in other epistles (Eph. 4:32; Col. 3:13; 2 Thess. 3:15). In 2 Corinthians 2:6–8, for instance, he corrected the church's refusal to restore a repentant brother. In the face of the Corinthians' tolerance, however, he encouraged the church to remove the man from the Christian community.

5:4. The procedures for church discipline of this public sin are straight-forward. First, the right setting must be attained. Christian discipline is not to be performed any way the church desires. It is a solemn occasion when the church is officially **assembled in the name of our Lord Jesus.** The apostle assured them that he also would be present **in spirit** and that the Holy Spirit's displays of **power** would be evident as well. Church discipline is too serious a matter to administer in an ordinary setting.

5:5. Second, the church must temporarily give the offender **over to Satan.** To do this is to exclude the wayward brother from the Christian com-munity and to treat him as "a pagan or a tax collector" as Jesus instructed (Matt. 18:17). It is to deliver him into Satan's sphere of influence (John 12:31; 16:11; Eph. 2:2). Paul used similar terminology to describe other church discipline cases as well (1 Tim. 1:20). The purpose of this action is destruction of **the sinful nature.** In Scripture Satan occasionally receives per-mission from God to test and trouble believers by weakening their physical conditions (Job 2:4–6; 2 Cor. 12:7), so it is possible that Paul referred to this type of destruction here.

In cases of church discipline, the goal of the process is that the person's **spirit** may be **saved on the day of the Lord.** Here Paul used an Old Testament term describing the day on which God destroys all of his enemies and blesses his people. The New Testament often uses this term for the second coming of Christ (1 Thess. 5:2; 2 Pet. 3:10). Although a true believer under discipline may endure hardship, the goal of that hardship is repentance that will lead to salvation on the day of final judgment. Discipline should ultimately be redemptive.

🅱 A Supportive Illustration (5:6–8)

SUPPORTING IDEA: *Paul persuaded the Corinthians that his instructions were appropriate by appealing to the common experi-ence of leaven and its effects. He then turned to the religious ana-logue of Passover celebration.*

5:6–7a. Paul's main concern here was for the church, which he was jeal-ous to protect from corruption. Thus, even though the incestuous man had sparked the occasion for Paul's rebuke, Paul insisted that the larger problem lay in the church itself. The church should have recognized that its toleration of such public sin transgressed its holy calling.

Paul had already identified pride as the source of this problem (5:2). Here he returned to that matter by asserting that the Corinthians' **boasting** was **not good.** Their attitude of boastful tolerance of scandalous sin in the church opposed the truth that boasting is to be done only to the Lord's glory (1 Cor. 4:7). This attitude also failed to understand common experience. The sin of this one man would have a deleterious effect on the entire church if it remained unchecked. On the basis of this common knowledge, Paul insisted that they deal with the sin.

The church is to be **a new batch** of dough without infectious impurity. As Paul pointed out, the church really is a pure, wholesome community of believers because it exists in Christ. Paul's command might be summarized, "You are pure, so start acting like it."

5:7b–8. The reason for removing the old leaven of the immoral person from the church is rooted in the significance of Christ's death. He is **our Passover.** As the lamb was slaughtered in the first Passover in the days of Moses (Exod. 12:21) and annually after that (Exod. 12:42), Christ **has been sacrificed** on the cross. His blood protects believers from the wrath of God like the blood spread on the entrances to Israelite homes in Egypt (Exod. 12:7). The Passover celebration anticipated the final atoning work of Christ's death (John 1:29; Rev. 13:8).

Building on this connection, Paul reminded his readers that one aspect of the Passover celebration was the removal of all leaven from the home and the baking of bread without leaven. The absence of leaven symbolized the hasty deliverance of the Hebrew people from the trials of Egypt (Exod. 12:33–34,39). In much the same way, Paul urged the Corinthians to remember that they had to remove the old leaven of immorality from their church because they lived in the age of Christ's Passover sacrifice. In this sense, the church is to **keep the Festival** of Passover every day without the old leaven of **malice and wickedness.**

All evil should be resisted and removed whenever possible so the people of God may metaphorically eat **bread** without leaven. Their lives are to consist of **sincerity and truth.** Immorality was unacceptable in the church because it introduced a corrupting influence among the people of God.

Paul said the Christian life was to be **without** the leaven **of malice.** He probably referred to those who opposed him in Corinth (4:18), or to those who caused division (1:10–12). "Malice" clearly did not describe the church's attitude toward the incestuous man. At this point, Paul was still thinking in broad terms. Rather than just correcting a problem of immorality, he was purifying, unifying, and protecting the church. Everything he had said so far in the letter was aimed at this goal. He saw the particular Corinthian problems as manifestations of deeper problems such as bad theology and bad attitudes. Thus, he urged them to avoid malice, a root problem, even though it did not pertain directly to the particular manifestation of that root problem which he happened to be addressing (proud tolerance of sexual immorality).

C A Point of Clarification (5:9–13)

SUPPORTING IDEA: *Paul clarified and reaffirmed a point he had made in an earlier letter: Christians should not associate with grossly sinful people in the church, such as the incestuous man who was the subject of the current controversy, but believers should not disassociate from all sinful people.*

5:9–10. Paul clarified one aspect of his instruction that may have been easily misunderstood. He referred to a previous letter in which he had written that believers were **not to associate with sexually immoral people**. This instruction could easily have been misunderstood (or purposefully twisted) to mean that believers should withdraw entirely from all immoral people. Paul ridiculed this misunderstanding of his earlier words by noting that avoiding all immoral people can only happen if Christians **leave this world**.

Since Christians must minister to the world, they must not separate themselves from all who are **greedy and swindlers, or idolaters**. These people are the church's mission field (see Matt. 9:10–13; Luke 15:1–32).

Possibly, those in Corinth who opposed Paul used this misunderstanding to undermine Paul's ministry and authority. They may have suggested that Paul called Christians to stay away from all sinners, and on that basis discounted all his teaching. Paul treated the Corinthians harshly for this misunderstanding for three reasons: it stemmed from a wrong reading of his prior letter; it had led to wrongful pride and corruption in the church; and it had allowed the church's toleration of the incestuous man.

5:11. Lest there be any confusion, Paul explained that he did not have in mind the sexually immoral people of this world (i.e., unbelievers), but **anyone who calls himself a brother** (people in the church). Such people may not truly be believers, even though they claim to be. If they fail to give evidence of new life in Christ, there may be sufficient reason to doubt their salvation. To protect the church from the corrupting influence of these so-called brothers, followers of Christ must not **even eat** with anyone in the church who is **immoral or greedy, an idolater . . . slanderer . . . drunkard or a swindler**. As Paul was to write in this same letter, "Bad company corrupts good character" (15:33).

5:12–13. Paul concluded that he and the Corinthians had no right **to judge those outside** the church. Such people make no pretense of being Christians, and **God** alone **will judge those**. Even so, the church must **judge those inside** the church. Those in the church submit themselves to the authority of the body of Christ. Church discipline is a difficult and troubling process, and many churches try to avoid it. Yet, the church must take action when its members flagrantly violate the ways of Christ. Consequently, as much as the Corinthian church did not want to take action, they had to **expel the wicked man**.

The phrase **expel the wicked man from among you** alludes to the legal language of Deuteronomy (Deut. 17:7; 19:19; 24:7). In all these occurrences of the phrase, the wicked are "expelled" or "purged" by being executed (Deut. 21:21). In Old Testament Israel, God ordained execution as the means by which the nation was to purge itself of severe wickedness.

Paul applied these standards of holiness to the church, God's New Testament people, but he applied the law somewhat differently by recommending excommunication rather than execution. Nevertheless, the fact that he used language typical of death sentences from the Old Testament reflects that he considered excommunication in the New Testament age to be quite serious. This form of church discipline should be reserved for the worst of circumstances.

MAIN IDEA REVIEW: *Paul received a report that the Corinthian church was taking pride in the fact that incest was occurring among them, and he responded to that report.*

III. CONCLUSION

An Unpleasant Task

The Corinthians had taken pride in their tolerance of a serious violation of Christian morality. In response, Paul insisted that the unpleasant task of church discipline was necessary. The purity of the church was at stake; the eternal soul of the sinner was at stake. For these reasons, excommunication was essential.

PRINCIPLES

- Sexual immorality is a sin.
- The church has the authority and obligation to exercise godly church discipline.
- The church offers protection against Satan.

APPLICATIONS

- Christians must not practice sexual immorality, including adultery, homosexuality, or other deviant sexual behavior.

- The church must stand guard against corrupting influences, being willing to discipline its members if necessary.
- We should grieve over the sins of others for the sake of the church's spiritual health and of the sinner who is moving toward destruction.

IV. LIFE APPLICATION

Sexual Dilemma

I was watching a nationally televised call-in show offering advice on moral issues. A twenty-two-year-old man posed this as his dilemma: "For the past six months, I have been having a sexual relationship with my step-mother. How do I break this news to my father?"

Although we might like to think otherwise, our world is not so different from Paul's Corinth. Of course, not all of us will have to deal with situations like this, but we can still apply many principles from this chapter to our lives.

First, we ought to keep close guard on our behavior. We must never engage in sexual immorality, such as fornication, adultery, homosexuality, or other deviant behaviors. Knowing that we have been made new in Christ—being sanctified, justified, and called to be holy—we need to behave in ways consistent with our new identity and nature. Ceasing from immorality and sin, we must live righteously.

Second, Paul also revealed many details about the nature of the church in this chapter. He taught us that believers share a spiritual union with other believers and that the actions of individuals affect the whole church. When these actions take the form of corruption, they run the risk of infecting the church. As a result, the church needs to stand guard against such wickedness, sometimes going so far as to discipline its members.

Discipline of this type cannot be carried out by individuals, or even by groups within a church, but only by the gathered corporate body. When the church meets in such an assembly, it carries the authority and power of Jesus in disciplinary matters. The most extreme form of discipline is excommunication, in which the church hands a professed believer over to Satan in the hope that the experience will be redemptive, causing the offender to repent.

Third, not only should this chapter of Paul's letter inform our behavior and knowledge, but also our emotions. Like Paul, we should be shocked and appalled when churches tolerate, condone, or take pride in heinous sins. Our proper response to terrible transgression should be grief—grief over the disrepute to which such sin subjects the church, and grief on behalf of the sinner who is moving toward destruction. We should fear excommunication and the power of Satan to which it submits us. Because of this fear, we should refrain from gross sin.

When necessary, however, we should not fear to inflict excommunication. God values the church so much that he commands us to put out those who jeopardize its purity. We should respect and love the church more, and develop a greater appreciation for the safety it provides us from Satan.

V. PRAYER

Lord Jesus, you are our Passover, and we want to celebrate you with purity and holiness. Give us hearts that are so devoted to you that we cannot take pride in our sins. Give us hearts that grieve over the sins of our brothers and sisters. And Lord, give us wisdom and love enough to know when we must actually discipline others in the body of Christ. Amen.

VI. DEEPER DISCOVERIES

A. Sexual Immorality (5:1)

In Greek culture, *porneia* ("sexual immorality") referred to prostitution, and was not necessarily frowned upon or considered immoral. Corinth in particular had a history of openly accepting it, as well as of accepting loose and open sexual lifestyles. To live like a Corinthian (*korinthiazesthai*) was proverbial for living a dissolute life. In hellenistic Judaism and the New Testament, however, *porneia* was always negative. This word referred to all extramarital and unnatural intercourse, including homosexuality.

B. Yeast (5:6–8)

In ancient times, yeast was scarce, and leaven was the popular alternative to yeast. Leaven was actually just an old piece of dough that had begun to ferment. When added to a new batch of dough, it spread its fermentation throughout the whole loaf, making the bread lighter. The longer this process continued, the greater the danger that the dough would become spoiled and poisonous. When the dough became bad, it all needed to be thrown away, and the process begun again.

Of course, the first batch of dough had to be made without leaven. This is why Paul spoke of cleaning out (*ekkathairo*) the old leaven (*zume*) and replacing it with a "new batch." Leaven by definition could never be "new"—only the batch could be new—and the older the leaven became, the more likely it was to be dangerous.

VII. TEACHING OUTLINE

A. INTRODUCTION

1. Lead Story: Sometimes We Should Be Shocked
2. Context: The Corinthian church had failed to discipline one of its members, who was living in a sexual relationship with his step-mother. The church even took pride in its tolerance of the man's sin. Paul was horrified by their tolerance, and he ordered the church to discipline the brother, warning that tolerance of the sin endangered the whole church and the man himself.
3. Transition: Sometimes the modern church also fails to exercise appropriate discipline, in part because it no longer perceives sin to be such a threat, and in part because it thinks excommunication to be an unloving act. Generally, the church does not value the church as it should, and therefore is not appropriately jealous to protect it. Further, the church often fails to realize that the loving thing to do with gross, unrepentant sinners is to discipline them. Proper discipline may be the means by which God redeems such people.

B. COMMENTARY

1. Report and Instructions (5:1–5)
   a. Immorality and pride reported to Paul (5:1–2)
   b. Paul's reaction: shock and judgment(5:1,3)
2. A Supportive Illustration (5:6–8)
   a. A little leaven leavens the whole lump (5:6)
   b. Get rid of the leaven to protect the lump (5:7)
   c. Christ's sacrifice parallels Passover (5:7)
   d. The church should get rid of the incestuous man's sin (5:8)
3. A Point of Clarification (5:9–13)
   a. God judges people outside the church (5:9–10,12–13)
   b. The church disciplines people within the church (5:11–13)

C. CONCLUSION: SEXUAL DILEMMA

VIII. ISSUES FOR DISCUSSION

1. How would you feel if you found out that a friend of yours, perhaps someone you had led to Christ, had been carrying on a sexual relationship with one of his or her parents? Would you be shocked? Disgusted? Grieved? Or would you be proud that, as an enlightened

Christian, you were open-minded enough to accept this person into your fellowship? Would you feel any differently if that person were involved in a homosexual relationship? An adulterous relationship? A sexual relationship with a boyfriend or girlfriend?

2. Who should judge believers when they engage in gross immorality? Does your church have a process that it follows in disciplinary matters? What is that process? What should be the ultimate goal of church discipline? Does your church have a process for restoring excommunicated members if and when they repent? How would you feel if you had to excommunicate a friend in your church?

3. How does this chapter relate to the first four chapters of 1 Corinthians? How does it further Paul's argument? What underlying ideas connect the material?

1 Corinthians 6:1–11

The Problem of Litigations

I. INTRODUCTION
Just a Symptom of a Bigger Problem

II. COMMENTARY
A verse-by-verse explanation of this section.

III. CONCLUSION
The Heart of the Gospel

An overview of the principles and applications from this section.

IV. LIFE APPLICATION
A River Runs Through It

Melding the section to life.

V. PRAYER
Tying the section to life with God.

VI. DEEPER DISCOVERIES
Historical, geographical, and grammatical enrichment of the commentary.

VII. TEACHING OUTLINE
Suggested step-by-step group study of the section.

VIII. ISSUES FOR DISCUSSION
Zeroing the section in on daily life.

1 Corinthians 6:1–11

> **Quote**
>
> "For the sake of the kingdom, Jesus wants his disciples to give up their rights, interests, benefits and safeguards ... This is not saying that the kingdom of God consists in having no property, or in the absence of rights ... But it means that God's kingdom represents something higher than a hierarchy of human values and interests, and that the 'righteousness of the kingdom' teaches us to subject everything to this."
>
> Herman Ridderbos

IN A NUTSHELL

Should Christians sue one another in public court? It happens throughout the world today, and it took place in Corinth as well. Paul argued that this practice had to end, and that it revealed that the Corinthian church really did not understand the gospel.

The Problem of Litigations

I. INTRODUCTION

Just a Symptom of a Bigger Problem

"*I*'m sorry, but the slight noise is just a symptom of a much bigger problem." Have you ever heard those words from an automobile technician? You go to the garage to have a squeak fixed and discover that you have to replace the transmission. You take your car in because of a rattle and you find out that you need a whole new engine. I do not know about you, but I just hate it when a little problem actually stems from a much bigger one.

In this passage, Paul addressed a squeak in Corinth. Some believers in the church were taking one another to court before unbelievers. But that problem was just a symptom of something much worse. It revealed another serious problem in the congregation: the Corinthians neither understood nor lived the gospel.

II. COMMENTARY

The Problem of Litigations

> **MAIN IDEA:** *Continuing his discussion on the proper sphere of Christian judgment, Paul expressed his shock and dismay over the fact that the Corinthian believers were taking one another to court before unbelievers. Such lawsuits contradicted Christian teaching and behavior.*

A An Incredible Problem: Mishandling Lawsuits (6:1–6)

> **SUPPORTING IDEA:** *This section begins with a series of questions indicating Paul's shock that the Corinthians would actually sue one another in public court rather than handle legal matters within the church community.*

6:1. In this question, Paul addressed those brethren who were willing to sue other Christians in public court. It was inconceivable to him that a believer would actually take a legal **dispute . . . before the ungodly . . . instead of before the saints.** Believers sometimes have legitimate disagreements that necessitate adjudication, but it astounded Paul that Christians would take their issues before unbelieving judges.

The concept of "judgment" found in this verse links it to the preceding material regarding the incestuous man and to the Corinthian divisions and opposition to Paul. Though the Corinthians considered themselves wise and this wisdom led to their divisions, the Corinthians lacked discernment. They judged when they should not have and failed to judge when they should have.

6:2–3. Whereas the first verse had addressed those believers who sued other believers, these verses addressed the whole church. Anticipating the objection that Christians were not competent to judge such legal or civil matters, Paul asked if they had forgotten two basic Christian beliefs that pointed to the contrary.

First, he wondered, with a note of sarcasm, if the Corinthians had forgotten that **the saints will judge the world.** Jesus himself taught that his followers would act as judges at the end of time (Matt. 19:28; see also Rev. 20:4). The language of the Greek Old Testament (Septuagint) also implies this in Daniel 7:22 where it says that judgment was given to "the saints of the Most High." This future role of believers reflects that they will be victorious over their enemies and enjoy the honor of ruling with Christ after he returns (cf. 2 Tim. 2:12). Paul believed that this demonstrated the church's competence to adjudicate its own problems internally. Not every believer at every moment is competent for such matters, but the church as a whole should be able to act.

Second, Paul reminded the Corinthians that believers **will judge angels.** Many angels fell from their positions of authority when they rebelled against God (2 Pet. 2:4). Followers of Christ will pass judgment on these angels when Christ returns. This fact demonstrated that the church's ability to make decisions about conflicts among believers should not be dismissed.

On the basis of the church's future role in such important matters, Paul argued that the body of Christ should also be **competent to judge trivial cases** such as those regarding worldly disputes between Christians over things that he defined as **the things of this life.** Though lawsuits may not seem trivial when they involve huge sums of money, all such disputes are trivial when compared to the weightiness of the final eternal judgment in which Christians will exercise authority.

By making the matter of public lawsuits a question of the Corinthians' competence (**are you not competent**), Paul further undermined the Corinthians' admiration of worldly wisdom. They were so impressed by the false wisdom of unbelievers that they had forgotten the wisdom the church had received from Christ.

6:4. That the Corinthians had **disputes** is clear, but the original language of the second portion of this verse—**appoint as judges**—is somewhat ambiguous. There are two possible interpretations of this portion. On the one hand, Paul may have been ordering the Corinthians to **appoint as judges even men**

of little account in the church because even men of little account in the church are better able to adjudicate than are the unbelievers of the public courts. On the other hand, Paul have been expressing astonishment that the Corinthians effectively appointed **as judges even men of little account in the church**—unbelievers—by taking their cases to public court.

It is not wise to be dogmatic on this interpretive issue, but either option fits well with the context. Practically speaking, because Christians should see things in light of the kingdom of God, and have true, spiritual wisdom, any Christian should have greater wisdom and be a better judge than even the wisest unbeliever. This does not mean that the disputants will necessarily like the judgments of Christians better, especially if they are as worldly-minded as the Corinthians. It does mean, however, that one should expect Christians' judgments to surpass worldly judgments in righteousness and ultimate perspective.

Moreover, because the church is so important and valuable, appealing to public courts demonstrates a lack of respect for God's holy institution, the church. In fact, this seems to have been the Corinthians' greatest problem, and thus may have been Paul's main point in this verse.

6:5–6. Paul asked another question to bring **shame** to his readers. Obviously, the Corinthians' shame was not his ultimate goal. Rather, he wanted to convince them to change their perceptions and behavior. He wondered if the Corinthian congregation that prided itself on eloquence and wisdom actually had no one **wise enough to judge** the disputes. Paul had already made it clear that such wisdom exists among believers, but the Corinthians had failed to search for such a one, probably because they had also failed to understand true wisdom. Instead, they were doing the unthinkable: they were going **to law against another—and this in front of unbelievers.**

There seem to be two problems indicated in verse 6. First, Christians appealed to **law** in disputes between themselves, and second, they sued one another **in front of unbelievers.** On the one hand, Paul argued that the secular law of the land enacted by unbelievers was inferior to God's wisdom for judging disputes between believers. Paul had already argued that human wisdom fell short of God's truth, and that the world considered the gospel foolish.

Christians, however, know that the gospel is supremely wise. Because the gospel includes things like unity in Christ and forgiveness, which worldly standards of justice ignore, the secular law of unbelievers is not equipped to adjudicate disputes between Christians. Unbelieving human law simply does not reflect true wisdom, godliness, or justice. Regarding public courts, it might be said that justice is blind not because it treats all people equally but because it cannot see the truth.

On the other hand, the Corinthians sued one another **in front of unbelievers.** What is so wrong with going before unbelieving judges? Paul reminded them that in these situations it is a **brother** who takes his brother to court. Christians are brothers and sisters of one another. They share the intimacy of belonging to the same spiritual family, and their loyalty to that family ought to outweigh their desire not to be defrauded. Thus, they should not go outside that family to settle disputes.

Further, bringing the disputes of the Christian family into the public eye damages the reputation and witness of the church. The gospel is supposed to reconcile believers in fellowship with one another in Christ. What will the world think when it sees Christians appealing to those without the gospel to solve the problems that the gospel should be correcting? Naturally, the world will think the gospel is ineffective. Even if a church court were to misjudge a case, this would be preferable to damaging the credibility of the gospel by going to public court.

B An Underlying Problem: Not Living the Gospel (6:7–8)

SUPPORTING IDEA: *The fact that the Corinthians mishandled lawsuits by taking them to public court was terrible, but this problem flowed out of an underlying difficulty. The Corinthians mistreated one another and failed to reconcile their conflicts in a Christian manner.*

6:7. Paul closed his expressions of dismay over lawsuits by pointing out how self-defeating they were. Anyone who brings a lawsuit against another person intends to win. But because public lawsuits between Christians damage the church's witness and reputation, those who participate in them cannot win. They do more damage to themselves by injuring the church in this way than they suffer by being wronged by other Christians. Whatever decision the public court reaches, the Christians **have been completely defeated already.**

Further, the fact that there were lawsuits in the church demonstrated that the Corinthians had lost sight of some of the most precious principles by which they were to live. Christ taught his church the law of love (Jas. 2:8). Christians should serve one another (Gal. 5:13). They should be a unified body in which every member works in harmony with the others (Eph. 4:16). For these reasons, and to protect the church, it would be better to be **wronged** and **cheated** than to struggle and fight with one another.

6:8. The Corinthians, however, were not only defeated by demanding justice and recompense. They failed to turn the other cheek (Matt. 5:39) and to submit willingly to lawsuits (Matt. 5:40), and they were wrongdoers themselves. They actually cheated and did **wrong** to one another, even to their **brothers**.

Ⓒ The Root Problem: Misunderstanding the Gospel (6:9–11)

SUPPORTING IDEA: *At the bottom of the Corinthians' legal problems was a misunderstanding of their identity in Christ, and of the behavior to which that identity called them. This misunderstanding led to their mistreatment of others, and then to mishandling disputes.*

6:9–10. The Corinthians had forgotten a basic Christian doctrine: there is a big difference between believers and unbelievers. **Wicked** people are not destined to **inherit the kingdom of God**—they face a future of divine judgment. They will not receive the blessings of God when Christ returns in glory (Rom. 2:5–10; Heb. 10:26–27). By reminding the Corinthians of the judgment that awaits the wicked, Paul again emphasized that the Corinthians were behaving like the unbelieving wicked. In verse 8, he had used the verbal form of "wicked" to say "do wrong." Believers must not allow themselves to **be deceived** in these matters.

To make his point more clearly, Paul offered a list of lifestyles that were common outside the Christian community. He did not speak of people who occasionally fell into these sins, but of those who made these sins the patterns of their lives. Similar lists of sinful lifestyles appear elsewhere in Paul's writings and in the rest of Scripture. Here he first mentioned sexual sins: (1) the **sexually immoral**, those who are involved in any kind of premarital or extramarital sexual relations; (2) **idolaters**, mentioned here because of the close association between sexual immorality and many pagan religions; (3) **adulterers**, those who break the sanctity of marital sexual exclusivity; (4) **male prostitutes**, those who served in pagan religious sexual rituals, and (5) **homosexual offenders**, those who practice homosexual relations in general.

He then turned to other social sins: (1) **thieves**, those who steal as a way of life; (2) **the greedy**, those who have unquenchable desire to possess for themselves; (3) **drunkards**, those who imbibe alcohol to excess; (4) **slanderers**, those who falsely accuse others; and (5) **swindlers**, those who take what is not theirs.

Except for the addition of **thieves** and the expansion of the **sexually immoral** into subclasses of **adulterers**, **male prostitutes**, and **homosexual offenders**, this list is identical to the list in 1 Corinthians 5:10–11. Paul hoped the Corinthians would remember that people who practice such things would not **inherit the kingdom of God**. He implied that professed believers in Corinth who lived such lifestyles should take care that they were truly in the faith, knowing that if they did not repent they would perish. He also pointed out the folly of taking lawsuits before these kinds of people, as if such wicked people could judge rightly between Christians.

6:11. Many of the believers in Corinth once lived in these patterns of life, but Christ had changed them so they became much more reliable as judges of disputes within the church. Since these patterns of life were in the past for those who truly believed, they could take confidence that they would inherit the kingdom of God. Those believers who still fell into these sins needed to remember that their new identities in Christ (**what some of you were**) protected them from judgment. At the same time, their new identities also required that they live no longer like the wicked, but like believers.

Believers are **washed**, cleansed from sin through faith in Christ as symbolized in baptism (Acts 9:17–18). They are **sanctified**, set apart from the world and brought into relationship with God (Acts 20:32; 26:18). They have been **justified**, declared innocent before God (Rom. 3:24; Gal. 2:16; Titus 3:7). This blessing comes to believers **in the name of the Lord Jesus Christ** as they call on Jesus' name and rely upon him for their salvation. They also come **by the Spirit of our God** as the Holy Spirit applies the work of Christ to believers (Rom. 15:16; Eph. 1:13–14; Titus 3:5). Followers of Christ differ fundamentally from the sinful world around them. Therefore, believers should not make it their practice to bring their lawsuits against one another before unbelievers.

> **MAIN IDEA REVIEW:** *Continuing his discussion on the proper sphere of Christian judgment, Paul expressed his shock and dismay over the fact that the Corinthian believers were taking one another to court before unbelievers. Such lawsuits contradicted Christian teaching and behavior.*

III. CONCLUSION

The Heart of the Gospel

In this passage Paul corrected the Corinthians for taking one another to court. He sought to convince them that there was no justification for this practice. But Paul also pointed out that this problem was just a symptom of a much deeper difficulty. The Corinthians had been mistreating one another and still had not understood the heart of the gospel.

PRINCIPLES

- Christians are more able than unbelievers to judge righteously in civil matters.

- Believers have a new identity in Christ, and this new identity requires new and appropriate behavior.
- Legal controversies between Christians can damage the reputation of the church and the gospel in the eyes of unbelievers.

APPLICATIONS

- Churches should establish procedures for settling cases where one believer has a claim against another believer.
- Believers should be willing to abide by the decisions of these mediators, and generally they should not appeal to secular courts to contest these decisions.
- Believers ought to be willing to be defrauded in order to protect the church's witness and the gospel's reputation.

IV. LIFE APPLICATION

A River Runs Through It

Exploring can be great fun. I had a friend who once went exploring to find the source of a river that ran past his home. He followed it for miles by car, and then by foot, until he came to the foot of a mountain at the river's head.

But his discovery was a gigantic disappointment. At the base of the mountain was a rural garbage dump. The small stream flowed right through the middle of it. That glorious river flowing by his house actually had a polluted source.

In this passage, Paul took the Corinthians exploring. What was the source of their need to litigate against one another before unbelievers? It was the pollution of mistreating one another and misunderstanding the gospel itself.

While the implications of Paul's teaching in this chapter may be readily apparent to many modern readers, the actual application of these principles is difficult. This difficulty arises from the fact that churches rarely establish church courts to handle matters other than church discipline. Church members no longer respect the judgment of the church enough to accept that judgment in civil matters, especially when money or property are involved. We ought to heed Paul's advice, but we generally aren't willing to do so. If we truly understand Paul's argument, however, our unwillingness may yield to submission.

V. PRAYER

Lord Jesus, we want to uncover the sources of our problems. Help us to look beneath the surface to the motivations and misconceptions that lead us into trouble. Bring us to a fresh awareness of the gospel and show us how it can be the source of faithful living in your service. Amen.

VI. DEEPER DISCOVERIES

A. Judgment (6:1)

When Paul was in Corinth, the Jews appealed to the secular court for redress against the Christians (Acts 18:12–17). They did so by dragging the Christians before the judgment seat (*bema*) (cf. Matt. 27:19; Acts 25:10). Judgment seats in the ancient world were typically located in public places such as markets, and archaeology suggests that Corinth was no exception. Thus, lawsuits in ancient Corinth would have been very public. Roman pro-consuls would have presided over such suits and would have judged them according to Roman law, which was not always righteous or just by Christian standards.

B. Wronged, Cheated (6:7–8)

"Wronged" (*adikeo*) is a generic term referring to all sorts of wrongdoing and injustice. It is cognate to the noun *adikos* which is translated as "ungodly" in 6:1 and "wicked" in 6:9. "Cheated" (*apostereo*), in turn, denotes defrauding or robbing, or more generally depriving someone of something to which he is rightfully entitled. In 1 Corinthians 6:7–8, the use of these terms in conjunction probably indicates any type of injustice, but emphasizes cheating in property or monetary matters.

C. Inherit the Kingdom of God (6:10)

The term "kingdom of God" (often also called the "kingdom of heaven" by Matthew) refers to God's kingship over creation (Isa. 66:23). In the New Testament, it particularly refers to God's assertion of authority in sending Christ to defeat his enemies and establish his eternal rule as heir to the Davidic throne and to the throne of heaven. The gospel depends upon the idea of the kingdom of God in that it promises that Christ will share his inheritance with believers (Gal. 3:26–29). His inheritance includes not only the full realization of the blessings of covenant-keeping promised in the restoration, but also Christ's own reign (2 Tim. 2:12).

VII. TEACHING OUTLINE

A. INTRODUCTION

1. Lead Story: Just a Symptom of a Bigger Problem
2. Context: The Corinthians had failed to understand that the gospel is about building God's kingdom, unity in Christ, and eternal blessings. It is not about petty earthly matters and worldly justice. Because they failed to realize this, the Corinthians mistreated one another. In so doing they had damaged the church's abilities to proclaim the gospel and to build the kingdom.
3. Transition: Like the Corinthians, most modern Christians fail to understand the breadth and depth of the gospel, and thus have a worldly value system. We fail to understand the gospel rightly, and we mistreat fellow Christians—often in the same way the Corinthians did: by taking them to court. We need to begin to grasp the full nature of the gospel and to behave properly in light of God's standards.

B. COMMENTARY

1. An Incredible Problem: Mishandling Lawsuits (6:1–6)
   a. Christian cases before ungodly judges (6:1,6)
   b. Christians should judge Christian cases (6:2–5)
2. An Underlying Problem: Not Living the Gospel (6:7–8)
   a. Lawsuits indicate a defeated lifestyle (6:7a)
   b. Christians should avoid dishonoring the church in public court (6:7b)
   c. Christians who cheat their brethren sin grievously (6:8)
3. The Root Problem: Misunderstanding the Gospel (6:9–11)
   a. The wicked will not receive the gospel's blessings (6:9–10)
   b. Christians are no longer among the wicked (6:11)

C. CONCLUSION: A RIVER RUNS THROUGH IT

VIII. ISSUES FOR DISCUSSION

1. Do you believe the church is more capable of rendering just decisions in matters of property and personal rights than the state is? Do you think most believers you know would render decisions more justly than public courts do?

2. When Christ returns, believers will judge angels and the world. But why should we trust them to judge righteously now, before Christ returns?

3. Would you be willing to let your own church judge between you and another believer in your congregation if you had a disagreement that would normally require legal intervention?

4. Do you value more highly the work of the church, or your rights and property? How are these values reflected in the way you spend your time, energy, and money? How are these values reflected in the way you respond when mistreated by Christians?

1 Corinthians 6:12–20

Prostitution

Quote

"Th' expense of spirit in a waste of shame
Is lust in action, and till action, lust
Is perjur'd, murd'rous, bloody, full of blame,
Savage, extreme, rude, cruel, not to trust,
Enjoy'd no sooner but despised straight,
Past reason hunted, and no sooner had,
Past reason hated as a swallowed bait
On purpose laid to make the taker mad:
Mad in pursuit and in possession so,
had, having, and in quest to have, extreme,
A bliss in proof, and prov'd, a very woe,
Before, a joy propos'd, behind, a dream.
All this the world well knows, yet none know so well
To shun the heaven that leads men to this hell." ?

William Shakespeare, Sonnet 129

1 Corinthians 6:12–20

I N   A   N U T S H E L L

In this chapter Paul exposed the pagan practice of religious prostitution for what it truly was. He called on the Corinthians to take on a Christian outlook and to reject the views of their surrounding culture.

Prostitution

I. INTRODUCTION

Cultural Blind Spots

A quick reading of church history reveals something very sad about the church in the past. Time and again we see that followers of Christ fell into beliefs and practices that were considered acceptable in their cultures. They thought they were following Christ and seeking his kingdom, but today we realize they were blinded by the norms of their cultures.

Examples appear in every historical period: the atrocities of the Crusades; executions of heretics; wars between Protestants and Catholics; the African slave trade. The list goes on and on. We read about these events and wonder how Christians could have stooped so low. How could they have endorsed such pagan practices?

It is easy to see these failures in Christians of the past, but it is important to realize that we face the same temptations ourselves. Christians are easily influenced by the standards of the world. When we grow up in a culture that tells us certain practices are good, we tend to embrace these practices even as we follow Christ. Every Christian has such cultural blind spots. We follow wrong cultural practices because we are blind to their evil.

In this section of 1 Corinthians, Paul addressed a cultural blind spot in the church at Corinth. He spoke about the practice of visiting religious prostitutes. Some in the church were convinced that religious prostitution was a benefit to their spiritual life. From our modern outlook, we find it hard to believe that any Christian could think this way. Involvement in prostitution is such a repulsive, heinous sin.

But be aware that while we may not have this cultural blind spot, we have many in our day that are just as evil. By looking at what Paul said to the Corinthians about their cultural blind spot, we can learn how to deal more adequately with our own.

II. COMMENTARY

Prostitution

MAIN IDEA: *Corinth was well known in the ancient world for widespread prostitution. Moreover, in Paul's day prostitution was often associated with pagan religious practices. Pagans believed that participating in such prostitution promised good fortune and blessings from the gods. Some believers within the Corinthian church continued to hold these views and practices. Paul responded by correcting their false views of prostitution, and by explaining several dimensions of the Christian view of sexual morality in general.*

A Opposing Their Slogans (6:12–14)

SUPPORTING IDEA: *The apostle began his treatment of prostitution by responding to two slogans that were floating around in the church. Paul opposed those who involved themselves with prostitutes by quoting their words back to them.*

6:12. The first slogan was, **everything is permissible for me.** Paul quoted these words four times in this epistle (6:12; 10:23). Apparently, this saying was used to justify a variety of illegitimate activities. Here it supported sexual immorality, while in 10:23 it referred to eating meat devoted to idols. Admittedly, there is a measure of truth in these words. Followers of Christ have been set free from the pedantic legalism of the world. Spirituality must not be confused with long lists of rules regulating what Christians may eat, drink, and touch (Col. 2:20–23). In these matters, believers have liberty of conscience.

Even so, this was not the sense in which the Corinthians meant these words. They used this slogan to support immoral practices, and Paul would not stand for that.

In this passage Paul countered the slogan with two responses. On the one hand, he asserted that **not everything is beneficial.** Whatever liberties believers have, choices must be carefully evaluated as to their spiritual benefit. Many practices, though lawful for Christians, will have detrimental effects on the believer's walk with Christ, on the lives of others, or on the church. This consideration must be brought to bear any time Christians contemplate a course of action.

On the other hand, Paul also insisted that he would **not be mastered by anything.** Sexual appetites are good and wholesome in the context of marriage. Yet, the Corinthians had become victims of their own desires. They had lost perspective and control over their own bodies as they gave themselves to sexual immorality. Their sexual desires had **mastered** them. Followers of Christ are to be free from the mastery of all earthly desires so they may serve Christ faithfully.

Paul generally used the word translated "is beneficial" (*sumphero*) with regard to a group rather than to an individual. For example, in 1 Corinthians 10:23 where Paul again quoted the slogan and offered the same counter, *sumphero* clearly refers to a benefit for the church, not for the individual—even though the slogan seems to be placed in the mouth of an individual and to be directed toward an individual ("nobody," 10:24).

Quite possibly, the first slogan and its counter refer back to the lawsuits of 6:1–11, which may have been lawful for Christians to bring, but which did not build up the church. In that case, the two occurrences of the slogan in 6:12 may relate to two topics, the first referring to the preceding material, and the second to the material following. Such a reading helps demonstrate the structural unity between 5:1–13; 6:1–11; and 6:12–20. All these passages deal with the damage the Corinthians' poor judgment caused the church. Interestingly, Paul used this word only in his Corinthian correspondence.

6:13a. The second slogan used in support of sexual immorality was, **Food for the stomach and the stomach for food.** From Paul's response to this slogan, it appears the Corinthians employed these words to mean that sexual pleasure was meant to be enjoyed just as food was meant to be eaten. In this line of reasoning, they defended sexual immorality as something natural, something that followed the natural course of biology. God created man as a sexual creature; therefore, sex is appropriate and good. To be sure, there is a measure of truth in this slogan. The enjoyment of sexuality is as natural as eating, but this truth does not legitimize every form of sexual pleasure.

Paul countered the universal application of this naturalistic slogan by reminding the Corinthians that God has the authority to limit and guide the way we live. He asserted that, despite the natural order of food for the stomach, **God will destroy them both.** In other words, the fact that God will one day destroy the natural order as it is now known proves that biological functions do not ultimately determine man's moral obligations. God is the ultimate authority for determining how humans must behave. He is the master over all nature, and his Word must regulate how humans live.

That God will destroy both food and the stomach does not necessarily imply that food and stomachs will not exist in the new heavens and the new earth. Paul probably meant that God would destroy stomachs and food as they are now recognized and experienced. He left unanswered at this point the question of the nature of the spiritual bodies that believers will receive in the resurrection (see 1 Cor. 15:35–53).

6:13b–14. To make his point more explicit, Paul replied with a proverb that resembled the Corinthians' slogan. Sexual immorality cannot be justified as a natural biological practice because the human **body is not meant for sexual immorality, but for the Lord, and the Lord for the body**. The revelation of God in Christ makes it clear that the natural order of things is very different from what is evident from mere biological observation. A singular relationship exists between our bodies and Christ. We are to serve him with our bodies (Rom. 12:1), and Christ redeems our bodies.

To explain this connection, Paul reminded his readers of Christ's resurrection. God did not simply raise the spirit of Christ from the dead. Through the **power** of the Holy Spirit (Rom. 1:4) God raised Christ's body. In the same way, on the final day of judgment **he will raise** the bodies of all believers from the dead. Believers' hope of future bodily resurrection from the dead demonstrates beyond doubt that the natural order of things is that Christians' bodies belong to Christ and must be used only in his service.

B The Nature of Sexual Union (6:15–17)

SUPPORTING IDEA: *Paul appealed to two truths that he expected his readers to have known already because of his earlier teachings. He focused on the union of believers' bodies with Christ and with prostitutes.*

6:15. First, he reminded them that their **bodies** were **members of Christ himself**. Paul's words make it clear that believers are not merely spiritually joined with Christ. Believers are so intimately joined to Christ on every level of their being that even their physical bodies are united to him, being parts of his body on earth. The Corinthians dismissed the importance of sexual immorality on the basis that God would destroy the body (6:13). They thought that bodies that would be destroyed could not possibly have any sort of eternal value.

Paul argued, however, that believers' bodies are valuable because they are already part of Christ. Their significance is not just eternal, but immediate and temporal. In fact, because believers' bodies are joined to Christ, believers involve Christ himself in their relationships with prostitutes. This physical union with Christ makes it inconceivable that union with a prostitute is legitimate. **Members of Christ** must not **unite** themselves **with a prostitute**.

6:16. Second, Paul anticipated an objection by referring to another teaching his readers should have known already. Everyone who joins himself to a prostitute becomes **one with her in body**. Relationships with prostitutes are not as casual as they may seem, but are similar to those sexual unions that occur between marriage partners. For this reason, Paul supported his claim by referring to the Old Testament.

Genesis 2:24 describes Adam and Eve in sexual union as being "one flesh." From a biblical perspective, even sexual relations outside the bonds of marriage create a union of flesh between the participants. Because a believer's flesh is united to Christ, when a believer becomes one flesh with a prostitute, he sexually joins Christ to that prostitute. This does not compromise Christ's holiness, just as Christ's union with sinful believers does not compromise his holiness. Still, it highlights the impropriety of believers living like unbelievers. Such mistreatment of Christ is unthinkable, and must be avoided.

6:17. Having already said that believers' "bodies are members of Christ himself" (6:15), Paul added that their union **with the Lord** makes them **one with him in spirit.** By asserting this oneness of spirit, Paul did not contradict his previous statement that believers are physically united to Christ. Rather, he distinguished between unions with prostitutes "in body" (6:16), and union with the Lord **in spirit.** This distinction is essentially the same as the distinction between being "one flesh" (in body) and the mystical union between believers and Christ (in spirit).

Ⓒ Uniqueness of Sexual Sin (6:18–20)

SUPPORTING IDEA: *Sexual sin is unlike other sins in that a Christian sins against his or her own body, violating the truth that the body belongs to and is united to Christ.*

6:18. Paul began his conclusion to this section with an abrupt command: **Flee . . . immorality.** It is likely that the apostle had in mind Joseph's example of fleeing Potiphar's wife (Gen. 39:12). Paul instructed the young pastor Timothy in a similar way (2 Tim. 2:22). Rather than moderate resistance to immorality, Paul insisted on radical separation.

Paul's radical advice rested on the uniqueness of sexual sin. In contrast with **all other sins,** immorality is **against** one's **own body.** The meaning of these words is difficult to determine. Many sins, such as substance abuse, gluttony, and suicide, have detrimental effects on the body. Paul's words do not refer to disease and/or other damage caused by sin. Instead, his words are linked to the preceding discussion of 6:12–17. There Paul established that Christians' bodies are joined with Christ so that they become "members of Christ" (6:15) himself.

Sexual union with a prostitute violates one's body by bringing it into a wrongful "one flesh" union, and by flaunting the mystical union with Christ (6:15). It is in this sense that sexual immorality is a unique sin against the body. It violates the most significant fact about believers' physical existence: their bodies belong to Christ.

6:19. For this reason, the apostle appealed once again to a teaching which he had already given the Corinthians. The Christian's **body is a temple of the Holy Spirit.** The Holy Spirit takes up residence in believers, making their bodies a holy place for the dwelling of God's special presence. That the Holy Spirit resides in believers points to the new nature of believers' bodies. Believers' bodies are sanctified and holy, being in union with Christ. When a person in Christ engages in sexual immorality, that immorality runs contrary to the new nature and new identity of his body. The Christian has been redeemed for good works (Eph. 2:10), so he ought to use his body for good deeds and righteousness, not for sin.

Paul also reminded the Corinthians that they did not have rights to their own bodies. They were not free to use their bodies any way they wished. He insisted that Christ bought them at a price—his own blood. As a slave was bought in the ancient world, Christ bought his followers, body and soul, through the price of his own death. Because they belong to him, believers do not have the right to rebel against him by using their bodies in ways the Lord has prohibited.

Further, because this purchase results in redemption and salvation, it ought to inspire grateful obedience, not rebellion. In this reminder, Paul chastised the Corinthians and pleaded with them to obey Christ eagerly and thankfully.

6:20. In conclusion, Paul insisted, **Honor God with your body.** Having already given the negative warning to flee immorality, Paul gave positive guidance through the gospel. Rather than merely resist sin, believers must see themselves as temples of God purchased by Christ. Of course, this purchase refers to Christ's atonement. Because Christ died for and purchased believers, believers owe him obedience and honor. They should search for ways to bring glory to God by using their bodies in the ways that God has commanded, and by refraining from using their bodies in ways God has prohibited. They should remember that their bodies have been united to Christ, and they must honor Christ by not dragging his members into union with prostitutes.

> **MAIN IDEA REVIEW:** *Corinth was well known in the ancient world for widespread prostitution. Moreover, in Paul's day prostitution was often associated with pagan religious practices. Pagans believed that participating in such prostitution promised good fortune and blessings from the gods. Some believers within the Corinthian church continued to hold these views and practices. Paul responded by correcting their false views of prostitution, and by explaining several dimensions of the Christian view of sexual morality in general.*

III. CONCLUSION

The Heart of the Gospel

In this passage, Paul addressed the deception of a cultural blind spot in the church at Corinth. Even though some Corinthians meant well as they visited prostitutes, they were actually violating some of the central teachings of the Scriptures as well as the core of their relationship with Christ.

PRINCIPLES

- Prostitution is always a sin.
- Christians' bodies are united to Christ; they are good and holy.
- Sexual immorality involving our bodies violates Christ.

APPLICATIONS

- Christians must not engage in sexual immorality.
- Christians must respect their bodies, valuing them as important parts of ourselves for which Christ died.
- Christians should remember that sexual immorality violates Christ by involving him in our sin.

IV. LIFE APPLICATION

Life as a Christian Communist

When I first became a Christian in my teenage years, I was very radical. I left my home church and joined a Christian commune. I did this because I could see how my home church endorsed practices that were culturally acceptable, but opposed to the ways of Christ.

"They're just a bunch of hypocrites," I thought smugly. "I'm going where people are *real* Christians."

As you can imagine, it did not take long before I realized something about that Christian commune. We were a bunch of hypocrites too. To be sure, we had a different set of sins that we endorsed, but we had them nevertheless. In many ways, these sins were just as opposed to Christ as those I rejected so strongly in my home church.

It's easy to point the finger at the cultural prejudices that lead to hypocrisy in other peoples' lives. It is easy to point the finger even at the Corinthians who were involved in religious prostitution. But as I learned in my early Christian years, you and I have sins in our lives that are just as terrible.

Hopefully, unlike the ancient Corinthians, most of us realize that prostitution is sexually immoral. We do not need to be told not to sleep with prostitutes in order to realize that such behavior constitutes sin. However, this isn't true of all Christians, especially those in liberal churches, and it certainly isn't true of many unsaved people who attend or belong to churches. Many people come from backgrounds that teach that morality is relative, so that, while prostitution and other forms of sexual promiscuity may be wrong for some people, they aren't wrong for everyone. They might maintain that moral standards vary from person to person, or from society to society, but the basic premises are the same.

Some people are more like the ancient Corinthians, believing that sexual behavior is simply a biological function, that it is amoral, whether or not it be within the context of marriage. Others realize the sinful nature of immorality, but do not properly understand what it means to be in Christ and to receive his standing before God. These people sometimes believe that God has accepted sinners as they are, without obligating them to live holy lives. We see this frequently in those churches that teach antinomianism.

Some professing Christians have gone so far as to say that sexual immorality does not include certain types of behavior that the Bible clearly condemns. They might say that sex outside of marriage is acceptable as long as it takes place between consenting adults, or between people who love one another—even if the people happen to be of the same gender.

Paul's teaching in this portion of 1 Corinthians ought to correct many of these erroneous views. First, Paul assumed categorically that prostitution is wrong. If ever there was a culture in which prostitution was acceptable on the basis of subjective standards, it was ancient Corinth. But Paul rejected prostitution out of hand. We should not forget that in chapter 6 Paul had also railed against all other forms of sexual immorality. He upheld the biblical standards of morality, and he did not bend to arguments favoring subjectivity.

By informing us that our bodies are united to Christ and that they are a temple, Paul let us know that our bodies are good and holy, that they are valuable, and that God is interested in what we do with them. In fact, Christ owns our bodies, having died to purchase them. Our bodies are important parts of our beings, and they are destined for redemption, not for destruction. In salvation, they are to be the instruments of good works, by which we help others and serve and worship God.

But this good relationship between our bodies and Christ makes our sexual sins even worse. Because sexual intercourse unites our bodies to our sexual partners, through our bodies we join Christ to our sexual partners' bodies. When our sexual unions are sinful, we violate Christ by involving him in our sin. In fact, so great is the weight of our sexual sin that Paul does not simply tell us to resist the temptation—but to flee from it.

We should rethink our attitudes toward our bodies so that we become more inclined to avoid sinful sexual relations. We can learn from Paul to value our bodies highly because they are joined to Christ, and be encouraged to respect and honor Christ properly. We ought to recognize that all sex outside marriage perverts God's intentions. We should be horrified at the idea of violating Christ through our sexual immorality.

V. PRAYER

Lord Jesus, we confess that we are prone to sexual sin, and that we fail to honor you properly with our bodies. Please forgive us, and give us strength through your Holy Spirit to flee sexual immorality. Amen.

VI. DEEPER DISCOVERIES

A. Body (6:13,15–16,18–20)

In Greek thought, man was composed of a body and a soul. His soul was his higher, immortal self, while his body was simply a shell that he wore until death freed him of its burden. Because the Corinthians seemed to adopt this attitude toward their bodies, they concluded that bodily matters such as sexual immorality were insignificant. Matters that did not involve their souls would perish with their bodies. Paul, however, saw the body not just as a temporary shell, but as an essential, permanent part of man's being, a part of him that Jesus is redeeming (Rom. 8:23) and which man would carry into eternity (John 5:29). In union with Christ, believers' bodies are joined to the Lord in this life and in the life to come, just as their souls are. Therefore, their bodily actions are significant.

The exact nature of believers' union with Christ is elusive and mystical. Similarly, the nature of the "one flesh" relationship established by sexual intercourse presents a difficulty for many modern thinkers. The biblical truth is that sexual intercourse unites the bodies of the participants so that they become "one flesh," joining them in such a way that the distinctive individual identities of their bodies become blurred.

If we cannot easily conceive of this, it does not change the fact that it was Paul's view, or that it influenced his theology and morals. Paul's goal in teaching this doctrine was to change behavior. His theological arguments were designed to refute faulty worldviews that led to sinful actions, in order that he might offer sound presuppositions to his readers and thereby encourage righteous lifestyles.

B. Temple (6:19)

The New Testament uses two different words for temple, *naos* and *hieron*. The latter term usually refers to the temple and its courts in a general way. *Naos*, in turn, most frequently designates those inner portions into which only the priests entered. In his letters, Paul employed *naos* almost exclusively, and used it as a metaphor for the church. He said that Christians are the temple both collectively and individually. Given the frequency with which Paul spoke of the church as the temple, and his doctrine of the church as a whole, his statement in 1 Corinthians 6:19 that each believer is a temple of

God probably derived from the idea that each believer makes up a part of the temple of all believers.

Paul's single use of *hieron* does not identify believers, but the physical building of an unidentified temple (1 Cor. 9:13). Historically, the believing community had tended to prefer *naos* to *hieron* when naming things associated with God because pagans primarily used *hieron*. By the time of the New Testament, however, this distinction had begun to fade. Still, it is worth noting that Paul chose to identify believers with the preferred term for the most holy places in the temple. Christians need to take seriously the implications of being the *naos* of God.

VII. TEACHING OUTLINE

A. INTRODUCTION

1. Lead Story: Cultural Blind Spots
2. Context: In the Corinthian church's culture, religious prostitution was a means of blessing, not an excuse for wickedness. Thus, the Corinthians did not naturally think of such prostitution as sin. Rather, they actually engaged in it with pride and thankfulness. Paul, however, knew the evil of all prostitution, and he responded by telling them that their prostitution was not innocent; it violated Christ himself.
3. Transition: In our culture, many forms of sexual sin are considered legitimate and right. Just as in Corinth, many Christians in modern times find themselves sympathizing, even agreeing, with the world's evaluations of sexuality, and of many other sins. We also need to hear Paul's call to become aware of our cultural blind spots so we can submit ourselves to God's teaching rather than continue in our immorality.

B. COMMENTARY

1. Opposing Their Slogans (6:12–14)
   a. The Corinthians' slogans (6:12–13)
   b. Paul's modifications of the Corinthians' slogans (6:12–14)
2. The Nature of Sexual Union (6:15–17)
   a. Believers' bodies are members of Christ (6:15)
   b. Sex creates a "one-flesh" union between sexual partners (6:16)
   c. A believer's union with Christ involves Christ in his "one-flesh" sexual unions (6:15–16)
   d. Believers are one with the Lord in Spirit (6:17)
3. Uniqueness of Sexual Sin (6:18–20)
   a. The nature of sexual sin (16:18b)
   b. Proper attitude and response to sexual sin (6:18a,19–20)

C. CONCLUSION: LIFE AS A CHRISTIAN COMMUNIST

VIII. ISSUES FOR DISCUSSION

1. Is it true that everything is permissible for believers? Why would Paul tell us not to do things that are perfectly legitimate just because they are not beneficial? Should we understand Paul's statements as universal absolutes, or as instructions specific to a particular situation?

2. What does it mean to be "mastered"? Did Paul intend this to refer only to things that master the body, or also to things which master us in other ways? Is there anything in your life that masters you?

3. What did Paul mean when he said that the body is for the Lord, and the Lord for the body?

4. How would you define sexual immorality? Why do you suppose Paul advocated fleeing sexual immorality instead of simply resisting it? Have you found sexual immorality easy to avoid in your own life?

1 Corinthians 7:1–40

Issues Related
to Marriage

I. **INTRODUCTION**
Sticking Out Like a Sore Thumb

II. **COMMENTARY**
A verse-by-verse explanation of this section.

III. **CONCLUSION**
Against the World

An overview of the principles and applications from this section.

IV. **LIFE APPLICATION**
Jalopies?
Melding the section to life.

V. **PRAYER**
Tying the section to life with God.

VI. **DEEPER DISCOVERIES**
Historical, geographical, and grammatical enrichment of the commentary.

VII. **TEACHING OUTLINE**
Suggested step-by-step group study of the section.

VIII. **ISSUES FOR DISCUSSION**
Zeroing the section in on daily life.

Quote

"Marriage . . . is a blessing for which good men dwelling with affectionate wives praise God every day they live. Marriage and the Sabbath are the two choice boons of primeval love that have come down to us from paradise . . . Oh, the joy, the true, pure, elevated peace and joy which many of us have received through that divinely ordained relationship! We cannot but bless God every time we repeat the dear names of those who are now parts of ourselves."

C . H . S p u r g e o n

1 Corinthians 7:1–40

I N A N U T S H E L L

Marriage is an institution observed by most of the human race. Yet, a number of important features make the Christian concept of marriage unique. In this passage, Paul focused on some practical matters related to Christians and marriage.

Issues Related to Marriage

I. INTRODUCTION

Sticking Out Like a Sore Thumb

*H*ave you ever thought you stuck out like a sore thumb? I guess most people find themselves standing out in a crowd from time to time. Most of the time, it is quite embarrassing.

I remember a pastor friend and his wife once telling me about a time when they stuck out. They had just moved from Dallas, Texas, to a small city in the South. When they first arrived, a kind family hosted a reception for the new pastor and his wife. The invitations read, "Come to our house and meet our new pastor." At the bottom of the invitation the instructions were written: "Dress—Casual."

"That's great," my friend thought to himself. He had been in a coat and tie all week. Now he had a chance to dress like he enjoyed it in Dallas. He and his wife donned blue jeans, snakeskin jackets, and big cowboy hats. That was how they dressed casually in Dallas.

But when the hostess of the reception opened the door, they learned something very quickly. She appeared in an evening gown and her husband stepped out in a suit and tie. Dressing casually in this town meant something slightly less than a tuxedo.

That evening the new pastor and his wife felt like they stuck out like a sore thumb. Everyone looked at them and rolled their eyes. As they shook hands, everyone tried their best to look straight in their eyes and not to give them the once-over.

"It was a nightmare," the wife told me. "I'm still embarrassed when I see those people."

As western culture continues to change by moving away from its Christian roots, Christians are going to feel like that new couple in town. In many ways, our lifestyles will seem increasingly odd and old-fashioned. This is especially true in the Christian practice of marriage. I cannot tell you how many people react with disbelief when I tell them that my wife and I have been married for twenty-five years. "Now you don't hear that very often these days," they reply.

It's true. As Christians commit themselves to observing what Paul said in this chapter about marriage, we will stand out from the crowd. We will stick out like a sore thumb.

II. COMMENTARY

Issues Related to Marriage

MAIN IDEA: *Who should marry? Who should remain single? How should husbands and wives relate to one another? These practical matters occupied the apostle Paul throughout chapter 7.*

A General Outlooks on Marriage (7:1–9)

SUPPORTING IDEA: *In this chapter Paul began to respond to a number of issues which the Corinthians had raised in their letter.*

7:1. The apostle focused on a particular statement sent to him. The fact that the Corinthians questioned Paul regarding this matter indicates that they disagreed over this issue. Some members of the Corinthian church had gone to the opposite extreme of those who had justified prostitution (6:12–20). They claimed that it was **good for a man not to marry.** The NIV translation obscures the meaning of the statement. The NRSV ("It is well for a man not to touch a woman") and NASB ("It is good for a man not to touch a woman") translate more literally ("touch" rather than "marry") this statement that sexual relations in and of itself are not good. It is stated without qualification, implying that the best choice for everyone in every circumstance is to abstain from sexual relations.

Some interpreters have understood this as Paul's own position. This position is less than convincing. In light of Paul's love for the Old Testament Scriptures that advocate marriage and children as blessings from God, it seems unlikely that Paul himself would have suggested celibacy for all people. In fact, Genesis 2:18 says, "It is not good for the man to be alone." He knew that God himself ordained marriage for the betterment of humanity. Like Jesus before him, Paul saw celibacy as an unusual condition. He probably paraphrased the position of others in this way to contrast it with the Old Testament outlook.

7:2. In contrast to the categorical denial of sexual relations, Paul insisted that **each man should have his own wife, and each woman her own husband.** The verb "have," used in a sexual context, does not suggest initiating a marriage, but continuing a sexual relationship. It is best to understand Paul not as exhorting unmarried people to marry, but rather married people to continue sexual relationships with each other (cf. 1 Cor. 5:1). In support of this view, the Corinthian statement spoke of men and women in general, but Paul selected a more specific word for males which the NIV rightly translates **husband.**

Paul went on to state his pastoral reason for this viewpoint. He focused on the fact that there was **so much immorality**. This is most reasonably seen as a reference to the Corinthian church's problems with prostitution (6:15–16) and incest (5:1). While some within the church justified incest and visiting prostitutes, others advocated abstinence even within marriage.

In Paul's mind there was a connection between these two problems. He believed that these opposite problems were caused by certain Corinthians who refused to have sexual relations with their spouses. To avoid the sexually immoral use of prostitutes, Paul insisted that married couples should fulfill each other's needs.

Some scholars believe that a faction of women within the Corinthian church may have advocated abstinence within marriage, and that Paul mainly addressed them here. If this is correct, then this division within the church would not only have split the body of believers, but the families within that body by estranging husbands from wives. Thus, Paul may have been working to reconcile families as well as to protect the sanctity of the church.

7:3–4. Marriage protects against the temptations of immorality only when it functions properly. For this reason, Paul spoke explicitly about the **marital duty** that enjoins partners. The Bible often speaks of sexual relations as a privilege and blessing (Prov. 5:18–19; Song 4:9–16), but married couples also have a duty not to refrain from sexual relations without just cause (Exod. 21:10).

The Corinthians were defrauding each other of their sexual rights, so Paul pointed out the obligations to sex that married couples bear. He also let them know that these obligations were mutual—the husband has a duty to have sex with his wife just as she has a duty to have sex with her husband. Neither partner has the right without good cause to refuse the other.

Paul expressed his view in a remarkable way. **The wife's body does not belong to her alone but also to her husband,** or as the NASB puts it, "The wife does not have authority over her own body, but the husband does." Unfortunately, these words have been used to justify physical abuse by husbands against their wives. They have also been used to compel women to submit to their husbands' sexual desires even when these women suffer from physical impairments and illnesses. We must recognize, however, that other teachings of Scripture, such as self-protection and the principle of love, inform us of limitations on Paul's statement.

Paul emphasized complete parity and mutuality of authority by adding, **The husband's body does not belong to him alone but also to his wife.** Wives have the same authority over their husbands' bodies that husbands have over their wives'. Sexual relations must be mutually agreeable. Couples should strive toward the ideal of marriage as they evaluate their specific situations and responsibilities.

7:5–6. In the Christian ideal, spouses must not deprive partners sexually except **by mutual consent and for a time**, and only for special religious purposes: **that you may devote yourselves to prayer.** Throughout the Old Testament, times of special religious devotion, such as prayer and fasting, included sexual abstinence (1 Sam. 21:4–5). Paul made it apparent that such practices were to be carried over into the New Testament as well.

Once the time of special religious devotion is over, the couple must return to normalcy **so that Satan will not tempt** them to be involved in illicit sexual relations. The longer couples abstain from sex, the greater the risk that one partner will fall into sexual immorality. In allowing couples to abstain from sexual relations for a time by mutual consent, Paul made a **concession.** He by no means intended to **command** periods of abstinence. His command was that they **not deprive each other.**

7:7. Paul also qualified his affirmation of marriage by admitting that in one sense he wished **all men** were as he. By the phrase **as I am,** Paul apparently referred to his unmarried status, and may also have meant to include the fact that he did not "burn with passion" (cf. 7:8–9).

Not much is known about Paul's marital history, though it is likely that he was married at one time because marriage was required of rabbis in his day. If Paul was an ordained rabbi, he must have been married for a while, but nothing is known about what happened to his wife. She may have died, or she may have left him when he converted to Christianity. Whatever the case, Paul was single and free from burning sexual passion when he wrote this letter, and he admitted that he saw advantages in this condition.

Even so, Paul recognized that God does not call all people to single lives unburdened by sexual passion, **but each man has his own gift from God.** In other words, God blesses one person with the call to be single, and another he calls to marriage.

While it is true that some gifts are greater than others (1 Cor. 12:31), this greatness does not depend upon an inherent superiority of the gift, but on the benefit it brings to the church (1 Cor. 14:1–4). In the particular time and situation that Paul addressed in Corinth, it appeared to him that singleness without sexual passion offered more benefits to the church than did marriage. This does not mean that he thought celibacy was necessarily a superior gift to marriage in all instances, and it does not diminish the high value of the gift of marriage. Instead, celibacy was more beneficial in Corinth's particular situation.

Further, by pointing out that God gifts different people in different ways, Paul subverted any possibility that reproach might fall on those who married. Thus, he removed the opportunity for those who remained single to become prideful in their ability to resist passion.

7:8. Paul concluded his general outlook on marriage by applying his views to the **unmarried and the widows.** He advised that **it is good for them to stay unmarried.** The language "it is good" again alludes to Genesis 2:18 where God said of Adam's singleness, "It is *not* good" (author's emphasis). In contrast with Genesis 2:18, Paul said that remaining single *is* good. Paul's viewpoint did not contradict Genesis. Genesis sets up marriage as a creational pattern that remains ordinary, proper, and good for human life in general. Yet, Paul recognized that celibacy had certain benefits over marriage in some situations. He did not state these benefits or situations, but revealed several complex ideas underlying his preference for singleness in 7:29–35.

7:9. Nevertheless, Paul also recognized that reality is usually not ideal. So, he conceded a hierarchy of preferences, with celibacy being the most desirable for the unmarried Corinthians. But "the unmarried and the widows" (7:8) were to **marry** if they could not **control themselves** sexually. Marriage was not as advantageous as celibacy, but it was better than burning **with passion.** Literally, Paul did not say, "If they are not able to control themselves," but "If they do not control themselves," that is, "If they lose control and fall into sexual immorality." Paul did not suggest that marriage would eliminate lustful thoughts, but that it could help believers abstain from sexual immorality.

𝔹 Divorce (7:10–16)

> **SUPPORTING IDEA:** *Paul addressed divorce between two believers and divorce between a believer and an unbeliever.*

7:10–11. Paul began by addressing divorce between two believers. He introduced his **command** with the notation that Jesus himself authorized his viewpoint. As an apostle, Paul had the responsibility to establish moral guidelines for the church. He did not need to appeal to Jesus (**not I, but the Lord**), but he did so here to give his words extra weight. The most relevant teaching of Christ on this subject appears in Mark 10:11–12 (see also Matt. 19:9).

Paul first stated the general policy to be followed: **a wife must not separate from her husband.** He followed with similar instructions to men: **a husband must not divorce his wife.** The terms **separate** and **divorce** were not distinguished in Paul's day as they are in many cultures today. To separate was to divorce. Jesus made fornication a legitimate grounds for divorce (Matt. 19:9). Paul argued that desertion was also grounds for divorce (7:15). With these exemptions in mind, Paul stated plainly that believers must not practice divorce.

Paul was realistic enough to know that illegitimate divorces happen among believers. For cases of illegitimate divorces, he offered two choices:

remain unmarried or **be reconciled** to the original spouse. Paul did not comment on what to do if attempts to reconcile are rebuffed. The rest of Scripture and prudence must guide believers in such situations.

7:12–13. Paul then addressed **the rest**, that is, believers married to unbelievers. In contrast with his previous directives, Paul admitted that this teaching was his own, **not** from **the Lord**. This qualification does not lessen the authority of the teaching because as an apostle Paul spoke on behalf of the Lord (14:37). Paul meant that, to his knowledge, Jesus had not spoken about marriages between believers and unbelievers during his earthly ministry.

Paul taught that believers should not divorce their unbelieving spouses if the unbelievers are **willing to live with** the believing spouses. This rule applies equally to men and women. Often religious differences between spouses will lead to serious tensions in the home, but Paul plainly stated that religious differences *per se* are not legitimate grounds for divorce.

7:14. Paul justified his position in two ways. First, the **unbelieving husband** and **unbelieving wife** have **been sanctified through** the believing **wife** and **husband**. The term *sanctified* denotes being made special or set apart for God's use or purposes (cf. 1 Tim. 4:5; Heb. 9:13; 1 Pet. 3:15). It does not mean that these unbelievers were redeemed or justified in Christ. If they had been redeemed or justified, they would not have been called **unbelieving**. Rather, **through** the believing spouses, the unbelieving spouses participate in the community of the sanctified people of God.

This sanctification process is different in each marriage. Some unbelieving spouses will eventually become believers through their association with their believing spouses (7:16). Others will not respond to this influence. In the very least, these unbelievers come into contact with the gospel and Christian graces in ways that ordinary people never experience.

Paul's viewpoint on the sanctification of unbelieving spouses does not rest on a long-standing or well-known tradition. Moreover, experience tends to convince many believers that they have little or no influence over their unbelieving spouses. For these reasons, Paul defended his position by noting a belief that he and the Corinthians shared. He said that **otherwise** (i.e., if it were not true that unbelieving spouses are sanctified) the **children** of these marriages **would be unclean.** But it was inconceivable both to the Corinthians and to Paul that the **children** of believers could be anything but **holy.**

The apostle's words assume a teaching that appears throughout the Bible: the children of believers are special in God's eyes, even though they are not redeemed. The term *holy* derives from the same root as *sanctified* earlier in this verse. These children are not necessarily believers, but they are the expected heirs of the covenant relationship which their believing parents enjoy with God (Ps. 89:29; Rom. 11:28).

7:15. Despite the potential for positive influence from believers in mixed marriages, Paul knew the reality that unbelievers often do not want to remain in these marriages. For this reason, he added that **if the unbeliever leaves, let him do so.** Believers are under no obligation **in such circumstances** to hold their marriages together. One interpretation of this verse suggests that to oppose the unbeliever's pursuit of divorce is to neglect the fact that **God has called us to live in peace.** Alternatively, the believer's call to live in peace may be seen as his or her call to remain with an unbelieving spouse.

In many Christian traditions, this passage has been used to support the idea that desertion is a legitimate ground for divorce. Since one who fails to provide for his families is "worse than an unbeliever" (1 Tim. 5:8), some believe that desertion may be legitimate grounds for divorce even when the deserting partner claims to be a believer. The act of desertion presumably disproves his or her profession of faith.

7:16. Why did Paul call for hesitation over divorcing unbelievers? In effect, he said that we cannot know how God will use us in the lives of unbelieving spouses. Often, believing spouses become the instruments through which unbelievers come to faith.

Stay Where You Are (7:17–24)

> **SUPPORTING IDEA:** *Paul digressed to discuss a guiding rule established for all the churches: each believer should retain the place in life that the Lord has assigned to him and to which God has called him.*

7:17. Throughout this passage Paul spoke of God's calls to believers, calls both to salvation and to various tasks. This emphasis on "call" expanded his statement in verse 15 that "God has called us to live in peace." Believers live in peace partly by knowing and following God's call.

It is important to remember that Paul did not suggest that believers should never change their status. He said that they should seek to know how **God has called** them, and to **retain** the places God has **assigned** them. His general rule was: Christians should remain as they are in relationships and service unless God assigns them new tasks.

7:18–19. Regarding circumcision, Paul stated plainly that a man should not automatically seek to change his condition. He insisted that **circumcision is nothing and uncircumcision is nothing.** Throughout his ministry, Paul opposed Jewish Christians who wanted to force Gentile converts to be circumcised. He reminded the Corinthians that he always defended the uncircumcised in the church, not allowing others to convince them that being circumcised was meritorious for salvation or for status in the church (cf. Gal. 6:13). At other times, Paul encouraged uncircumcised Gentile believers not to despise their Jewish brethren (Rom. 11:13–18).

Whether circumcised or uncircumcised, believers should remain as they are and not let others press them to change. No one should take pride in his circumcised or uncircumcised status. At one point, Paul encouraged Timothy to be circumcised for the sake of peace in the church, though never allowing that circumcision might be thought meritorious for salvation. In general, however, he believed that the uncirmcumcised should remain so. The only truly important thing is obedience to **God's commands** (cf. Rom. 2:25–29).

By comparing marriage and circumcision, Paul indicated that marital status was insignificant for a person's standing before God and within the church. Just as believers should not change the status of their circumcision to gain approval before God or man, they should not change their marital status for these reasons.

7:20. This verse serves mainly a rhetorical function, reasserting Paul's main point. Its repetition here and in verse 24 emphasizes that this is the primary thing Paul intended this entire section to prove.

7:21. Regarding slavery, Paul reminded the Corinthians that he had a similar policy. If someone was a **slave** when he or she became a believer, then that person should not feel compelled to change his social status. Paul conceded, **If you can gain your freedom, do so.** He knew that slavery is not the ideal condition for human beings, and he wished that no one be enslaved to anyone but Christ (Rom. 6:18; Eph. 6:6). Nevertheless, he insisted as a general policy, **Don't let it trouble you.**

One cannot help but wonder how the suggestion that slaves obtain freedom accords with Paul's argument that each believer should remain as he was called. In some cases, however, there are legitimate reasons to change one's situation. For example, freedom is objectively better than slavery, and marriage is better than falling into sin (7:9).

7:22. Paul explained why slaves should not be despondent with their condition: Any believer who is a **slave** is **the Lord's freedman.** In a day when slavery was widespread throughout the Mediterranean world, Paul gave great comfort to those who were unable to become legally free. He pointed to their inner spiritual condition of freedom in Christ. The status of slave carries no dishonor; rather, slaves are equal in Christ to those of higher social status in the church (cf. Gal. 3:28; Col. 3:11). In fact, Paul raised the status of slaves by asserting that the believing **slave** ought to consider himself a **freedman,** and the **free man** ought to consider himself **Christ's slave.** In Christ, the ground is level. Every believer is both free man and slave.

7:23. It would have been difficult for a slave to accept Paul's viewpoint. So Paul closed this discussion by repeating a doctrine he had mentioned in 6:20: all believers have been **bought at a price**—the price of Christ's blood. Believers have been set free from sin's dominion through the death of Christ.

This spiritual freedom came at the price of Christ's sacrificial death. Consequently, believers must **not become slaves of men**.

Paul spoke metaphorically here. He did not want slaves within the church to accept the outlook of those who would have enslaved them, tyrannizing them with false views that Christian slaves were not equals to Christian masters (Rom. 6:16; Phlm. 16). Instead, he wanted them to think of themselves, whatever their condition, as free men and women because Christ had set them free at the cost of his own blood. As in 6:20, Paul also emphasized that Christ's purchase of the church meant that the church's new identity in Christ required different behavior on the part of believers.

7:24. Affectionately calling the Corinthians **brothers**, Paul repeated the general rule of remaining in the station to which one is called. Yet, he added that Christians must live **as responsible to God**. These words draw attention to the fact that one can know when to change his or her situation only if he or she depends on God. No rule can cover all the circumstances involved in such decisions.

Virgins and Marriage (7:25–28)

> **SUPPORTING IDEA:** *Paul applied the principle developed in the previous section to the question of whether virgins should marry. He told the unmarried not to change their stations to improve their status. Moreover, because of the crisis in Corinth, he encouraged them to remain unmarried unless God called them to do otherwise.*

7:25–26. In verse 25 Paul responded to a different question from the Corinthians' letter. The term *virgins* probably refers to virgin women who were engaged but not yet married (see 7:36). Apparently, there was a controversy in the Corinthian church over whether engaged couples should go ahead and marry. Paul admitted that Jesus had not taught on the matter (**no command from the Lord**). Quite possibly, Paul meant that the Corinthians' **present crisis** presented a unique problem which neither Jesus nor the Old Testament had addressed. Even so, Paul's view as an apostle was authoritative. **By the Lord's mercy**, he was **trustworthy** to speak sound advice.

By qualifying his answer with the words **I think**, Paul offered a preference or opinion, not an absolute rule. In effect, Paul said that the rule of "remaining as you are" which he had just illustrated should also be applied to those contemplating marriage. Remaining unmarried **is good** (7:26). Paul did not contradict God's assessment of singleness and marriage in Genesis 2:18: "It is not good for the man to be alone." He made it clear that his preference stemmed from the unique circumstances which the church, and perhaps only the Corinthian church, faced in his day. He said that the unmarried should remain unmarried **because of the present crisis** (7:26).

It is difficult to know for certain what Paul meant by **the present crisis**. Paul may have been pointing to the crisis associated with the return of Christ. In this passage he referred to the nearness of Christ's return.

A more likely understanding is that Paul referred to famines in Greece that caused great trials for the people of Corinth. Some of the Corinthian Christians were hungry as they came to the Lord's supper (11:21,34), and historical research has demonstrated that famines were occurring in the land near this time. In light of the hardships these famines caused the church, Paul strongly suggested that unmarried people should remain unmarried.

In support of this reading, note that Paul nowhere suggested that virgins should never marry, or that this judgment was to be perpetual. In fact, in 7:36 he qualified his advice by suggesting that it might be better to marry people who were getting on in years. This suggests that Paul did not advise perpetual singleness but a temporary moratorium on weddings.

7:27. Paul expanded his advice by telling those bound to wives **not** to **seek a divorce**. Paul did not use the word *married* (NIV) here, but rather the phrase "bound to a woman/wife" (cf. NASB and NRSV "bound to a wife"). In all likelihood, Paul had in mind those who were betrothed or promised in marriage. In ancient Israel betrothal was practically equivalent to marriage (see Deut. 22:23–24).

Paul did not want betrothed parties to break off their engagements, but only to postpone them. Further, he did not want those who had been released from marital obligations to **look for a wife**. The NIV is somewhat misleading here in its reference to the **unmarried**. As the NASB ("Are you released from a wife?") and NRSV ("Are you free from a wife?") reflect, the text literally speaks to those who have been released from women/wives. His main points were that those already engaged should not yet wed, and that those who had broken off their engagements should not yet seek to enter new marriage contracts.

7:28. Though he thought marriage inadvisable because of the present crisis, Paul conceded that it was no sin (**have not sinned**). Yet, those choosing marriage were to do so with eyes wide open to the **troubles in this life** they would **face**. Though "in this life" is a common translation (NIV, NASB, NRSV), the KJV renders the phrase more literally as "in the flesh." The KJV translation should be preferred here since Paul did not mean that married life is always more difficult and troublesome than single life. After all, God ordained wives to be partners of their spouses, not hindrances (Gen. 2:18).

Given the famines in the area, Paul probably meant that marriage would make it harder to put food on the table. This is especially understandable when one considers that marriage leads to children, and therefore to more mouths to feed. Such lack of food would truly be "trouble in the flesh." Paul encouraged caution to those who were unmarried because he wanted **to** spare them these troubles. His sensitivity to the practical needs of the Corinthians was evident, yet he was also plainly aware that he needed to allow them to follow God's call in such matters on an individual basis.

E The Implications of an Eternal Perspective (7:29–35)

SUPPORTING IDEA: *Paul wanted the Corinthians to discard their worldly perspectives that emphasized personal spiritual status and led to arrogance and divisions. He taught them to adopt an eternal perspective, which would help them weather their time of crisis.*

7:29–31. Paul's reference to the Corinthians as **brothers** reflected his deep concern for their well-being. His concern caused him to ponder the conditions of life faced by all believers—married, divorced, widowed, engaged, and single alike. He began and ended with acknowledgments that this life is fleeting: **time is short . . . this world in its present form is passing away.**

Between these opening and closing thoughts, the apostle reflected poetically on the nature of life in this fleeting time. His poetry followed the patterns of parallelism found in Old Testament poetry. Because this material is poetic, it is not surprising to find that the apostle spoke in hyperbole. He mentioned several kinds of people: **those who have wives, those who mourn, those who are happy, those who buy something,** and **those who use the things of the world.** As in 5:1 and 7:2, **those who have wives** probably does not refer to the engaged virgins, but to those who maintain sexual relationships with their wives.

All of these activities are legitimate and honorable in Paul's view, but they are oriented toward this earthly life. Paul was concerned that believers not invest themselves too deeply in such matters. For this reason, he balanced each category of activity by encouraging an eternal perspective. Christians **should live as if** they have no wives, no mourning, no happiness, no permanent possessions, and no engrossments.

Paul's words should not be taken in an absolute sense. Elsewhere he affirmed balanced views of marriage responsibilities and sexuality (Eph. 5:22–33), happiness (1 Thess. 5:16), mourning (Phil. 3:18), and possessions (1 Tim. 6:8). In this passage, he reminded all Corinthians that these legitimate aspects of life are not everything.

Paul defended this attitude in verse 31: the world to which these things belong is **passing away.** To handle matters of this life properly, Christians must remember that these things are not permanent. On the one hand, believers live in this world with its pleasure, pain, and responsibilities. On the other hand, they belong to the next world that will replace this life forever. This is why Paul described his own life in paradoxical terms: dying but living, beaten but not killed, sorrowful but rejoicing, poor but making others rich, having nothing but owning everything (2 Cor. 6:9–10).

7:32. Paul continued to address all varieties of Corinthians by explaining that he gave the instructions in 7:29–31 in order to keep them from anxiety. He wanted them **to be free from concern.** The word translated "free from concern" is *amerimnous,* which may be positive ("caring") or negative ("worrying or being anxious"). The same is true of its cognate verb *merimnao,* here translated "is concerned." Given the fact that Paul said he wants people to be *amerimnous,* it seems best to understand a negative force in this passage.

Traditionally, *amerimnous* has been taken to mean "free from concern over worldly matters." This reading probably arose because of the context of the immediately preceding verses (7:29–31). As a result, *merimnao* has been interpreted positively in reference to "the Lord's affairs," but negatively in reference to affairs of this world (7:33). Paul did not offer this qualification, however, and the word itself does not mean this. Moreover, people in every station of life, whether married or unmarried, are susceptible to concern and anxiety when they lose the eternal perspective.

As Paul pointed out, even **an unmarried man** may worry over **the Lord's affairs.** Elsewhere in this letter, Paul made it clear that the Corinthians placed heavy emphasis on human merit (4:7). The Corinthians: misunderstood what it meant to be "in Christ" (15:18–22); thought their spiritual gifts were meritorious and status-worthy (12:1–31); and strove for spiritual status through their own efforts and associations (3:21; 5:6). Because they thought pleasing God depended on their own works, they had good reason to worry about pleasing him.

7:33–34a. Paul declared that **a married man** without an eternal perspective has even more trouble than an unmarried man because he must worry about pleasing **his wife** as well as the Lord. To fulfill their moral responsibilities, married men must pay attention to all kinds of things that may distract them from their efforts to please the Lord. The **affairs of this world** crowd their lives and their **interests are divided.** If they lack an eternal perspective, they worry about pleasing God and about very real problems like putting food on the table even in times of famine.

7:34b. Similarly, **an unmarried woman or virgin** (engaged woman) who lacks an eternal perspective may worry that her efforts to please **the Lord** will fail, or will not be enough to satisfy his holiness. It is the duty of unmarried women to refrain from fornication, **to be devoted to the Lord in . . . body** as well as in **spirit.** This was probably hard to do in the sexually loose world of Corinth, particularly for those who had once been part of the promiscuous crowd. Keeping sexually pure was certainly as stressful as it was difficult, especially for those who thought their acceptability before God depended upon it. While a married woman had an outlet for her sexual needs, she also had the added worries of nurturing a relationship with **her husband** and of fulfilling her household responsibilities.

7:35. Paul did not encourage the postponement of marriage or the adoption of an eternal perspective in order **to restrict** the Corinthians' behavior. He did not intend them to interpret 7:29–31 as instructions against conjugal relations, mourning, happiness, or participation in the marketplace or in life. Given the Corinthians' propensity to twist Paul's words, Paul was probably wise to make this point explicitly. Paul knew that postponing marriage and adopting an eternal perspective would benefit the Corinthians by helping them **live in a right way in undivided devotion to the Lord.**

Though the NIV uses the word *devotion* here and the word *devoted* in verse 34, this is somewhat misleading since the Greek words *euparedron* ("devotion" NIV) and *hagios* ("devoted" NIV) are completely unrelated. Paul certainly did not mean to say that postponing marriage would help engaged virgins refrain from fornication. In fact, he apparently intended *euparedron* ("devotion" NIV) to refer to men and women, whether married or unmarried. The devotion of which he spoke was probably the eternal perspective he encouraged and the willingness to alter behavior on the basis of that new perspective, such as by postponing marriage.

F Final Concessions (7:36–40)

> **SUPPORTING IDEA:** *Paul intended to help the Corinthians live in proper devotion to the Lord, not to restrict them by giving them new rules to follow. To make sure they understood this, he offered two final concessions regarding marriage between those who were already engaged and those who had been widowed.*

7:36. Paul acknowledged that "better" is not necessarily the only right choice. Paul advised singleness over marriage for the time of the present crisis, but the fact that God ordained marriage meant that its legitimacy could never be denied. So Paul once again qualified his advice, suggesting that the marriage of engaged women who were **getting along in years** not be postponed. **Anyone** is somewhat ambiguous here. It may refer either to a young woman's fiancé or to her father. The NIV and NRSV understand fiancé, and are most likely correct given that 7:25–28 put the responsibility for keeping or breaking engagement on the groom. Whether Paul referred to fathers, fiancés, or both, however, the basic idea is the same. If someone is convinced that marriage is right before God, **he should do as he wants. He is not sinning.**

7:37–38. At the same time, the man who has decided **not to marry the virgin . . . also does the right thing.** Refraining from marriage is right only if the decision is **settled** in the man's **own mind.** Paul found this qualification so important that he rephrased it several times. There must be **no compulsion.**

The person must have **control over his own will**, and must have **made up his mind not to marry.**

Apparently, some members of the Corinthian church sought to control others in these matters, perhaps by pressuring them to pursue the "highest" spiritual status. Paul knew the error of such concepts of status, and he refused to let Christians dominate and abuse their brothers' and sisters' freedom of conscience. Paul had expressed strong personal feelings about postponing marriage. Yet, he knew each individual had to settle this issue personally.

Many aspects of Christian living are of this nature. Advice may be given, but in the end each Christian must make a decision in good conscience before God. For this reason, Paul closed his discussion of this matter on a conciliatory note. Those who married did **right**, and those who did not did **even better**. Both options were acceptable.

7:39–40. In 7:8 Paul had advised "the unmarried and the widows" that it was "good for them to stay unmarried." In these verses Paul returned to matters concerning widows. He began with the well-known policy that marriage bonds continue throughout life, but only until the death of a spouse (cf. Rom. 7:2). Paul went on to say that, upon the death of her husband, a widow **is free to marry.**

In much the same way, Paul told Timothy that he wanted young widows to remarry (1 Tim. 5:14). The only qualification he offered was that the new husband must **belong to the Lord.** Later, Paul reiterated that Christians should be bound only to other Christians (2 Cor. 6:14). He did not want believers to divorce unbelievers, but he also did not want believers knowingly to marry unbelievers.

As he had done a number of times in this chapter, Paul allowed marriage, but clearly made known his own judgment or opinion that a widow would be **happier** if she stayed as she was (i.e., unmarried). Clearly this was occasional advice tailored to Corinth's peculiar situation. Paul did not give contradictory advice to the Corinthians and to Timothy (1 Tim. 5:14). Because his opinion may have sounded contrary to general biblical principles favoring marriage, Paul wanted to make sure that no one dismissed his opinion too quickly. Thus, he reminded the Corinthians that he also had **the Spirit of God.**

In this passage Paul did not command the Corinthians authoritatively as he did on other matters, but these final words appealed to the Corinthians to take Paul's opinions very seriously.

MAIN IDEA REVIEW: *Who should marry? Who should remain single? How should husbands and wives relate to each other? These practical matters occupied the apostle Paul throughout chapter 7.*

III. CONCLUSION

Against the World

This chapter touches on several important aspects of Christian marriage. In the Corinthians' world, the temptation to depart from biblical teaching on marriage confronted the Christian church on every side. In our world, the same is true. We must look carefully at the apostle's words to evaluate our own outlooks and practices in marriage.

PRINCIPLES

- Sex within the covenant of marriage guards against sexual immorality and infidelity.
- Marriage is sacred to God.
- Marriage is a great blessing.
- The children of believers are holy to God, obligated to keep God's covenant.

APPLICATIONS

- Married couples should maintain healthy sexual relationships.
- Sometimes marriage is inadvisable, but barring such circumstances we should desire and practice it.
- The children of believers must come to faith in order to receive the blessings of God's covenant.
- Christians should maintain an eternal perspective.

IV. LIFE APPLICATION

Jalopies?

Some people love to drive old cars. I have friends who spend lots of time and money renovating and driving around in antique automobiles. They enjoy it, but I have seen people stop and stare at them like they're crazy. All dressed up in costumes from the earlier decades of this century, they drive about with big smiles on their faces. Meanwhile, modern, faster cars line up behind them waiting for the opportunity to pass and go on their way unhindered by these throw-backs to yesteryear.

Let us face it. When Christians today take seriously the teachings of this chapter and apply them to marriage, they seem as out of touch with the modern world as antique car enthusiasts. People gawk at us, waiting for us to move our jalopies so they may go on their way unhindered.

Despite the attitudes of the world, we must look at Christian marriage not as a jalopy but as a precious antique, a treasure from the past. In the beginning God ordained marriage and commanded it in Scripture. This gift from God is not to be despised, but cherished as the blessing of our Creator.

Knowing the great value of marriage, we have to be careful when we apply Paul's principles from this chapter. We cannot simply reiterate Paul's advice because our situation is not the same as the situation in Corinth. It is simply not true that, as a general rule, Christians ought to be single, or that widows ought not to remarry. Paul believed that marriage was a great blessing, but he also recognized that sometimes conditions in life compel us to postpone our pursuit of this blessing. For this reason, we must gather from Paul's specific teaching on marriage the principles he held that led him to issue this advice. Knowing his fundamental principles, we then have to use our own judgment to know how to apply these principles in our own lives.

Paul's first principle was that married people should maintain healthy sexual relationships with their spouses. They should not abstain from sex unless they do so temporarily by mutual consent for the purpose of prayer. We should realize, as Paul did, that poor sexual relationships in marriage make spouses more susceptible to sexual temptations. Healthy sexual relationships in marriage satisfy normal sexual needs, thereby guarding against adultery.

Regarding divorce, Paul taught that believers may not divorce other believers except in the case of marital infidelity. (Some also believe that if an unbeliever abandons a believer, the abandoned spouse may also remarry.) If believers divorce for any other reason, they must remain unmarried or be reconciled. Besides learning legitimate regulations for divorce, we ought to realize from this that God considers marriage sacred. We ought to respect our marriages, not taking them lightly as the world often does, and to see them as lifelong covenants and commitments.

Regarding widows, we ought to learn from Paul that their marital obligations died with their spouses. They are free to remarry without condition, just as single people. Virgins, too, may marry at will. We should include all legitimately single people in this category even if they have previously fallen into sexual sin, as long as they have repented. Of course, any Christian who marries must marry a believer.

V. PRAYER

Lord Jesus, we live in a day when the ideals of Christian marriage are attacked on every side. Teach us your ways for marriage and grant us strength to delight in the treasure. Amen.

VI. DEEPER DISCOVERIES

A. Unmarried (7:8,11,32,34)

The word translated "unmarried" (*agamos*) appears in the New Testament only in 1 Corinthians 7. Traditionally, it has been understood as a generic term referring to anyone not currently married. This would include single men and women, widowed men and women, and divorced men and women. Others, however, have suggested that *agamos* probably does not include people who have never been married, but only unmarried people who used to be married. The suggestion has also been made that *agamos* was not only a generic term for formerly married people, but also the typical word used in the New Testament period for "widower."

B. Virgins (7:25,28,34,36–38)

Most likely, the term *parthenos* applied not only to virgins, whether male or female, but also to engaged women. Thus, the NRSV translates "fiancée" in 7:36–38. The NRSV is almost certainly correct in its assessment of these verses. The groom, not the bride's father, appears to have had control over whether or not he married in 7:27–28, though this does not preclude the possibility that the groom, the bride, and the bride's father all needed to agree. The moral responsibility for marriage also falls on the bride ("she has not sinned," 7:28), but nowhere is there explicit mention that the bride's father has not sinned, or even takes part in the decision process. This context favors the reading that the groom, not the bride's father, is the subject of 7:36–38, and therefore that *parthenos* here means "fiancée."

C. Divorce (7:27)

The marriage contract between a groom and a bride was considered so binding that to break that contract was considered divorce. Matthew's gospel illustrates this well in that Joseph, who had not yet married Mary, sought "to divorce her" (Matt. 1:19). Moreover, the context of 7:25–28 deals with virgins ("now about virgins," 7:25), so it seems much better to understand 7:27 also to apply to female virgins and their male counterparts. Thus, divorce here refers to the breaking of the marriage contract prior to the consummation of the marriage.

VII. TEACHING OUTLINE

A. INTRODUCTION

1. Leading Story: Sticking Out Like a Sore Thumb

2. Context: The Corinthians lived in difficult times. In their world, society did not value marriage as God does. The Corinthian church was to maintain views and standards on marriage that looked downright silly to its culture, and the Corinthians were not sure whether or not they should agree with the worldly system on certain points. To complicate matters, the famine Corinth suffered made some traditional Christian emphases temporarily impractical. The Corinthians had trouble figuring out which teachings on marriage they were to maintain at all costs, and which they were able to modify as needed.

3. Transition: The modern church finds itself in constant conflict with its culture when it comes to issues of marriage and family. Our culture, too, finds our values foolish, unnecessarily troublesome, and often even offensive. Sometimes we also have trouble distinguishing between important principles and their applications. On the one hand, we want to remain loyal to God and to obey him. On the other, we do not want to be stricter and harsher than God by putting on our people and our cultures a burden that is too heavy for people to bear.

B. COMMENTARY

1. General Outlooks on Marriage (7:1–9)
   a. Marriage and sex (7:1–6)
   b. Singleness (7:7–9)
2. Divorce (7:10–16)
   a. Between believers (7:10–11)
   b. Between believer and unbeliever (7:12–16)
3. Stay Where You Are (7:17–24)
   a. The rule of all the churches (7:17,20,24)
   b. Circumcision (7:18–19)
   c. Slavery (7:21–23)
4. Virgins and Marriage (7:25–28)
5. The Implications of an Eternal Perspective (7:29–35)
6. Final Concessions (7:36–40)

C. CONCLUSION: JALOPIES?

VIII. ISSUES FOR DISCUSSION

1. What were the circumstances in Corinth at the time Paul wrote? Why are those circumstances so important to understanding almost everything he wrote in this chapter?
2. Why should married couples maintain a sexual relationship? Are there exceptions to this?

3. When is divorce acceptable? Under what conditions is remarriage acceptable for divorced people? Under what conditions is remarriage acceptable for widows?
4. How does the material in this chapter relate to the material immediately before it and after it in the letter? Why do you think Paul chose to talk about these issues at this particular point in the letter?

1 Corinthians 8:1–13

Food for Other Gods

I. **INTRODUCTION**
Go Tell Him

II. **COMMENTARY**
A verse-by-verse explanation of this section.

III. **CONCLUSION**
True Precision

An overview of the principles and applications from this section.

IV. **LIFE APPLICATION**
A Matter of Principle

Melding the section to life.

V. **PRAYER**
Tying the section to life with God.

VI. **DEEPER DISCOVERIES**
Historical, geographical, and grammatical enrichment of the commentary.

VII. **TEACHING OUTLINE**
Suggested step-by-step group study of the section.

VIII. **ISSUES FOR DISCUSSION**
Zeroing the section in on daily life.

> ## Quote
>
> "Liberty of conscience is not without restrictions or qualifications. There is an over-ruling principle delimiting Christian freedom—the concern one ought to have for a fellow-believer who is weaker in the faith."
>
> John Currid

1 Corinthians 8:1–13

 IN A NUTSHELL

Christ has given his followers much freedom in many areas of life, but this freedom was never intended to be used to harm others. Paul applied this principle to a controversial question in the Corinthian church: Should Christians eat food sacrificed to idols?

Food for Other Gods

I. INTRODUCTION

Go Tell Him

*R*alph had grabbed the guitar and microphone twenty minutes ago and he would not let go of them. At first, everyone at the party was polite enough, maybe just a little too polite. But now patience was wearing thin.

"Go tell him!"

"No, you tell him."

"I can't . . . you."

"What am I supposed to say? 'Ralph, sit down; you're making a fool of yourself'? . . . He thinks he's really good."

So everyone kept silent as Ralph continued to play and sing. Horrifying sounds came from his mouth. He could not get a single tune right; none of his chords fit. It was all everyone could do not to laugh him out of the room. But Ralph went on, so full of himself, so confident of his musical talent that he thought he was the life of the party.

In this chapter Paul addressed some of the Corinthian believers who acted like Ralph. They had learned a few things about Christian theology. But in their self-assurance they insisted that doctrinal exactitude was all that mattered. They became so full of spiritual pride that they lost sight of more important teachings, such as the responsibility to love and edify others. Paul, however, could not let them continue. As one who cared for them, he had to tell them.

II. COMMENTARY

Food for Other Gods

> **MAIN IDEA:** Should Christians eat meat that has been offered to idols? Paul dealt with this controversial matter forthrightly, saying that eating such meat was acceptable because pagan gods actually amount to nothing. Yet, he added that Christians ought not to eat such meat if it caused other believers to sin against their consciences.

A Love, Not Knowledge (8:1–3)

> **SUPPORTING IDEA:** Before dealing with the question of food sacrificed to idols, Paul commented on related matters: the danger of knowledge about such things, and the primacy of love over knowledge as the guiding principle of Christian behavior.

8:1. Paul plainly stated another topic about which the Corinthians had questioned him (the formula **now about** indicates a response; see also 7:1,25; 12:1; 16:1,12): **food sacrificed to idols.** In the Greek culture of Paul's day, families often participated in religious sacrifices, offering sacrificial animals in pagan temples. In many rituals only part of the meat was burned. The priest and the family making the sacrifice took the rest. This consecrated meat was taken home and eaten, or sold in the marketplace.

The Jerusalem council had forbidden Christians to eat these foods (Acts 15:29). Yet, controversy still existed in the Corinthian church over whether believers could participate in these meals or eat the consecrated meat sold in the market. This particular chapter deals primarily with meals actually eaten in idols' temples. Given the famines in Greece at the time, the Corinthians' interest was probably more than a casual inquiry.

It is likely that Paul first quoted the Corinthians themselves, perhaps from their earlier letter to him. **We all possess knowledge,** they have said to Paul. Verse 4 indicates the content of their knowledge: they knew idols were nothing and that there is only one God. But not everyone understood these truths. Therefore, Paul warned the knowledgeable ones that **knowledge puffs up, but love builds up.** Paul forbade arrogance in his other writings and in this letter and set up edification of the church as a high goal (Rom. 15:2; Eph. 4:29). In effect, the apostle asserted the superiority of love over knowledge because the latter so often leads to sin if not handled carefully.

In making this comment, the apostle did not reject the importance of sound doctrine and knowledge of the things of Christ. He asserted that knowledge is not a good thing in and of itself. Knowledge can result in humility and love, but often it produces unsympathetic arrogance. In a word, knowledge—even of holy things—is not all that Christians must pursue.

8:2. Paul countered the tendency toward pride through knowledge by revealing the true nature of the person **who thinks** that **he knows something.** He did not oppose people thinking themselves to have a measure of knowledge or insight. Rather, he warned that those who believe they have mastered a subject may become prideful. Paul said that such people do **not yet know as** they **ought to know.** They have not realized that all human knowledge is faint and fragmentary—hardly the kind of knowledge from which they should take arrogance and pride.

8:3. Paul wanted the Corinthians to place a premium on **love,** not on knowledge. He indicated the superiority of love by reminding them that the one **who loves God** (God himself and the kingdom of God) **is known by God.** The expression "known by God" appears elsewhere in Paul's writings (Gal. 4:9) as a description of redemption. Paul meant that, unlike the prideful people who center their religious lives around knowledge, those who focus on love demonstrate that they have been redeemed. This warning against prideful knowledge and this encouragement to love undergird Paul's entire discussion of food offered to idols.

B Believers' Knowledge (8:4–6)

SUPPORTING IDEA: *Paul affirmed the Corinthians' position that food sacrificed to idols was not corrupted by the act of sacrifice. Such meat escaped corruption because the idols to which it was offered did not exist.*

8:4. Paul returned to the main topic of concern: **eating food sacrificed to idols**. He acknowledged what he and the informed ones at Corinth understood (**we know**). They knew that idols are **nothing at all** and that there is **no God but one**. With these statements he resolved the issue of meat dedicated to idols on a technical, factual level. There could be no problem with eating this meat since it had been offered to something that did not exist.

Now we have to be careful here not to misunderstand Paul's intentions. Paul believed in an evil spiritual reality behind pagan idolatry. In accordance with other portions of Scripture he believed that idolators worshiped demons (Deut. 32:16–17; Rev. 9:20). Later in this epistle he acknowledged as much when he said that "the sacrifices of pagans are offered to demons" and warned against participating too closely with demonic rituals (10:18–22). For this reason, we can be sure that when Paul said that idols are nothing at all in this verse, he did not make a straightforward assertion. Instead, he spoke by way of comparison with the glory and honor of the true God of Israel.

In comparison with the Creator and his divine Son Jesus, the demons are nothing. They need not be feared; Christians have no reason for superstitious avoidance of things associated with idolatry such as meat offered to idols. As the apostle John put it in 1 John 4:4, "The one who is in you is greater than the one who is in the world." For this reason, Paul felt free to permit the Corinthians to eat meat sacrificed to idols.

8:5–6. Of course, it would have been easy for Paul's opponents to argue that there was a sense in which other gods exist. Paul admitted this himself in 8:5 where he said that there **are so-called gods** . . . **indeed there are many "gods" and many "lords"** which people all over the world worship. Even so, for Christians **there is but one God**. This **one God** is **the Father** who is the source and goal of all things. Moreover, **there is but one Lord, Jesus Christ**. These verses take the form of an early catechism or hymn of praise to the Father and Christ.

To emhasize the singularity of the true God, this hymn of praise attributes similar qualities to both the Father and the Son: all things have their origin in them; and we live in and through them. Simply put, the God of Christianity so overshadows all others who may be called "gods" or "lords" that those others are entirely insignificant.

With this kind of knowledge in hand, it is easy to understand why some believers at Corinth did not hesitate to eat food that had been dedicated to idols. As far as they were concerned, these religious ceremonies were insignificant. Paul affirmed this theology and conclusion to a degree. The Corinthians surmised that Christianity's monotheism precluded the existence of other gods, and thus nullified the significance of the pagan sacrifices.

Ⓒ Dealing with Others' Ignorance (8:7–13)

SUPPORTING IDEA: *Paul agreed with those who were knowledgeable on this issue, but he insisted that their correct theological conclusions did not justify their practices. They sinned by eating meat sacrificed to idols—not because of the idols, but because of the damage done to their fellow believers.*

8:7. While Paul agreed that idols are nothing, he pointed out that the Corinthians had wrongly assessed their own church. They thought that all possessed the knowledge that idols were nothing, but they were wrong. Apparently, a number of believers in Corinth were **still so accustomed to idols** that they had a hard time thinking in new ways about food offered to idols. Old superstitions died slowly. So, when these people ate, they still believed that the food had been devoted to a significant power or god, and they may have expected to benefit from the sacrifice as a result. Thus, when they ate, **their conscience**, being **weak** in this area, was **defiled**. They violated their sense of loyalty and devotion to Christ.

8:8. This verse is difficult to understand, unless it is another quote from the knowledgeable believers in Corinth. Neither the knowledgeable Corinthians nor the superstitious Corinthians would have thought that eating meat sacrificed to idols somehow brought them closer to, commended them to, or dedicated them to the real God. While the NIV translates the first part of the verse, **But food does not bring us near to God**, it is also possible (and more literal) to translate, "Food does not bring us near to the god" (i.e., the idol to which the food in question was offered). In light of the preceding context, this seems to be the better option. This verse probably represents the opinions of the knowledgeable ones in Corinth, whether actually expressed in their letter or anticipated by Paul as their response to his teaching that the weaker brothers' consciences were defiled.

The phrase **we are no worse if we do not eat, and no better if we do** probably expands the meaning of **bring us near**. It probably refers to the lack of prosperity an idol worshiper might anticipate if he failed to eat of the sacrifice, and to the abundance he would expect to receive if he did eat. Those of weak conscience in Corinth may have sinned partly by thinking that eating the food sacrificed to idols would give them a better chance for the material prosperity they needed to see them through the current famines.

The knowledgeable Corinthians who realized that idols were not gods at all and that idols did not control one's prosperity would have found the weaker Christians' consciences downright culpable for their superstitions. As a result, they probably would have dismissed those of weak conscience as foolish and ridiculous.

8:9. Paul responded to this imagined objection, warning them to **be careful**. He did not dispute the facts; he did not object to the theological perspectives of the knowledgeable ones. Rather, his pastoral concern for those with weak consciences led him to restrain the knowledgeable Corinthians' behavior. He warned that the **freedom** enjoyed by those who understood the situation might **become a stumbling block to the weak.**

Those who understand have freedom, but they also have the responsibility to use that freedom in service to others (Gal. 5:13) and to restrain that freedom when it threatens to damage others. Those who understand sound doctrine must also take into account the weaknesses of others around them. Their knowledge must not overshadow their love for the brethren.

8:10–11. Paul presented a potential scenario to illustrate his concern. If a knowledgeable Christian eats **in an idol's temple** and one with **a weak conscience** (i.e., misinformed) sees him eating there, then the misinformed one will be **emboldened to eat.** He will think that the knowledgeable one believes that eating the idol's sacrifice offers a real benefit, and that idolatry is compatible with Christianity.

Thus, the brother with the weak conscience will be emboldened to engage in idolatry himself. Whereas the knowledgeable Christian would not eat with idolatrous intent, the weaker one would, thereby being drawn into syncretism through the observation of his brother. As a result, the **weak brother** would be **destroyed** by the **knowledge** of his brother—by the act of freedom based on knowledge.

Paul did not explain in what sense this destruction would take place. He may have had in mind something as simple as discouragement and confusion, or something worse such as death, or even apostasy and judgment by God. The word translated "is destroyed" generally refers to death or absolute destruction. It is probably wise, however, to temper this passage with Paul's parallel statements, where he spoke of a defiled conscience (8:7), a wounded conscience (8:12), and falling into sin (8:13).

In any event, Paul reminded the knowledgeable ones that **Christ died** for those brothers and sisters of weak conscience. Therefore, knowledgeable believers should not be indifferent to weak ones. Weak Christians are so precious to Christ that he laid down his life for them. Therefore, they should be precious to other followers of Christ as well.

8:12. To drive home his perspective, Paul intensified the connection between these actions and Christ. Christ did more than die for these people.

He united them to himself in such a way that Paul could say, **When you sin against your brothers in this way . . . you sin against Christ**. Sinning against believers who are in Christ, who are part of his body, is sinning against Christ himself. Safeguarding the conscience of weaker brothers is no small matter; it is a service of honor to Christ himself.

8:13. For this reason Paul drew a firm conclusion: out of love for fellow Christians and for Christ himself, he would **never eat meat again** if eating caused his **brother to fall into sin**. In Corinth at this time, most butchered meat would have been dedicated to some idol. So Paul may not have been exaggerating when he said, **never eat meat again**. The immediate context, however, refers more specifically to dining in idols' temples. Further, Paul later wrote that believers should eat meat in certain circumstances (10:27).

Still, his point should not be blunted. Paul insisted that even drastic self-denial of all meat is worthwhile if it protects others from falling into sin. Protecting those in Christ takes precedence over exercising freedom.

MAIN IDEA REVIEW: *Should Christians eat meat that has been offered to idols? Paul dealt with this controversial matter forthrightly, saying that eating such meat was acceptable because pagan gods actually amount to nothing. Yet, he added that Christians ought not to eat such meat if it caused other believers to sin against their consciences.*

III. CONCLUSION

True Precision

The apostle called for Christians to care about one another so much that they put the good of others over their own rights. Theological precision must be so extensive that it factors the personal and relational dimensions of church life in addition to theological facts.

PRINCIPLES

- We have great freedom in the gospel.
- Christian freedom grows as Christian understanding grows.
- Our Christian freedom must be sacrificed when it leads others to sin.
- When we cause other believers to sin, we sin against Christ.

APPLICATIONS

- We must be aware of our weaker brothers and sisters in Christ, and not exercise our freedom in ways that cause them to sin.

- We must always seek to improve our understanding of truth so that we may experience more freedom under the gospel.
- We must not resent those for whom we limit our freedom, but rather love them.
- We must not condemn those whose freedoms in the gospel are greater than our own.

IV. LIFE APPLICATION

A Matter of Principle

The weary couple sat as far apart as they could, and the therapist's chair formed an equilaterial triangle with theirs. "I'm right about this. It's a matter of principle," the husband insisted.

"No, I'm right about this, and I think it's a matter of principle too," the wife retorted.

"Well," the therapist interrupted. "I think we just discovered the problem. The problem is that principle is more important to you than the other person. Maybe we need to expand your strong commitments to principle to include kindness to one another."

In this chapter Paul addressed a group of Corinthians who insisted on following a narrow set of principles. Paul did not want them to give up their strong commitments to principles. But he wanted them to expand their commitments to include a Christlike love and concern for others.

There are two common errors to which this understanding of Paul's teaching on this matter has led, and both must be avoided. First, some interpreters have determined from Paul's stance that the weak do not need to be educated. If this were true, Paul would not have referred to them as "weak." He obviously considered the properly informed position superior (though he did not say the knowledgeable *people* were superior). If Paul believed that knowledge was insignificant, he would not have wasted his time trying to correct the fundamental understandings of the Corinthians on such areas as divisions and the resurrection of the body.

Second, many people have understood this chapter to teach that Christians should not do things that offend other believers. This is simply wrong. Paul's point was that Christians not cause other believers to sin, not that they refrain from doing things with which other Christians disagree. His fear was that the weak would sin by wrongly interpreting and copying the example of the strong, not that the weak would think less of the strong or take offense at their actions.

Finally, we need to hear again in this passage the same message that Paul taught throughout the letter thus far: believers are in Christ. Because of

Christ's mystical union with all believers, Christ is one recipient of every action we take toward one another. When we hurt one another, we hurt Christ himself. We cannot attack Christ's body without also attacking Christ. We need to gain a greater respect for our fellow Christians, even for those who are foolish in their beliefs and prone to stumble into sin. We also need to love them more, just as we love Christ.

V. PRAYER

Lord Jesus, we are delighted that you were so principled that you cared about the lost, the weak, and the weary. We are so grateful for your tender mercy. Now, O Lord, grant us the same concern for others, that we may honor both you and them. Amen.

VI. DEEPER DISCOVERIES

A. Worse, Better (8:8)

In keeping with the rest of the New Testament, Paul often used the word translated "we are worse" (*hystereo*) to mean "to be lacking" or "to be in need" (cf. 2 Cor. 11:9; Phil. 4:12). The word translated "we are better" (*perisseuo*) appears to carry the meaning "abound, overflow" in every other Pauline usage. In 8:8 these words most probably refer not to moral or spiritual benefit or damage, but to material prosperity. This corresponds well with the idea in the ancient world that sacrifices procured material blessings from the gods. This seems an even more likely reading in light of the famines in Greece at the time of this letter.

B. Destroyed (8:11)

In the New Testament, "destroyed" (*apollumi*) generally refers to physical death or to final judgment. It is often also translated "perish" or "die." Paul's usage of the word generally reflects this same range of meaning.

In light of the fact that Paul in 1 Corinthians 5:5 referred to the destruction of the "sinful nature" or "flesh" of the immoral man (perhaps referring to his physical death), in 8:11 he could have meant something as extreme as that God might physically kill the brother drawn into idolatrous eating. Like the immoral brother, if his spirit were truly saved, he would not perish eternally, but he would suffer the physical judgment of death. On the other hand, *apollumi* might simply be a strong metaphoric parallel to the statements in 8:7,12–13 regarding defiled/wounded consciences and falling into sin, or a statement of lostness similar to the gospel writers' depictions of those who go astray.

VII. TEACHING OUTLINE

A. INTRODUCTION

1. Lead Story: Go Tell Him
2. Context: Some of the Corinthians had proper knowledge regarding pagan gods. As a result, they felt comfortable eating food that had been sacrificed to idols. In fact, they were satisfied with too little knowledge. What they did not know was that their actions were improper even though their understanding of pagan gods was correct. They also needed to know that love for other Christians ought to have overridden their desire for freedom of action. By their eating, they actually sinned against immature believers.
3. Transition: Modern believers do not have to worry about food sacrificed to idols. However, we do sometimes sin against others who have less knowledge than we do. We must always be aware that our actions are not always justifiable even if they are not sinful in certain contexts. By our actions we sometimes encourage other Christians to do what for us is not sin but for them is sin. When we do, we sin against those Christians and against Christ.

B. COMMENTARY

1. Love, Not Knowledge (8:1–3)
   a. Knowledge puffs up (8:1–2)
   b. Love builds up (8:1,3)
2. Believers' Knowledge (8:4–6)
   a. Idols are not true gods (8:4–5)
   b. There is only one true God, the Father (8:4–6)
   c. There is only one true Lord, Jesus Christ (8:6)
3. Dealing with Others' Ignorance (8:7–13)
   a. Some Christians have a weak conscience (8:7–8)
   b. Christian behavior and weak believers (8:9–13)

C. CONCLUSION: A MATTER OF PRINCIPLE

VIII. ISSUES FOR DISCUSSION

1. How does knowledge "puff up"? Do you find that your natural tendency upon attaining new knowledge is to feel proud of your accomplishment? Is this wrong?
2. Who does love "build up"? How does love "build up"?

3. Is it more important to love or to know? Can we get by with only one or the other? Why or why not?

4. How far should we go in giving up our rights when it comes to causing others to stumble? At what point do we draw the line? How do we keep believers with the weakest consciences from ruling the church?

1 Corinthians 9:1–27

Freedom and Rights

Quote

"*Of* free choice and zeal and love to Christ, [Paul] had an insatiable desire for the salvation of mankind."

John Chrysostom

1 Corinthians 9:1–27

IN A NUTSHELL

In this passage the apostle continued his thoughts on the importance of love and service over dogmatic doctrinal attitudes. He did so by illustrating from his own life the importance of serving others.

Freedom and Rights

I. INTRODUCTION

"So Long As I Don't Hurt Anybody"

*I*t's almost a universal belief among Americans that we should be able to do whatever we want—so long as we don't hurt anybody. I grew up in America, and one of the most sacred words of American ideals is the word *freedom*. In America, our freedoms include the rights to "life, liberty, and the pursuit of happiness." You have heard the songs lyrics: "the land of the free" and "let freedom ring." Freedom is our highest good.

Unfortunately, the premium we place on personal liberty often does not disappear when we become followers of Christ. In fact, we often transfer our freedom ideals into our faith. We think we should follow Christ any way we see fit, so long as we don't hurt anyone.

In this passage, Paul said just the opposite. Followers of Christ are to overcome their devotion to personal freedom. It is the only way to serve Christ and to spread his gospel.

II. COMMENTARY

Freedom and Rights

MAIN IDEA: *In order to encourage the Corinthians to forfeit their rights for the sake of other Christians, Paul described his entire ministry as one of sacrifice and accommodation to others.*

A Christian Rights (9:1–14)

SUPPORTING IDEA: *Paul had insisted in the previous chapter that Christians often have to forfeit their legitimate rights in loving service to others. He continued this argument by affirming his own rights—rights which the Corinthians knew he had given up.*

9:1–2. Paul began his discussion of forfeiting rights with a series of four questions to which he expected positive responses. He asked if it were not true that he was **free** and **an apostle**. Apostles were central leaders of the church; they and the prophets were the foundation of the church (Eph. 2:20). Consequently, certain rights, freedoms, and responsibilities came with the office. In a very powerful sense, Paul was in charge of the church, not the other way around.

Paul also asked if it were not true that he had **seen Jesus** on the road to Damascus (Acts 9:3–8). No one should have doubted that he met the requirements of apostleship mentioned in Acts 1:21–22. Paul directed the final question to the Corinthians themselves, reminding them that they had come to Christ by Paul's own **work in the Lord.** The church at Corinth directly resulted from Paul's ministry (Acts 16:1–11). Those unfamiliar with Paul might have had grounds to doubt reports about him, but the Corinthians knew the truth because they themselves were **the seal,** or proof, of Paul's **apostleship in the Lord.**

These questions indicate that Paul's opposition in Corinth may have challenged the authenticity of his apostleship. The power of the Holy Spirit had so attended his preaching in Corinth that the Corinthians should have respected Paul's apostleship. Elsewhere Paul even called the Corinthian believers his letter of recommendation (2 Cor. 3:2). Their own conversion certainly should have been sufficient to satisfy the Corinthians in this regard.

9:3. Paul was about to give a **defense** against people who sat **in judgment** on him. To understand his defense, one must first understand the accusation. From the preceding and following contexts, it would appear that some people were displeased with Paul's refusal to eat meat sacrificed to idols. They particularly did not like his teaching that others should do the same. Those judging Paul knew that he understood the practice was theologically justifiable—it was a freedom that every knowledgeable, mature Christian had. To them it must have seemed that Paul contradicted the straightforward truth when he insisted that stronger Christians should not eat for the sake of weaker Christians.

To defend his actions, Paul drew upon the larger practices of his life. His position on eating meat sacrificed to idols was not a sign of weakness or inconsistency. Rather, it accorded with the basic Christian principles that guided his life. For this reason, the Corinthians who opposed him on the matter of meat sacrificed to idols actually opposed the fabric of Christian ethics.

9:4–6. Paul introduced his defense through a series of questions and considerations, establishing a set of true premises about the apostolic ministry. First, he asked questions directly about himself and Barnabas. The answers to these questions are so obvious that one can easily sense Paul's sarcasm.

1. Did he and Barnabas **have the right to food and drink** as they ministered? Yes.
2. Did he and Barnabas **have the right** to have **believing** wives with them like **other apostles?** Yes.
3. Were he and Barnabas the only apostles not worthy of pay for their work? No.

Evidently, those who sat in judgment against Paul thought his refusal to take advantage of these rights proved that he actually lacked these rights. They must have reasoned that he did not exercise these advantages because he was not truly an apostle.

To counter this thinking, Paul affirmed his apostolic rights. Even though he supported himself making tents, he had a right to be fed and paid by the Corinthians. Similarly, even though he remained single for the sake of those to whom he ministered, he had a right to be married.

9:7. Paul led up to the question of why he and Barnabas did not take advantage of what they had rights to enjoy. Before he reached that point, however, he built his case even more strongly. He appealed not only to the example of the other church leaders but also to common daily life.

1. Does any soldier serve at his own expense? No.
2. Do farmers eat from their produce? Yes.
3. Do shepherds drink milk from their flocks? Yes.

Common sense dictates that people have a right to make a living from their work. By appealing to these ordinary life analogies, Paul continued to assert his rights, and thereby led to questions surrounding his refusal to take advantage of these rights.

9:8–10. Finally, Paul asked a serious question. Were these expectations **merely from a human point of view**, or did God confirm them as well? Paul insisted that God agreed to these rights and that Scripture proved the point. He asked, **Doesn't the Law say the same thing?** Paul believed that Old Testament law actually undergirded his moral right to receive a livelihood from his ministry. To support his argument, Paul quoted Deuteronomy 25:4, **Do not muzzle an ox while it is treading out the grain.**

In biblical times, at least two methods of treading grain were practiced. At times, stalks of grain were spread out over a flat hard surface called a threshing floor. Oxen or horses dragged a weighted board across the grain by walking around and around a central post. At other times, the animals simply walked on the grain with their feet. Old Testament law did not allow farmers to muzzle the treading animals. God's law permitted the animals to eat as they worked.

Paul applied this Old Testament law to the issue at hand, insisting that **God** was **concerned** about more than oxen. God said this **for us** (human beings). Paul knew that the law pertained to oxen treading grain, but also that a deeper moral principle undergirded this law. He summarized the principle in this way: **when the plowman plows and the thresher threshes, they ought to do so in the hope of sharing in the harvest.**

9:11–12. With biblical support for his views, Paul returned to his own situation. Since he had **sown spiritual seed** in Corinth, he had every right to **reap a material harvest** of reasonable pay for his work. This passage is used today to support the idea that ministers of the gospel should be paid for their efforts. Paul argued that the Corinthians benefited from his ministry. For this reason, he had an even greater **right to support** than the other church leaders whom the Corinthians evidently supported.

In verse 12b the apostle hinted at the forfeiture of rights that he would talk about in later verses. He had every right to be paid, **but** he did **not use this right.** Instead, he **put up with** all kinds of troubles **rather than** do anything that would **hinder the gospel of Christ.**

9:13–14. In a final effort to demonstrate the doctrinal correctness of his right to be paid, Paul noted that in the Old Testament the priests and Levites got **their food from the temple** and shared **in what** was **offered on the altar.** He concluded that, **in the same way, the Lord** (not mere humans) **has commanded that those who preach . . . should receive their living from the gospel.** This may also be a reference to Jesus' instructions to the apostles in Matthew 10:10 or to the seventy-two in Luke 10:7. Paul's conclusion could not have been put in stronger terms.

It would be difficult to overemphasize the force of Paul's argument. He created a watertight case for the fact that he should be paid for his apostolic ministry. Common fairness supported him. Current social practices agreed with his contention. Most importantly, the Old Testament law itself clearly taught his view. There was no reason that Paul should not be paid.

𝕭 Forfeited Rights (9:15–27)

SUPPORTING IDEA: *Just as Paul forfeited his right to be paid so the gospel might have greater success, the Corinthians should forfeit their rights to eat meat sacrificed to idols so they would not injure weaker brothers and sisters.*

9:15. Paul declared, **I have not used any of these rights.** He had forfeited his right to making an honest living from his ministry, but he quickly countered any misunderstandings of his motivations in building such a strong case. He had not defended his rights in order that the Corinthians might begin to pay him, but rather to defend his apostleship.

The statement **I would rather die than have anyone deprive me of this boast** is not a single sentence. In the original language, the phrase **I would rather die than** is an incomplete exclamation that is interrupted by the statement "No one will **deprive me of this boast.**" On occasion Paul could not complete sentences because his emotions overcame him (see Rom. 3:25; 8:32). This was one such instance. He could not finish his sentence because he was overwhelmed by how important preaching the gospel was to him. He would never allow anyone to **deprive** him of the **boast** that he preached voluntarily—it was his reason for living.

9:16–17. Paul wanted to continue the practice of preaching without pay. He explained that he could not **boast** simply because he preached the gospel. He insisted, **I am compelled to preach.** In other words, he had no choice.

God had called him to preach, and he had to fulfill that obligation or fall under divine judgment.

How did Paul enhance his preaching ministry? He preached **voluntarily** so he might receive **a reward**. Paul frequently spoke of himself and of other Christians being motivated to service by a desire for reward and praise (Rom. 2:29; Gal. 6:4–10; Col. 3:24). Eternal reward motivated him as it should all believers. Paul did not want to lose his eternal rewards for preaching willingly and eagerly and without pay. If he preached begrudgingly or received pay, he believed he would be doing nothing more than **simply discharging the trust committed** to him. To raise his preaching above the level of mere obedience, Paul voluntarily gave up his right to remuneration.

9:18. To sum up the matter, Paul asked what his **reward** was. This verse presents a number of complexities. If one reads the verse as a question and answer, then two understandings are possible. First, many interpreters have understood Paul to say that preaching was a reward in itself. To preach the gospel **free of charge**, and in so doing **not** to **make use of** his **rights** for pay, was sufficient reward. But in the light of 9:17, it seems better to understand Paul in another way. The second interpretation is that Paul knew he would one day receive a reward for having preached without remuneration. Christ would reward Paul for not seeking his own benefit in this world.

This verse may also be translated entirely as a question. It would thus read, "What then is my reward so that, when I preach the gospel, I offer it free of charge so as not to make full use of my rights in the gospel?" Paul may have been asking what great reward motivated him to forfeit his rights by offering the gospel free of charge. In this case, his answer would come in 9:23: "I do all this for the sake of the gospel, that I may share in its blessings."

9:19. As a missionary in the Mediterranean world, Paul had to deal with many different cultural standards. In these varying circumstances, he committed himself not to exercise his right to pursue the norms of his own cultural preferences, and not to insist on his freedoms under the gospel. This argument is much like his forfeiture of his right to eat meat.

The apostle began this discussion with a strong assertion: **I am free and belong to no man.** In the ancient world, a slave had little freedom. Masters dictated most of what their slaves did. By asserting his free status, Paul restated an indisputable truth: he was free and did not have to conform himself to the preferences of others.

Nevertheless, Paul voluntarily made himself **a slave to everyone.** He gave up his rights to his own preferences in order to serve other people. He did this **to win as many as possible,** to further the kingdom of Christ. The desire to see many people come to faith in Christ overrode Paul's desire for his individual rights.

9:20–21. To illustrate just how far he was willing to follow this policy, Paul described two extremes of his multicultural ministry. First, he ministered **to those under the law** and **to those not having the law**—Jews and Gentiles. In the ancient world, the differences between these two groups could be enormous. Clothing, holidays, eating habits, religious beliefs, family practices, etc. were often very different between Jews and Gentiles. This diversity required great flexibility from Paul because he wanted **to win those under the law** and **to win those not having the law.**

Paul's description of these groups was not precisely symmetrical. He did not speak of those who had the law versus those who did not have it. Rather, he spoke of those who were **under the law** and **those not having the law.**

Under the law, on the one hand, was Paul's technical terminology for people under the curse of the law because they sought justification before God through obedience to the law of Moses (Rom. 6:14–15; Gal. 5:18). Paul understood the ways of Jews who sought to find favor with God through obedience to the law. They did not merely have the law, but they actually became its victims because reliance on obedience to the law always leads to frustration and failure.

Even so, many Jews in Paul's day were so committed to this lifestyle that they filled their lives with all kinds of biblical and extrabiblical observances of law. Although Paul knew these practices had nearly condemned him to God's judgment early in his life (Rom. 7:8–11), he cared so much about the Jewish community that he observed their customs and laws when he was with them so the gospel might take root in them.

On the other hand, **not having the law** meant that the Gentiles were "excluded from citizenship in Israel and foreigners to the covenants of the promise, without hope and without God in the world" (Eph. 2:12). They did not have the extensive rules of Scripture, but followed pagan rituals and lifestyles free of Jewish restrictions. Although Paul did not approve of all pagan lifestyles, he observed their customs and laws when he was among them so the gospel might spread among the Gentiles.

Paul was very flexible as he went from one community to another, but he knew where to draw the line. When he was with religious Jews, he always remembered that he did not seek justification through the law and was not subject to its curse (**though I myself am not under the law**).

Likewise, when with Gentiles who did not observe the laws of Scripture, Paul conformed his outward behavior to theirs in many ways, but he did not stray into paganism. Rather, he always remembered that he was bound to keep the law in Christ (**though I am not free from God's law but am under Christ's law**).

Christ's law is not opposed to the law of Moses. Jesus himself said, "Do not think I have come to abolish the Law or the Prophets; I have not come to abolish them but to fulfill them" (Matt. 5:17). Christ's law is the moral teachings of all the Scriptures as they were taught by Christ and his apostles. Paul often affirmed that God's law was designed as a guide for Christians (Rom. 2:26–29; 8:7; 1 Tim. 1:8). Yet, here he made it clear that God's law for Christians is interpreted in the light of Christ's coming, and thus has become **Christ's law.** While he sought to help others by becoming like them, Paul refused to fall into sin for the sake of others.

9:22. Paul added another class of people to whom he condescended besides Jews and Gentiles, one that drew attention to his concern for the Corinthian church—**the weak.** The strong and knowledgeable people in the Corinthian church refused to make allowances for the weak among them. The strong insisted on eating meat sacrificed to idols because they correctly understood their freedom to do so, but thereby they sinned against weaker brothers and sisters.

In contrast to them, Paul **became weak** by willingly conforming his behavior to that of **the weak.** By limiting his freedom in this way, Paul made certain that he did not cause weaker brothers and sisters to fall into sin.

In summary, Paul claimed that he had **become all things to all men.** Foregoing his rights to pursue his own preferences, he submitted to everyone **so that by all possible means** he might bring some to salvation. Paul's chief concern was to build the kingdom of Christ through the conversion of the lost. He refused to allow his own freedoms to prevent others from following the ways of Christ. In this regard he exemplified the principle with which he had begun this section: knowledge alone "puffs up" and makes a person not care about the well-being of others, but "love builds up" (8:1). Love for others leads a person to perform those actions that bring as many people as possible into the kingdom of Christ.

9:23. Paul was motivated for the sake of other people and **for the sake of the gospel.** He was concerned to see the good news of salvation in Christ proclaimed and believed throughout the world. He wanted the kingdom of God to come in full. He made himself the servant of all people in order to further these ends. Yet, Paul's motivation for this course of action was not entirely altruistic. He knew that God would reward him for his service. He sacrificed his own rights so that he might **share** in the gospel's **blessings.**

Paul's last words raised the stakes in the matter of meat sacrificed to idols. Those who pursue their own rights even when this results in the destruction of the weak reveal the true condition of their hearts. As the apostle John put it, "Anyone who does not love his brother, whom he has seen, cannot love God, whom he has not seen" (1 John 4:20). The strong and knowledgeable at Corinth had correctly understood their rights, but they had forgotten the importance of love for others. Disregarding the weak in the Corinthian church would eventually bring the judgment of God.

9:24–25. Paul next turned to an analogy that illustrated the seriousness of this matter. He appealed to the athletic event of **a race.** Because of the Corinthians' sponsorship and familiarity with the Isthmian Games, the analogy of a **race** spoke to an experience that Paul had shared with the Corinthian believers. Paul drew several comparisons between the Christian life and a race.

First, not everyone wins, just as not everyone who begins the Christian life endures to the end. Therefore, everyone who claims to be a Christian must always **run . . . to get the prize.** Christians must be "eager to do what is good" (Titus 2:14). They will express their faith through good works (Eph. 2:10; Jas. 2:17).

Second, every athlete **goes into strict training.** Christians must devote themselves to self-denial, such as forfeiting their rights for the sake of weaker brothers and sisters, and to spiritual development and self-discipline.

Third, unlike athletes who work hard **to get a crown that will not last,** a ceremonial wreath, Christians will receive **a crown that will last forever** (cf. 2 Tim. 4:8; 1 Pet. 5:4). By this latter crown Paul referred to eternal rewards such as everlasting life, not to temporal blessings. Christians endure for eternal glory (Rom. 2:7; 2 Tim. 2:10).

9:26–27. Paul drew some moral implications for his life from the foregoing analogy. First, he did not live his Christian life **like a man running aimlessly.** He had a definite goal—winning the prize—and he ran to achieve it.

Second, shifting the analogy slightly, Paul commented that he did **not fight like a man beating the air.** Later, in a letter to Timothy, Paul again metaphorically wrote of running and boxing for the purpose of gaining a crown (2 Tim. 4:7–8). Here, he pointed out his care not to miss with his "spiritual punches."

Third, he declared his determination to **beat** his **body** (literally, to give himself a "black eye"). Paul did not mean that he actually afflicted or beat his body. He was speaking metaphorically. When boxers fight vigorously, they usually end up with bruises. Paul probably meant that he followed Christ so vigorously that it sometimes caused him physical harm, such as being lashed, beaten with rods, stoned, and shipwrecked (2 Cor. 11:24–25).

Fourth, he made his body his **slave.** This is a metaphor describing the rigor of his spiritual life. He conditioned himself spiritually, denying himself as athletes deny themselves for the sake of winning the contest (cf. Titus 2:12).

Paul concluded this athletic analogy by restating his goal. He worked hard to make sure that **after** he had **preached to others,** he would **not be disqualified for the prize.** Again, Paul did not speak of losing salvation. Yet, he was aware that even he could fall away from Christ and prove he had never truly been regenerated. Paul knew that the **prize** is received only by those who endure to the end.

In this analogy the apostle spoke generally about his entire spiritual life. He lived like an athlete in every area of his life. In the context of this chapter, however, the more immediate reference is the way Paul gave up his rights for the sake of others. Self-denial in service to others is a difficult practice. Yet, Paul knew that it was necessary if he wanted to attain the prize of eternal life. By implication, the same is true of every believer, just as it was true of the knowledgeable ones in the Corinthian church. Paul used himself as an example for them to follow. Since he, an apostle, had been willing to make such sacrifices, the Corinthians should be willing as well.

> **MAIN IDEA REVIEW:** *In order to encourage the Corinthians to forfeit their rights for the sake of other Christians, Paul described his entire ministry as one of sacrifice and accommodation to others.*

III. CONCLUSION

Responsible to Serve

This passage challenged the strong and knowledgeable Corinthian believers to go even further. Rather than lord their knowledge over others, they were to realize their responsibility to serve others. It was their responsibility to give up their rights and freedoms for the sake of others.

PRINCIPLES

- Paul had authority that no modern minister shares.
- Christian ministers deserve a living wage for their work.
- Expressing our freedom in Christ may hinder the gospel at times.
- Lost souls are more important than our rights.
- Saving faith produces good works.

APPLICATIONS

- We must submit to apostolic teaching.
- We should pay our pastors and other full-time Christian ministers a living wage.
- We need to cultivate a love for others that motivates us to place their need for the gospel above our desire for freedom.
- We need to be active to produce good works and to confirm our salvation.
- We should obey God's law with understanding, applying it to our day.

IV. LIFE APPLICATION

The Most Toys

You have seen the bumper sticker: "The one who dies with the most toys wins!" What a sad description of life. Yet, in the day-to-day affairs of our lives, we often live by the principle: get everything you can get out of life. There is some value in this principle. It motivates us to work hard and to plan for success. Yet, as Christians we are called upon to think in another way as well: give all you can give to life. In some ways, "The one who dies with the least toys wins!"—so long as he has given them in service to others.

This passage brings this perspective to bear on our relationships with other people, especially fellow believers. We should not seek our own rights and privileges but the good of others.

Christian ministers have used this passage to show that they should be paid for their labors, and this is one legitimate application. The thrust of Paul's argument surrounding payment for ministers, however, is not that they should be paid, but that ministers should forfeit their pay if accepting their wages hinders the gospel.

Ministers may be prone to ignore legitimate reasons that they should refuse pay. Legitimate reasons might include ministry in areas where people have been hardened to the gospel because of the monetary abuses of other Christian ministers or television evangelists. Congregations, in turn, particularly those with small budgets, might be tempted to use Paul's example to suggest that their own ministers be self-supporting—not because paying their ministers hinders the gospel, but because their members do not contribute enough to the church.

Ministers also have a right to be married. As with Paul, there may be situations in which marrying would hinder a minister's ability to preach the gospel, and these circumstances would contribute to an argument against marrying. Ultimately, though, marriage must be a personal judgment call.

Paul mentioned these rights in order to prove his apostleship. He also declared that he forfeited these rights in order to show the Corinthians how to interact with one another. We need to learn from Paul to value lost souls more than we value our rights, and to give up our rights for the sake of gaining an audience for the gospel. This means not only giving up our rights to be married or to receive pay for our ministries, but also being willing to adapt to unfamiliar—perhaps even unpleasant—cultural norms.

Exactly how can we be all things to all people? First, we need to develop a love for others that motivates us to seek their good above our rights. We need to repent of our self-centeredness and cold hearts and begin to feel a compassion for the lost that makes us eager to do whatever it takes to bring them the gospel.

Second, we should be motivated by the fact that God has promised us eternal rewards for doing what he has commanded, such as proclaiming the gospel. Our eternal rewards will far outweigh the rights we forfeit.

Third, we need to realize that a desire to advance the gospel is a fundamental quality of Christians. If we lack this desire, we should examine ourselves to make certain we are in the faith.

Fourth, we need to recognize that true belief leads to good works and that failing to produce good works may demonstrate that we are not saved.

V. PRAYER

Lord Jesus, we are taught from the beginning of life to protect our freedom and rights. Grant us wisdom, Lord, to know when to set those privileges aside for others. Grant us grace to live up to the call to live for others. Amen.

VI. DEEPER DISCOVERIES

A. Apostle (9:1–2,5)

The modern tendency is to equate the term *apostle* with one of "the Twelve," with the subsequent addition of Paul. This position understands "apostle" as an office, and accords well with most of the New Testament uses—particularly with those that describe the qualifications of an apostle (1 Cor. 9:1–2; 2 Cor. 12:12; Gal. 1:1). The qualifications appear to include these: seeing the Lord Jesus; working signs, wonders, and miracles; and being commissioned by God himself. Acts 1:20–26 also suggests the existence of the office of apostle, and the qualification of having been with the original apostles from the beginning. The problem with this last qualification is that it excludes Paul.

Other passages, however, call people beyond the Twelve and Paul "apostle," namely: Andronicus, Junias (Rom. 16:7); Barnabas (1 Cor. 9:5–6); unnamed brethren (2 Cor. 8:23); James (Gal. 1:19); Epaphroditus (Phil. 2:25); and Silas and Timothy (1 Thess. 2:6–7). All these could not have fulfilled the apostolic requirements above because Timothy at least was converted by Paul.

It seems likely that the word *apostle* was used in a variety of ways. Sometimes it referred to a miracle-working, authoritative, Christ-commissioned office, while at other times it referred to those commissioned and sent by the church for the work of the ministry or as messengers. Such a distinction is possibly reflected in the qualification of Paul and Peter as apostles of Jesus

Christ (Eph. 1:1; 2 Tim. 1:1; 2 Pet. 1:1), while certain unnamed brethren are apostles, or messengers, of the churches (2 Cor. 8:23).

In 1 Corinthians 9:1–5, verses 1–2 seem to imply an official, authoritative apostleship. Given the context and the lack of any indication that Paul changed his use of the word within the passage, a shift in meaning in verse 5 would be misleading at best. While verse 5 would seem to label Barnabas an apostle, the surrounding verses make clear that Paul's point was to defend his own apostleship, not Barnabas's. Thus, the phrase "other apostles" means "other than Paul" rather than "other than Paul and Barnabas."

B. What Then Is My Reward? (9:18)

This verse is best translated in its entirety as a single question: "What then is my reward so that, when I preach the gospel, I offer it free of charge so as not to make full use of my rights in the gospel?" Though this seems awkward in English, it makes better grammatical sense of the word *hina* (translated "that;" the NIV inserts "just this" to help the flow of the English). *Hina* is a conjunction that introduces subordinate clauses, so it is more proper to see the NIV's answer (**Just this . . . in preaching it**) as a subordinate clause, making it part of the question itself.

C. Race, Prize, Crown, Beat (9:24–27)

The Corinthians loved athletics. They sponsored the biannual Isthmian Games, which were second in importance only to the Olympic Games. They held these games only ten miles from Corinth, so most people in Corinth would have been familiar with the goals and practices of the games. They also would have had the opportunity to observe these games. Paul was in Corinth in A.D. 50–52, so he would have been present for the Isthmian Games held in the spring of A.D. 51.

The games included six events: wrestling, jumping, javelin and discus throwing, and, most importantly for Paul's analogy, racing and boxing. Competitors in the Olympic Games were required to train for at least ten months before the games in order to qualify for participation. It is possible that a similar requirement existed for the Isthmian Games, which may explain Paul's references to strict training and disqualification. Winners received crowns either of pine or of celery, both perishable materials.

VII. TEACHING OUTLINE

A. INTRODUCTION

1. Lead Story: "So Long as I Don't Hurt Anybody"

2. Context: The Corinthians, for the most part, thought more in terms of "I" than "we." As a result, when they considered their freedoms in Christ, they focused on the benefit they received personally from those freedoms. They failed to consider the repercussions their exercise of those freedoms might cause. Paul had to teach them that, while freedoms are valuable, they are not as important as the gospel or the kingdom of God. Christians ought to discard their freedoms readily and eagerly when they do so to further the gospel of the kingdom.

3. Transition: Christians in America and other parts of the Western world tend to value their freedom. We are often unwilling to give up our rights for the sake of others. When we are willing to give up our rights, we frequently do so to meet people's physical needs. Unfortunately, like the Corinthians, we cling to our rights when the only benefit to forfeiting them is spiritual.

B. COMMENTARY
1. Christian Rights (9:1–14)
   a. Paul was an apostle (9:1–2)
   b. Paul had apostolic rights and freedoms (9:3–14)
2. Forfeited Rights (9:15–27)
   a. For Paul's own sake (9:15–18,23–27)
   b. For the gospel's sake (9:19–23)

C. CONCLUSION: THE MOST TOYS

VIII. ISSUES FOR DISCUSSION

1. How did Paul prove his apostleship? Why did he need to defend his apostleship? How did Paul's apostleship make his sacrifices even greater?
2. When should ministers be willing to give up their rights? When should Christians be willing to give up their rights?
3. What does it mean to be "all things to all people"?
4. How much effort do you put into being a Christian? Do you work as hard for the gospel as Olympic athletes train to win a medal?

1 Corinthians 10:1–11:1

An Essential Lesson from the Old Testament

I. **INTRODUCTION**
Condemned to Repeat It

II. **COMMENTARY**
A verse-by-verse explanation of this section.

III. **CONCLUSION**
Freedom That Leads to Sin

An overview of the principles and applications from this section.

IV. **LIFE APPLICATION**
This Is London?

Melding the section to life.

V. **PRAYER**
Tying the section to life with God.

VI. **DEEPER DISCOVERIES**
Historical, geographical, and grammatical enrichment of the commentary.

VII. **TEACHING OUTLINE**
Suggested step-by-step group study of the section.

VIII. **ISSUES FOR DISCUSSION**
Zeroing the section in on daily life.

Quote

"*Those who cannot remember the past are condemned to repeat it.*"

George Santayana

1 Corinthians 10:1–11:1

IN A NUTSHELL

Paul applied Old Testament examples of Israel's idolatry to the Corinthians' situation. He warned them against idolatry and gave them practical instructions on how to avoid causing others to stumble.

An Essential Lesson from the Old Testament

I. INTRODUCTION

Condemned to Repeat It

*S*ome people find history interesting, but at least as many people think it is just plain boring. "Why do I have to learn all of these dates?" the teenager complains to her parents. "This is just old stuff that nobody cares about any more," another child says to his history teacher. "What's it got to do with me today?"

The famous Harvard philosophy professor George Santayana wrote, "Those who cannot remember the past are condemned to repeat it." History can teach us where other people have made mistakes as they met the challenges of life. If we fail to learn from their examples, we too may fall when circumstances present us with similar challenges.

Paul judged that the history of Israel provided many important lessons for the church. In this chapter he drew from history to alert the Corinthians that their knowledge regarding meat sacrificed to idols might cause them to become arrogant. Calling their attention to Israel's wilderness wanderings in the days of Moses, Paul warned that the Corinthian church risked repeating Israel's idolatries.

II. COMMENTARY

An Essential Lesson from the Old Testament

> **MAIN IDEA:** Dining in an idol's temple is an act of demon worship that Christians should shun. Christians should learn from Israel's bad example that they must avoid idolatry.

🅰 A Historical Example (10:1–5)

> **SUPPORTING IDEA:** Paul had just used analogies from racing and boxing to demonstrate that Christians must be diligent in living the Christian life. Here, he offered scriptural support for his position.

10:1–2. Once again, Paul used the term **brothers** to indicate his concern for the Corinthians. Paul taught them harshly because he loved them and was concerned for their welfare. The believers in Corinth who ate meat offered to idols had a measure of knowledge, but Paul feared they were **igno-rant** of the lessons of Old Testament history and the imminent dangers that idolatry posed.

The apostle elucidated these dangers by drawing two comparisons between the Corinthian Christians' experiences and the wilderness wanderings of Israel. First, the Israelites **were all under the cloud** and **all passed through the sea**. All the Israelites, young and old, male and female, faithful and unregenerate, were **baptized into Moses** in this way. The use of the word *baptized* points to an implicit analogy. The Israelites had been baptized into Moses just as the Corinthians had been baptized into Christ. Paul pointed out this similarity in order to identify Israel with the Corinthians, and thereby to apply Israel's lessons to Corinth.

He strengthened this association by referring to the Israelites as **our fore-fathers**, even though the Corinthians were Gentiles. In Paul's mind, sufficient continuity existed between the covenant people of God in the Old Testament (Israel) and in the New Testament (the church) that the Old Testament Israelites were the spiritual forefathers of all New Testament believers.

10:3–4. Second, the Israelites **ate the same spiritual food and drank the same spiritual drink**. This **food** and **drink** were not ordinary, but **spiritual**. Paul did not mean that these items were nonphysical but that they came from the Spirit and had spiritual power for God's people.

Specifically, Paul spoke of the manna that God provided to Israel for forty years (Exod. 16:12–35), and the water he provided them at least twice (Exod. 17:6; Num. 20:11). A **spiritual rock**, one miraculously provided by the Spirit and empowering the people, **accompanied them** in the sense that water-giving rocks appeared on at least these two occasions. John explained that the manna foreshadowed Christ (John 6:31–58). Here, Paul symbolically connected Christ and the water-giving rock. The **rock was Christ.**

In the Old Testament, "rock" frequently appeared as a metaphor closely associated with God. It focused on his life-giving role as a victorious warrior-king who saved his people from their enemies. Water flowing to refresh the earth and its inhabitants is a figure also closely associated with God as king. For example, in Ezekiel 47:1–12, water flowing from the temple (God's earthly throne) gives life to every creature near it (cf. Ps. 65:9; Jer. 17:13). It was in this sense that Paul spoke of the water-giving rocks in the wilderness as types of Christ. Christ poured forth the life-giving water of salvation on his people (cf. John 6:35; Rev. 22:1–2).

Israel's **spiritual food** and **spiritual drink** were similar to the Corinthians' partaking of Christ's body and blood symbolized in the Lord's supper (10:14–22). The Israelites in the wilderness had lived through the Old Testament foreshadows of Christian baptism and the Lord's Supper. By describing these Old Testament events as "baptism" and "spiritual food and drink," Paul emphasized the similarity between the situation of the Corinthians and of the Israelites under Moses.

10:5. Next, Paul addressed his chief concern. Five times in four verses (10:1–4) he mentioned that "all" of the Israelites shared these common experiences. All the Israelites were joined together in their experiences of God's grace, just as all the Corinthians were joined together in their experiences of Christian baptism and the Lord's supper.

Despite the experience of grace enjoyed by all Israel, **God was not pleased with most of them.** As a result, most of them died in **the desert** and were not permitted to enter the Promised Land. Paul mentioned this to draw attention to a similar possibility within the Corinthian church. Everyone in the Corinthian church had begun a spiritual journey in Christ, and everyone had participated in baptism and the Lord's Supper—but these experiences did not guarantee that each of them would complete the journey and receive eternal life.

We must not think that Paul believed it was possible to lose salvation. Paul taught that those who have saving faith in Christ will never lose their salvation (Rom. 5:8–10; Eph. 1:5,13–14). Yet, he also knew that not all people who profess faith in Christ and partake of baptism and the Lord's Supper have saving faith.

B Relevance of the Old Testament Example (10:6–13)

> **SUPPORTING IDEA:** *The events of Israel's exodus from Egypt occurred as examples or "types." A type is an Old Testament event that foreshadows a spiritual reality revealed in the New Testament. Paul's application of these Old Testament texts divides into two parts: five examples and a concluding exhortation.*

10:6. Five times Paul warned the Corinthians against acting **as they did** ("as some of them," 10:7; "as some of them did," 10:8–10). Five times he showed how Israel's experiences under Moses provided negative examples of Christian behavior. Each of these examples drew attention to specific aspects of Paul's main concern in this passage: how to deal with meat offered to idols.

First, the Corinthians were to avoid setting their **hearts on evil things.** This terminology occurs only twice in the Old Testament (Num. 11:34; Prov. 1:22), so Paul may have been alluding to Numbers 11:4–6 where the Israelites valued Egypt's food above loyalty to God. Israel committed so many sins that all but two of the adults who originally left Egypt died in the wilderness (Num. 14:22–30; 32:11–13). Even Moses was not allowed to enter the Promised Land (Num. 20:12).

In general, Paul meant these examples to warn the Corinthians of the conditional nature of God's blessings. If they failed to obey God, if they continued to abuse one another, God might judge them as he had judged Israel.

God had already killed some of the Corinthians for these things (1 Cor. 11:30). Specifically, Paul wanted the Corinthians not to allow their desire for meat sacrificed to idols to override their loyalty to God, again to avoid judgment.

10:7. Second, Paul warned believers not to **be idolaters, as some of them were.** Here he had in mind the specific event of Exodus 32:6, and he quoted it to illustrate his point. When Moses went to Sinai to receive the Ten Commandments, Israel began **to indulge in pagan revelry** before the golden calf, which evidently included pagan cultic meals like those the Corinthians ate in pagan temples (8:10). Because of this idolatry God nearly destroyed the entire nation of Israel. As it was, he had three thousand men put to death (Exod. 32:28). Paul warned the Corinthians to take this temptation to idolatrous eating seriously.

10:8. In the third example, Paul warned against **sexual immorality,** referring to the time when **twenty-three thousand of them died** after engaging in idolatry at Baal-Peor and involving themselves in fertility rituals (Num. 25:1–9; 31:16). Numbers 25:9 mentions that twenty-four thousand died as a result. Paul approximates this number (just as the original twenty-four thousand was an approximation rather than an exact count), but his point is clear. Many died because of involvement in pagan fertility rites.

Fertility religions believed that participating in religious prostitution and orgies brought health, fertility, and prosperity. The idolatry practiced in Corinth in Paul's day involved similar fertility practices. Paul's warning was plain: eating meat sacrificed to idols may lead to sexual immorality—to which some of the Corinthians were prone (1 Cor. 6:15–16)—and such immorality stirs the wrath of God.

10:9. Fourth, Paul warned the Corinthians **not** to **test the Lord, as some of them did,** and he mentioned **snakes** which killed many in Israel. This alludes to Numbers 21:4–9 where the people blasphemed God by rejecting his manna. Paul drew upon this parallel because some in Corinth were not satisfied with what God had given them in Christ. As the Israelites before them who desired food other than manna, the Corinthians desired meat so much that they disregarded all other considerations. God's retribution against the Israelites warned the Corinthians against these practices.

10:10. Paul's fifth warning was that the Corinthians not **grumble, as some of them did.** Complaining against God and his leaders took place many times in the wilderness (Exod. 15:24; Deut. 1:27). But Paul had in mind a time when **the destroying angel** killed those who grumbled. Although the Scriptures do not mention a particular time when such an angel appeared in the wilderness, similar concepts appear in many places in the Old Testament (Exod. 12:23; 1 Chr. 21:15). The rabbis of Paul's day taught that God had a particular angel who destroyed and killed. Apparently, Paul agreed with this teaching.

Paul may have referred to Numbers 16 where the people rebelled against Moses' leadership and many thousands died, or perhaps to Numbers 14:28–30 where God issued the curse that only Joshua and Caleb would enter the Promised Land. Those who opposed Paul on the matter of meat offered to idols risked committing against him the kind of rebellion against Moses which brought death to the Old Testament Israelites.

10:11. Paul again exhorted the Corinthians that the sins and judgments in the wilderness **happened to them as examples and were written down** in the Old Testament **as warnings** for Christian believers. This does not mean that the only reason the Israelites experienced these things was to provide an example for later Christians, but it does mean that in God's providence this was part of the reason. Similarly, these events were not recorded just for the sake of the New Testament church; the Old Testament covenant people of God also benefited from these lessons. Followers of Christ are always in danger of taking their Christian experiences of grace as a license for sin (cf. Rom. 6:1), but the Old Testament example prohibits such license.

The apostle qualified his description of followers of Christ by calling them those **on whom the fulfillment of the ages has come.** The Corinthians lived after the earthly ministry of Christ, and therefore lived in the "latter days" or **fulfillment of the ages.** The writer of Hebrews said explicitly what Paul implied by this reference: the responsibilities of those in the age of Christ are even greater than those of the Old Testament age (Heb. 10:26–30).

10:12. Followers of Christ who are overly confident and **think** they are **standing firm** should **be careful** not to **fall** as the Israelites did in the desert. Again, Paul did not mean that one's salvation can be lost. Rather, he meant that some who wrongly think they are saved might prove themselves not to be (see Heb. 3:12–13).

He probably directed this comment to those who ate in idols' temples. These would have been the people who had confidence they would not fall, and the ones who had put themselves in jeopardy of idolatry. Paul may also have been thinking of the weak brothers and sisters who gained the confidence to eat in pagan temples by observing others do the same. He had already expressed concern that these brothers and sisters might be destroyed by such activity.

10:13. The warning to be careful not to fall raised another issue that Paul addressed. What if Christians are so tempted that they cannot resist turning from Christ? Perhaps he had in mind the attraction some Corinthians had toward the idolatrous fertility rituals practiced in Corinth. What if they were not able to resist?

First, all temptations that Christians experience, including that of idolatry, are **common to man**. Others had resisted the temptation toward idolatry, and the Corinthians could do so as well.

Second, **God is faithful**, and he will not desert his people (see Deut. 7:9; 1 Thess. 5:24; Heb. 10:23; Rev. 1:5). God can be trusted not to allow temptations **beyond what** Christians **can bear**. God will always **provide a way out** of temptation so believers **can stand up** and not fall into apostasy. He himself tempts no one (Jas. 1:13), but he is in control of Satan, who tempts believers to sin (Matt. 4:1; 6:13). Because of his great love for his children, God does not allow temptations to be so great that they overcome us. Instead, Christians sin because they do not search for **a way out**.

Ⓒ Prohibition Against Idolatry and Further Explanation (10:14–22)

> **SUPPORTING IDEA:** *Paul drew several conclusions from the previous discussion, further explaining the dangers and idolatrous nature of dining in idols' temples.*

10:14. Paul appealed to the Corinthians in friendly terms, calling them **my dear friends** a strategy he employed in a number of passages. Paul's basic advice was simple but dramatic: **flee from idolatry**. On several occasions, Paul instructed his readers to "flee" from sin when he saw that they were in grave danger (1 Tim. 6:11; 2 Tim. 2:22). As the preceding verses make clear, idolatry is a serious matter. Christians should never flirt or toy with it.

10:15. Next, he compared idolatrous festival meals to the Lord's Supper. Paul assumed the Corinthians were **sensible people**, and he encouraged them to **judge** the matter for themselves. Rather than assert his authority on the matter, he thought the reasonableness of his argument would win them to his position. Thus, he asked a series of questions about the Lord's Supper to which he assumed they knew the correct answers.

10:16. Paul's first question spoke of **the cup of thanksgiving** and **the bread that we break**. These expressions parallel the language in the accounts of the Lord's Supper (Matt. 26:26–28; 1 Cor. 11:23–26). This particular passage places special significance on drinking and eating. Drinking from the cup is **a participation in the blood of Christ** and eating the bread is **a participation in the body of Christ**. The word *participation* (*koinonia*) may also be translated "sharing in" (NASB, NRSV) or "communion of" (NKJV). The New Testament teaches that believers have at least two types of communion. Believers experience fellowship with Christ (1 John 1:3,6) and with one another (1 John 1:7).

10:17. Paul added another type of fellowship to explain his concern in this matter. He noted that believers, **who are many, are one body**, and that this is true **because there is one loaf** of which **all partake.** In Paul's writings, **one body** (*hen soma*) is a technical phrase that refers to mystical union (cf. Rom. 12:5). Because all believers are in spiritual union with Christ, all believers share spiritual union with one another in him.

Paul could have said that believers partake of one loaf because they are one body, because this is also true—but he did not. Rather, he said that believers **are one body** because they **partake of the one loaf.** Paul assumed a similar spiritual effect also took place between the demons and the worshipers in the idols' temples, and he forbade participation in pagan ceremonies as a result.

10:18. Paul added a comment about **the people of Israel** in the Old Testament. Some interpreters have taken his words negatively, as if they referred to the revelry at the foot of Mount Sinai (Exod. 32:1–6). Others have suggested that Paul spoke of the Passover celebration of peace offerings. In the thanksgiving or peace offerings of the Old Testament, the Israelites ate portions of what they sacrificed (Lev. 7:15–16). The Passover meal exemplified the kind of sacrifice of which worshipers ate (Exod. 12:1–14), and the Christian Lord's Supper had its roots in the Old Testament Passover ceremony (Mark 14:12–24). Paul referred the Corinthians to the Old Testament practice of Passover as historical support for his views of the Lord's Supper in 10:16–17.

Once again, he emphasized the fact that those who eat such sacrifices **participate** in the spiritual significance of **the altar** of the temple. Paul did not consider eating the Old Testament thanksgiving offerings to be empty symbolism. Rather, he believed that spiritual fellowship between believers and their God occurred as they partook. In the same way, those who partake of the Lord's Supper fellowship with God.

10:19–20. Paul warned the Corinthians to "flee from idolatry" (10:14), and he supported his command with the fact that participants in biblical sacrificial meals have spiritual communion with God and with one another (10:16–18). Paul's point is clear. If such communion takes place in biblical sacrificial meals, then in some sense it also takes place in pagan sacrificial meals—but Paul anticipated an objection. Did he mean that **a sacrifice offered to an idol is anything, or that an idol is anything?** No, he replied.

Paul had already argued that pagan religions are false and that their sacrifices are not made to true gods, and at the same time had qualified that statement by saying that many so-called gods exist. In the verse at hand, he explained his meaning more fully. Pagans are greatly mistaken about sacrifices to their so-called gods, but something supernatural is involved: **the sacrifices of pagans are offered to demons.**

Unlike the pagans and the unknowledgeable Christians in Corinth, Paul realized that pagans do not sacrifice to great gods whom Christians should fear. In this sense, an idol is nothing. Yet, the sacrifices of pagans are made to real **demons**, and Paul insisted that the Corinthian believers not **be participants with demons.**

10:21. It is inappropriate for Christians to **drink the cup of the Lord** and also **the cup of demons.** Drinking the cup of demons is a sharing of fellowship with evil supernatural beings, and somehow effects a mysterious spiritual union with them, just as sexual intercourse between a man and a prostitute brings about a similar union. Demons have no power over Christians even when Christians eat in idols' temples, but such union with demons corrupts the sanctity of the believer's relationship with Christ just as fornication with prostitutes does.

10:22. Paul made this clear when he wondered if the Corinthians wanted to **arouse the Lord's jealousy**, and if they were **stronger than** the Lord. God is often portrayed in Scripture as a jealous, possessive husband (Jer. 31:32; Hos. 2:1–13). He requires exclusive communion from his people. The Corinthians were to flee the practice of idolatry because they risked incurring the wrath of God much like the Israelites under Moses.

Ⅾ Practical Directions on Meat Offered to Idols (10:23–11:1)

> **SUPPORTING IDEA:** *Paul had argued that idols are not divine and should not be treated with pagan superstition; that idolatrous practices involve demons, so Christians should flee them; and that the guiding moral imperative is love for others, not asserting one's own rights. At this point, he offered practical guidelines based on these principles.*

10:23–24. This section begins with a slogan that Paul had already mentioned: **everything is permissible.** There is a measure of truth in the slogan; Christians have much freedom in Christ. Yet, the slogan must be balanced for practical implementation. Paul did so with the qualifications that **not everything is beneficial.**

Beneficial and **constructive** are ambiguous terms at first glance. Did Paul mean beneficial to oneself or to others? In line with his previous discussion of the importance of love and humility toward others, Paul made the meaning of these terms clear: **nobody should seek his own good, but the good of others.** Freedom in Christ must be balanced by a desire to build up and benefit Christians.

10:25–26. Christians may eat any meat they buy in the market so long as the issue of idolatry does not come up. Yet, if the matter of sacrifice to idols is mentioned, then believers should refrain from eating for the sake of others. In the meat markets of Greece, some meat was sold after being dedicated to an idol, while other meat had never been so dedicated. Apparently, the distinction was not always made evident by shop keepers.

The rabbis placed many restrictions on Jews who lived in pagan cities like Corinth. Jews had to be sure they bought meat only from shops that were kosher. But this was not Paul's policy. Believers could **eat anything sold . . . without raising questions** about whether the meat had been sacrificed to an idol. Paul supported his counsel by quoting Psalm 24:1: **The earth is the Lord's, and everything in it.** Jews often used this phrase in mealtime prayers. Paul used it to assert that the Lord is the only true God of all things, and that idols are insignificant. Followers of Christ could eat without **raising questions of conscience**—without asking questions about the meat's history that might trouble the conscience of others.

10:27–29a. After speaking of the marketplace, Paul turned to the situations in which believers were guests in unbelievers' homes. His first statement was similar to the marketplace advice. Christians may **eat whatever** they receive **without raising questions of conscience.** Even so, the policy changed if someone said that the meat had **been offered in sacrifice** to an idol. When this fact was known, the situation became more complex. Followers of Christ were **not** to **eat** under these circumstances **for the sake of the man who told** them.

Paul's outlook is clear. Knowing that meat has been sacrificed to idols raises issues of **the other man's conscience**, perhaps by offending him, but more likely by encouraging him to participate in the sinful practices of idolatry.

It is significant that Paul offered instructions on dining with unbelievers. Apparently, this was not a scenario he imagined would be played out in a believer's home. If the Corinthians followed Paul's advice, they never would have known whether the meat they purchased had been sacrificed to idols, and thus would not have been in a position to tell their guests the meat's history. Further, Christian guests should not suffer a moral quandary on this issue.

10:29b–30. It is difficult to understand this portion of Paul's argument. Was he defending his own actions against those who opposed him in Corinth, or was he speaking hypothetically of himself as if he was in a situation like the one he posited in 10:27–29a? In any event, the two questions in this section seem designed to justify his policy regarding eating in unbelievers' homes.

First, Paul wondered why he should do anything that would allow his **freedom** to **be judged by another's conscience.** Christians have freedom to eat meat sacrificed to idols, but they should not exercise that freedom when it threatens the conscience of another. If an unbelieving host does not mention the meat's history, his conscience evidently is not threatened by that history, and Christians are free to eat. If believers ask questions about the meat, however, it indicates to their unbelieving hosts that idols are significant.

Thus, when Christians eat such meat after asking its history, their hosts' conscience may be encouraged toward idolatry (cf. 8:7). Alternatively, hosts may consider believers hypocritical if believers eat meat they know had been sacrificed to idols. This seems to be the point of his second question, **Why am I denounced?** Questions can only lead to the unnecessary forfeiture of Christian freedom, or to the harm of unbelieving hosts' consciences. For the same reason, Christians should not eat meat when their hosts volunteer the information that the meat has been sacrificed to an idol.

Nevertheless, Paul said Christians may legitimately give thanks for and eat meat that has been sacrificed to idols. They may **take part in the meal with thankfulness.** This is most likely a reference to the prayer of thanks in 10:26. In any case, Paul did not argue here for the forfeiture of Christian freedom, but for the protection and careful exercise of Christian freedom. He suggested abstinence only when such freedom had been compromised by the actions of others.

10:31–32. Paul summarized his outlook into two principles. First, whether or not believers partake, they must **do it all for the glory of God.** The chief end of human beings is the glory of God; his honor should be the principle concern of those who love him (Deut. 6:5; Matt. 22:37).

Second, whether believers partake or not, they should **not cause anyone to stumble.** They should neither cause anyone to sin nor hinder receptivity to the gospel. The principle of love for neighbor goes hand in hand with love for God (Lev. 19:18; Matt. 22:39). This concern for others applies to **Jews, Greeks,** and **the church of God.** Paul mentioned these groups because each raised different considerations. Both **Jews** and **Greeks** are unbelieving, but each group has different standards and expectations. Moreover, the principle of love for neighbor must also extend to **the church,** which has still different issues.

10:33–11:1. Paul closed this section by reminding his readers that he did not require of them something he himself was unwilling to do. He reminded them that he sought **to please everybody in every way.** Of course, as he had said earlier, Paul did not carry his service to others to the point of sin. He sought to serve others because he was **not seeking** his **own good but the good of many,** or more specifically, **that they may be saved.** Paul's commitment to seeking the salvation of the lost led him to subjugate his personal preferences and freedoms to the good of others.

As a result of the consistency with which Paul fulfilled this service, he felt capable of encouraging the Corinthians to **follow** his **example** as he followed **the example of Christ.** Christ gave up his freedom and honor, humbling himself to the point of death on a cross, in order to save others (Phil. 2:5–8).

Paul encouraged the Corinthians to remember Christ's great sacrifice as the perfect model of love and concern for others (see Eph. 4:32–5:1).

> **MAIN IDEA REVIEW:** *Dining in an idol's temple is an act of demon worship that Christians should shun. Christians should learn from Israel's bad example that they must avoid idolatry.*

III. CONCLUSION

Freedom That Leads to Sin

In a day when many temptations toward idolatry surrounded Christians, Paul insisted that mature and knowledgeable believers should consider the effects of eating meat sacrificed to idols. Both unbelievers and believers may be led into sin by Christians exercising freedom in these matters. Moreover, mature Christians needed to remember that idolatry was a serious temptation even for them.

PRINCIPLES

- The whole Bible is relevant and applicable today.
- God's covenant blessings and curses are conditioned upon covenant obedience and disobedience.
- Believers are counted as covenant keepers in Christ.
- God does not allow us to be tempted beyond our ability to endure temptation.

APPLICATIONS

- We must learn from the examples given to us in the Bible and not repeat the sins we see there.
- We must seek the good of our neighbor above our own good.
- We must resist the temptation to engage in idolatrous practices.
- We must actively seek to escape evil.

IV. LIFE APPLICATION

This Is London?

"Man, I can't believe this is London," my fellow traveler said to me. He referred to the fact that London today is so multiethnic and multireligious. "I always think of London as a Christian city. Why are there so many mosques?"

I think we all know that the world is no longer neatly divided into monolithic cultures. It used to be in many parts of the world that a person could live and die without coming in contact with other religions. Now it is hard to get through a day without facing different cultural and religious norms.

In many ways, our situation is similar to that of the Corinthian believers. We face the challenge of figuring out how to interact socially with other faiths without compromising our own.

Similarly, people of other world religions often convert to the Christian faith, but they bring with them all sorts of baggage from other religions that hinders their spiritual development. Some of these converts come from religions that offer food to idols. For example, a sacred Hindu book teaches that the devotees of Krishna are released from all kinds of sins because they eat food that is offered first for sacrifice. When interacting with believers from this type of background, the situations Paul described may parallel our lives far more closely than we might first imagine. But even if we never meet such people, we can still learn many valuable lessons from this chapter.

First, Paul has shown that we cannot go through our Christian lives reading only the New Testament. One of the lessons Paul taught from the Old Testament is that God's blessings and curses are conditional. He offers blessings when we are faithful to him, but threatens temporal judgments when we disobey. We cannot assume that God will never bring judgment on us just because we are part of the church, or because we have been baptized or have taken the Lord's Supper, or because we have made a profession of faith. God killed many professed believers in the Old Testament, and he will also subject Christian believers to his wrath.

We should also learn from this chapter that God has not allowed us to be tempted beyond our abilities to resist. Some people point out that God gives us a way out by strengthening us through the Holy Spirit. While this is true, Paul emphasized our responsibility to withstand sin. He implied that God will manipulate circumstances so there will be something we can do to avoid the situation of sin, not just that we will be able to grit our teeth and bear it.

Since Paul's main point concerns idolatry, we should consider the actual idolatry we encounter in life. Many Christians do not realize that some of their activities are idolatrous. Some actually eat in idols' temples (perhaps at a free vegetarian buffet at the local Hindu shrine), while others enjoy astrology or seances. Many forms of pagan rites and worship are accessible in the modern world. If we fail to recognize them for what they are, we may affiliate ourselves with them. Though we may not realize it, we will be tempting God's wrath, and he may destroy us.

Still, some things related to idolatry we may enjoy without incurring God's wrath—just as the Corinthians could eat meat that had been sacrificed to idols—as long as we refrain from sin. At the same time, we need to remain aware of the weaknesses of believers and unbelievers so we do not send the wrong signals to those of weak conscience.

V. PRAYER

Lord Jesus, we yearn for wisdom as we face other religions. We want to remain loyal to you; keep us from all temptations to become corrupted by other ways of life. We also want to be servants of believers and unbelievers alike. Give us the wisdom to form all of our actions toward others so that you are honored and they are encouraged to come to faith in you. Amen.

VI. DEEPER DISCOVERIES

A. Participation, Participate (10:16,18,20)

In Paul's writings, "participation" (*koinonia*) and "participate" (*koinonos*) have multiple meanings, though all their meanings seem to revolve around the idea of "fellowship" or "mutuality." Some occurrences speak of a mysterious union that believers share with Jesus and the Holy Spirit and with one another through Jesus and the Spirit: "called . . . into fellowship with . . . Jesus Christ" (1 Cor. 1:9); "the fellowship of the Holy Spirit be with you all" (2 Cor. 13:14); and "fellowship with the Spirit" (Phil. 2:1).

Philippians 3:10 relies on this underlying conception in saying that believers share in Christ's sufferings ("fellowship of sharing in his sufferings"). Colossians 1:24 expresses the same thought, saying that believers "fill up in [their] flesh what is still lacking in regard to Christ's afflictions." That is, Christ completes his own suffering through his union with suffering believers. Akin to this is Paul's statement, "You share in our sufferings" (2 Cor. 1:7), which in context means not that the Corinthians suffer the same kinds of things that Paul suffers, but that their union with him means that they experience his suffering with him (cf. 1 Cor. 12:26).

In Philippians 1:5, Paul referred to his readers' "partnership in the gospel." The context of this statement suggests better translations would be "participation" (NASB), "sharing" (NRSV), or "fellowship" (NKJV), because Paul did not mean that the Philippians shared in the work of the gospel, but that they were in the process of being changed by the gospel.

B. Anything Sold in the Meat Market (10:25)

In Paul's day, most of the meat available for purchase in the market had been butchered by pagan priests, and much of what those priests butchered they also sacrificed to idols. It should have been fairly easy to question vendors regarding the history of the meat they sold. Still, not all may have known whether particular cuts had been sacrificed to idols, even if the vendors knew that the meat had been butchered by pagan priests. Pagans also offered other foods to their idols, and many of these also found their way into the marketplace. Paul's exhortation "whether you eat or drink" (10:31) reflects the understanding that much of the food and drink available for purchase by the public came from idols' temples.

VII. TEACHING OUTLINE

A. INTRODUCTION

1. Lead Story: Condemned to Repeat It
2. Context: The Corinthian church lived in a very idolatrous society. Many Corinthian Christians had been converted from paganism. Further, much of the food available for purchase in the market had associations with paganism. The opportunities for Christians to fall back into pagan practices abounded. Sometimes when Christians exercised their freedom in Christ without falling into sin themselves, others observing their actions were affected. Thus, Paul argued that in order to protect others, Christians should forfeit their freedom in certain contexts.
3. Transition: Similar temptations to sin exist for Christians today. Many Christians are tempted by or interested in pagan practices such as astrology or psychic readings. Many others have been converted from other religions. They associate certain innocent practices with their former idolatries. Not only must these Christians resist the temptation to engage in idolatrous activities, but all other Christians must be aware of these struggles, restricting their own freedoms so they do not cause their weaker brothers and sisters to stumble.

B. COMMENTARY

1. A Historical Example (10:1–5)
   a. Baptized into Moses (10:1–2)
   b. Spiritual food and drink (10:3–4)
   c. God killed them (10:5)
2. Relevance of the Old Testament Example (10:6–13)
   a. Christians should not set their hearts on evil things (10:6–10)
   b. Christians may fall as Israel did (10:11–13)
3. Prohibition Against Idolatry and Further Explanation (10:14–22)
   a. Lord's Supper (10:15–17)
   b. Jewish sacrifices (10:18)
   c. Pagan sacrifices (10:19–20)
   d. Flee/resist idolatry (10:14,21–22)

4. Practical Directions on Meat Offered to Idols (10:23–11:1)
   a. Seek the good of others (10:23–24,32–33)
   b. Do all for God's glory (10:31)
   c. Follow Paul's example (11:1)
   d. Eating marketplace food (10:25–26)
   e. Eating with unbelievers (10:27–30)

C. CONCLUSION: THIS IS LONDON?

VIII. ISSUES FOR DISCUSSION

1. What things in the Corinthian church did Paul think had been fore-shadowed by the Israelites' baptism into Moses, and by their eating and drinking of spiritual food and water? What happened to the Israelites? What does this imply about Christians in the New Testament age?

2. What sins did Israel commit? How did God respond to their sins? How does God's response to these sins serve as an example to the church? Were these sins evident in the Corinthian church's past? Do you see any of these sins being committed in the modern church, especially in your church?

3. Exactly what promise does God make regarding the support he will give us in times of temptation? How is this promise commonly misunderstood or abused?

4. How does your church interpret the Lord's Supper? Are you satisfied with your ability to understand or explain this reality?

1 Corinthians 11:2-16

Honoring Others in Worship

Quote

"*W*orship is a time to care for one another, to build up the unity of our fellowship in Christ."

J o h n   F r a m e

1 Corinthians 11:2–16

I N   A   N U T S H E L L

*P*aul began a long discussion about worship in this chapter by focusing first on the importance of men and women honoring Christ and each other in worship.

Honoring Others in Worship

I. INTRODUCTION

A Cold Winter Day in Tasmania

I stood there behind the pulpit in a small town in Tasmania, Australia. It was the middle of July, but it was their winter—a very cold winter. As I stood there shivering in the pulpit, I could not believe what happened. It was just an innocent comment, a general application of the Bible. I think I simply said, "We should all be careful to be patient with one another."

But suddenly a woman in the congregation jumped up and shouted. "Don't tell me that until you have told my husband to get a job!"

She sat down as quickly as she stood up, but I remember everyone in the church turning around to look at her husband. His face turned bright red, and he hid his face in his hands. He did not look up again for the entire worship service.

I was only a guest, so I do not know what family dynamics were displayed at that moment. But one thing was sure. The woman did not feel the least obligation to honor her husband during their public worship.

Less extreme examples of such dishonor take place in worship all the time. A husband elbows his wife as the preacher says something that touches on an argument they had earlier in the week. A parent threatens a child with severe punishment in front of the congregation.

Put simply, we do not seem to realize that worship is a time to honor other people. We come to worship Christ, but we could care less about the others who join us in worship. But the fact is that we cannot honor Christ in worship while we dishonor our fellow worshipers.

II. COMMENTARY

Honoring Others in Worship

MAIN IDEA: *Paul began a discussion of yet another area of controversy and problems among the Corinthians: worship. He addressed three important subjects: the question of head coverings for women in public worship, the observance of the Lord's Supper, and the gifts of the Holy Spirit in worship.*

◬ Words of Praise (11:2)

SUPPORTING IDEA: *Paul began on a positive note. He knew the value of congratulating believers when they were doing well.*

11:2. One can only imagine the relief that came to the Corinthians when they heard the opening words, **I praise you for remembering me in everything.** "Everything" in this sense means "all kinds of things." As Paul's mind moved toward matters of worship, he apparently was satisfied that many of his teachings were being followed by a majority of the Corinthian believers. So he praised the church **for holding to the teachings** he had **passed on** to them. "Pass on" was technical rabbinical terminology for the official, sacred transmission of religious traditions (cf. 11:23). Paul probably hoped this positive word would help them attend to the corrections he was about to offer.

Paul was dealing with a somewhat controversial matter (11:16). Apparently, some people in the Corinthian church had rejected the common practice of the church that wives should cover their heads in public worship. Paul was satisfied that many understood and practiced this policy, but he still felt the need to explain the reasons that everyone should continue it.

Paul was particularly concerned with how men and women treated each other in public worship. Although having implications for everyday life, his words focused on prayer and prophecy (the teaching and preaching of God's Word) (11:4–5), which would have taken place primarily when believers gathered.

Paul's instructions derived from three basic concerns. First, he was committed to honoring God by applying the principles of Scripture to worship. Second, he was concerned that believers show due regard for one another in their worship times. Third, he was concerned with the testimony of the Corinthian worship meetings before unbelievers. This chapter focuses on how the practice of head coverings for women reflects these three concerns. Why were women to cover their heads in worship? Paul's answer was threefold: (1) it was true to divine commands; (2) it honored husbands in worship; and (3) it reflected the cultural expectations of decency in their day.

In this passage Paul shifted without notice between the relationships of men and women in general, and husbands and wives in particular. In Greek the terms usually translated "man" and "woman" are flexible enough to be used in both senses. We must remember that Paul's words at any moment may apply generally to men and women, to husbands and wives, or to both. But his central focus was on the behavior of husbands and wives in worship.

B The Divine Order (11:3)

SUPPORTING IDEA: *Paul asserted that three parallel relationships exist: (1) Christ in relation to every man; (2) man in relation to woman; and (3) God (the Father) in relation to Christ.*

11:3. Much disagreement arises because Paul did not explicitly complete these metaphors. He described all three forms of headship: Christ is the head; husbands are heads; God is the head. Yet, he did not state the roles of the corresponding analogues (men, wives, and Christ). If one member of each pair is the head, what roles do the others play? Most interpreters have sought to answer this question in the same way for all three relationships. As a result, two major interpretations have risen.

First, some have argued that **head** in this passage means "source," as the "head" of a river is the source from which the river flows. In this view, Christ is the source of males in the sense that Christ created Adam from the dust (Gen. 2:7). In a similar fashion, males are the source of females in the sense that Eve was taken from Adam (Gen. 2:22). God the Father is the head of Christ because Christ "came from the Father" (John 16:27–28).

In support of this view: (1) ancient Greeks frequently used the term *head* metaphorically to indicate the source from which something came; and (2) in this passage, Paul specifically mentioned that "man did not come from woman, but woman from man" (11:8).

Second, others have argued that **head** implies that a chain of authority extends from God the Father, to Christ, to husbands, and to their wives. This interpretation gains support primarily from the Hebrew term *head* in the Old Testament (Josh. 11:10; 1 Sam. 9:22; Isa. 7:8–9; only in Hab. 3:13–14 does the Greek word *head* appear in the Septuagint. Here it clearly refers to the literal head of a body in a metaphor). It is also supported by Paul's uses of "head" in Colossians 2:10 and Ephesians 5:23. This is also the meaning behind "head" as a metaphor in Ephesians 1:22. In addition, several New Testament authors quoted Psalm 118:22 which uses "head" to mean "main" or "chief" (Matt. 21:42; 1 Pet. 2:7).

An alternate interpretation suggests that Paul purposefully did not complete the metaphors because the parallels among Christ, husbands, and God are not precisely the same. Recognizing that these analogies could easily be stretched too far by treating the parallels too strictly, Paul himself qualified these metaphors in the next portion of this chapter (11:11–12). Christ, husbands, and God are all sources and/or authorities in different ways. The term *head* has a variety of connotations, including "source" and "authority." In some respects the connotations of "source" should be emphasized, and in other respects "authority" appears more clearly in view.

This variation should be self-evident. Husbands are never the heads of their wives in precisely the same way that Christ is the head of men. After all, Christ created human beings and is the perfect and absolute authority. No man could or should be that for a woman. Nor is Christ the head of men precisely in the same way that God is the head of Christ. The Father did not create the Son, nor is Christ simply the subordinate of the Father. The differences among the various members of these analogies make precise comparisons impossible.

What then was Paul telling the Corinthians in 11:3? To know more precisely what headship means in these various relationships, we must look beyond the mere term *head* and understand the unique features of each relationship.

On the other hand, we must remember that Paul's chief concern here was not to specify what he meant by headship. He commended the Corinthians for understanding this doctrine (11:2), and apparently felt little need to explain himself. His primary concern was much more practical. In this passage, the headships of Christ, husbands, and God had one thing in common to which he drew attention: each head should be honored. This practical concern comes to the foreground in the repetition of the word *dishonor* (11:4–5). By their actions in public worship, men are expected to honor Christ (11:4), and wives are expected to honor their husbands (11:5), just as Christ brings honor and glory to his heavenly Father (15:24).

Ⓒ Responsibilities to Heads (11:4–12)

SUPPORTING IDEA: *In Corinthian society, male head coverings dishonored God, and female head coverings honored husbands. Therefore, wives were to wear head coverings in worship, and men were not to wear head coverings in worship.*

11:4. Paul addressed men first, saying that **every man who prays or prophesies** while **his head** is **covered dishonors** Christ, **his head.** Perhaps Paul had in mind that men dishonor their own physical heads, but this interpretation seems unlikely from the context. In the Roman Empire, men commonly covered their heads with their togas as they performed pagan worship rituals. It is not known for certain that this practice had reached Corinthian pagan worship. But it seems likely that Paul at least warned against adopting this practice in the church.

In a word, for a man to cover his head in the worship of Christ was to worship in the same way pagan men worshiped their gods. Imitating this practice mixed false religion into the worship of Christ, and therefore dishonored him. It is not possible that Paul intended this as an absolute statement rather than a culturally specific statement because God himself commanded

Aaron the high priest always to wear a turban when ministering. This would have included prophecy and prayer (Exod. 29:6). Moreover, throughout church history Christian men have covered their heads in worship for the sake of warmth and decoration. Paul's teaching responded to the particular pagan influence in Corinth.

11:5–6. Turning to women, or more specifically to wives, Paul affirmed that sometimes a woman **prays or prophesies** in public worship. The practice of public prayer would certainly include congregational and silent prayer, but Paul did not limit women to these kinds of prayer. Moreover, prophecy in the New Testament included the expression and explication of God's word to his people. Although Paul forbade women to serve in the ordained positions of pastor, elder, and teacher (1 Tim. 2:12), he did not restrict women from more informal forms of speaking the truth of God's word, even in worship.

Nevertheless, Paul insisted that any wife praying or prophesying in public worship should do so with her head covered. If she spoke in worship **with her head uncovered**, then she **dishonor[ed] her head**. Once again, Paul may have had in mind a woman's own physical head, but this seems unlikely. He almost certainly meant that she dishonored her husband. Many commentators have suggested that, in the Mediterranean world of Paul's day, it was customary in some circles for women of good repute to wear a veil or head covering in public, and that this practice honored husbands. While this was certainly true in some areas, there is some reason to doubt that this was the case in secular Corinth. It was, however, for reasons not entirely clear, a practice which honored husbands in the church, and which the churches of God universally practiced (11:16).

To convince dissenters of his view, Paul drew a connection between women having their heads uncovered and having their heads shaved. Wives who did not cover their heads in worship brought shame to their husbands **as though** their **head[s] were shaved**. Here Paul may have referred to the custom in the Mediterranean world of the first century that adulterous women were punished by having their heads shaved in disgrace. One can only imagine the shame this practice brought to women. If these women were married, it would also have brought dishonor to their husbands.

Consequently, Paul argued that **if it is a disgrace** to her husband for a woman to have her head shaved, then **she should cover her head** in public worship. In a culture that did not see any shame in women with uncovered heads, this would have been an ineffective argument. Paul probably felt confident arguing this way only because the church's subculture differed from the secular world on this point.

11:7a. Paul supported his views with Scripture. First, he argued that **a** man should not imitate a pagan head covering because **he is the image and**

glory of God. According to Genesis, both Adam and Even were created in the image of God (Gen. 1:27). What then did Paul mean by saying that man is the **image . . . of God** in contrast with woman? He probably meant that Adam held a special status (**glory**) as God's image because he was created first. God made Adam directly from the dust, but he made Eve from Adam's body. This gave Adam and his male descendants a unique role on earth that could not be held in the same way by women (cf. 1 Tim. 2:12–13).

This perspective seems even more likely because Paul not only described man as the **image** of God, but also as the **glory of God.** Adam was not designed for his own glory, but for God's. Before making Eve, God placed Adam in the garden of God and commissioned him to work the land in his service (Gen. 2:15). In this sense, therefore, the male descendants of Adam have a more direct responsibility to serve God in the fulfillment of his creation mandate.

This special role for males does not diminish in the least the responsibilities of females. They are also made in God's image and render service to him. Even so, males are in the unique position of being the same gender as the one who first stood before God and served him. They have the serious responsibility to bring honor to God in all things, but especially in worship.

11:7b. Whereas husbands are the "glory of God," **woman is the glory of man.** Paul did not mean that woman is not the glory of God, for all of creation is for the glory of God (Rom. 11:36). More likely, he meant that woman is the glory of both man and of God, and not just of God. Therefore, determining whether wives should wear head coverings was more complicated than it was for men. In fact, this was exactly the point he was trying to prove: women should wear head coverings even though men should not.

Paul called women **the glory of** their husbands because this is one of their unique roles in the creation order. According to Genesis 2:18,20, God created Eve to make it possible for the human race to fulfill the task originally given to Adam. For this reason Moses called Eve "a helper suitable for [Adam]." The Hebrew word *helper* does not mean "inferior," but "aid" or "assistant." It can even be used of social superiors. Moreover, the term "suitable for" means "corresponding to" or "the mirror image of." Eve was the **glory** of Adam in a special way. With her joining Adam, the human race would become all God had intended it to be. Both she and Adam would receive honor as a result.

This unique role held by Eve and her married female descendants gives wives a responsibility to bring honor or glory to their husbands. As followers of Christ, all Christians must seek the good of others above their own (1 Cor. 10:24). The special relationship between wives and husbands intensifies this responsibility (for husbands too, Eph. 5:25–31). Because of this responsibility, wives must honor their husbands in public worship.

11:8–9. Paul further supported his argument that woman is the glory of man by appealing to another aspect of the creation account. He reminded his readers that **man did not come from woman** and that man was not **created for woman**. He thereby implied that husbands are not the glory of women. Instead, the **woman** came **from man** and was created **for man**. Because she was created **from** and **for man**, a wife is to bring glory to her husband.

11:10. At this point in Paul's argument, one might expect him to have concluded that wives ought to cover their heads in public worship. In fact, this is what the majority of the translations suggest, but it may not be precisely what he said. Paul concluded that women **ought to have . . . authority** over their heads.

This passage presents a number of difficulties. Most major translations add to the original text the words "a sign of" or "a symbol of" so that the verse reads "a sign of authority." If this approach is correct, then it probably means that women ought to wear head coverings as symbols that they are under their husbands' authority. Generally, most interpreters prefer this option. Even if this option is correct, we must remember that head coverings were a culturally specific symbol of man's authority. Modern Christians cannot simply put veils on their wives and believe they have fulfilled the intention of Paul's teaching.

It is possible, however, that the major translations have erred by inserting the words "a sign/symbol of." It is more in keeping with the Greek original to translate the verse "the woman ought to have authority over her head," meaning that women ought to exercise authority over their physical heads. This understanding indicates that Paul wanted women to act responsibly and on their own in the matter of head coverings. This more literal reading is confirmed by the next statement, "However, woman is not independent of man" (11:11). This clause appears to qualify an assertion of the women's authority encouraged in 11:10.

Paul also argued that women should have **a sign of authority** over or on their heads **because of the angels**. Two interpretations of this expression are widespread. First, "angels" could refer to actual celestial creatures. The New Testament hints that churches have angels who attend to the church and represent the church to God (Rev. 2:1; 3:14). Even individuals may have such angels (Matt. 18:10). If Paul referred to these angels, then he meant that supernatural angels watched the worship in the church at Corinth to make sure this was acceptable.

Alternatively, the term *angels* may be translated "messengers," referring to human messengers (Luke 9:52; Acts 12:15). If this is the correct understanding of this passage, then Paul may have referred to human messengers who reported to him. In this case, Paul warned the Corinthians to remember that their behavior in worship was monitored by people who would report to him, and that he would hold them accountable.

Paul may also have referred to messengers from other churches. Some of the churches who held to the practice of head coverings for women did so on the basis that their societies required such attire for reputable women. Paul may have been worried that the messengers would be offended, and would carry bad reports about Corinth back to their own churches. This might have become an opportunity for stumbling. The Corinthian women might have negatively influenced the behavior of other churches.

11:11–12. Paul's statements about men and women were easily misunderstood in his day, even as they are today. Thus, having affirmed the responsibilities of husbands and wives to honor their heads in worship, he feared his instructions might be taken as a complete statement on the relations of men and women. Therefore, Paul qualified what he had said.

His qualification began with the expression **in the Lord,** a phrase he used elsewhere to identify people in the body of Christ (Rom. 16:8; 1 Cor. 4:17). In other words, the qualifications he was about to express should always be remembered by those who serve Christ.

Without the rest of Christian teaching, some interpreters might conclude from the preceding passage that men bear no responsibility to honor their wives in worship. Others might think that wives bear no direct relationship to the Lord. Paul wanted to make clear that such assumptions had no basis in his teaching. In the Christian church, men's and women's different roles in worship must be guarded by other considerations.

Paul brought two considerations to the foreground. First, neither husbands nor wives are independent from each other. Paul restated that **woman** (a wife) **is not independent of man** (a husband), a principle evident from 11:3–10. Her authority was always meant to complement man's, so she must not think herself autonomous. Next, Paul added the corollary that **man** (a husband) is not **independent of woman** (a wife). Husbands must not think that their headship implies independence from or superiority over their wives. Their dependence on their wives qualifies their roles as heads.

To support this claim, Paul referred to the biological interdependence of men and women. To be sure, **woman came from man** when Eve was made from Adam's rib (see Gen. 2:22), but it is also true that **man is born of woman.** Every male has a mother, and this biological fact mitigates against any man's temptation to think himself free from the obligation to honor women. The principle of honoring mothers (Deut. 5:16) implies that husbands ought to have high regard and honor for their wives.

Second, lest anyone mistake his description of headship in 11:3, Paul made it clear that wives also have a relationship with God. He reminded the Corinthians that **everything comes from God.** In other words, the fact that

Eve came from Adam's rib does not contradict the fact that God himself fashioned the first woman. To be sure, husbands have a headship role, but this role does not eliminate the need for wives to cultivate their own relationships with Christ. Wives worship and honor God directly because "there is neither . . . male nor female, for you are all one in Christ Jesus" (Gal. 3:28). Moreover, this common origin implies a commonality of worship; the distinctions between the sexes in their worship roles do not imply complete separation. Both men and women must fulfill their proper roles together if worship is to be acceptable.

Cultural Considerations (11:13–16)

> **SUPPORTING IDEA:** *Paul returned to the issue of head coverings, but used a new strategy. He appealed to nature and to the common practices of the church.*

11:13. This section begins with an unusual expression: **judge for yourselves.** By these words Paul did not encourage the Corinthians to ignore his instructions. Rather, he meant that they should not blindly obey his directives. They were to think through the issue. Paul said this because he was convinced the believers in Corinth had the ability to think properly on this issue. He hoped they would reason through issues with him and see how he came to his conclusions. In fact, since this was an area in which he knew the church was following his instructions, he probably expected the majority of his readers to agree with his position.

His direction that they **judge** for themselves may have been a rhetorical nudge to get the Corinthians to compare notes with one another. Paul may have wanted this statement to begin a dialogue between the Corinthians so the majority would influence the dissenters in a positive way.

Paul put the matter to them plainly, asking if it were **proper** for women to pray in public worship with their heads **uncovered.** By stating the question in terms of propriety, Paul avoided speaking directly of sin. Though some improprieties are also sin, the two are not so closely related that one absolutely must refrain from all impropriety (cf. Eph. 5:3; Heb. 2:10). Paul consciously chose to argue from what was appropriate rather than from what was righteous. He appealed to the Corinthian's own notions. Knowing their worldview, he expected strong agreement with his position.

11:14–15. This portion of Paul's argument is difficult to discern. He clearly led the Corinthians to the correct answer by posing another question, asking them to consider if it were not true that **the very nature of things** taught his particular view on the matter. The meaning of this question, however, is puzzling. Several explanations have been advanced, but none seems adequate.

The expression "the very nature of things" may also be translated "nature itself." On this basis, some interpreters have argued that Paul's question was an appeal to creation ordinances. They have assumed either that Paul thought the created order demonstrated that men should have short hair and women long hair, or that he believed that God actually created men with shorter hair than women. Some have suggested (though wrongly) the latter view to have been the opinion of the Stoic philosopher Epictetus, and thereby have suspected that this might have been the Corinthians' view. Given that the Old Testament says nothing about the length of hair, however, it is unlikely that Paul endorsed a particular view of hair length at the time of human origins.

Paul expected the Corinthians to recognize that men should have short hair and women long hair. He also expected them to see that the glory of women's long hair implied the propriety of women's head coverings in worship.

11:16. Paul anticipated resistance to his argument, admitting that some Corinthian believers may have wanted to be **contentious about this.** The term *contentious* means "eager to argue or fight." Contentions could come from **anyone**—from men or women. Paul sought to settle the matter by appealing to the widespread practice of the church, saying, **we have no other practice.** This phrase may also be translated "we have no such custom."

Some interpreters have understood Paul to say that no approved custom of arguing or contention existed in the church. It is better, however, to understand Paul as the NIV suggests. Paul meant that he and other church leaders, and **the churches of God** had **no other practice** than having women cover their heads in public worship. The widespread practice of the church should have caused dissenters at least to hesitate over their objections.

> **MAIN IDEA REVIEW:** *Paul began a discussion of yet another area of controversy and problems among the Corinthians: worship. He addressed three important subjects: the question of head coverings for women in public worship, the observance of the Lord's Supper, and the gifts of the Holy Spirit in worship.*

III. CONCLUSION

Honor in Worship

Many details of this passage remain obscure for modern readers, but some aspects are clear. Paul instructed the Corinthian men and women to honor each other in worship. To do otherwise was to present unacceptable worship before God.

PRINCIPLES

- There is a God-given order within creation as regards men and women.
- Cultural standards are relevant to worship practices.
- In the Lord, men and women are interdependent.

APPLICATIONS

- Men and women are to worship with an orderliness that reflects the order of creation.
- We should take cultural norms into account when applying the gospel in a specific culture.
- Men are to honor Christ in worship; women are to honor their husbands.
- We must develop cultural awareness and sound biblical thinking in order not to impose cultural standards as biblical standards in worship.

IV. LIFE APPLICATION

Looking for an Excuse

Have you ever met someone who was just looking for an excuse to ignore the Bible? Well, here is one of the most overlooked chapters in the New Testament. "That's just a cultural thing," we tell ourselves. "We don't have to take this part of the New Testament seriously."

As we have seen in the comments above, this chapter speaks from deep within the framework of Corinthian culture. As a result, its specific teachings are oriented toward the Corinthian situation. Nevertheless, when we dismiss this chapter as merely cultural, we lose sight of its abiding and universal principles.

It is important for modern Christians to distinguish between the principles Paul espoused here and the applications of those principles to the Mediterranean culture. The apostle was concerned that men honor Christ and that wives honor their husbands by their behavior in public worship. We should follow that principle in all places and times. Yet, Paul chose this particular application of the principle because head coverings had specific significance in the culture he addressed.

Paul sought to apply the gospel to each culture (1 Cor. 9:19–23). In imitating Paul, we should not mimic precisely what he or the Corinthians were supposed to do in their cultural settings. Rather, the Christian must find ways to express in his behavior the principles Paul endorsed here. Men must avoid the practices of other religions in Christian public worship today and always, for they will dishonor Christ if they do not. Similarly, women must find ways to express honor for their husbands as they worship.

Beyond the specific issues Paul addressed, we can learn several things about the roles of men and women from this passage. First, Paul did not introduce the issue of headship in order to tell women that they should submit to their husbands. Some have interpreted this passage as teaching that a man's authority over his wife is equal to Christ's authority over the church: absolute. Obviously, similarities exist between Christ's headship over the church and husbands' headship over their wives. But Paul did not teach that the similarities ran so deeply. Rather, he taught that "in the Lord" husbands and wives are interdependent. In fact, he did not introduce the subject to give husbands confidence to assert power over their wives, but to encourage both men and women to honor Christ, husbands, and the church in their worship.

We should also recognize that women are not second-class citizens in the church. They have certain God-given authority to govern themselves in worship. Just like single women, wives have direct relationships with Christ, not relationships mediated through their husbands. Women also have the freedom to pray and prophesy in church. While Paul taught that women should not hold ordained positions (1 Tim. 2:11–12), he expected them to take active roles in public worship. He required that they do it in ways that honored their Lord, their husbands, and the church's reputation.

V. PRAYER

Lord Jesus, we are people who love to worship you while we ignore the needs and honor of other people. Grant us grace to see how you want all of us, men and women, young and old, to worship you in ways that honor you and those around us. Amen.

VI. DEEPER DISCOVERIES

A. Women with Uncovered Heads (11:5)

Many artifacts recovered from the Corinth of Paul's day—including figurines, statues, and coins—present women without veils or head coverings. One may speculate on this basis that bareheadedness was not a sign of a socially disapproved lifestyle in Corinth. None of these artifacts, however, shows women engaged in religious activity.

In contrast to this, Dio Chrysostom (A.D. 40–about 120), writing to Paul's hometown Tarsus shortly after Paul's day, suggested that in public women veiled themselves completely, such that they could not see. It may be that Paul came from a culture (Tarsus) in which dishonor attached to women who did not veil themselves in public, but wrote to a church in a culture that did not share this view. While many women may have worn veils in public worship according to the custom of the church, some preferring Corinth's practices may have stopped wearing veils.

B. Women with Shaved Heads (11:5)

Dio Chrysostom indicated that a woman's shaved head might indicate adultery and prostitution prior to Paul's time, while Lucian indicated that after Paul's time it may have been a mark of lesbianism. Lucian also associated short hair with a potentially adulterous woman. Beyond this, the Bible seems to indicate that shaving a woman's head was dishonorable or humbling (Deut. 21:12–14), though without reference to adultery or prostitution.

C. A Sign of Authority (11:10)

The Greek text literally says that a woman ought to have "authority" (*exousia*) on/over (*epi*) her head." The NIV inserts the words "a sign of" because it assumes Paul is speaking about a head covering that represents authority. While *epi* often means "on" or "upon," the evidence from Greek usage elsewhere in the Bible suggests that *epi* when used after *exousia* refers to the realm in which authority is possessed (i.e., " authority on earth," Luke 5:24), or to the thing over which authority is possessed (Rev. 2:26). The grammatical evidence suggests that Paul meant that women ought to exercise authority over their own heads.

D. Long Hair on Men (11:14)

Contrary to popular myth, the evidence from Greek philosophy of Paul's day is that nature did not teach that long hair on men was disgraceful. Epictetus is often cited as proof that nature distinguished men from women by giving men beards (Epictetus 1.16.9–14). In fact, Epictetus himself probably wore long hair (Epictetus 4.8.5). Evidence from Dio Chyrsostom concurs that no stigmas attached to men with long hair, whether from culture, religion, philosophy, or the natural world.

VII. TEACHING OUTLINE

A. INTRODUCTION

1. Lead Story: A Cold Winter Day in Tasmania
2. Context: The Corinthians were engaging in practices that dishonored one another in worship, and that dishonored Christ. Specifically, some wives were not wearing veils. In their culture, this dishonored their husbands. Not only did this corrupt their worship, but it damaged the church's witness to the world.

3. Transition: The modern church may not have the same practices as early Corinth, but the same principles of worship apply. We must honor one another in worship. When we do not, we fall into the same trouble as the Corinthians. Like them, we must heed Paul's warning to honor not only God, but also others in worship.

B. COMMENTARY
1. Words of Praise (11:2)
2. The Divine Order (11:3)
   a. God is the head of Christ (11:3)
   b. Christ is the head of man (11:3)
   c. Husbands are the heads of wives (11:3)
3. Responsibilities to Heads (11:4–12)
   a. Men must not cover their heads as pagans (11:4,7)
   b. Women ought to cover their heads to give honor (11:5–6)
   c. Reasons for behavioral differences between men and women (11:7–12).
4. Cultural Considerations (11:13–16)
   a. The need for judgment and discernment (11:13–14)
   b. The practice of the church (11:15–16)

C. CONCLUSION: LOOKING FOR AN EXCUSE

VIII. ISSUES FOR DISCUSSION

1. For what did Paul praise the Corinthians? Does this section of Scripture sound like praise to you? Why or why not?
2. What does it mean to be a "head"? What do the various heads have in common? Why did Paul use this metaphor?
3. In what parts of his argument did Paul appeal to culture? In what parts did he appeal to Scripture?
4. What roles do women play in your church's public worship?

1 Corinthians 11:17–34

The Lord's Supper

I. **INTRODUCTION**
"Step to the Side"

II. **COMMENTARY**
A verse-by-verse explanation of this section.

III. **CONCLUSION**
Honoring Christ in the Lord's Supper
An overview of the principles and applications from this section.

IV. **LIFE APPLICATION**
Bored to Tears
Melding the section to life.

V. **PRAYER**
Tying the section to life with God.

VI. **DEEPER DISCOVERIES**
Historical, geographical, and grammatical enrichment of the commentary.

VII. **TEACHING OUTLINE**
Suggested step-by-step group study of the section.

VIII. **ISSUES FOR DISCUSSION**
Zeroing the section in on daily life.

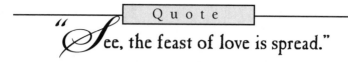

> **Quote**
>
> "*See*, the feast of love is spread."
>
> William H. Bickersteth

1 Corinthians 11:17–34

 IN A NUTSHELL

In this passage Paul admonished the Corinthians about another part of worship: the Lord's Supper. The Corinthians had turned this celebration inside out by using it as an opportunity to divide from and to abuse one another. The celebration that was supposed to unify the church actually brought disunity.

The Lord's Supper

I. INTRODUCTION

"Step to the Side"

I want to tell you about two times I stood in line. The first experience was in Poland during the last few years of communism. There I stood with some friends in a long line that stretched around several city blocks. It was a line for a precious commodity at that time—toilet paper. I was amazed at the patience everyone seemed to have. Having worked all day, they now stood in line for nearly the entire evening, waiting to get an item I took for granted. Everyone was kind and gracious. Young people held places in line for the old. Men stood in the place of women. It was a tremendous expression of solidarity among the people of that oppressed nation.

Another time, however, I had just the opposite experience. I was in an airport in Asia, and had arrived three hours early because I was afraid I might miss my plane. At that point I was third in line. A long line slowly grew behind me, but I still felt safe because I was still number three. But when the ticket agent walked up to the counter and I stood up from the floor, I suddenly realized I was fiftieth in line. The people behind me had pushed past me.

Many people throughout the world live by the principle known as "step to the side" every day of their lives. We compete in sports, business, and even in our home lives. When we get the opportunity to be first, we rush for that position.

Paul faced a terrible situation in Corinth. The Corinthian Christians were pushing their way to the table of the Lord's Supper. Elbowing their way to the bread and wine, they said to others, "Step to the side. You're in my way."

II. COMMENTARY

The Lord's Supper

MAIN IDEA: *The Corinthians had so twisted the celebration of the Lord's Supper that it was hardly recognizable. To correct this problem, Paul applied the three principles which he employed in each subject related to worship. He appealed to: (1) the honor of God in worship, (2) proper regard from one believer to another, and (3) the testimony of the church to outsiders. Paul insisted that the Lord's Supper at Corinth no longer met these criteria.*

Words of Rebuke (11:17)

SUPPORTING IDEA: *Paul criticized the Corinthians for their disrespectful worship practices.*

11:17. In the preceding section, Paul had begun with words of praise. But here he said, **I have no praise for you**. Paul's disgust with the Corinthians focused on how their **meetings**, or public worship gatherings, did **more harm than good**. Paul did not condemn them absolutely and categorically—he had already praised them for holding to many of his teachings on worship (11:2). Yet, his assessment was that the **harm** of their worship times outweighed the **good**.

What kinds of things would yield this kind of condemnation? The Corinthians had corrupted one of the most sacred events in Christian worship: the Lord's Supper. They had not given due regard to the honor of Christ, nor had they honored or edified one another in the celebration of the Lord's Supper.

B Divisions at the Table (11:18–22)

SUPPORTING IDEA: *In their observance of the Lord's Supper, the Corinthians discriminated against the poor. Paul condemned this perversion, stating that Christ would not accept their act of worship.*

11:18. Paul began with **in the first place**, but never moved on to a second or third matter. His words should be understood to mean "the most important way this is true is." He also added, **I hear**. Paul did not reveal his source, but elsewhere he said that Chloe's household had informed him of similar matters (1:10–12). Others from the church had also reported to him (16:17). Though he could not be sure, Paul knew the church well enough that he believed the reports were true at least **to some extent**.

Paul's criticism was that there were **divisions** among the Corinthians, but he had already addressed this issue extensively in chapters 1–4. Here, he focused on the divisions that existed when the Corinthians came **together as a church**. Paul's chief concern was that divisions perverted public worship.

11:19. Two interpretations of this verse seem likely. On the one hand, it may concede that some divisions are necessary because the visible church contains both true believers and false professors. In this view, Paul affirmed that it is sometimes necessary for true believers to establish **differences** from the false teachings of others. Doing so makes clear who has **God's approval**. This view is supported by the fact that the word "differences" (*hairesis*) is not the same as "divisions" (*schisma;* 11:18).

On the other hand, Paul did not actually say that he approved of these differences. He may have spoken facetiously, recognizing **differences** as a subset of the divisions. "Divisions" is clearly negative ("I have no praise for you," 11:17); therefore, "differences" may be also. Sinful **differences** might explain why the church allowed some of its members to go hungry. The poor may not have been considered "approved," and perhaps may even have been counted as "dispensable."

11:20. Paul returned abruptly to the issue at hand. **When** the Corinthian Christians came **together** to celebrate the Lord's Supper, divisions so corrupted it that it could **not** be called **the Lord's Supper.** Although this terminology is common in the church today, this passage contains the only expression of the phrase "Lord's Supper" in the New Testament. It may connote a number of ideas: "the Supper belonging to or hosted by the Lord"; "the Supper which the Lord ordained" (Luke 22:19–20); or "the Supper at which the Lord's body and blood are shared" (Matt. 26:26–28).

11:21. Paul explained his remark by describing the report he had received. As the Corinthians ate, each of them went **ahead without waiting for anybody else.** This phrase **each of you goes ahead** may be translated as "each one takes his own supper." Paul may have intended this identification of each person's "own supper" to explain why it was not the "Lord's Supper." Some in the church had lost the corporate aspect of the ritual and had come to focus mainly on themselves.

The descriptions of hunger and intoxication in this passage may sound strange to modern readers. Churches today generally observe the Lord's Supper much differently from the way the first century church did. Now, Christians observe the ordinance with a pinch of bread and a modicum of drink, but the early church celebrated the Lord's Supper with great banquets. According to the Book of Acts, the early church often ate meals together (Acts 2:46). These meals came to be known as "love feasts." They probably climaxed in an observance of the Lord's Supper.

In their meals, the Corinthians favored the privileged and rich. If the Lord's Supper was observed in Corinthian homes, the rich and powerful may have been allowed to eat first. Since **one** remain[ed] **hungry** while **another** got **drunk,** they obviously ate and drank to excess. This would have been bad enough, but they magnified the harm by leaving nothing for the others. Such social practices were so common that it would have seemed natural for the church to do the same. The gospel, however, demanded a radical departure from custom. This is why the New Testament warns against giving special honor to the wealthy (Jas. 2:1–26).

11:22. Paul began his correction by asking several questions. First, he asked if they did not **have houses** in which to **eat and drink** ordinary meals. It may have been that Paul's question was an indirect way of saying, "If this is what you do at the Lord's Supper, then stay home." Paul did not approve of discrimination against the poor, but it would have been less offensive for someone to disregard others in an ordinary meal than in the midst of Christian worship.

Second, Paul expressed the evil of this practice by asking those who abused the poor if they **despise[d] the church of God.** The church consists of those people gathered out of the world because they belong to God. They are his special, prized people. When believers disregard the sanctity of the Lord's Supper by keeping the poor among God's people from partaking, they look down on God's people. Because the poor are an integral part of the church community, one cannot hate the poor without despising the church. Those who mistreat the people of God are destined for God's judgment (Deut. 32:43; Isa. 3:13–26; Ezek. 13:9–10; Rom. 12:19). In fact, Paul was about to address this issue directly.

Third, Paul asked if the rich members of the Corinthian church actually wanted to **humiliate those who** had **nothing.** The poor of the ancient world were mocked and humiliated by the wealthy. According to the Old Testament and Jesus, however, this was not to be the situation of the poor in God's kingdom. In fact, Jesus blessed the poor (Luke 6:20–21) and warned the rich of the difficulties that accompanied their social status (Mark 10:25). The poor already had nothing in human, worldly terms. In Corinth they also had their sense of dignity stolen by fellow believers—and this at the Lord's Supper. Sarcastically, Paul asked if they thought he should **praise** them for their behavior. He then answered his own questions with a determined **Certainly not!**

Ⓒ The Central Focus of the Lord's Supper (11:23–26)

> **SUPPORTING IDEA:** *Paul reminded the Corinthians that the central focus of the Lord's Supper is the remembrance and proclamation of Christ's saving work. Remembering this should lead the Corinthians to correct their misconduct.*

11:23a. Paul explained that he could not praise the Corinthians for their behavior because they had failed to observe the teachings about the Lord's Supper he had **passed on** to them. The expression "pass on" was technical terminology among the rabbis of Paul's day for the official, sacred transmission of religious traditions. This passage stands in stark contrast to Paul's earlier praise of the Corinthians for holding the teachings he had "passed on" to them (11:2). Regarding the Lord's Supper, they already knew the proper way, but they had not carried out the teaching.

Their failure to hold Paul's teaching was all the more tragic since the apostle had not concocted the Lord's Supper himself. He had only passed on what he had **received from the Lord.** He did not specify the precise manner in which he received this teaching from **the Lord,** but it may have come supernaturally from Christ himself during Paul's early years in Arabia (Gal. 1:15–17). It is also possible that Paul received the teaching indirectly through other apostles (e.g., Gal. 1:18).

11:23b–24. Paul next described how to observe the Lord's Supper. These instructions are so simple and straightforward that they appear abbreviated. Yet, this simplicity was needed to correct the Corinthian situation.

Paul revealed the proper way to observe the Lord's Supper by recounting how **the Lord Jesus** himself had observed it on **the night he was betrayed.** Four verbal ideas described the activities surrounding the bread: **took bread; had given thanks; broke it;** and **said.** Jesus **took bread,** that is, he picked it up. The term *bread* may also be translated "loaf." It is likely that Jesus used a single loaf of bread to symbolize the unity of those who partook together. Then he gave **thanks.**

Then Jesus **broke** the bread. Hosts customarily broke the bread for their guests (Mark 6:41; John 6:11). It is not likely, therefore, that the breaking of the loaf portrayed the breaking of Christ's body. In fact, John's Gospel comments on the fact that Christ's bones were not broken (John 19:33–36).

Jesus then spoke to his disciples about the symbolism of the bread. Paul summarized Jesus as having **said** three things.

First, **This is my body.** This expression has been the source of much controversy throughout church history. With the help of Aristotelian philosophy, Roman Catholic tradition has interpreted this passage in a literal fashion, arguing that the bread and wine actually change their physical substances to become the body and blood of Christ. Their view is called "transubstantiation."

The Lutheran tradition of "consubstantiation" contends that Christ's body and blood are present in, with, and under the bread and wine, but that the substances of the bread and wine do not change. Calvinism has purported that Christ himself is spiritually present in a mysterious way, but not that his physical body and blood are somehow present. Other groups have argued that the elements of the Lord's Supper are symbols that encourage a focus on Christ's body and blood. Neither this passage nor the Gospel records answer this question, but most Protestants hold one of the last two views.

Second, **which is for you.** Christ suffered death on the cross on behalf of others. The atoning power of Christ's death is of infinite value and is offered to all. It is available to anyone in the world who turns to Christ in faith, confession, and repentance (1 John 1:9–2:2). Yet, in these words of the Lord's Supper, Christ said he laid down his life for a particular group of people: his followers. His suffering atoned only for the sins of those who believe in him.

Third, **do this in remembrance of me.** The Lord's Supper was ordained as an event when God's people were to remember the death and resurrection of Christ. The last meal Jesus shared with the apostles was set within the context of Christ's betrayal, arrest, and eventual death.

The Lord instituted this ritual at the Passover, which commemorated the Exodus (Exod. 12:14–27). By telling the disciples to perform the new ritual in his own remembrance, Jesus made a bold statement, appearing to claim significance at least equal to the Exodus. This third portion of Christ's words occurs again in association with the blood of Christ. The centrality of Christ in the Lord's Supper is the main point of this entire section.

11:25. Paul turned next to **the cup.** He noted the parallel between the distributions of the bread and of the cup by saying that the latter occurred **in the same way.** Whereas 11:23–24 mention talking, thanking, breaking, and speaking, 11:25 mentions taking and speaking. The expression "in the same way," however, indicates that Paul intentionally abbreviated his description of the procedures with regard to the cup. In 10:16 Paul called this cup "the cup of thanksgiving for which we give thanks." This description makes clear that **in the same way** includes a separate blessing for the cup. Paul emphasized by repetition the one element that was absent from every Gospel account: **Do this . . . in remembrance of me.** Paul saw the honor and remembrance of Christ as central to the Lord's Supper.

The **cup** was taken **after supper.** In the ritual meals of Jews during the first century, it was customary to have several courses of food and drink. Matthew and Mark recorded that Jesus took the wine after bread (Matt. 26:26–28; Mark 14:22–24). Luke, however, mentioned that Jesus gave the cup to his disciples, broke bread, and then gave the cup (Luke 22:17–20). The Gospel writers relate different portions of a ritual involving drinking from four different cups. The third cup was known as "the cup of thanksgiving." Paul had this cup in mind.

Paul's record of Jesus' words closely parallels Luke's account. The main point is that the wine represents **the new covenant in** Jesus' **blood.**

The expression "new covenant" derives from Jeremiah 31:31. In this passage the prophet Jeremiah described the covenant arrangement that God would make with the remnant of his people after they returned from exile. Ezekiel and Isaiah called the same restoration covenant the "covenant of peace" (Isa. 54:10; Ezek. 37:26). Other prophets described it as an "everlasting covenant" (Jer. 32:40), and a "covenant of love" (Dan. 9:4). The New Testament derives its name from this new covenant. It tells us that the covenant renewal that took place through Christ's ministry was the fulfillment of the promise for a great covenant after the restoration following Israel's exile.

Paul also reported that Jesus defined the **new covenant** in terms of his **blood.** Christ's sacrificial death paid the debt for sin. His death made it possible for people to enjoy forgiveness and new life in him. The expression "in my blood" recalls the importance of blood rituals in covenant-making. Not every covenant in the Bible is connected to sacrificial blood, but blood sacrifice has been the way of good standing before God from the earliest times (Gen. 4:4; cf. Heb. 9:22).

Perhaps the clearest expression of this principle appears in the institution of Moses' covenant (Exod. 19:1–24:18). The whole ceremony of covenant ratification at that time revolved around the sprinkling of sacrificed blood (Exod. 24:6–8) and the celebration of a fellowship or peace meal after the covenant had been ratified (Exod. 24:11). In fact, Paul's terminology recalls Moses' words in Exodus 24:8: "This is the blood of the covenant that the LORD has made with you." The prophet Zechariah also announced that the remnant of God's people would be restored after the Exile because of "the blood of my covenant" (Zech. 9:11). The cup of the Lord's Supper symbolizes the centrality of Christ's blood as covenant sacrificial blood (cf. Heb. 10:29).

Echoing what he said about the bread, Jesus exhorted his disciples, **Drink it, in remembrance of me.** The main purpose of the Lord's Supper is to draw the participants' attention to the centrality of Christ's saving work on their behalf. The importance of this motif for Paul is evident from the fact that Paul repeated it three times.

11:26. Paul closed his account of the institution of the Lord's Supper with an explanation of his unique repetition of the remembrance of Christ. Why should eating and drinking in the Lord's Supper focus on the remembrance of Christ? It is because **whenever** the church participates in the Lord's Supper, Christians **proclaim the Lord's death until he comes.** The expression "proclaim" (*katangello*) occurs many times in the New Testament to describe the ministry of the church to the unbelieving world. It is the prophetic announcement to those outside the church that Christ is the only way of salvation.

When the world sees the church eating and drinking in order to remember the significance of Christ's body and blood, the word of the gospel is made visible. The expression "the Lord's death" represents the whole of Christ's saving ministry on behalf of the church: his life, death, resurrection, and ascension.

Take Great Care (11:27–34)

SUPPORTING IDEA: *To mistreat the brethren in the Lord's Supper is to show contempt for Christ's death, to malign the gospel, and to tempt the judgment of God.*

11:27. Whenever people participate in the Lord's Supper **in an unworthy manner,** they are actually **guilty of sinning against the body and blood of the Lord.** To participate in the Lord's Supper in an **unworthy manner** has traditionally been interpreted broadly to mean to participate while having unconfessed sin. This may be due in part to a misinterpretation that understands "unworthy" as describing the sinner rather than the manner of partaking.

To be sure, it is valuable for believers to confess their sins, and appropriate to prepare for worship by doing so. But Paul's focus in this passage was much narrower. The unworthiness he had in mind was participating in the Lord's Supper in a way that failed to exhibit the unity of the church in Christ. That this was his meaning can be seen quite clearly in his exhortation in 11:33–34. To prevent unworthy eating and subsequent judgment, he did not advise the Corinthians to confess their sin, or even to recognize Christ's presence in the elements, but to wait for one another and to eat at home.

The Corinthians' unworthy observance was no small matter. One can imagine them thinking that they had just been inconsiderate of their poor brothers and sisters in Christ. That much was true enough. Yet, Paul insisted that something much worse was happening. Because remembering and proclaiming Christ is the purpose of the Lord's Supper, violators actually sin **against the body and blood of the Lord**. That is to say, their offense violates the central, sacred purpose of the Lord's Supper: honoring Christ for his work of salvation. To sin against **the body and blood** is to sin against the very hope of salvation. They also sinned **against the body and blood of the Lord** by sinning against Christ's church, or more particularly against the poor Christians who were not granted admission to the Lord's Supper. To sin against those for whom Christ shed his blood and gave his body is to sin against Christ himself.

11:28–29. To avoid such serious offenses, every believer **ought to examine himself**. Christians must scrutinize their motives and actions to see that they match the significance of the Lord's Supper. This self-examination is to take place **before** eating and drinking. The reason for taking time for self-examination is evident: He who participates **without recognizing the body of the Lord** brings divine **judgment on himself**.

This verse does not say that the Lord's Supper should be observed introspectively, with participants focusing mainly on their own hearts. Rather, Paul offered this instruction as a corrective for a specific problem. In general, the Lord's Supper should be a time of celebration in which Christians focus on Christ's honor, the church's unity, and the proclamation of the gospel. The focus should be on others, not on oneself. It is only in the preparation for the Lord's Supper that individuals must turn their attention inward.

The meaning of **recognizing the body of the Lord** is difficult to discern. Most of the best manuscripts do not contain the expression "of the Lord," but this has little bearing on the interpretation of **the body**.

At least two outlooks seem reasonable. First, **the body** may refer to the church. If this is the proper reading, Paul warned participants to treat their fellow members in the body with proper regard while participating. This interpretation agrees with Paul's instructions that the Corinthians should treat one another well in the Lord's Supper in order to avoid judgment.

Second, **the body** may also be an abbreviation for "the body and blood." The proximity of 11:24–27, in which "body" and "blood" refers to Christ's physical body and blood, supports this reading. If Paul intended this, he was warning participants to give proper consideration to the sanctity of Christ's body and blood—the focal points of the Lord's Supper. By implication he also would have meant that partakers should recognize and honor the church for whom Christ gave his body and shed his blood. In either case, Paul pointed once again to the seriousness of violating the Lord's Supper. Those who did so would not escape God's **judgment.**

11:30. Paul continued explaining the seriousness of violating the Lord's Supper by pointing out the judgment the Corinthians were experiencing as a result of their failure to observe the Lord's Supper properly. He wrote, **Many among you are weak and sick.** Paul probably received information about illnesses in the church from messengers sent to him. Second, he remarked, **A number of you have fallen asleep.** Some in the church had died as a result of God's judgment against them because of their sin against the body of Christ. Sickness and death do not always happen as a result of personal sin. They come to believers and unbelievers alike for many reasons (Job 2:1–7; John 9:2–3; Rom. 8:36). But in this situation, Paul had apostolic authority to support his pronouncement.

11:31–32. Paul added the comment that if the Corinthians **judged** themselves, they **would not come under judgment.** In other words, if the Corinthians took time to evaluate themselves before the Lord's Supper and changed their actions based on this evaluation, God would not judge them with sickness and death. God disciplines his church so the true believers will take notice and turn back to Christ in repentance, **so that** they **will not be condemned with the world.**

11:33–34. Paul closed this section with a general summation, giving some final instructions. He appealed to the Corinthians with familial affection by calling them his **brothers.** Paul yearned for them to turn from this serious sin. To avoid God's **judgment,** they needed to do two things.

First, they needed to **wait for each other.** Instead of the rich eating first and the poor not eating at all, all participants in the feast were to eat at the same time. This would show proper honor to the poor, and thereby to Christ.

Second, in order to eliminate any justification for not waiting for others, Paul added that **anyone** who was **hungry . . . should eat at home.** He did not chide the poor for coming to the Lord's Supper hungry—they could not avoid it. Those of means who were hungry were to eat at home so there would be enough food for the poor. The feast was a time when the gospel could be demonstrated not only in the elements of bread and wine, but also in the loving treatment of the poor.

Why should this practical advice be followed? If the church would gather for the Lord's Supper in harmony and mutual consideration, then their meetings would **not result in judgment.** The discipline that God was inflicting on the church would cease because the Corinthians would have begun to celebrate the Lord's Supper in a way that pleased God, honored Christ, respected the church's unity, and proclaimed the gospel.

Paul had touched on the most vital aspects of his teaching on the Lord's Supper. Even so, he knew the Corinthians needed to learn much more about the matter. So he told them that when he came to visit, he would **give further instructions.**

MAIN IDEA REVIEW: *The Corinthians had so twisted the celebration of the Lord's Supper that it was hardly recognizable. To correct this problem, Paul applied the three principles which he employed in each subject related to worship. He appealed to: (1) the honor of God in worship, (2) proper regard from one believer to another, and (3) the testimony of the church to outsiders. Paul insisted that the Lord's Supper at Corinth no longer met these criteria.*

III. CONCLUSION

Honoring Christ in the Lord's Supper

In this passage Paul confronted the Corinthians with their serious violation of the Lord's Supper. They had failed to live up to the symbolism of the Lord's Supper by mistreating one another, especially the poor. He reminded them of the Christ-honoring way to proclaim the Lord's death in the Lord's Supper.

PRINCIPLES

- The Lord's Supper is to focus on the church's unity in Christ.
- In the Lord's Supper we proclaim the gospel and honor Christ and his sacrifice.
- Dishonoring fellow believers during the Lord's Supper also dishonors Christ.

APPLICATIONS

- We must "get right" with our fellow believers before we partake of the Lord's Supper.

- We should not focus so much on ourselves during the supper, but on Christ and what he has done for all believers and the church.

IV. LIFE APPLICATION

Bored to Tears

I grew up in the church, and I remember those first Sundays of every month—Lord's Supper week. I hated it. It meant that the worship service would last even longer than usual. When I think about it, I believe a lot of adults around me felt that way too. The looks on their faces told me they had lost sight of the wonder of the Lord's Supper. They were bored to tears.

The Corinthian Christians had also lost sight of the wonder of the Lord's Supper. But they were not bored. They had turned the Lord's Supper into a drunken party. They had forgotten that the Lord's Supper was a celebration of Christ.

The Lord's Supper has been the subject of doctrinal dispute and division over the centuries. It is ironic that the one ceremony Christ gave us that symbolizes and builds our unity has been so abused that it has actually resulted in our disunity.

By and large, Protestants have encouraged our churches to focus on confession of our individual sins, and thereby on our individual worthiness to partake of the Lord's Supper rather than on Christ. As a result, believers tend to approach the Lord's Supper timidly, tuning out the rest of the congregation so they may "get themselves right with God."

The Lord's Supper is not so much an opportunity for all the members of the church to engage in personal piety at the same time, but for all the members of the church to experience together their relationships with Christ and with one another and to proclaim the gospel. Before we partake of the Lord's Supper, we need first to ask, "How am I treating my brothers and sisters right now?" not, "What sins have I committed since my last confession?" To put it a bit differently, Christ says to us, "Come be with your family," not, "Go take a bath."

The Lord's Supper signifies Christ's atonement for sin. We should come to the Lord's Supper, discerning the Lord's body in the company of others for whom he offered himself. When we do, we proclaim his death until he returns.

V. PRAYER

Lord Jesus, we take your body and blood so often without our hearts attuned to what we are doing. Grant us the power of your Spirit to approach this sacred, wonderful meal in a way that honors and pleases you. Amen.

VI. DEEPER DISCOVERIES

A. Broke (11:24)

It has been common to see the breaking of the bread in the Lord's Supper as a symbolic action representing the breaking of Christ's body. This may be because the KJV quotes Jesus as saying, "This is my body, which is broken for you," and the NKJV follows this tradition ("This is My body which is broken for you"). Some of the ancient texts contain a Greek word that these versions translate as "broken" (*klao*). But the best manuscripts do not contain this word.

Further, the New Testament contains fourteen occurrences of *klao,* not counting this disputed appearance, and in all of these *klao* takes some form of bread as its object. This implies strongly that *klao* refers specifically to the breaking of bread. According to Luke, when Jesus instituted the Lord's Supper, he did not say that his body was "broken," but that it was "given" (*didomi*) (Luke 22:19). The alleged use of *klao* in 1 Corinthians 11:24 takes "body" as its object, not "bread." Therefore, it is likely to be an interpolation by an ancient scribe who was unfamiliar with the New Testament's use of the verb, but familiar with the close association between Christ's body and the broken bread.

B. This Is My Body (11:24)

One dominant Protestant doctrine of the Lord's Supper stems from the Reformers Calvin and Zwingli, who believed that Christ was spiritually present in the Lord's Supper. The other more modern view sees the Lord's Supper as a mere memorial. In fact, these two views share much in common. The differences between these doctrines stem mostly from different understandings of 1 Corinthians 10:16–17, not from different interpretations of 1 Corinthians 11:17–34 or of the Gospel accounts.

Unlike Roman Catholics and Lutherans, Calvinists and memorialists believe that Christ's body and blood are not physically present in the Lord's Supper. In this sense, both interpret Christ's identification of the bread with his body and of the wine with his blood as metaphors. Likewise, both agree that the Lord's Supper is a memorial, and that it benefits believers only when they partake of it by faith. Both recognize the Lord's Supper as a visual portrayal of Christ's death, and thus understand that the ritual can strengthen the faith of those who take part in it, just as hearing the gospel preached may strengthen faith. Further, both believe that Christ would not have ordained the Lord's Supper if the things it symbolized—Christ's atonement and the unity of the church—were not true.

VII. TEACHING OUTLINE

A. INTRODUCTION
1. Lead Story: "Step to the Side"
2. Context: The Corinthian Christians tended to see themselves in individual relationships with Christ, not as participants in a corporate relationship between Christ and the church. When they came to the Lord's Supper, they demonstrated this attitude by neglecting the poor among them. Though this was in keeping with societal norms in Corinth, it contradicted the church's call to unity in Christ.
3. Transition: Many modern Christians also misunderstand the corporate nature of believers' relationships with Christ and with one another. This sometimes gives them a wrong attitude toward other believers, so that they do what is socially acceptable. By mistreating the brethren, the modern church tempts God's temporal judgment just as Corinth did.

B. COMMENTARY
1. Words of Rebuke (11:17)
2. Division at the Table (11:18–22)
   - a. Division (11:18–19)
   - b. Not the Lord's Supper (11:20)
   - c. Mistreatment of the poor (11:21–22)
3. The Central Focus of the Lord's Supper (11:23–26)
   - a. Instituted by Jesus at the last supper (11:23)
   - b. The bread (11:24)
   - c. The cup (11:25)
   - d. Proclaims the Lord's death (11:26)
4. Take Great Care (11:27–34)
   - a. Eating in an unworthy manner (11:27,29)
   - b. Examination to prevent eating in an unworthy manner (11:28,31)
   - c. Judgment for eating in an unworthy manner (11:29–32)
   - d. Eating in a worthy manner (11:33–34)

C. CONCLUSION: BORED TO TEARS

VIII. ISSUES FOR DISCUSSION

1. Why do we celebrate the Lord's Supper? Of what does the Lord's Supper consist? What is the significance of its elements? What is the significance of its observance?

2. Does your church's theology of the Lord's Supper match more closely with the Roman Catholic view, the Lutheran view, the Calvinist view, or the Zwinglian view? Which do you think is most biblical? Why?

3. When you celebrate the Lord's Supper in your church, do you focus more on personal introspection and confession, or more on the unity and loving fellowship of the church?

4. Is your church in danger of discipline? Has it perhaps experienced discipline that no one has recognized yet?

1 Corinthians 12:1–30

Spiritual Gifts in Worship

Q u o t e

"*Let* us all then, considering these things, imitate the love of these members; let us not in any wise do the contrary, trampling on the miseries of our neighbor and envying his good things. For this is the part of madmen and persons beside themselves. Just as he that digs out his own eye hath displayed a very great proof of senselessness; and he that devours his own hand exhibits a clear evidence of downright madness."

J o h n   C h r y s o s t o m

1 Corinthians 12:1–30

I N   A   N U T S H E L L

In this chapter the apostle Paul turned to the issue of spiritual gifts in the church. He touched on a number of matters but especially on the value of all spiritual gifts.

Spiritual Gifts in Worship

I. INTRODUCTION

"That Little Piece Is Worth That Much?"

We have seen many changes in technology during the last fifty years. One of the most important changes is the shift from "bigger is better" to "smaller is better." It used to be that the biggest computer in the school was the best computer. Now the smallest computer in a briefcase is the best computer.

I once had a computer crash in the worst way. It was not something big that broke. It was one of the smallest pieces. I remember the technician explaining it to me. He drew a picture of the defective part, then commented: "You understand that this part is only this big . . ." He then drew a circle smaller than a dime.

Then I asked the big question. "How much is it going to cost me?" When he told me, I laughed. "That's more than I paid for the entire computer. That little piece is worth that much?"

"Yup," he replied. "This piece may be small, but what it does is vital to the computer. The computer just can't work without it."

Paul pointed out in this chapter that every gift God gives to his church is valuable. The Corinthians looked at appearances to determine which gifts were more important than others. But Paul declared that the smallest and least spectacular gifts are essential to the work of the church.

II. COMMENTARY

Spiritual Gifts in Worship

> **MAIN IDEA:** *Paul explained the role of the gifts of the Spirit in worship, beginning with the value of diverse gifts in the worship of God. He discussed the issue in three main sections: identifying the Spirit, the unity and diversity of the Spirit's manifestations, and the unity and diversity of members in the body.*

Much controversy exists over whether the supernatural manifestations of the Holy Spirit listed in this passage continue today. The controversy generally centers around the issue of special revelation. Some interpreters believe that special revelation continues today, while others deny the giving of new special revelation. Evangelicals take many different positions on this subject, but for the sake of convenience evangelical positions can be categorized under three basic headings.

Continuation. Some traditions affirm that the *infallible* transmission of special revelation ceased with the closure of Scripture. Even so, God continues to speak to his church through apostles and prophets and through other supernatural means such as tongues, word of knowledge, word of wisdom, etc. These groups apply Paul's discussion of spiritual gifts such as tongues, interpretation of tongues, and prophecy directly to their situations because they believe these manifestations of the Spirit continue in modern times.

Modification. Other traditions hold that significant changes have taken place between the days of Paul and our day. First, the offices of apostle and prophet were foundational offices of the church (Eph. 2:20), designed specifically to transmit special revelation to the church in its early stages. In this view, these offices have ceased.

Second, manifestations such as tongues, prophecy, and messages of knowledge and wisdom have gone through modifications with the cessation of the apostles and prophets. In this view, none of these gifts provides direct infallible special revelation. Through fallible pastors, teachers, and the like, God leads the church into proper application of his Word in Scripture through preaching, intuitions, advice, and evaluations of circumstances. Nevertheless, at every point the teachings of these officers must be evaluated carefully by the Scriptures. These groups apply these passages only indirectly to their churches, adjusting the meanings of the passages to account for the current circumstances wherein infallible special revelation no longer occurs. Paul's words still give the church guidance for managing current manifestations of the Spirit analogous to those in Corinth.

Cessation. Some branches of the church assert that all supernatural special revelation has ceased and that God communicates with his church today only through the Scriptures. These people usually hold that the miraculous gifts seen in the New Testament have ceased, believing that miracles existed to demonstrate the authority of God's infallible spokespersons. When God stopped sending infallible spokespersons, the Spirit stopped bestowing miraculous gifts. For the most part, Paul's comments on the supernatural gifts are largely irrelevant because these gifts no longer exist. Preachers and teachers of the word today have the responsibility of reasoning carefully through the logical implications of Scripture.

To meet the needs of each position, this commentary will focus primarily on Paul's original meaning to the Corinthians in this passage. Different readers must apply these matters to their situations according to their orientations toward *Continuation, Modification,* and *Cessation.*

🅰 Identifying the Spirit (12:1–3)

> **SUPPORTING IDEA:** *The Corinthians' pagan background made them susceptible to being misled by supernatural manifestations. Paul told them how to identify those who spoke by the Spirit.*

12:1. Paul began with the expression **now about spiritual gifts.** The terminology *now about (peri de)* indicates that Paul responded to questions or issues raised by the Corinthians themselves. He did not reveal their precise concerns, but stated emphatically that he did not **want** them **to be ignorant** or unaware of this topic. Once again, Paul created a familial mood by addressing the Corinthians as **brothers.**

12:2–3. Paul provided a central criterion for distinguishing the Holy Spirit's work from the experiences of pagan religion. He did this by setting up a contrast between the times **when** the Corinthians **were pagans . . . and led astray to mute idols,** and their Christian experience of **speaking by the Spirit of God.**

The precise nature of this contrast is debated. Some interpreters argue that Paul contrasted the fact that pagans were led by idols, and Christians by the Holy Spirit. Others have argued that Paul specifically contrasted the extraordinary supernatural experiences of ecstatic speech in pagan religion with the supernatural work (esp. tongues and prophecy) of the Holy Spirit in the church.

Although the former outlook may not be ruled out entirely, several considerations support the latter view: (1) Mystery religions popular in the Mediterranean world at that time practiced ecstatic speech. (2) In this passage, Paul did not focus on Jews, but on Gentiles who were likely to have been involved in such idolatrous religions. (3) Paul said that the Gentile believers were formerly **influenced and led astray** by someone or something. (4) He described the idols as **mute,** which in this interpretation would be a great irony. (5) The general context of this verse focuses on the nature and restrictions that apply to speaking in tongues, a Christian experience similar to the ecstasy of pagan religions. It would appear, therefore, that Paul reminded the Corinthians about their past extraordinary religious experiences of idol worship.

Paul drew attention to these past experiences to deduce general instructions on distinguishing the Holy Spirit's gifts from pagan religious experiences. First, the Holy Spirit never leads anyone to say, **Jesus be cursed.** If someone in the church at Corinth spoke such words (even under supernatural influence), he was not speaking by the Spirit of God. Second, the Holy Spirit empowers those who proclaim that **Jesus is Lord.**

If a religious experience does not honor Christ as Lord, then it is not from the Spirit. If it does, then the Holy Spirit may be behind the experience.

B Diverse Spiritual Gifts (12:4–11)

SUPPORTING IDEA: Paul warned against identifying the Spirit with only one manifestation in the church. The gifts of the Spirit are manifold, and each is important in the worship of God and the ministry of the church.

12:4–6. Paul spoke of gifts in association with the Spirit, service ("ministries" NASB, NKJV) in conjunction with the Lord Jesus, and working ("effects" NASB; "activities" NRSV, NKJV) in association with God the Father. Diversity and unity coexist. There are **different kinds of gifts, different kinds of service**, and **different kinds of working.** Yet, each variety is associated with a person of the Trinity: **the same Spirit; the same Lord;** or **the same God.** The authorization by the triune God indicates the unity that exists within the great varieties.

The three terms—**gifts, service,** and **working**—relate closely to one another, but they are not synonymous. Each item is the source of the one that follows: service comes from gifts, and working from service. The term *gifts* appears frequently in this epistle with reference to the various manifestations of the Holy Spirit in the lives of believers. The **gifts** of the Spirit empower each Christian to function in the body of Christ. **Service** derives from terminology that Paul used frequently to describe a variety of ministerial activities occurring within the church (*diakonia*).

Working (*energema*) is an uncommon noun in the New Testament. Its verb form generally connotes effectual work. Thus, it may be better to translate the noun as "results" or "effects" rather than as "working." Although humans perform services in the church, only God the Father brings about the results of the **gifts** that are used in **service.**

Not only is there diversity in unity, but also broad distribution of gifts. God causes all these results **in all men.** In other words, all kinds of people—men, women, old, young, Jew, Gentile—receive gifts of the Spirit and perform ministries in the church through which God produces results. The Old Testament prophet Joel predicted this democratization of the Spirit's blessings (Joel 2:28–29), and Peter saw this Old Testament hope fulfilled in the church (Acts 2:17–18).

Paul's outlook spoke powerfully to the Corinthian church because some believers felt that their particular gifts (especially tongues) were more important than others. Because all Christians are part of and necessary to the body of Christ, God blesses all Christians with gifts, ministries, and results.

12:7. Paul elaborated on the themes of unity, diversity, and distribution, first stating that God gives a **manifestation of the Spirit** to each person. The Holy Spirit is the down payment or guarantee of every believer's future inheritance (Eph. 1:13–14). So all believers receive the Spirit. Paul did not speak only of the Spirit's indwelling presence here, but of **the manifestation of the**

Spirit. This terminology indicates that every believer has some display of the Holy Spirit's presence in his or her life.

Also, **the manifestation of the Spirit** has a particular goal: **the common good** (cf. 1 Pet. 4:10). The gifts of the Spirit are not principally for the edification of the individuals who receive them, but for the **good** of all believers.

12:8–10. Paul next listed several manifestations of the Spirit's gifts. He mentioned **the Spirit** four times in these verses to remind the Corinthians that all of these gifts come from one divine source: the Holy Spirit. But the list indicates that **the same** or **one Spirit** manifests his presence with great variety. Comparisons with other lists of the Spirit's manifestations (Rom. 12:6–8; Eph. 4:11) reveal that this catalogue is only a sampling that probably corresponded to the gifts which Paul knew the Corinthian church manifested.

Paul listed nine manifestations of spiritual gifts that interpreters have attempted to group in different ways, but no pattern can sustain scrutiny.

Message of wisdom. Some Corinthians exalted the wisdom of this age. But Paul rejected the wisdom of the world as folly. He found true wisdom in the gospel of Christ's saving work. It is unlikely that Paul meant anything like "good advice," "special intuitions," or "deeper insights." His use of **wisdom** more closely related to the declaration and explanation of Christ in a culture that emphasized human wisdom.

Message of knowledge. Here Paul contrasted the manifestation of the Spirit with claims to "knowledge" which some had made. Little evidence exists for thinking that Paul had in mind the ability to gain factual knowledge through supernatural means. He probably meant knowledge of God in Christ that comes from direct revelation, or the ability to teach correctly.

Faith. This is not saving faith because it is only given to some believers. It is probably the kind of "faith" that Jesus described as "faith as small as a mustard seed" (Matt. 17:20)—the strong conviction that God will move in one way or another in a specific circumstance.

Gifts of healing. Supernatural healing of the sick is well attested in the ministry of Jesus and the early church. Healing the physical body was a foretaste of the resurrection of the body on the last day. The plural form of **gifts** may indicate that this manifestation of the Spirit takes different forms at different times.

Miraculous powers. This general term probably refers to an assortment of supernatural powers other than healings.

Prophecy. Old Testament prophets spoke God's word under direct inspiration from God. There is no justification for thinking that the office of prophet in the New Testament was substantially different in this regard from the Old Testament office of prophet. Joel prophesied that in the final chapter of redemptive history, prophecy would be widespread among different classes of people (Joel 2:28–29). The words of true prophets of the Spirit were to be received as the word of God himself.

Both the apostolic and prophetic offices solidified the teachings of the church in its early years through special unquestionable revelation. All who declared words contrary to these foundational teachings were to be judged and rejected. To be sure, the Corinthians lived in the times of the apostles when such special revelations still occurred. So Paul could have had this manifestation of the Spirit in mind.

At the same time, Paul encouraged the church to "test" or "critique" prophecy. Thus, although he used the same terminology, it would appear that here he intended "prophet" in the more generic sense of "spokesperson who is not beyond question."

Distinguishing between spirits. Even in the Old Testament Israel had false prophets and teachers whose true character had to be discerned (Deut. 18:20–22). The same has been true of the church from its inception. Behind these false teachers are demons and evil spirits (2 Thess. 2:9–10; Jude 4; Rev. 16:13–14). It was valuable for someone to have the ability to discern the spirits at work in any verbal or nonverbal display of supernatural power. Of course, Scripture provided the Corinthians with guidelines for distinguishing between the Holy Spirit and other spirits. Yet, the deception of evil spirits could be so extensive that supernatural ability was also necessary, especially in the early church where the Scriptures were scarce.

Tongues. This gift is at least as controversial today as it was in Paul's day. Much of the controversy centers on whether **tongues** were known human languages spoken by someone who did not know the language, or ecstatic utterances not known to humans, perhaps even "the tongues of angels" (1 Cor. 13:1). A few interpreters have even argued that **tongues** included language that could be understood by listeners as if it were their own native language, though it was not (Acts 2:11).

A crucial consideration lies in the fact that Paul did not say **tongues**, but **different kinds of tongues** (12:10). Paul appears to have been intentionally ambiguous, allowing for a broad range of phenomena under the rubric of **tongues**. This breadth appears in the way Paul drew a comparison between Christian tongues and pagan religious ecstatic speech earlier in this chapter (12:2–3).

It is important to add that there is little or no reason to think that **tongues** always involved infallibly inspired speech, even in the apostolic period. It is likely that some of the **different kinds** may have included infallible speech by apostles and prophets, when the Spirit inspired them infallibly. Yet, it is also likely that not all **tongues** were infallibly inspired any more than all preaching or proclamation was. If infallible **tongues** did once exist, they no longer continue in the modern church.

At least four characteristics of speaking in tongues must be remembered: (1) The speakers were not delirious; they were able to control how and when they spoke. (2) Both the speakers and at least some hearers were unable to understand what was said. (3) The Holy Spirit enabled someone in the church to interpret or translate the tongues. (4) Paul preferred that people speak in church in languages that everyone in the church could understand.

Interpretation of tongues. The word translated "interpretation" (*hermeneia*) may also be rendered "translation" in the usual sense of the word. The ability to interpret tongues apparently differed in ways that corresponded to the kind of tongues uttered. But even when a known human language was spoken, this gift was more than the ordinary ability to translate a language known to the translator. It must have been a supernatural ability to translate an unknown language. If **tongues** involved ecstatic or angelic speech, **interpretation** would have involved translating the tongue into understandable human speech. Paul later gave instruction that when tongues occur in worship they are to be interpreted, if at all possible, so that all may benefit from what is spoken (14:5–28).

12:11. Having covered a short catalogue of spiritual manifestations, Paul closed this list with another general comment. As Paul pointed out in the preceding verses, all spiritual gifts come from **one and the same Spirit.** They are all legitimate and important to the church because they come from the Holy Spirit. Beyond this, **each one** in the church has received different gifts, not because of differences in qualifications or circumstances, but according to only one standard: **just as** the Spirit **determines.**

Simon Magus (Acts 8:18–19) exemplified the error of thinking that human will determines the manifestations of the Spirit. His fate demonstrated the inaccuracy of such a view. Although Christians desire the manifestations of the Spirit, the Spirit alone decides to whom gifts are given. For this reason, no one should feel superior to others because he possesses a particular manifestation.

C Unity and Diversity of Members in the Body (12:12–30)

> **SUPPORTING IDEA:** *Paul pointed out the importance of each spiritual gift in the church by means of an extensive analogy. He likened the church, the body of Christ, to the physical human body.*

12:12–13. The apostle issued three statements which set up the basic structure of his analogy. First, the human **body is a unit.** It is **one body,** even though it has **many parts.** Second, just as one human body has many parts, so it is with the body of **Christ.** Paul often called the church "the body of Christ" (Rom. 7:4). Here he pointed to the unity in diversity that exists in the church as Christ's body. Third, Paul explained how Christ's body resembles the human body. To emphasize the diversity within the church, he mentioned racial and social diversity first; **Jews, Greeks, slave,** and **free** all contribute to the church. No matter what had previously separated these people, they all had been joined together in **one body** by means of the **one Spirit.**

Paul emphasized two experiences of the Holy Spirit that all believers share and that bring unity among them: (1) they are all **baptized by one Spirit**; and (2) they are all **given the one Spirit to drink**. Many interpreters argue that Paul was not referring to baptism and the Lord's Supper. They divide baptism of the Holy Spirit from water baptism, and note that drinking of the Spirit is a metaphor for receiving the Spirit at conversion (John 7:37–39).

Also, in the modern church people often profess faith in Christ and remain unbaptized for long periods of time. As regenerate believers they have the Holy Spirit even though they have not been baptized. Thus, interpreters hesitate to equate **baptized** too closely with **given the one Spirit**. Further, no account of the Lord's Supper refers to partaking of the Holy Spirit in the cup.

Even so, the text implies these ordinances and the New Testament church could hardly have conceived that followers of Christ would remain unbaptized or refrain from participating in the Lord's Supper. Such believers would have been considered odd (Acts 10:47–48). These ordinances were signs and seals of the new covenant that all true believers were expected to undergo. For this reason, Paul spoke of baptism and the Lord's Supper as experiences shared by all true believers that symbolized their union with one another in the Spirit and in the body of Christ.

Note the way these verses present Paul's argument. Specifically, Paul assumed the unity of the church on the basis of the Spirit. Verses 14–24a especially do not argue for the church's unity so much as they assume it. They argue for diversity. In the modern, fragmented church, many people consider diversity an obstacle to be overcome in the quest for unity. But from Paul's perspective, unity was to be sought in the Spirit, not in uniformity. The church's fullness and ability to function properly depend upon its diverse manifestations of the Spirit.

12:14–17. Paul turned next to human body imagery to illustrate the importance of proper regard for all parts of Christ's body. After repeating the motif of 12:12, **the body** has not **one part** but **many**, he presented two scenarios that conveyed his outlook on the disharmonies in the Corinthian church. First, he imagined parts of the body thinking too lowly of themselves. A **foot** may say to itself that it does **not belong to the body** because it is **not a hand**. Even so, even if it thinks this way about itself, it does not **cease to be part of the body**. The same would be true of **an ear** which felt it did not **belong to the body** because it was **not an eye**.

By analogy, Paul meant that Christians are not cut off from the body of Christ because they think they have no importance or place of service. Each part of the body makes unique contribution to the whole. How foolish it would be for the whole body to be one part. **The sense of hearing** would vanish if the **whole body were an eye**. **The sense of smell** would disappear **if the whole body were an ear**.

One might expect Paul to have reversed the perspective of this section, attacking those who valued themselves too highly rather than addressing those who had low opinions of themselves. Paul probably took this approach for two reasons. First, he wanted to make doubly certain that the arrogant Corinthians had no basis to discriminate against other Christians. Second, he recognized the harm that such discrimination does to its victims, and he saw the need to build up those who had been abused.

12:18–20. The foolishness of these scenarios indicates that **God has arranged the parts** of the human body according to his divine wisdom. He made them **just as he wanted them to be**—their composition being designed to fulfill his purposes—and God's wisdom in so doing should not be questioned. This divine coordination of diverse parts is so essential to the function of a body that Paul asked a final question: "If every part of the body were **one part**—all eyes, all ears, all feet—**where would the body be?**" Clearly, there would be no body. To drive home this point, Paul repeated the theme of this section: human beings have **one body**, but that body needs its **many parts**. Every part is important in its own right.

12:21–24a. Paul then presented scenarios in which the body parts questioned the value of others. Paul insisted it would be inconceivable for an eye to tell a hand, "**I don't need you!**" The same inconceivability would apply to the head speaking that way to the feet. Common sense demands that the opposite is true. The eyes need the hands, and the head needs the feet. The **parts of the body** which appear to be **weaker** are actually **indispensable**.

Ironically, those parts of the body that people consider **less honorable** they actually **treat with special honor**. This expression probably refers to clothing and ornaments placed on fingers, feet, toes, and other so-called "minor" parts of the body. Likewise, the church should give special honor to its members who do not naturally attract honor themselves. Moreover, people take great care to treat **unpresentable** private portions of their bodies **with special modesty** as they give comparably little **special treatment** to their **presentable parts**. The church should behave similarly, going out of its way to honor and exalt those people whom we tend to overlook.

12:24b–26. Paul contended that God himself had given **greater honor** to the members of the body that lacked obvious honor. He did this for the purpose of making sure that there would be **no division in the body** and so that all parts **should have equal concern for each other.** The interdependence of all parts evidences this design. If **one part suffers** from pain or disease, then **every part suffers with it**. Most people have experienced how things as small as toothaches and ingrown toenails can wreak havoc on their bodies. The appendix may be small and have no apparent function, but when it suffers it jeopardizes the life of the entire body.

Moreover, when **one part is honored** and treated with great care, then every other part of the body **rejoices with it**. For example, soaking one's feet in cool water after a long walk brings delight to the entire body. God exhibits his design in these common experiences. He has arranged the human body so that every part is important to every other part.

In the same way, every Christian is important to the church and to every other Christian. Because of the union that believers share with one another in Christ, what happens to one believer happens to everyone. The Corinthians needed to learn this lesson, so Paul designed this portion of his argument to address the situation of their divisions.

12:27. Paul next applied the analogy of the human body to the church as the body of Christ. He began with the declaration, **Now you are the body of Christ**. Paul used this metaphor for the church many times in this letter and in other epistles (Rom. 12:5; Eph. 3:6). Here he focused on the diversity and honor of the various members of Christ's body, starting with this general assertion and then pointing to each person in the church at Corinth. **Each one** is a **part** of the **body**. Without exception every person who has trusted Christ receives a place in **the body of Christ**.

12:28. To illustrate God's arrangement of the body of Christ, Paul listed seven appointments that God had made in the church. It appears that he listed the first three of these in order of importance, but listed the last five without indicating any priority other than their subsequence to **teachers**. He probably intended this variation because **apostles, prophets,** and **teachers** have relatively well-defined leadership roles in the church, while the other gifts of **miracles, healing, help, administration,** and **tongues** do not.

Apostles were very special leaders in the church. Jesus called twelve apostles (Matt. 10:2–4), and Matthias replaced Judas (Acts 1:23–26). Paul was added to the Twelve as the apostle for the Gentiles (1 Tim. 2:7). Other people such as Barnabas (Acts 14:14), James (Gal. 1:19), possibly Silas, Timothy (1 Thess. 2:6 with 1:1), Andronicus, and Junias (Rom. 16:7) were also called "apostles" in the informal sense of "ones who are sent," which is the term's most basic meaning.

Prophets in the New Testament, like their counterparts in the Old Testament, were instruments of special revelation from God. The more prominent examples of prophets in the New Testament are Agabus (Acts 21:10), Judas, and Silas (Acts 15:32). Philip the evangelist's daughters were also known as prophetesses (Acts 21:9). Prophets are second to apostles. All who claim to be prophets must be evaluated in light of the apostolic word. They were listed beside apostles because their office was also foundational to the church.

Teachers are of third importance. In the New Testament, teachers were like Jewish rabbis. They studied the Scriptures and taught the church sound doctrine. In Ephesians 4:11 Paul associated the office of teacher with that of pastor. This office is not an office of special revelation, but an office of interpreting special revelation.

Workers of miracles is not an altogether clear classification. In the church certain people apparently had the ability to perform miracles. **Healing** is a special kind of miracle in which the sick or dying are brought back to health. **Help** is not well understood because the word occurs only this one time in the entire New Testament. It probably indicates service as an assistant to others in the church. The character of this gift must have varied from place to place and person to person. **Administration** (*kuberneseis*) also occurs only here in the New Testament. It expresses the idea of "leader" or "guide." Finally, Paul listed **different kinds of tongues**. The same phrase appears in 12:10.

12:29–30. Paul next issued a series of rhetorical questions to which he expected negative responses. No gift is possessed by everyone in the church. The church is not made up of any one of these appointments. He repeated much of the list from 12:28, but replaced "help" and "administration" with the interpretation of tongues. Paul intended the Corinthians to conclude the analogy themselves. Just as the human body consists of different but interdependent parts, so the body of Christ consists of diverse but interdependent parts.

MAIN IDEA REVIEW: *Paul explained the role of the gifts of the Spirit in worship, beginning with the value of diverse gifts in the worship of God. He discussed the issue in three main sections: identifying the Spirit, the unity and diversity of the Spirit's manifestations, and the unity and diversity of members in the body.*

III. CONCLUSION

Every Gift Is a Blessing

Paul went to great lengths in this passage to establish proper attitudes toward every gift of the Spirit. The Corinthians tended to exalt some gifts over others, but Paul urged them to recognize all gifts as the blessings of the Spirit of God.

PRINCIPLES

- Every Christian is a necessary, beneficial member of the church.
- Spiritual gifts are primarily for the purpose of building up the church.
- Because we are members of one another, the spiritual states of our fellow believers affect us personally.
- We do not receive spiritual gifts according to merit or ability, but as God sees fit according to his grace.

APPLICATIONS

- We must look for ways to use our gifts in the service of the church and encourage others to do so as well.
- We must not take pride in our spiritual gifts
- We must not feel inferior if our spiritual gifts are not as impressive as the gifts of others.
- We should actively pursue spiritual gifts.

IV. LIFE APPLICATION

Free Amputations

Do you want to know how important it is to honor all the gifts the Spirit has provided the church? Think with Paul about how important it is to honor all the parts of your physical body. Imagine someone coming up to you and saying, "I will be glad to cut off any normal, healthy part of your body. Just tell me which part."

No person would have a normal, healthy part of his body removed. Why then do we treat some believers as dispensable? Why are we so willing to dishonor normal, healthy parts of the body of Christ?

The idea of the church as the body of Christ was an important metaphor for Paul because it represented the unity that believers share in Christ in a way that most people could understand.

We learn many things from Paul's metaphor. First, we realize that every Christian is a necessary, beneficial member of the church. The church cannot function properly if it does not enlist the contributions of each of its members. This does not mean that we allow unqualified people to lead or teach because they think they are gifted in these areas. But we should keep in mind that these situations are the exceptions, not the rule. If people do not know their gifts, we have a responsibility to help them discover their gifts. God can always find new ways to use believers to accomplish his work, and he is willing to bestow new gifts to fit the needs of his people.

God calls us to be excited about spiritual gifts. He wants us to recognize their value and to thank him for their wonderful blessings. At the same time, he wants us to remember that he gives us gifts so we can build up the church, bear witness to the gospel, and honor and glorify him.

V. PRAYER

Lord Jesus, give us eyes to see that every part of your body is valuable. Give us hearts that yearn to honor each member of your body. Give us the desire to glorify you by exalting the gifts of others. Amen.

VI. DEEPER DISCOVERIES

A. Speaking (12:3)

Besides Christianity, many pagan Greek and Roman religions featured "inspired" prophetic and ecstatic speaking. Some speakers spoke in understandable languages, while others such as the Delphic oracle of Apollo uttered incomprehensible sounds that Apollo's priests interpreted for the people. In almost every case, those in false religions who prophesied or spoke in tongues did so in trance-like states brought on by their gods. They spoke not for the "common good" (12:7), but for their own fulfillment.

B. Service (12:5)

By "service" (*diakonia*) Paul probably had in mind various acts of ministry to the church. For example, in Luke 10:40, both this noun and its cognate verb *diakoneo* appear in the context of preparing and serving a meal. Several times, such ministry includes the sharing of material wealth (Acts. 11:29). It also refers to the apostolic and evangelistic ministry (Rom. 11:13; 2 Tim. 4:5), including devotion to "the word" (Acts 6:4). Paul probably had many of these things in mind when he referred to "different kinds" of *diakonia*. In general, though, it appears to refer to actions and measures a person takes to care for others.

C. Weaker (12:22)

Paul's word for "weaker" here is the comparative form of *asthenes*, an adjective he used many times in this epistle. Paul meant his readers to associate the "weaker" parts of the body with the "weaker" members of the church.

Paul suggested that "weaker" Christians are of three main types: (1) those without human merit; (2) the weak in faith; and (3) the physically ill. Paul tended to define the first category as those who were "not . . . wise by human standards, not . . . influential, not . . . of noble birth" (1:26). He grouped the "weak" with those without honor (4:10), and with the poor (4:11). In the second category, he placed those who did not have a proper understanding of idols, and who were prone to falling into sin because they were encouraged to violate their consciences (8:7–13). The third category applied to those who had fallen ill as a result of mistreating the brethren in the Lord's Supper (11:30).

VII. TEACHING OUTLINE

A. INTRODUCTION

1. Lead Story: "That Little Piece Is Worth That Much?"
2. Context: The Corinthians had a very skewed view of spiritual gifts. They took personal pride in their gifts as if they had earned them or deserved credit for showing them. They were more interested in

using their gifts for personal fulfillment than for the good of the body. They failed to realize the importance of the smallest gifts. They also failed to recognize the importance of those people whose gifts were seemingly least useful.

3. Transition: The same thing can often be said about the modern church. We respect and honor those in church who do the most for the ministry. We act as if they do God's work by their own human abilities and not by God's grace. We fail to see the importance of every member of the church, focusing attention instead on those whom God is using most visibly at the moment. Like the Corinthians also, when we exercise our spiritual gifts, we frequently do so because it gives us a sense of personal fulfillment and enjoyment— not for the good of the body.

B. COMMENTARY

1. Identifying the Spirit (12:1–3)
   a. False spirits (12:1–3)
   b. The true Spirit (12:3)
2. Diverse Spiritual Gifts (12:4–11)
   a. There are many different gifts (12:4–6,8–10)
   b. One God determines and works all these gifts (12:4–6,11)
   c. All gifts are given for the common good (12:7)
3. Unity and Diversity of Members in the Body (12:12–30).
   a. The church is a unit made up of many parts (12:12–13)
   b. No one should think too lowly of himself (12:14–20)
   c. No one should think too highly of himself (12:21–26)
   d. The church is the body of Christ (12:27–30)

C. CONCLUSION: FREE AMPUTATIONS

VIII. ISSUES FOR DISCUSSION

1. Why do some people have certain gifts of the Spirit, while other people have different gifts? Is this a good thing? What is the purpose of gifts of the Spirit?
2. Why did Paul include this chapter in his letter? Do you think it was to correct a particular problem? If so, what was the problem? If not, why does the argument appear here?
3. What is the point of the "body" metaphor? Did Paul emphasize diversity or unity, or did he treat both equally? Can you defend your answer with explicit examples from the text?
4. Are there any people in your church who do not belong there? Is it always bad when people leave a church? Why or why not?

1 Corinthians 12:31–13:13

The Most Excellent Way

I. INTRODUCTION
It's the Best Way There

II. COMMENTARY
A verse-by-verse explanation of this section.

III. CONCLUSION
Gifts Without Value

An overview of the principles and applications from this section.

IV. LIFE APPLICATION
"Not My Daughter!"

Melding the section to life.

V. PRAYER
Tying the section to life with God.

VI. DEEPER DISCOVERIES
Historical, geographical, and grammatical enrichment of the commentary.

VII. TEACHING OUTLINE
Suggested step-by-step group study of the section.

VIII. ISSUES FOR DISCUSSION
Zeroing the section in on daily life.

1 Corinthians 12:31–13:13

Quote

"If we love Christ as we think we do, as we pretend we do, we shall love his church and people."

Charles Haddon Spurgeon

IN A NUTSHELL

Paul pointed out that Christian love is the most important of all gifts from the Spirit of God. He called the Corinthians to pursue love, without which all of their spectacular gifts amounted to nothing.

The Most Excellent Way

I. INTRODUCTION

It's the Best Way There

*W*hen you plan your family vacation, how do you decide which roads to take? Do you sit with the map and search for the most convoluted, indirect way to go? Do you choose roads that are small and treacherous? Or do you look for the most pleasant way? Perhaps the fastest way? Or the most scenic way?

Whatever choice you make, unless you are very unusual, you choose what you think is the best way. To be sure, there are usually many different routes to follow as you travel from one place to another. The options are there before us on the map. But we take the time to map out our route, and we depart with the conviction that we have chosen the best way there.

The apostle Paul continued to speak of spiritual gifts in this chapter. As he did, he invited the Corinthians to look at a map. They had been traveling this way and that with little concern for direction. Paul called them to examine their situation and to find the best way to exercise their spiritual gifts.

II. COMMENTARY

The Most Excellent Way

> **MAIN IDEA:** *This chapter focuses on love, a theme found throughout Paul's discussion of worship, and emphasizes the importance of the edification of others.*

A Introduction (12:31)

> **SUPPORTING IDEA:** *Paul introduced the idea that love is the greatest of all gifts.*

12:31. The apostle closed the last chapter and opened this one with a statement that would carry through chapter 13. He told the Corinthians they should **eagerly desire the greater gifts.** The original language is ambiguous at this point. Some interpreters have suggested that Paul stated a fact ("but you are eagerly desiring the greater gifts"), and then rebuked the Corinthians for this fact in chapter 13. This interpretation seems unlikely because in this same context he encouraged the Corinthians to desire spiritual gifts and prophecy. Moreover, 13:13 indicates that love is "the greatest" of all things to be desired. This verse introduces the positive pursuit of greater gifts. Paul was about to show the Corinthians **the most excellent way** to live as a member of the body of Christ.

It would be difficult to overemphasize Paul's commitment to love among Christians. The principle of love for others guided his discussion of worship. He urged believers to restrict their freedoms for the sake of others. He argued that concern for their husband's honor should guide wives' behavior, and he told rich believers to make sure the poor received the Lord's Supper.

B Priority of Love (13:1–3)

SUPPORTING IDEA: *Paul expressed his commitment to the priority of love over other aspects of life in the Spirit.*

13:1. First, Paul touched on speaking in **tongues**. This issue topped his list because of the overemphasis some Corinthians had placed on this gift of the Spirit. He described the gift here as **tongues of men and of angels**. The grammatical construction of the original language does not indicate that Paul was claiming to have done this. He spoke entirely hypothetically, without reference to whether he had done any of these things. Obviously he had not surrendered his "body to the flames" (13:3) as he said later. Further, neither he nor anyone else but the omniscient God ever had, could, or would "fathom all mysteries and all knowledge" (13:2). On the other hand, he did have the "gift of prophecy" (13:2), and he did "speak in tongues" (14:18). Grammatically, no evidence exists that Paul believed it was possible to speak in the **tongues . . . of angels**. Nowhere else does the Bible provide evidence of such a possibility.

Even so, such an extraordinary gift would profit nothing without love. Paul put the matter in striking terms, confessing that without **love** accompanying such an extraordinary gift, he would amount to nothing but **a resounding gong or a clanging cymbal**. His special gift, devoid of love, would amount to meaningless clamor. This must have shocked the Corinthian readers. Those who exalted themselves because of their gift of tongues must have looked like fools.

13:2. Second, Paul spoke of **prophecy**. Paul held this gift in high esteem. But he imagined the gift in a greater form than it had ever appeared in human history. Suppose he were to have the **gift of prophecy** to such a degree that he could **fathom all mysteries and all knowledge**. Prophets know things that are hidden from others because they receive revelation from God, but no prophet has ever had such omniscience. Yet, without **love** he would be **nothing**, even if he knew every divine secret.

Third, Paul raised the gift of **faith**. In this case, he did not have in mind saving faith that every believer exercises. Instead, he spoke of a special ability to trust and believe God to do great miracles. Paul described this **faith** as the ability to **move mountains.** The allusion to Jesus' words is evident (Mark 11:23). It would be astonishing for Paul to have had the ability to move mountains through his faith. Nevertheless, even this dramatic ability would amount to **nothing** without **love** for others.

13:3. Fourth, Paul imagined himself giving **all** he possessed **to the poor.** This may allude to Jesus' words to the rich young ruler (Mark 10:21), or it may refer to the early church's practice of selling their possessions to feed the church (Acts 2:44–45). Paul, however, was not wealthy. He had also demonstrated his willingness to go hungry and homeless. In all likelihood, Paul focused more on the benefit to others that such an act would produce, not on the sacrifice. Even such a beneficial act would profit him nothing if he did not do it out of love.

Fifth, Paul imagined that he might **surrender** his **body to the flames.** Some textual evidence supports an alternative reading followed by the NRSV: "hand over my body so that I may boast." It seems most likely that he imagined a situation of religious persecution in which he would be called upon to die. Or, Paul may have thought of his own trials and persecutions short of death. The words, **I gain nothing,** may apply to one situation as well as to the other.

Throughout this portion of the chapter, Paul addressed several hypothetical situations in which he might do the most remarkable things imaginable. It seems commonsensical that these experiences should have value in themselves. But Paul responded that without Christian love these experiences amount to nothing, just like the person who performs them.

Paul followed Jesus, who placed "love your neighbor as yourself" second only to "love the Lord your God" (Matt. 22:37–40). The command to love one another is the second most important law of Scripture. It is no wonder Paul argued that without love for others all spiritual gifts are worthless.

🅲 The Characteristics of Love (13:4–7)

SUPPORTING IDEA: *Paul focused on love between brothers and sisters in Christ. These fourteen characteristics of love also apply to many other human relations.*

13:4. Paul's deep concern for the unity of the church at Corinth caused him to address several aspects of Christian love. The first quality Paul listed was **love is patient.** Patience is a quality of love that the New Testament frequently mentions by this or closely related terminology. It signifies forbearance, slowness to repay for offenses. God is patient because he does not immediately punish those who offend him. God's patience slows down the judgment process and opens the way for reprieve from punishment altogether. Believers should behave similarly because of their love for one another.

One must be careful to distinguish patience from indifference. Patience bears with an offense, but indifference ignores it altogether. When an offense takes place that is harmful or destructive to oneself or to others, it must not be entirely overlooked. Paul, for instance, loved the Corinthians. He patiently bore with them and worked with them slowly and carefully to edify them and honor Christ.

Love . . . is kind. The term *kindness* (*chrestotes*) appears many times in Paul's epistles. It is connected with patience again in Galatians 5:22, apparently because these concepts are similar. Paul's distinction between patience and kindness was probably similar to that of English speakers. Patience has a more temporal focus, while kindness refers to the manner in which a person treats others.

Kindness takes many forms. In general, it is soft and gentle. Occasionally, however, kindness must take the form of a careful rebuke designed to bring about a good result. Paul demonstrated this as he dealt kindly, but firmly, with the Corinthians. Jesus' own life demonstrated such kindness (Luke 13:15–17).

Love . . . does not envy. One may admire another for something that person is or has, and he may desire many of the same good things for himself. Jealousy and envy begin when admiration and desire turn to resentment of others for what they have. They are the attitudinal roots of many terrible actions in the world. The Bible illustrates this time and again. To envy is not to display the love of Christ, who gave up all for the sake of others (Phil. 2:3–8).

Love . . . does not boast. Paul's word for "boast" (*perpereuomai*) appears only here in the New Testament, and infrequently in the rest of hellenistic literature. The meaning seems to be "bragging without foundation," and may also encompass sinful acts that Paul elsewhere called *kauchaomai*. The NIV also translates *kauchaomai* as "boast," but *kauchaomai* does not always carry a negative connotation.

At the same time, loving other people does not mean failing to acknowledge the good God has done in oneself and in others. Paul was not beyond complimenting the Corinthians. He even asserted his own standing on occasion. Love does not mean lying about human accomplishments. Rather, it means not exalting ourselves over others as if our accomplishments were based on our own merit and ability.

Love . . . is not proud. To be proud is to be overly self-confident or insubordinate to God and others. The Scriptures of the Old and New Testaments condemn pride as the source of much destruction and pain in the world. When one cares about other people, he does not find himself full of self-importance or arrogance toward others.

Unfortunately, many Christians avoid pride so studiously that they deprecate themselves. Whether in ourselves or others, the image of God must be held in high regard. Pride reproaches other images of God. Self-hatred reproaches oneself as the image of God.

13:5. Love . . . is not rude. Paul at least expressed the need to follow customary decorum. The definitions of "rude" vary from culture to culture. At the heart of rudeness is a disregard for the social customs that others have adopted. When one does not concern himself with the likes and dislikes of others, he shows a disrespect for them. Proper regard, on the other hand, indicates love for other people.

Nevertheless, love does not always require a person to go along with the crowd. When the customs of a culture contradict the higher ideals of the Christian faith, it is not unloving to break these social mores. In fact, it may actually show Christlike love to break with such cultural norms. For instance, every loving Christian bears the responsibility to break the customs that perpetuate racial discrimination.

Love . . . is not self-seeking. Paul probably had in mind here the practice of always putting oneself in first place without due consideration of others. Many situations in life call upon Christians to choose between benefit to themselves and to others. The loving person puts the benefit of others over his or her own good. Paul exemplified this practice when he refused to receive money for his work as an apostle (9:6–15). Jesus' humiliation was the greatest expression of putting others' benefit above one's own (Phil. 2:4–8).

It is also important to realize that this practice does not mean ignoring one's own legitimate needs. Jesus himself withdrew from the crowds for his own benefit, sometimes just to get away and other times to pray (Luke 5:16; 22:41).

Love . . . is not easily angered. The NIV probably catches the sense of Paul's expression even though the text says nothing explicit about the ease with which one becomes angry. Those who love others do not normally become irritated and angry whenever others do wrong, but rather are slow to anger. They are patient.

Still, there are times when anger is appropriate. Paul himself became angry when he saw the idols of Athens (Acts 17:16). Luke described him with the same word Paul used here (*paroxunomai*). Even Jesus became angry when he saw people's hardness of heart (Mark 3:5) and the money changers in the temple (John 2:14–17). We must never allow an avoidance of anger to become indifference to the suffering of others or to the honor of God.

Love . . . keeps no record of wrongs. People who love others do not keep meticulous records of offenses. They offer forgiveness time and again. Both

Jesus (Luke 23:34) and Stephen (Acts 7:60) demonstrated this type of love by forgiving the people who put them to death.

But Paul did not speak absolutely here. With no record of offenses, one cannot help others with many of their problems. Paul received reports on the wrongdoings in the Corinthian church. Someone had to keep a record in order to give him these reports. Yet, the purpose of the records was restorative, not vengeful or begrudging.

13:6. Love . . . does not delight in evil but rejoices with the truth. Paul juxtaposed **evil** and **truth** in this description of **love**. This contrast suggests that the term *truth* means something like "living according to the truth." In other words, those who truly love do not enjoy seeing their loved ones stumble into evil. They rejoice when their loved ones try to live according to the truth of the gospel. Sin destroys people's lives, so to rejoice in their sin is to rejoice in their destruction.

13:7. Love . . . always protects. Major English Bible versions translate the term *protects* (*stego*) very differently from one another. The word can mean "to endure" or "to cover, protect." If Paul had in mind the concept of endurance, he meant that love bears with many offenses and does not stop loving even under the strain of difficulties imposed by others, even going so far as to love enemies (Luke 6:27). If he had in mind the concept of covering, then he may have meant that love will not seek to expose the sins of others. Love handles the sins of others in ways that will not bring exposure or shame.

It is evident that Paul limited such endurance or protection. For example, he instructed Timothy that "those who sin are to be rebuked publicly" (1 Tim. 5:20). Likewise, he called public attention to the strife between Euodia and Syntyche (Phil. 4:2). He commanded the Corinthians to stop tolerating the man who had his father's wife (1 Cor. 5:1–13). Wisdom is required to know when and how to protect or to expose, and love always tends to protect.

Love . . . always trusts. Perhaps this characteristic of love is best expressed in contemporary English idiom as: "Love gives the benefit of the doubt." Suspicion and doubt toward others do not indicate affection or love. On the contrary, when someone loves with Christlike love, he entrusts himself to the person he loves time and again. Still, love does not demand that a person trust even when the basis for trust has been destroyed. Love does not give the "benefit" when there is no "doubt." In these circumstances trust is folly. Yet, the general practice of those who love is to trust the good intentions of others as much as possible.

Love . . . always hopes. Loving someone requires maintaining a measure of optimism on that person's behalf. Hope is an attitude that good will eventually come to those who may now be failing. Failure invades every Christian's life, and it often causes others to give up on the one who fails. Yet, Christians who love continue to hope for the best. This optimism encourages others to keep moving forward. This hope is based not on the Christian, but on Christ. The hope of each Christian is that Christ will preserve him to glory. When a brother falls, it is Christ who picks him up and makes him stand (Rom. 14:4). Christ is the one who promised to finish the work he began. Optimism can also become foolishness and wishful thinking. For example, Paul did not believe that the incestuous man at Corinth would repent without undergoing church discipline.

Love . . . always perseveres. Loving someone is easy when the other person does not challenge one's affections by offending or failing. Love's quality becomes evident when it must endure trials. The New Testament encourages Christians to persevere in their Christian walks (1 John 5:2–5). Here Paul had in mind particularly the need to persevere in love for others. Christians should look to the length and perseverance of Christ's love as the standard for their own.

Ⓓ The Superiority of Love (13:8–13)

> **SUPPORTING IDEA:** *Paul compared love to the spiritual gifts the Corinthians valued so highly.*

13:8a. Paul contrasted Christian love on the one hand, and prophecy, tongues, and knowledge on the other. These were the same topics with which he began this chapter. In this verse, he asserted that **love never fails.** By this expression Paul indicated that those who devote themselves to Christian love involve themselves in something beyond the ordinary. They participate in the grace of God. The apostle John wrote that "God is love" (1 John 4:8,16). As followers of Christ, believers receive the grace of God to express this divine love in human form.

In fact, the love Christians express in this life will extend to eternity. Even after Christ's return in glory, Christians will continue to share in the love God has for his own. For this reason, Paul exalted love to a special place. The experience of Christian love as Paul defined it is one of the few ways that Christians taste in part the perfection that awaits in full in the new heavens and new earth.

13:8b–9. In contrast to love, Paul described three other Christian graces as temporary. **Prophecies, tongues,** and **knowledge** will not carry over to eternity in the same way that love will. **Prophecies . . . will cease; tongues . . . will be stilled; knowledge . . . will pass away.** These gifts are as temporary as they are partial. Spiritual gifts do not divulge full knowledge or prophecy, so believers only **know in part** and **prophesy in part.** Paul did not justify his assertion that **tongues . . . will be stilled.** Rather, he implied that

tongues was another partial gift by grouping it with the related gifts of prophecy and knowledge. Prophecy, tongues, and knowledge were from the Holy Spirit and therefore were valuable in the church, but the nature of the gifts made their value only temporary. Not being of eternal value, they would eventually stop.

13:10. The **imperfect** understandings Christians gain through gifts of prophecy, tongues, and knowledge will disappear at the coming of **perfection**. Even though Paul alluded to the gifts of prophecy and message of knowledge in the previous verse, he avoided speaking directly of them. Instead, he spoke of the benefit Christians derive from them. The gifts do not disappear; **imperfect** understanding **disappears**. Christians will put the gifts behind them when their need for the gifts is gone.

Paul said that when **perfection** came he would see "face to face" (13:12), implying that "perfection" included his meeting a person. Moreover, he indicated that he would meet a person when "perfection" came by saying that he would know in the same way that he was known. When **perfection** came, Paul would gain a greater personal knowledge of someone who already had such knowledge of him—someone of whom he was already learning through prophecy, tongues, and messages of knowledge. That person was Christ. The coming of **perfection** coincides with meeting Christ in person; therefore, for the church as a whole, it must take place at Christ's second coming—at the consummation of all things in him (Eph. 1:10).

When Christ returns, there will be no need for prophecy, tongues, or the limited knowledge the church gains in this world. All these gifts only provide glimpses and foreshadows of the perfection that will come. Just as the shadows of the Old Testament sacrificial system no longer continue—now that Christ to whom they pointed has come (Heb. 10:1–14)—the shadowy, **imperfect** gifts of the Spirit will disappear **when perfection comes**.

13:11. Paul supported his view with two analogies. First, he appealed to a parallel with the human experience of maturation, explaining that as a **child he talked, thought,** and **reasoned like a child**. But when he **became a man**, he got rid of **childish ways**. The gifts of prophecy, tongues, and knowledge are so limited by the constraints of this life and their partial nature that they may be compared to childish things. Just as it is unimaginable that a mature adult would resort to childlike immaturity, so it is unimaginable that these gifts will endure beyond their usefulness into eternity.

13:12. The second analogy involves the experience of looking at a **poor reflection as in a mirror**. In Paul's day Corinth was well-known for its mirrors. Because their mirrors were made of polished brass, some interpreters have argued that Paul referred to the fact that metal mirrors reflect one's image only imperfectly. Corinth, however, made high-quality mirrors that probably provided good reflections. More likely, Paul meant that a reflection is no substitute for a real person. A modern parallel would be the photograph. Modern believers enjoy clear photographs of loved ones, but those pictures barely begin to portray the wonderful people they depict.

For Paul the gifts of the Spirit are the photographs the church has access to **now**. When Christ returns, however, **then** everyone will see **face to face**. Everything of which the gifts now speak in part will then be revealed in full. Just as a reflected image outlives its usefulness when the thing it portrays can be seen **face to face**, the gifts will have outlived their usefulness "when perfection comes" (13:10) at Christ's return.

Repeating the contrast between **now** and **then**, between the present age and the time after Christ's return, Paul said that he knew **in part,** but in the end he would **know fully . . . even as** he was **fully known.** By this he meant that he and other believers would know God intimately and personally in heaven, just as God already knows all believers. Human knowledge is imperfect in at least two ways: it is finite and corrupted by sin. In the world to come, believers will be fully redeemed from sin and its effects (Rom. 8:29–30), but they will still be finite. Paul did not mean that believers will fully comprehend God in eternity. That would be impossible. Instead, he focused on the personal and direct nature of believers' future knowledge of God.

13:13. Paul closed his discussion of "the most excellent way" (12:31b) with a summary statement that must have been familiar to the Corinthians. Paul spent much of his ministry emphasizing the importance of **faith** and **hope.** He presented **faith** primarily as the means by which believers are joined to Christ and thereby receive the blessings of salvation (Gal. 2:20; Phil. 3:9). **Hope,** in turn, Paul described mainly in terms of the glories of salvation that believers receive in heaven, including things like bodily resurrection. For Paul, **faith** and **hope** represented the means of obtaining the blessings of the gospel **(faith),** and the ultimate blessings themselves **(hope).** In this context, he placed even more value on **love.**

Paul also said that **faith, hope,** and **love** remained **now.** Although some commentators understand **now** to introduce only a logical conclusion, it is difficult to disregard it completely as a temporal marker because of the present tense verb **remain.** Thus, Paul meant that **faith** and **hope** existed at the time he wrote, not that they would always continue to exist. **Hope** does not continue when its object has been realized (Rom. 8:24). **Faith** similarly relates to that which is yet unseen (Heb. 11:1).

To show the importance of Christian **love,** Paul included it alongside **faith** and **hope.** The centrality of **love** would have been evident if Paul had stopped at that point, but instead he raised **love** to an even higher level. While **faith, hope,** and **love** stand above all spiritual gifts (displacing the Corinthians' favorites: prophecy, tongues, and knowledge), **the greatest of**

these is love. In this statement Paul raised a crucial question for the Corinthians. As their church struggled in its worship, especially in the practice of prophecy and tongues, what was its highest priority? Paul's position was plain. The highest virtue for them to pursue was love for one another.

> **MAIN IDEA REVIEW:** *This chapter focuses on love, a theme found throughout Paul's discussion of worship, and emphasizes the importance of the edification of others.*

III. CONCLUSION

Gifts Without Value

In this passage Paul affirmed that Christians receive many wonderful gifts from the Spirit of God. Yet, he also insisted in the strongest terms that these gifts are without value unless they are coupled with the greatest gift—love. Love is the most excellent way in which the other gifts must be manifested.

PRINCIPLES

- Unless motivated by love, spiritual service and gifts do not benefit the believer.
- Love is eternal.
- Spiritual gifts are temporary devices for ministering to the church until Christ returns.

APPLICATIONS

- We must refocus our priorities, setting love of others as a higher standard than effective service, and as a higher standard than spiritual gifts.
- Our love for others must be demonstrated in the way we treat them.
- Our spiritual gifts should remind us that we await the perfect realization of the blessings of the gospel.

IV. LIFE APPLICATION

"Not My Daughter!"

A friend of mine once told me about one of the first sermons he preached. He was very young at the time, and was substituting for the pastor of his home church in the South. Being unsure of himself, he picked a text that he could not possibly get wrong: 1 Corinthians 13. He spoke carefully, avoiding controversial subjects, and made only the broadest applications. After the sermon, a delegation approached him in anger. "Do you mean that we have to let our white daughters date black men?" they demanded. My friend was taken aback. Although he agreed with this application, he had said nothing of the sort in his sermon. Still, without him explicitly making this application, the Holy Spirit had pricked the consciences of the people who heard him speak. When he reminded them of the nature of love, they saw in their hearts some specific ways they failed to love their Christian brothers.

Like the people who heard my friend speak, most of us cling to actions and attitudes that are unloving. Rather than repent, we try to justify ourselves by redefining either "sin" or "love." One way that we typically redefine "love" is by describing it in terms of what we "do." We say that to love we must express patience, act kindly, and desist our envy and boastful language. But Paul was not interested solely in the way we act toward one another. He was also concerned with the way we feel toward one another. He wanted the Corinthians to begin to care for one another, and he wanted their actions to flow from a true feeling of love. Hypocrisy was not an option.

Perhaps some of us can say that we treat other Christians well, and that we conduct ourselves properly in church. Some of us may even have learned to let love guide our use of spiritual gifts. But precious few of us use our gifts primarily because we love the church. We tend to exercise our gifts because service gives us a sense of personal fulfillment. And what of the rest of us? According to Paul, the good that we do profits us nothing if we do not do it out of love. This means that the good that most of us do might as well be so much rubbish. This does not mean that we have not done some good things, or that people have not benefited from our ministry. But we can forget about receiving any eternal reward for our efforts. If we serve for the wrong reasons, we lay up our treasures on earth, not in heaven.

V. PRAYER

Lord Jesus, was there ever one who loved so deeply as you? Give us eyes to see that your life of love is to be our goal, our destiny, our ideal. Help us to see that of all things we have in this life, the greatest of these is love. Amen.

VI. DEEPER DISCOVERIES

A. Love (13:1–4,8,13)

No word for "love" other than *agape/agapao* appears frequently in the New Testament. Whereas *philia/phileo* was the dominant word group used to describe all sorts of love in the classical period, *agape/agapao* dominated in the New Testament. *Agape* describes many types of love, having a range of meaning similar to that of the English word "love," so one should not place exegetical weight on an author's use of *agape/agapao* as opposed to other words available to him—it was simply the general, all-encompassing word for love. Agape may be anything from the hypocritical Pharisees' love of the best seats in the synagogue (Luke 11:43), to the love between husbands and wives (Eph. 5:25–33), to God's loving act of sending Christ to die for sin (John 3:16).

B. Perfection (13:10)

The Greek word translated "perfection" (*teleios*) appears in the neuter gender, so it should not be translated "perfect one," even though its coming coincides with personal, intimate knowing. Matthew used the word twice, first meaning something closer to "flawless" (Matt. 5:48), but then more closely meaning "whole" (Matt. 19:21). James also used it both of these ways ("flawless," Jas. 1:17; 3:2; "whole," 1:4), and also in an ambiguous way (Jas. 1:25). John used it in a similarly ambiguous fashion (1 John 4:18), as did the author of Hebrews (Heb. 9:11).

For Paul, *teleios* most commonly means "mature" (Col. 1:28), though occasionally it appears to be closer to "flawless" (Rom. 12:2). Judging from the metaphor of maturity in 1 Corinthians 13:11 and Paul's dominant usage, *teleios* almost certainly means "mature" in 13:10. Of course, with the article *to*, the adjective *teleios* functions as a noun ("maturity").

C. Mirror (13:12)

Though mirrors (*esoptron*) in the ancient world were made of metal, they were not considered to render poor images. In fact, they rendered good images by most ancient accounts. Paul's metaphor relies on the ancient opinion of the reflective qualities of mirrors, so his metaphor probably did not assume that the famous Corinthian metal mirrors provided blurry or unclear reflections.

VII. TEACHING OUTLINE

A. INTRODUCTION

1. Lead Story: It's the Best Way There
2. Context: Paul was in the middle of teaching the Corinthians about the proper use of spiritual gifts. He knew they needed more than new information regarding the gifts; they needed a new framework in which to think about gifts. Before he wrote to them, they were interested in their personal fulfillment and prestige, not in building up the church. In this chapter, Paul gave them a new orientation toward life

that focused on putting other people first. He taught them to love, knowing that if they loved rightly, they would also use their gifts appropriately.

3. Transition: If there is any similarity between the modern church and the ancient church, it lies in our failure to love. In fact, by most accounts, we are often worse than the Corinthians. At least the Corinthians had managed to remain united as a single church. They had not split their fellowship, even though they had abused it. Most Christians today tend to be self-centered. They do not place others first, and they certainly do not commit themselves to living the love of which Paul spoke.

B. COMMENTARY

1. Introduction (12:31)
2. Priority of Love (13:1–3)
   a. Without love, a believer is nothing (13:1–2)
   b. Without love, a believer gains nothing (13:3)
3. The Characteristics of Love (13:4–7)
   a. Patient (13:4)
   b. Kind (13:4)
   c. Not envious (13:4)
   d. Not boastful (13:4)
   e. Not proud (13:4)
   f. Not rude (13:5)
   g. Not self-seeking (13:5)
   h. Not easily angered (13:5)
   i. Keeps no record of wrongs (13:5)
   j. Does not delight in evil (13:6)
   k. Protects (13:7)
   l. Trusts (13:7)
   m. Hopes (13:7)
   n. Perseveres (13:7)
4. The Superiority of Love (13:8–13)
   a. Prophecy, tongues, and word of knowledge are temporary (13:8–12)
   b. Faith, hope, and love (13:13)
   c. Permanent and superior value of love (13:8,13)

C. CONCLUSION: "NOT MY DAUGHTER!"

VIII. ISSUES FOR DISCUSSION

1. What intrinsic value do gifts of the Spirit have? Can a gift benefit the church even if it does not benefit the person who demonstrates it? How does love relate to the value of spiritual gifts?

2. How would you describe love? Does your definition look anything like Paul's? Was Paul's definition meant to be exhaustive?

3. Does Paul's definition of love look more like something you feel or something you do? If you did the things in his definition, would that qualify as love? Why or why not?

4. Why are gifts like prophecy, tongues, and knowledge only "partial"? What does your church teach about the continuation, cessation, or modification of spiritual gifts?

1 Corinthians 14:1–40

Gifts for Others

I. INTRODUCTION
That's What Money Is For

II. COMMENTARY
A verse-by-verse explanation of this section.

III. CONCLUSION
Glory, Edification, and Conversion

An overview of the principles and applications from this section.

IV. LIFE APPLICATION
Chaotic Worship

Melding the section to life.

V. PRAYER
Tying the section to life with God.

VI. DEEPER DISCOVERIES
Historical, geographical, and grammatical enrichment of the commentary.

VII. TEACHING OUTLINE
Suggested step-by-step group study of the section.

VIII. ISSUES FOR DISCUSSION
Zeroing the section in on daily life.

Quote

"The possession of gifts for service in Christ's church constitutes a call for their use. . . . We use our gifts in order to serve God, not in order to advance ourselves, attract the admiration of others, or even find satisfaction and fulfillment."

Edmund P. Clowney

1 Corinthians 14:1–40

I N A N U T S H E L L

Paul continued his discussion of spiritual gifts, focusing on their proper use in worship. God designed spiritual gifts for the edification of others. This principle should guide the ways we exercise them in worship.

Gifts for Others

I. INTRODUCTION

That's What Money Is For

A couple of years ago a friend called me on the phone and said, "Richard, I've got some money. Do you want it?"

We talked for a while about the kinds of ministry opportunities in which the money could be used. In the end, he gave a large check and we devoted it to the work of the kingdom.

I saw my friend recently and thanked him again for the blessing he was to me. "Thank you again for your gift," I said as I left. "We're using it to serve a lot of people."

Then he responded in a way true to his Christian character. "That's what money is for," he replied.

He believed that. God had given him success and money, but he understood that God's gifts to us are to be used in the service of others. The Christians at Corinth had many gifts of the Spirit that they used in worship. But these gifted believers had lost sight of the purpose of their gifts. They thought their spiritual gifts were for their own pleasure. Paul reminded them that every gift from God is intended for service to others.

II. COMMENTARY

Gifts for Others

> **MAIN IDEA:** *Paul argued that the principles of love and edification must guide the use of gifts in worship. He urged the Corinthians to devote themselves to using their spiritual gifts for others.*

Paul's discussion of spiritual gifts focused again on the extraordinary gifts of revelation (tongues, prophecy, interpretation). As mentioned in a previous chapter, the manner in which Christians understand these verses for today depends on whether they hold to the continuation, modification, or cessation of these gifts.

Love and Gifts Together (14:1–5)

> **SUPPORTING IDEA:** *Paul rejoiced that the Corinthians had been blessed with spiritual gifts, but he wanted them to use these gifts to edify the church.*

14:1. In what practical ways could the Corinthian church bring together love and spiritual gifts? The NIV obscures the fact that there are actually three verbs in Paul's solution: **follow, desire,** and "you may prophesy" (NASB). The believer who seeks both love and gifts will be **especially** desirous of **the gift of prophecy.** Having previously made the points that all gifts in the church are from the same Spirit, and that all members of the body are vital to the life of the church, Paul's encouragement that the Corinthians **especially** pursue **prophecy** required further explanation. As he went on to explain, the reason lay in the nature of prophecy as opposed to tongues.

14:2. The person who **speaks in a tongue** says things that no one can understand without an interpretation. For this reason, tongue-speakers do **not speak to men but to God** alone. The most that can be said of them is that they utter **mysteries with** their **spirit[s].** It is not clear whether Paul had in mind the spirit of the person speaking in tongues or the Holy Spirit. The **mysteries** that tongue-speakers utter are incomprehensible to the human mind, or at least they remain incomprehensible when delivered in this manner (1 Pet. 1:10–12). If no one interprets, the church cannot be edified.

14:3. To speak to God in worship is a good thing, but Paul was concerned with using spiritual gifts to edify others. He encouraged prophecy as a way to join love and spiritual gifts because prophets speak **to men for their strengthening, encouragement, and comfort.** This assessment of God's Word in worship is more positive than the one in 2 Timothy 3:16, but similar to the description in 1 Thessalonians 2:13. Prophecy in the early church resembled contemporary preaching in many ways. It was a message from God to his people, delivered in the language of the people. Prophecy benefited people in countless ways and was used in the service of love.

14:4. When a person **speaks in a tongue**, he only **edifies himself.** Nothing is wrong with being edified. As Paul would suggest later in this chapter, there is a place for tongues in self-edification at home. The edification Paul talked about appears to have been the edification of his spirit, not of his mind. But in the public worship of God, the gifts of the Spirit are for the edification of **the church.** Such corporate edification takes place only when what is said can be understood by the worshipers.

14:5. Paul did not deprecate tongues. In fact, he would have liked **every one** of the Corinthians **to speak in tongues.** The gift of tongues in the early church came from the Holy Spirit. Yet, Paul preferred that they **prophesy: he who prophesies is greater than one who speaks in tongues.** The former is greater because the employment of that gift more connects with the greatest of all gifts to the church—love for others. Prophecy is superior to tongues in this sense, unless the person who speaks in tongues also interprets **so that the church may be edified.** The one who prophesies is greater because he uses his gift in love, whereas the selfish demonstration of tongues without interpretation is done apart from love.

Paul had already mentioned interpretation of tongues as one of the gifts of the Spirit. When tongues are interpreted, they instruct and edify like prophecy. The guiding principle throughout this discussion is that the pursuit of spiritual gifts must be joined with a pursuit of love for others.

🅱 The Limitations of Tongues (14:6–12)

SUPPORTING IDEA: *Paul appealed to several analogies to build a case for his application to the Corinthians. Without interpretation, tongues are ineffective.*

14:6–8. Paul opened with the familial term **brothers** to help them lower their defenses. He was about to say some things with which they would agree. First, he spoke of a hypothetical visit he might pay them. Paul declared that even a visit from him would do no **good** for the Corinthian church **unless** he came with **some revelation or knowledge or prophecy or word of instruction.** The precise meaning of these expressions is not clear, but they are examples of the same kind of thing. Each term refers to the communication of God's word to the church in a way that can be understood. The only benefit from a visit from Paul would be the edifying teaching he would bring.

Second, Paul mentioned how no one can discern **a tune** on **a flute or harp** unless there is a distinguishable series of **notes.** Third, he referred to a **trumpet** used to call for battle. The signal will not be understood unless the trumpet puts forth **a clear call.** The purpose of these illustrations is clear: tongues without interpretation do not reveal anything. They do not communicate knowledge; they do not prophesy; and they do not give instruction. Instead, they are like untuned instruments, making sounds that benefit no one.

14:9. All of these analogies point out that in order to benefit others, a person must communicate clearly and effectively. Paul applied this principle to the Corinthian situation. When the Corinthians spoke in public worship, they had to be careful to **speak intelligible words.** Otherwise no one would **know what** they were **saying.** Speaking in ways that make no sense to anyone is the same as **speaking into the air.**

14:10–12a. The apostle continued to speak about tongues in these verses, using a closely related analogy. He recognized that there were **all sorts of languages in the world.** Yet, he also emphasized that the purpose of these languages was to communicate among people because **none** of these languages was **without meaning.** If, however, someone does not **grasp the meaning of what someone is saying**—if they do not speak the same language—then the listener and the speaker consider one another **foreigner[s].**

Their attempts to communicate with one another are doomed to failure, and they benefit no one. This analogy closely paralleled tongues-speaking in the Corinthian church. By speaking in tongues without interpretations in their public worship, the Corinthians became **foreigners** to one another rather than the brothers and sisters they should have been. Their tongues failed to benefit the church. Such self-centered use of tongues was unloving and unacceptable.

14:12b. Paul repeated the theme with which he had begun the chapter. He approved of the Corinthians' **eager** pursuit of **spiritual gifts**, including tongues. But he wanted them to realize the true purpose of spiritual gifts, and to **try to excel in gifts that build up the church.** The edification of others is the primary goal of using spiritual gifts in public worship. The Corinthians needed to make this goal their primary principle.

C Tongues and Edification Within the Church (14:13–19)

SUPPORTING IDEA: *Because uninterpreted tongues edify only the spirit of the person who speaks them, they are self-indulgent and of no use to the church. Tongues must speak to the mind of the church. This can happen only when they are interpreted.*

14:13–14. From the preceding description of the limitations of tongues, Paul drew the conclusion that anyone who spoke **in a tongue should pray that he may interpret.** When one prayed **in a tongue,** his prayers involved only his **spirit,** not his **mind.** While this benefited the person who prayed in tongues, it was not as beneficial as if he also prayed to interpret the tongues so his mind might be edified.

This juxtaposition of **spirit** and **mind** is unique in the Scriptures. It is not clear what Paul meant. He seems to have been saying that tongues without interpretation are unintelligible to everyone, including the speaker. The Holy Spirit uses the believer's spirit as he or she speaks in tongues, but the believer's rational ability is **unfruitful** in the process. If Paul did not understand what he said when he prayed in tongues, how could anyone hearing him understand and benefit from the practice? Since spiritual gifts are manifested in worship primarily to edify others, interpretation is crucial to their proper use.

14:15. In light of the limitations of praying in tongues, Paul had decided to **pray with** both his **spirit** and his **mind.** In a similar way, he determined to **sing with** his **spirit,** as well as with his **mind.** He believed that singing and praying unintelligibly (with the spirit) was appropriate in private worship, but not in public worship.

14:16–17. While it is important to consider the orientation of worship toward God, one must not ignore the church's edification. Those who hear only uninterpreted tongues can never say **Amen** to the praise they do **not understand.** Because the church cannot understand uninterpreted tongues, it can neither profit from nor confirm what is said. It may be true that a tongues-speaker is **giving thanks** to God, but the **other man is not edified.** The need to edify others makes it necessary to pray and sing in comprehensible ways.

14:18. Paul revealed the intensity with which he held this conviction with two final sentences. He was grateful to **speak in tongues more than all** of the Corinthians. He understood and experienced the blessings of this gift in remarkable ways in his private worship. This report of Paul's personal life may also indicate that the preceding "hypothetical" situations were drawn from Paul's personal experiences, including his relationship with the Corinthians.

14:19. Paul had another strong conviction that balanced his enthusiasm for tongues. In the public worship of **church,** he **would rather speak five intelligible words** than **ten thousand words in a tongue.** Why did he place so much weight on **intelligible words?** It was because words that can be understood **instruct others.** Love's focus on the edification of others governed Paul's attitude toward tongues in a remarkable way. For him, public worship did not honor God if it did not edify the church—no matter how earnest, dynamic, and personally fulfilling that worship might be.

Tongues and Unbelievers (14:20–25)

SUPPORTING IDEA: *Paul asked, "What effect do tongues have on the unbelievers who visit the public meetings of the church?" He provided a caution against the practice of speaking in tongues in public worship.*

14:20. Paul appealed again to the Corinthians as **brothers.** This address indicates the intensity with which he appealed to them. At the same time, he told them to **stop thinking like children.** The allusion to the preceding chapter on love is evident. For Paul, the Corinthians' preoccupation with tongues indicated their spiritual immaturity. They fixated on their temporary gifts— "childish ways" in the grand scheme of things—failing to maintain an eternal perspective.

Of course, the Bible sometimes commends childlike attitudes in believers. Jesus presented a child's trust as a model of faith (Mark 10:15). Even here, Paul insisted that believers should be as naive as **infants . . . in regard to evil.** But Paul did not want believers to be naive about evil. Rather, Christians must be wise as serpents (Matt. 10:16). The ideal is that believers should be inexperienced in and separated from evil, and that they should not know much about it. While he found it appropriate to be innocent regarding evil, Paul insisted that believers should still be **adults . . . in** their **thinking.** In other words, with respect to Christian doctrine and practice, Paul wanted the Corinthians to be mature in their perspectives.

14:21–22. Paul demonstrated the Corinthians' need to think maturely about tongues by paraphrasing Isaiah 28:11–12. The prophet Isaiah warned northern Israel that God would exile them to a place where he would use **strange tongues** and **lips of foreigners** to **speak to this people.** Even while suffering this punishment, however, they would **not listen** to the Lord.

As the church spread throughout the Gentile world, unbelieving Jews heard the message of the Messiah Jesus in foreign Gentile languages. People of strange languages proclaiming God's gospel in tongues throughout the world signified judgment against many Jews' continuing unbelief. Paul concluded that **tongues . . . are a sign . . . for unbelievers** because God designed them to communicate the gospel and Christian teaching across linguistic boundaries. They are **a sign** in the prophetic sense of the word: as a curse against those who do not believe.

Prophecy, however, is **for believers** because it edifies them and builds them up in the faith. For rhetorical effect, Paul spoke in absolute terms about something that was relative. Tongues are more for unbelievers, while prophecy is more for believers, **not for unbelievers.**

14:23. On the basis of this distinction, Paul depicted two potential scenarios. On the one hand, he imagined **the whole church** at Corinth gathering for public worship with **everyone** speaking **in tongues.** In fact, this scenario might have represented the reality of Corinthian worship. The result was that visitors who did **not understand** or who were **unbelievers** would think the Christians were out of their minds.

14:24. On the other hand, Paul suggested that if **an unbeliever or someone who** did **not understand** came to the worship service and **everybody** was **prophesying** in ordinary languages, then that visitor would **be convinced.** Paul had in mind **everybody . . . prophesying** in sequence, one at a time, not simultaneously. If order was observed and ordinary language was used, the visitor would discover himself or herself to be **a sinner.**

Paul also declared that visitors would **be judged by all.** The meaning of these words is not clear, but Paul did not contradict Jesus, who warned against self-righteous judgment of others (Matt. 7:1–5). Paul probably meant that prophecy would judge unbelievers by virtue of its content, not that believers would condemn unbelievers.

14:25. As a result of the intelligible proclamation of God's word, sinful **secrets** hidden in the **heart** of the unbeliever would **be laid bare.** Even things of which the unbeliever may not have been conscious would suddenly come to his or her awareness. Many unbelievers would **fall down and worship**

God. In other words, they would confess their sins and pledge their loyalty to Christ. These new converts would be so astonished at the word of God proclaimed in the Christian assembly that they would proclaim, **God is really among you.** The conversion of the lost is part of the purpose for Christian gatherings.

E The Practice of Worship (14:26–40)

SUPPORTING IDEA: *Paul turned to some practical instructions about worship, concluding that everything in worship should be done in a fitting and orderly way.*

14:26. Paul began with another appeal to his readers as **brothers** to continue his plea for their compliance. He asked, **What then shall we say?** In other words, "What practical conclusions should we draw from the preceding discussion?" The answer was that "everything should be done in a fitting and orderly way" (14:40). As he began to define this, he pronounced a policy that **everyone** should come to worship ready to use his or her spiritual gifts, whether it be **a hymn, or a word of instruction, a revelation, a tongue or an interpretation** of tongues.

The distinction between **instruction** and **revelation** is not clear because Paul did not use these terms very often. **Instruction** probably meant ordinary, fallible preaching and teaching. **Revelation** is more than likely infallibly inspired proclamation. This list is just a sampling of the spiritual exercises that might take place in a worship service. Paul's point was that there should be no bystanders in worship.

At the same time, this policy needs to be qualified. **All** activities in worship must be practiced **for the strengthening of the church.** The Spirit grants gifts to believers for the purpose of building up the church. To exercise a spiritual gift in a way that does not build up other believers is to abuse the gift and to corrupt the worship of God.

14:27–28. Paul gave directions for **anyone** who spoke **in a tongue.** For the sake of order and edification, Paul insisted that only **two—or at the most three—should** be allowed to **speak.** Even these few were not to speak simultaneously, but **one at a time,** and only if there was an interpretation. In the absence of such order and interpretation, those speaking in tongues should **keep quiet** in the worship service, speaking only to themselves **and God,** not expressing within the church what is unintelligible.

14:29–33. Paul focused in this section on **prophets.** Once again, **two or three prophets** sufficed. Others were to **weigh carefully** all prophetic speech. Paul was concerned that the prophets follow a protocol of generosity toward one another. If someone received **a revelation** while another was speaking, then **the first speaker** was to **stop**. Prophets were to wait for their **turn so that everyone** might **be instructed and encouraged.**

Anticipating the objection that prophets cannot control themselves when the Spirit comes on them, Paul added that **the spirits of prophets** were under **the control of prophets.** In other words, within limits prophets can control how and when they prophesy. Paul explained why this is true: **God is not a God of disorder but of peace.** God would not inspire prophets to bring chaos to public worship in Corinth.

14:34–35. The instruction to "weigh carefully what is said" (14:29) by a prophet raised an issue for wives. How should wives honor their husbands who prophesy and at the same time weigh what their husbands said?

Three times Paul said that women should remain quiet: **women should remain silent; they are not allowed to speak;** and **it is disgraceful for a woman to speak in church.** Yet, he also qualified this to some degree by adding, **if they want to inquire.** Paul did not believe that women should not speak at all in church. In 11:5,13 he acknowledged their right to pray and prophesy. Rather, they should not ask questions. By suggesting that they ask their questions of **their own husbands at home,** he also implied that **their own husbands** were the ones who knew the answers. In this context, he seems specifically to prohibit wives from questioning their own husbands in church.

It seems best to read this passage as returning to the issue of wives honoring their husbands in public worship. Wives must behave in worship in ways that honor their husbands. In effect, Paul told wives not to question their husbands' prophecies in the public meeting. Instead, **if they want[ed] to inquire,** they were to **ask their own husbands at home.** Paul's reason for this was the same as in 11:6: it is **disgraceful** for a wife to behave otherwise. It was important for wives not to embarrass their husbands by challenging their prophecies in public.

14:36–38. Closing his discussion of spiritual gifts in worship, Paul objected to those who asserted leadership in other directions. He asked if the **word of God** had come from them first, and if the Word had **reached** only them. Of course, the answer to these questions was an emphatic "No!" The Corinthians had received the Word from others, including Paul himself, and the church throughout the world had the Word.

For this reason, Paul reminded the Corinthians of the proper attitude toward the apostles of Christ. Everyone who considered himself or herself **a prophet or spiritually gifted** was to remember that Paul was an apostle and that what he wrote was **the Lord's command.** Prophecies must be weighed and tested, but the apostolic word is the Word of Christ.

Neglecting apostolic authority carries serious consequences. Anyone who **ignores** Paul's authority **will be ignored** or rejected by God.

14:39–40. In conclusion, Paul appealed to the Corinthians once again as **brothers** to show that love and concern motivated his plea for their compliance. He hoped the Corinthians would **be eager to prophesy** because it benefited the church. He was less enthusiastic about tongues, saying that the church should **not forbid speaking in tongues**, but not that **tongues** should be sought eagerly. In all these and other matters related to worship, all activities should take place **in a fitting and orderly way**.

> **MAIN IDEA REVIEW:** *Paul argued that the principles of love and edification must guide the use of gifts in worship. He urged the Corinthians to devote themselves to using their spiritual gifts for others.*

III. CONCLUSION

Glory, Edification, and Conversion

In this passage, Paul closed his discussion of spiritual gifts in the Corinthian church. He provided many specific instructions, especially about prophecy and tongues. Yet, in all of this discussion his central focus was that the gifts of the Spirit were to be used in worship not only for the glory of God, but also for the edification of believers and the benefit of the unconverted.

PRINCIPLES

- Individuals may approach God in worship only because they belong to the body of Christ.
- Spiritual gifts in worship are for the purpose of building up the church, not for individual fulfillment.
- Disorderly worship does not build up the church or present a good witness to the gospel.

APPLICATIONS

- Our worship must praise and honor God and build up and honor the church and its members.
- We should refrain from doing things in worship that do not edify the church, even if those things edify us personally.
- Our worship must be orderly.
- We should desire and pursue spiritual gifts to use in worship.

IV. LIFE APPLICATION

Chaotic Worship

Many of us live chaotic lives. Take a look at your work place, your home, or your car. If you keep these things in order all the time, you are an unusual person. Now imagine how Christian worship would be if our worship services were as chaotic as these aspects of your life. What would we accomplish in worship? What good would come of it? Chaotic worship soon becomes no worship at all. This is why Paul insisted that whatever we do in the worship of God must be done in an orderly and decent way.

The way we apply this chapter will depend to some degree on our theology of spiritual gifts. But we can draw some universal principles from the text that apply to all situations.

Paul taught that worship must not only be directed toward God; it must also be "corporately aware." That is, we do not worship as individuals, but as a church. Corporate worship should emphasize and build up corporate unity in Christ.

Even if we enjoy worship, sing loudly, give proper thanks, and feel personally fulfilled, our worship may still fail to please God. Singing the songs with everyone else and listening to sermons alongside everyone else are not enough to make worship "corporate." We can do these things without speaking to another person or without thinking about the unity the body shares in Christ. We can do these things without benefiting anyone else in the body. Worship must have at its core an awareness that the church is the body of Christ and that individuals participate in corporate worship because they belong to that body. Moreover, our worship must be directed not only toward praising and honoring God, but toward building up and honoring the body and its members.

This means that most of us need a major renovation of our concept of worship. We tend to determine whether a worship service was "good" on the basis of our enjoyment of it. We even pick the church we will join on the basis of whether the worship fulfills our needs. This concern for meeting our needs is not entirely improper, but focus on meeting *our* needs is inappropriate for believers. Worship is good if it builds up the church as a whole by benefiting the individual members and uniting them to one another.

There is another point in this chapter that often falls between the cracks. Paul told the church to desire spiritual gifts so it could better minister to itself. We must not only stop our wrong behavior and redirect our focus, but we must also seek ways to build up one another.

V. PRAYER

Lord Jesus, so often we come to worship for what we can get out of it. Grant us your mercy, Lord, so that we may come to give glory to you and edification to others. Amen.

VI. DEEPER DISCOVERIES

A. Two—or at the Most Three (14:27)

In pagan worship services in Paul's time, tongues were personal indulgences in ecstasy. Worshipers worked themselves into trances. When they spoke in their tongues, they were not interested in the other worshipers. Pagan services often led to many people speaking in tongues simultaneously, each without regard to the rest of the congregation. Paul wanted to make certain that Corinth's worship services did not exhibit this chaos. He wanted tongues speakers to conduct themselves temperately, speaking for the congregation's benefit, one at a time, and in limited numbers.

B. Control of Prophets (14:32)

When pagan worshipers prophesied, they behaved much as they did when they spoke in tongues. Their prophecies constituted "madness" according to Socrates. This was also Philo's (about 20 B.C.–A.D. 50) understanding. Although he was a Jew, he also drew heavily from hellenistic thinking, such as Platonism.

When Paul argued that the spirits of prophets were under the control of prophets, he meant to distinguish true prophecy from pagan prophecy. Unlike pagan prophecy that required the prophet to abandon himself to some supernatural power, Christian prophecy required that the prophet remain in control of himself and his spirit.

VII. TEACHING OUTLINE

A. INTRODUCTION

1. Lead Story: That's What Money Is For
2. Context: The Corinthians had many good gifts to use in worship, but they did not know how to use them properly to edify others. Paul gave them some very practical instructions to help them use their gifts and to maintain orderly worship services.
3. Transition: The modern church, like the Corinthian church, is full of gifted people. Yet, like the Corinthians, many of us do not know how to use our gifts properly in worship to edify others. We need to learn from this chapter that we must use our gifts in worship not for

personal fulfillment, but to build up the church and to present a godly witness to the world.

B. COMMENTARY

1. Love and Gifts Together (14:1–5)
    a. Tongues do not benefit others unless they are interpreted (14:2,4–5)
    b. Prophecy is superior to uninterpreted tongues (14:1–5)
2. The Limitations of Tongues (14:6–12)
    a. Illustrations (14:6–11)
    b. Application: excel in gifts that build up the church (14:12)
3. Tongues and Edification Within the Church (14:13–19)
    a. Those who speak in tongues should pray for interpretation (14:13,15)
    b. Uninterpreted tongues edify the speaker's spirit, but not his mind (14:14)
    c. Uninterpreted tongues do not edify others (14:16–19)
4. Tongues and Unbelievers (14:20–25)
    a. Uninterpreted tongues will not convert unbelievers (14:20–23)
    b. Prophecy will convert unbelievers (14:22,24–25)
5. The Practice of Worship (14:26–40).
    a. All gifts must be practiced for the good of the church (14:26)
    b. The orderly practice of tongues (14:27–28)
    c. The orderly practice of prophecy (14:29–33)
    d. Orderly, silent women (14:34–35)
    e. Paul's summary call for order in worship (14:36–40)

C. CONCLUSION: CHAOTIC WORSHIP

VIII. ISSUES FOR DISCUSSION

1. Why should we desire spiritual gifts? Is this something your church teaches you to do? Why or why not?
2. What benefits do tongues provide? How do prophecy's benefits compare with these? Why is prophecy more beneficial to the church than tongues? Under what situations can tongues be as beneficial as prophecy?
3. Why did Paul thank God that he frequently spoke in tongues? Where and when did Paul imply that he spoke in tongues? What did he prefer to do in church? Why?
4. How were the Corinthians thinking like children? How did their thinking need to grow and mature?

1 Corinthians 15:1–58

Controversy Over
the Resurrection

I. INTRODUCTION
"One Thing I Know for Sure"

II. COMMENTARY
A verse-by-verse explanation of this section.

III. CONCLUSION
Raised with Him

An overview of the principles and applications from this section.

IV. LIFE APPLICATION
"Who Did He Think Was in the Casket?"

Melding the section to life.

V. PRAYER
Tying the section to life with God.

VI. DEEPER DISCOVERIES
Historical, geographical, and grammatical enrichment of the commentary.

VII. TEACHING OUTLINE
Suggested step-by-step group study of the section.

VIII. ISSUES FOR DISCUSSION
Zeroing the section in on daily life.

Quote

"*J*esus lives and so shall I:

Death, thy sting is gone forever!"

Christian F. Gellert

1 Corinthians 15:1–58

I N   A   N U T S H E L L

*I*n this chapter Paul dealt with another problem in the Corinthian church. He affirmed that the Christian faith rests upon the resurrection of Christ and has a sure conviction of the resurrection on the final day of all who believe in him.

Controversy Over the Resurrection

I. INTRODUCTION

"One Thing I Know for Sure"

*W*hen Christians speak to unbelievers, they often discover that the truths of Scripture that we hold so dear are disbelieved, even mocked by unbelievers. Now in many circles it is not so strange that we believe in God. It does not even seem odd to many people that we give our allegiance to Christ. Many people understand that Jesus was a good man and a great moral teacher.

But all around the world, one doctrine sticks in the throats of non-Christians: the doctrine of the resurrection. I can remember sharing my faith with a man. He was kind and listened attentively, but at one point he had to interrupt me.

"I can go along with you on most of what you said," he admitted. "The world is a mess and we need a Savior . . . But there's just one thing I can't get past."

"What's that?" I asked.

"It's just not possible that Jesus was resurrected from the dead," he replied. "Dead people don't come back to life . . . That's one thing I know for sure. Besides, why do I need to believe in that anyway?"

The challenge of our belief in Christ's resurrection is not something that began with the rise of modern science and naturalistic thinking. It has been a foolish notion to many people from the day Jesus rose from the grave. In this chapter, Paul called on the Corinthians to lay hold of their faith in Christ's resurrection and to realize why it was so important that they live in the light of the hope it brings.

II. COMMENTARY

Controversy Over the Resurrection

> **MAIN IDEA:** *Having dealt with a number of problems related to worship in the church at Corinth, Paul turned to a doctrinal controversy over resurrection. Both Gentile and Jewish opponents could have influenced the believers at Corinth to deny the doctrine of resurrection.*

The Reality of Christ's Resurrection (15:1–11)

SUPPORTING IDEA: *Paul reminded the Corinthians of the importance of the gospel they had believed. He included the resurrection as an important element of the gospel.*

15:1. Paul appealed once again to the Corinthians as **brothers** as he began to talk about the resurrection. By this affectionate term Paul affirmed the Corinthians in their basic commitments to Christ's resurrection, wanting to **remind** them of the elements of the **gospel**, not to challenge their acceptance of it.

The **gospel**, or good news, is the message of God's saving work in Christ. Up to this point, Paul had oriented the gospel message around Christ's death, but here he **preached** the gospel by emphasizing the resurrection. He also affirmed his belief that the Corinthian Christians had **received** this gospel message and had **taken** their **stand** on it. In Paul's day being a Christian was more than intellectual assent to a group of doctrines. The social price that followers of Christ paid forced them to take a stand in a hostile world.

15:2. Anticipating the importance of what he would say about the resurrection, Paul made it clear that anyone who did not hold to the gospel he had preached could not be **saved**. Only **by this gospel** could they be **saved** from God's judgment. Salvation comes through belief in the good news of Christ's death and resurrection.

Yet, Paul added an important qualification. They **are saved, if** they **hold firmly to the word**. As he indicated throughout this epistle, Paul believed that saving faith would set itself apart from insincerity through time. True believers persevere in their commitments to Christ. Paul did not mean that truly regenerate people could lose their salvation, nor that truly regenerate people were without sin and failure. He understood, as the entire Bible teaches, that saving faith proves itself over a lifetime.

Paul warned that if the Corinthians had once trusted the gospel of Christ but did not hold fast to that gospel, then they **believed in vain**. In other words, their temporary commitments to Christ would not benefit them as they had hoped. Anyone who turns away from belief in the resurrection of Christ puts himself in a precarious position. He or she stands in line for God's judgment, not for his eternal salvation.

15:3–4. Paul next explained why it was important for the Corinthians to believe his teaching about the resurrection. He justified his insistence that they hold fast to the gospel, insisting that the resurrection was central to the gospel message. Why was this so important? Why was the resurrection a necessary element of the gospel?

First, Paul **received** and **passed on** this gospel. In rabbinic Judaism this terminology described the transmission of authoritative religious teachings.

Paul told the Corinthians to maintain the gospel as he had given it to them because it was a sacred tradition, not a human tradition.

Second, he delivered this gospel teaching as a matter **of first importance.** In other words, nothing was more central or more important in Paul's conception of gospel than these teachings.

Paul summed up his gospel as having two main concerns: the death and the resurrection of Christ. Both of these took place **according to the Scriptures.** Paul repeated this phrase to emphasize the importance of the scriptural witness and to demonstrate that the resurrection's importance paralleled the centrality of Christ's death.

He spoke first of Christ's death, declaring, **Christ died for our sins.** Christ's substitutionary death on behalf of believers brought salvation to those who would otherwise have been lost. When Paul said that Christ's death was **according to the Scriptures,** he probably had in mind Isaiah's prediction that the son of David would suffer on behalf of the people of God (Isa. 53:1–12).

Second, Paul referred to the resurrection. Christ was **buried,** but **he was raised on the third day.** Paul never said that Christ raised himself. Instead, the apostle taught that God the Father raised Christ by the power of the Holy Spirit (Rom. 1:4; Gal. 1:1). The resurrection was also **according to the Scriptures.** Paul probably had in mind Isaiah 53:10–12. The prophet explained that the son of David would come back from the grave to bring great blessings to God's people. Paul also may have thought of Psalm 16:10, a passage in which David recorded that God would not allow his Holy One to see decay. Jesus defended the idea of resurrection in the Old Testament by asserting that God was the God of the living (Matt. 22:31–32). By including both Christ's death and resurrection as essential elements of the gospel, Paul precluded those who denied the resurrection from claiming salvation in Christ.

15:5–8. Paul continued by adding a third element that expanded the second. Christ was not simply raised from the dead. He also **appeared;** people saw and heard him. Paul did not repeat the refrain "according to the Scriptures" here because no particular prophecy focused on appearances of the resurrected Son of David. But Paul did note that several people saw the resurrected Christ. These included **Peter, the Twelve, more than five hundred of the brothers . . . most of whom** were **still living, James, all the apostles,** and Paul himself.

Although Paul's main idea was that all of these people bore witness to the resurrection of Christ, his list had at least three major concerns. Christ appeared to: (1) figures of central authority in the church (**Peter, the Twelve, James, all the apostles**); (2) large numbers of people (**Twelve, five hundred, all the apostles**); and (3) to Paul himself.

Paul declared that Christ had appeared to him on the road to Damascus **last of all . . . as to one abnormally born.** The expression "last of all" probably indicates that Paul was the last person to see the resurrected Christ. Viewing the resurrected Savior was a requirement for apostleship (Acts 1:21–22). Yet, Paul admitted that his own situation had been extraordinary because Christ came to him in a miraculous manner after the ascension.

Thus, Paul saw himself as having been **abnormally born.** This expression is difficult to translate because it occurs only here in the New Testament. In an effort to express his humility, Paul compared himself to an untimely born child, indicating some degree of inferiority to those who had lived with Jesus during his earthly ministry.

15:9. In explaining why he spoke of himself in this way, Paul admitted to being the **least of the apostles,** not even deserving the title because he **persecuted the church of God.** This probably resonated strongly with his detractors. They most likely thought, "Obviously he is the least, that is why we favor Apollos and Cephas."

15:10. But Paul went on to defend his apostolic authority by pointing to God's choice of him. As Paul considered his background, he had no doubts that he had been called as a Christian and as Christ's apostle (**I am what I am**) only by the **grace of God.** Paul taught elsewhere that the Christian life begins by grace and continues through God's grace received by dependent faith. Here the apostle evaluated his own life in these terms. Not only had he initially believed because of God's grace, but every good thing in his Christian life also came from the grace of God.

At this point, Paul concerned himself with one particular aspect of God's **grace** in his life. Divine mercy had great **effect,** or result, on his service to the body of Christ. This is the same type of argument he used in 9:1–27 to defend his apostleship. The one who had once persecuted the church **worked harder than all** the other apostles. Paul assessed the situation honestly, not speaking proudly as if he had accomplished anything on his own. He reiterated that he did nothing in his own power. He performed only by **the grace of God that was with** him. Paul knew himself too well to take credit for the good he had done in Christ's service. He knew that the only source that could produce these good works through him was **the grace of God.** Because he relied so strongly on God's grace, he became one of the most effective apostles.

15:11. Paul closed this section by bringing his readers back to the main idea. The Corinthians must believe that Christ had been resurrected. On this all the apostles agreed—Christ's resurrection was central to the gospel. All of the apostles continued to **preach** this message, and the Corinthians at one time had **believed** it as well. Paul hoped they would reaffirm their commitment to Christ's resurrection.

B The Hope of Believers' Resurrection (15:12–19)

SUPPORTING IDEA: *Paul addressed opponents who opposed the idea of human bodies being resurrected into glorified bodies.*

15:12–13. Paul introduced this line of reasoning by posing a dilemma. If he had **preached that Christ** had **been raised from the dead** and the Corinthians had believed it, how could they deny the **resurrection of the dead?** He introduced the idea that this was an inconsistent way of thinking. Christ had been dead, and he was subsequently resurrected from the dead. The Corinthians had believed as much. It was illogical for them also to believe that resurrection of the dead does not take place.

While this Corinthian heresy probably arose around the general resurrection of believers on the last day, Paul referred more generally to the idea of resurrection. The phrase "resurrection of the dead" (*anastasis nekron*) appears in the Book of Acts without reference to a general resurrection (Acts. 26:23). Paul duplicated this use in Romans 1:4. Moreover, in 1 Corinthians 15:21 he used it as counterpart to physical "death." He did not use this terminology solely as a technical term for the general resurrection.

The New Testament makes it clear that, like the Sadducees, Greek philosophers resisted the gospel because they rejected the idea of bodily resurrection. The argument that **there is no resurrection of the dead** may have been advanced by those Corinthians who had become enamored with such worldly wisdom. Perhaps these were the same opponents Paul addressed throughout the letter. Some commentators argue that these Corinthians spiritualized the resurrection of believers.

Such errors of spiritualization can be easily understood when one considers Jesus statement, "I am the resurrection" (John 11:25). Such language might be misconstrued to mean that bodily resurrection was a metaphor for true spiritual life. The vocabulary of a resurrection "in Jesus" (Acts 4:2) might also have been misinterpreted to teach this. In this error, the Corinthians may not have denied the possibility of restoration of life to dead bodies such as took place with Lazarus (John 11:43–44), but rather resurrection to an eternal state in which a person would never die (Rom. 6:8–9).

As far as Paul was concerned, any argument that opposed bodily resurrection denied Christ's bodily resurrection. Because believers' eternal resurrections and Jesus' are of the same type, one cannot be possible and the other impossible. If people cannot be resurrected bodily, then Jesus was not resurrected. The fact of Christ's resurrection invalidated any philosophical objection to the possibility of resurrection.

15:14–15. The Corinthians' denial of the possibility of a general resurrection denied Christ's resurrection. This meant the Corinthians' position also resulted in other unacceptable denials. If there were no resurrection of bodies, then: (1) the apostles' **preaching** would be **useless**; (2) the Corinthians' own **faith** would be in vain; and (3) the apostles would be **false witnesses**.

Bodily resurrection was essential to the gospel. Without Christ's resurrection the gospel would be false. Therefore, **preaching** it and believing it would be **useless**. In addition, anyone who preached the gospel would be guilty of propagating a lie and of testifying falsely **about God**. All these implications of denying bodily resurrection would make Christianity a senseless religion. Why should a person waste his time believing in a false religion, or making himself a liar? According to Paul, it would be foolish to do so.

15:16. Paul paused in his list of implications that result from denying bodily resurrection. He did so in order to reassert that if the **dead** cannot be **raised**, then **Christ has not been raised**. This point was so important to Paul that he felt compelled to emphasize it by repetition. This break in the list of ridiculous conclusions divides the list in 15:14–15 from that in 15:17–19. The first list describes reasons it would be foolish to be a Christian if Christ were not raised; the second list describes the pain and loss that Christians would suffer.

15:17–19. Continuing his list of unacceptable conclusions drawn from denying bodily resurrection, Paul added that (4) the Corinthians' **faith** would be **futile**; (5) the Corinthians would **still** be **in** their **sins**; (6) those who had **fallen asleep** [died] **in Christ** would be **lost** forever; and (7) believers should **be pitied more than all men**.

That the Corinthians' **faith** would be **futile** duplicates Paul's point that it would be useless, but this time with a different implication—their futile faith would leave them **in their sins**. Not only would they gain no benefit from their faith, but they would still be under the curse of God's wrath. This argument probably struck home with many Corinthians. Paul had previously indicated that their radically changed lifestyles had come through the gospel. Their new lives proved that Christ must have been raised.

Likewise, if faith were in vain, then every Christian who had died would never receive an eternal benefit for having repented and believed. All who had died in Christ would never realize any part of the salvation for which they hoped; everything would have been a lie. These implications of denying bodily resurrection addressed the emotional aspect of Christian living. The gospel provides hope and comfort to those who cling to it. If the Corinthians insisted that bodily resurrection could not occur, however, they would undermine their own reasons for hope for themselves.

Further, Christians would be the most pitiful and pitiable people on earth. Modern Christians sometimes see Christian living as so beneficial that they think it would be better to live as a Christian than not, even if Christianity were false. This is true because, for many Christians, commitment to

Christ does not require much suffering. In the early church, however, believers sacrificed a great deal to follow Christ. They lost families, friends, jobs, homes, and even their lives. Thus, Paul could say that Christians would deserve great pity if their hope for resurrection proved to be false. Not only would they receive no benefit from their religion, but they would also forfeit the pleasures their brief lives on earth offered.

Ⓒ Christ Has Been Raised; Therefore, Believers Will Be Raised (15:20–28)

SUPPORTING IDEA: *Because Christ has been raised, Paul declared, the believing dead must be raised because of their relationship to Christ.*

15:20. Paul insisted that it was a fact that **Christ . . . indeed** had **been raised from the dead**, but Christ's resurrection was more than one person's triumph over death. At the very heart of Christ's resurrection was the idea that he was **the firstfruits of those who have fallen asleep.** Paul drew an analogy between Christ's resurrection and the Old Testament ritual of firstfruits. The firstfruits were the first portions of the harvest, and they were given as offerings to God (Lev. 23:15–17). The firstfruits indicated that the entire harvest was soon to follow.

In Paul's outlook, Christ's resurrection was not an isolated event. It represented the beginning of something much larger. His resurrection promised the rest of the harvest. The full harvest, of which Christ is the first sign, is the harvest of those **who have fallen asleep.**

The New Testament frequently uses the euphemism "sleep" for the death of believers to emphasize that their deaths are only temporary conditions. Christ himself had **fallen asleep** in death, but in his resurrection he left that state and entered eternal life. His entry into the "newness of life" (Rom. 6:4, NASB) was the firstfruits representing much more to come—the resurrection of all believers who have died.

15:21. Paul next explained in what sense Christ was raised as the firstfruits of all who would be raised, arguing for a symmetry in God's dealings with the human race (see also Rom. 5:12–19). In the first place, the record of Genesis makes it plain that **death came through a man.** Adam's sin was more than a personal transgression; it brought guilt and the divine judgment of death on all humanity. **Since** it was through Adam that death came, it should not be surprising that **the resurrection of the dead comes also through a man.** In many passages Paul pointed out that God considered Christ's experience on earth much more than one person's experience. What happened to him in his death and resurrection happens to all who believe in him.

15:22. Restating his previous explanation, Paul once again relied on the symmetry between Adam and Christ: **In Adam all die . . . in Christ all will be made alive.** Paul drew a parallel between Adam and Christ (**as in Adam . . . so in Christ**), but we must be careful not to misunderstand this comparison. From the rest of Paul's writings, we must conclude that the similarity between Adam and Christ is not numerical but functional. That is to say, Paul did not suggest that the number of people who receive salvation equals the number of people who suffer death. In other passages Paul made it very plain that he did not believe in universal salvation (Rom. 2:5–12; Eph. 5:6; 2 Thess. 1:6–10).

Paul's main concern in this passage was to show that Christ's resurrection was more than his own resurrection. It foretold the general resurrection of all believers. Paul did this by pointing to the theological beliefs that he and the Corinthians shared. They believed that Adam's personal life had affected everyone joined to him. In the same way, Paul argued, Christ's personal life affected everyone joined to him, everyone **in Christ.**

The expression "in Christ" appears in Paul's letters to describe the union between believers and Christ. In this verse, Paul used the expression to indicate those united to him by faith. As he put it in 15:23, those who are in Christ and receive resurrection through him are "those who belong to him." The inevitability of the general resurrection explains why Paul could describe Christ as the firstfruits. His life, death, and resurrection bring countless blessings to those who are in him—including resurrection from the dead.

15:23. Having given a theological justification for calling Christ the firstfruits, Paul continued the analogy. The term *firstfruits* suggests a certain order. Resurrection will happen **to each in his own turn.** First, **Christ** as the **firstfruits** has already been resurrected. Second, **those who belong to him**—those who have exercised saving faith in Christ—will be raised along with Christ. This second resurrection will occur **when he comes** in the second advent. Thus far, Paul had not taken the analogy of firstfruits beyond his discussion in the preceding verses. But at this point, he turned to an additional dimension of the analogy.

15:24. After Christ returns, **then the end will come.** It will be time for the final judgment and the formation of the new creation. At this time, Christ will give **over the kingdom to God the Father.** Just as the firstfruits of the Old Testament sacrificial system were symbolic of the giving over of an entire harvest to God, Christ's resurrection was symbolic of a much greater harvest to be given to God the Father—the harvest of the entire kingdom. Just as an entire harvest exceeds the firstfruits, so the harvest of the dominion given to the Father will be beyond measure.

This handing over to the Father will occur only after Christ **has destroyed all dominion, authority and power.** Elsewhere Paul used this terminology to describe both human authority (Rom. 13:1–3) and demonic powers (Eph. 1:21). In this context he had in mind the destruction of all powers that are raised against the kingdom of Christ, whether human or supernatural.

15:25. Paul had just set forth a complex scenario that pointed to Christ as the firstfruits: Christ's resurrection, then believers' resurrection, then the destruction of authorities and the deliverance of the kingdom to the Father. To explain this scenario further, Paul pointed out that Christ **must reign until he has put all his enemies under his feet.** This verse recalls Psalm 110:1. This psalm spoke of the promise of great victories given to the descendants of David. Every time a Davidic king experienced victory over an enemy, he saw this dynastic promise realized in his life. Paul applied this psalm to Christ, since Christ is the great and final son to sit on David's throne (Mark 11:10). In Christ all the promises to David's family come to full realization.

Paul focused here on reigning in victory. The New Testament explains that Christ was seated on the throne of David at the time of his resurrection and ascension (Eph. 1:20–21). God once promised that David's family would rule over the entire earth (Ps. 89:20–29), and this promise now applies to Christ. Thus, it is necessary that Christ eventually reign over everyone and everything.

15:26–27a. Of course, **the last enemy** that Christ will destroy is **death** itself. Adam introduced death into the human race (Rom. 5:12–14), but Christ has come to eliminate death. Yet, this destruction of death will take place gradually. The elimination of death is the last great work of Christ. This will occur when he raises believers to everlasting life and frees them from the power of death (Heb. 2:14–15).

How can we know death will be destroyed? Paul referred once again to Psalm 110:1, emphasizing that Christ would dominate everything. He considered it an indisputable fact that the great son of David would reign over all things, including death itself. Since Christ would reign over death, those in Christ would not be subjected to death's dominion. For this reason, the general resurrection of all believers is a certainty.

15:27b–28. Realizing that he had pushed the term *everything* to the limits, Paul qualified himself to avoid confusion. He noted that it was **clear** or obvious to those reading Psalm 110 that the term *everything* did **not include God himself,** because God the Father is the one **who put everything under Christ.** In other words, Psalm 110:1 makes it plain that God puts everything under the feet of David's son. For this reason, the Father remains superior to the Christ. As a result, when all is accomplished **the Son himself will be made subject** to the Father. In perfect harmony with the idea of Christ as the firstfruits that honor God as the one who gives harvest, Christ will remain in subjection to the Father **so that God may be all in all.**

D If There Is No Resurrection, the Christian Life Is Meaningless (15:29–34)

SUPPORTING IDEA: *Paul pointed out that it would be meaningless to live as a Christian if there were to be no resurrection.*

15:29. First, Paul raised a point that his original readers clearly understood. But this point has confounded interpreters for almost two millennia. He pointed to the absurdity of believing there would be **no resurrection** of believers in light of the practice of being **baptized for the dead. If the dead are not raised**, there is no reason for others to be **baptized for them.**

The greatest difficulty with this verse is that there are no other biblical references to anything like a baptism for the dead. Explanations for this verse are varied, and none is convincing. Perhaps the most likely explanation is that Paul identified a practice of which he did not approve. He referred to the practitioners in the third person (**people**) rather than in the first ("we") or second person ("you"), probably avoiding close association with them. If this outlook is correct, then Paul pointed out the inconsistency between this practice and the denial of the general resurrection. He asked what sense it would make for people to deny the final resurrection while practicing vicarious baptism for the dead.

15:30–32. Second, Paul appealed to the sacrifices that he and other apostles made for the sake of Christian work. He asked for some explanation for the fact that they **endanger[ed]** themselves **every hour.** Those who first bore the gospel of Christ did so at great personal risk. They were imprisoned, beaten, stoned, and murdered. Paul elaborated on his sacrifices by saying that it was as if he **die[d] every day.** To ward off the accusation of exaggeration, Paul added, **I mean that, brothers.** Paul's entire ministry involved daily danger and sacrifice. His personal loss was just as sure as the fact that he took **glory** or delight **over** the faithful Corinthian believers **in Christ Jesus** the **Lord.**

Paul next referred the Corinthians to an event that they knew from his life. He had **fought wild beasts in Ephesus.** Acts 19:1–20:1 records Paul's difficulties during his three-year stay in Ephesus. He faced serious troubles there. Although some interpreters have suggested it, Paul probably did not have to fight animals as a civil punishment. He would have been protected from such persecution because he was a Roman citizen. In all likelihood, Paul spoke figuratively by describing his persecutors as vicious beasts.

Whatever event he had in mind, Paul made it plain that he would never have endured such a trial **for merely human reasons**—without the goal of resurrection in mind. **What** would he have **gained** from that? Nothing. If it were true that **the dead are not raised**, then Paul would not have lived such a hard life. Instead, he would have subscribed to the philosophy **Let us eat and**

drink, for tomorrow we die. These words allude to Isaiah 22:13, where the prophet rebuked his listeners for not taking the warnings of divine judgment seriously. Paul said that irresponsible sensual revelry would be the only reasonable approach to life if there were no hope of resurrection.

Paul appealed to the Corinthians to consider his own life as strong evidence that the future resurrection of believers was an essential Christian belief. It is not possible to justify the sacrifices involved in living for Christ without the hope of resurrection.

15:33–34. Paul closed this portion of his discussion with a stern warning. He worried that those who denied the resurrection of the dead would corrupt sincere Corinthian believers. He reminded them of a well-known proverb from the Greek poet Menander: **Bad company corrupts good character.** The Corinthian believers associated with people who scoffed at the notion of a future resurrection, and Paul wanted them to break off these associations. These associates probably advocated Greek philosophy, not only denying the resurrection, but also influencing some Corinthians to pursue worldly wisdom.

Thus, Paul called the Corinthians to **come back to** their **senses,** to start thinking clearly about the resurrection by adopting the view he had elaborated in the preceding verses. This was no small matter. To deny the resurrection was to sin and rebel against God. Those who denied the future resurrection of believers were **sinning** and **ignorant of God.** They did not understand the basic things of the gospel revealed in Christ.

Paul was also concerned that associating with such unchristian thinkers would corrupt not only the Corinthians' doctrine but their behavior as well. In fact, it seems evident throughout this epistle that the sectarian thinking of the Corinthians, probably based in Greek thinking, became the basis for all sorts of sins, including: divisions, immorality, lawsuits, mistreatment of one another at the Lord's Supper, and abuse of spiritual gifts. Yet, the Corinthians continued to associate with these ignorant sinners. For this reason, Paul remarked that he gave these instructions **to their shame.** They should have been ashamed of accepting these false teachers and their ways.

Ⓔ The Nature of Resurrection (15:35–58)

SUPPORTING IDEA: *Paul turned to some specific issues regarding the idea of a general resurrection.*

15:35. The phrase **someone may ask** indicates that Paul had either heard about this objection or he anticipated that someone might raise it. Paul listed two specific issues: **how . . . the dead are raised;** and **what kind of body** the dead will have when **they come** back to life. Both of these questions presented the same objection in different terms. Paul saw them as cloaked objections arguing for the impossibility of a general resurrection.

These objections probably stemmed from Greek dualism, which taught that the soul is good but the body is corrupt. In this view, death allowed the soul to liberate itself from the body. Some interpreters suggest that the Corinthians understood that Christians would be resurrected in the same bodies they possessed before death, but they thought God would not perfect these bodies. For them, the resurrection presented an awful scene of reanimated, unrestored corpses. Paul's opponents apparently thought they had pointed out the odious nature of Paul's position.

15:36. As a result, Paul responded quite harshly, **How foolish!** Literally, he called his hypothetical opponent a "fool." He considered these objections foolish because they disregarded God's incomparable abilities.

To demonstrate how foolish his opponents were, Paul appealed to a regular natural occurrence that demonstrated the future resurrection of believers. Responding to the first objection, "How are the dead raised?" (15:35), Paul answered that a seed that is sown **does not come to life unless it dies.** Before a seed can grow into a tree or a plant, it must be buried as if it were dead. The ability of a seed to overcome its burial should be reason enough for everyone to believe that human beings may be resurrected by God's supernatural power.

15:37–38a. Second, Paul answered the objection, "With what kind of body will they come?" (15:35). Again, the apostle used the example of a normal seed. When people plant seeds, they **do not plant the body that will be.** In other words, a seed does not bear the shape and size of the full-grown plant. In fact, a seed does not look anything like the plant into which it grows. Instead, **God gives it a body as he has determined.** As God causes the dead seed to come to life as a plant, he also shapes it into the appropriate form. In his sovereignty, God chooses what each plant will look like.

In the resurrection, Paul said in effect, believers will have the kind of body that God has determined they will have. Resurrected bodies will be different from mortal bodies, just as a seed differs from the plant into which it grows. Though Paul did not answer the immediate question, "What kind of body," he did answer the objection that God could not raise the dead. God displays his sovereign ability and desire to raise the dead each time he grows a seed into a plant.

15:38b–41. To prove further that God is capable of giving resurrected bodies to followers of Christ, Paul listed various natural objects by which God shows his ability to create different types of bodies. Paul demonstrated this first by pointing out that **each kind of seed** receives from God **its own body.** He pressed the point by noting that **all flesh is not the same.** The bodies of **men, animals, birds, fish, heavenly bodies, earthly bodies, the sun,**

the moon, and the stars all differ from one another. God does not have any problem coming up with shapes, sizes, and substances for each item in his universe. For this reason, believers should not worry that the lack of an appropriate body type will prevent the resurrection of believers. God is able to overcome this problem.

15:42–44a. Paul concluded that just as it is with the varieties of bodies that God has made in the universe, so will it be with the resurrection of the dead. He then mentioned four differences that believers may anticipate between their present mortal bodies and those they will receive at the resurrection. First, mortal bodies are perishable, but resurrected bodies will be imperishable. Mortal bodies are subject to illness and death, but resurrected bodies will have no such difficulties.

Second, mortal bodies carry dishonor, but resurrected bodies carry glory. Since Adam's fall into sin, all human beings have been born into a dishonorable existence wherein sin corrupts even their bodies (cf. Rom. 7:17–25). Resurrected bodies, however, will be glorious and splendid.

Third, mortal bodies suffer weakness, but resurrected bodies will be filled with power. Human beings originally received the power and honor of dominion over creation (Gen. 1:26–28). Through sin, however, man and the rest of creation were drawn apart (Rom. 8:20–23). In the resurrection, however, believers will reign with Christ in great power over his creation (2 Tim. 2:12).

Fourth, mortal bodies are natural, but resurrected bodies will be spiritual. These terms are difficult to define precisely, but there is no justification for believing that Paul meant to contrast the material and immaterial or the physical and nonphysical. Christ's appearances in his resurrected body demonstrated that he continued to be physical and material, but this physicality had special characteristics. For example, he was able to appear suddenly (Luke 24:36), even in rooms with locked doors (John 20:19,26), and to vanish just as quickly (Luke 24:31). At the same time, however, he was able to break bread (Luke 24:30), to eat fish (Luke 24:42–43), and to cook and distribute food (John 21:9,13). Moreover, people were able to touch him (John 20:27).

It is best to take the term *spiritual* not as "immaterial," but as a reference to the Holy Spirit. In other words, believers' resurrected bodies will be spiritual because they will be renewed by the Holy Spirit. Christ himself was raised by the Spirit (Rom. 8:11), and in the same way the bodies of believers will be resurrected by the power of the Spirit.

15:44b–49. To make his position perfectly clear, Paul stated that the existence of a natural (ordinary) body necessitates the existence of a spiritual (renewed by the Holy Spirit) body. He supported this belief with five observations about Adam written in the Scriptures. From these five observations Paul drew five conclusions about Christ. Assuming the truthfulness of his earlier comparison between Adam and Christ, he argued from the lesser to the greater that if something were true of Adam, then something greater must be true of Christ.

First, Paul paraphrased Genesis 2:7, which states that **Adam became a living being.** Then, turning to **the last Adam,** he asserted that Christ did not merely become a **living being.** In his resurrection Christ became something much greater than a living being. He became **a life-giving spirit.** In other words, as much as Adam was a wondrous creature able to transmit life to his offspring, he did not compare to the wonderful Christ, who gives eternal life to all who trust in him.

Second, Paul noted that the order of the biblical account was important. Historically, the **natural** body for the human race came before **the spiritual** body given by Christ. This supports Paul's earlier argument that God will provide a body renewed by the Spirit in the resurrection of believers.

Third, Adam was **of the dust of the earth,** but Christ is **from heaven.** Adam was an ordinary human being, but Christ exceeds Adam's glory because Christ came from heaven (John 6:38). Fourth, Paul argued that Scripture indicates that those who are **of the earth** (i.e., Adam's descendants) are like **the earthly man** (i.e., Adam). They inherit his natural physical nature. Yet, **those who are of heaven** (i.e., born from above in regeneration) become like **the man from heaven** (i.e., Christ). **From heaven** (*epouranios*) does not refer to Christ's location of origin, or even to his current location, but to his nature. The regenerate inherit Christ's spiritual nature.

Fifth, Paul pointed out that the biblical record teaches that all people bear **the likeness of the earthly man.** The Old Testament not only teaches that human beings are the image of God, but also that they are the images of their human ancestors, including Adam (Gen. 5:3). So Paul concluded it must be true that Christians **bear the likeness of the man from heaven.** Elsewhere, Paul described the ultimate state of salvation as being "conformed to the likeness of [God's] Son" (Rom. 8:29). To **bear the likeness** of Christ is to reach the zenith of human existence.

15:50. Paul concluded that **flesh and blood, the perishable** physical bodies that people receive from Adam, cannot **inherit the kingdom of God** which is **imperishable.** God designed something much greater to take place in Christ. This greater thing is the resurrection of the bodies of every believer at the return of Christ. Moreover, Paul asserted that those bodies inherited from Adam **cannot inherit the kingdom of God.** Unless a person receives a resurrected body of a different nature, he or she cannot receive the full blessings of the gospel. Paul appealed to the Corinthians as **brothers** to indicate the intensity with which he wanted them to accept his conclusion.

15:51–52. Continuing with the idea that only those with resurrected bodies can inherit the kingdom of God, Paul assured the Corinthians that believers do not have to die to inherit the kingdom. He mentioned this probably because they were concerned over the imminent return of Christ. The natural Corinthian worry over Paul's prior arguments would have been, "But what if Christ comes back before I die? If I haven't died, how can I be raised in a heavenly body and thereby inherit the kingdom of God?"

Paul assured his brothers and sisters that they would **not all sleep** (i.e., die), but they would **all be changed—in a flash, in the twinkling of an eye, at the last trumpet**. Although Paul did not mention Christ's return here, **the last trumpet** clearly indicates this event, as does the raising of **the dead**. In 15:22–23 Paul had made it clear that the general resurrection would occur at Christ's return. Those believers who are still alive at the time of Christ's return will be **changed** instantly. Without passing through death, they will receive heavenly, spiritual, **imperishable** bodies.

15:53–54a. These verses look back to the statements of 15:50 that "flesh and blood cannot inherit the kingdom of God," and "the perishable" cannot "inherit the imperishable." Because the **perishable**, corruptible, **mortal** bodies that believers possess according to their nature in Adam cannot inherit the kingdom of God and live in perfection forever, they must be changed. Believers must have imperishable and immortal bodies to carry into eternity. While Paul did not say exactly what composition these bodies would have, he did indicate they would be qualitatively different. They would not be subject to death.

15:54b–55. Paul looked forward in these verses to the fulfillment of two Old Testament prophecies at the general resurrection: **Death has been swallowed up in victory** (see Isa. 25:8); and **Where, O death, is your victory? Where, O death, is your sting?** (see Hos. 13:14). Though he did not quote either of these texts precisely, these were unmistakably his references. These quotes may represent Paul's own rendering of these verses from the Hebrew. Of course, his point is clear: because believers' resurrected bodies will be immortal and imperishable, death will never affect them. Death will not be able to destroy them or to plague them. Instead, believers will live eternally, free from the worry of physical deterioration and death.

Paul issued these taunts to death in the present tense. Although the general resurrection had yet to occur, Paul's confident hope in Christ to bring about the resurrection removed all fear of death. Further, because he understood believers' resurrections to be an outworking of Christ's own resurrection, and because Christ's resurrection had taken place, he saw death already in the process of being defeated.

15:56. Paul introduced some new ideas into the argument at hand and the letter as a whole. First, he asserted that **death** results from **sin**. Disease, decay, violence, and other means may cause death, but these secondary causes would not exist or have **power** without sin as their source.

Second, he declared that **sin** inflicts its **sting of death** through **the law**. With the first assertion, Paul began to bring the argument to its conclusion by returning to the issue with which he had begun: the gospel. The resurrection is essential to the gospel that saves believers from their sin. If there is no resurrection, neither is sin defeated. The emergence of the second theme regarding the law, however, seems to have no real antecedent in this letter. It may be that Paul brought in this concept simply because the verse itself was a known slogan. Alternately, or perhaps concurrently, Paul may have associated **the law** with **sin** and **death** so closely that he thought of sin working through the law when he thought of death working through sin.

15:57. This brief doxology of **thanks** to God solidifies the gospel allusion in the preceding verse. Of course, the **victory** of which Paul spoke was the resurrection of believers, not forgiveness. The **victory** comes through **Jesus Christ** not because he died, but because he was raised from the dead. Because believers are united to Christ, they must be resurrected like him.

15:58. In concluding this argument, Paul expressed his concern and love for the Corinthians by calling them his **dear brothers**. This was to remind them that love had motivated him to criticize their thinking so severely in the preceding argument. He had been concerned that they were abandoning the gospel.

Thus, Paul exhorted them to **stand firm**, to hold firmly to the word he had preached to them, to guard their belief in the gospel and in the resurrection of believers. He exhorted the true believers to **let nothing move** them because those who denied the resurrection undermined the gospel itself. If the Corinthians let themselves be dragged away by false teaching, they would deny their only hope for salvation. No matter how persuasive the opposing arguments sounded, the Corinthians were to remember the truth of Christ's resurrection, their union with Christ, and their future resurrection.

Paul also exhorted them to **give** themselves **fully to the work of the Lord**, knowing that their **labor in the Lord** was **not in vain**. While this encouragement may pertain to godly works in general, it is tempting to see it as a more direct command to minister the gospel. The language here closely approximates Paul's question in 9:1: "Are you not the result of my work in the Lord?" There, "work in the Lord" clearly refers to the work of preaching and ministering the gospel.

By telling his **brothers** that their **labor in the Lord** was **not in vain**, Paul alluded once more to the opening verses of this chapter, encouraging the Corinthians that they had not believed the gospel in vain and did not hope in it vainly. With these words his argument came full circle, affirming the Corinthians' salvation on the condition that they believed the gospel and stood firm in it.

> **MAIN IDEA REVIEW:** *Having dealt with a number of problems related to worship in the church at Corinth, Paul turned to a doctrinal controversy over resurrection. Both Gentile and Jewish opponents could have influenced the believers at Corinth to deny the doctrine of resurrection.*

III. CONCLUSION

Raised with Him

In this chapter Paul defended the Christian doctrine of the resurrection of the body. His defense reached into the very heart of the gospel of Christ. We are saved by a risen Lord so that we may be raised with him.

PRINCIPLES

- Our bodies are important parts of us, not just shells that we discard at death.
- We will spend eternity in resurrected bodies.
- Our resurrected bodies will be perfect, not subject to death, disease, or weakness.

APPLICATIONS

- We should see death as unnatural and as an enemy, not just as another phase of life.
- We should be courageous in death, knowing that Christ has conquered death.
- We should look forward to receiving our perfect, resurrected bodies as the time when our salvation will be completed.

IV. LIFE APPLICATION

"Who Did He Think Was in the Casket?"

A few years ago a dear friend of mine died in his twenties of sickle-cell anemia. I remember that the minister who preached the funeral told us not to worry about my friend. Pointing to the open casket, the minister told us that the body we saw was not my friend, that he had gone to be with the Lord. After the service, my pastor remarked to me, "You know, I don't understand . . . Who did he think was in the casket? When I looked in the casket, I saw my friend. I saw the ravages of sin. I saw the work of the last enemy death. I saw a wrong that Jesus died and was raised to set right."

Of course, he did not mean that my friend was not enjoying the immediate presence of the Lord. His point was that our bodies are important parts of us. They are not just shells that we discard at death. Our bodies are essential parts of us. Being separated from them is a terrible tragedy that Christ will rectify in the resurrection. Further, although God will change our bodies in the resurrection, continuity exists between the bodies we leave in our caskets and the bodies we will have in the resurrection. They are in fact the same bodies—only better.

As believers we can learn many things from this chapter. It teaches us more about the resurrection that awaits believers than any other chapter of Scripture. We know that there is nothing inherently evil about our flesh and that we are created in the image of God. Even so, compared to the glorious resurrected bodies we will receive, our earthly, physical bodies are dishonorable and weak. In this life many of us suffer illness and handicaps, and all of us grow old. When we age, our bodies lose strength; they become more susceptible to injury and disease. Eventually we deteriorate to the point where our bodies can no longer sustain life. Sin wreaks these ravaging effects on our bodies. Since we are sinful, fallen creatures, there is nothing we can do to avoid this.

The gospel, however, promises that in the resurrection our bodies will be renewed, remade by the Holy Spirit, so that we will never suffer any weakness or sickness and we will never die. For eternity we will enjoy life in bodies that never grow old—bodies that are far more amazing, powerful, and glorious than the ones we have now.

The promise that we will receive resurrected bodies is an important part of the gospel. To deny our resurrection is to deny Christ's resurrection and our union with him. The first of these is deadly because it constitutes a denial of the gospel itself. The second of these is not quite as deadly, but it makes for a terrible misunderstanding of salvation and life in Christ. This appears to have been the problem in Corinth that spawned many of their divisions and much of their mistreatment of one another.

From the Corinthians' errors we should learn to defend Christ's resurrection at all costs and to remember our unity with him as a guiding principle for our behavior. If we fail to do the first, we may be led into deadly error. If we fail to do the second, we may mistreat the church as badly as the Corinthians did. This means that we also need to pay attention to the company we keep.

Of course, Paul's statement that bad company corrupts good morals can apply to many areas of life, but we should not lose sight of his main point: we should avoid the company of those who would corrupt our faith in the resurrection. For Paul, belief in the resurrection was a matter of morals. To fail to believe was to sin. If it was so for Paul, then it is so for God, and we should reckon our own lives accordingly.

V. PRAYER

Lord Jesus, we long for the day when we will be free of these bodies of death. We yearn for the day when we are resurrected and receive new bodies. What a glorious time that will be! Amen.

VI. DEEPER DISCOVERIES

A. Baptized for the Dead (15:29)

If one reads the Greek text naturally, the most obvious meaning of this phrase is that some Corinthians were getting baptized on behalf of others. But this reading raises significant theological questions. The fact that the Bible refers to this practice only here also complicates the matter, as does Paul's noncritical stance toward it. As a result, many interpreters understand this verse to mean something other than its apparent surface meaning. The suggested solutions fall into several broad categories.

The first solution redefines "baptized" (*baptizo*) so that it does not identify the Christian rite of water baptism, but metaphorically represents some other experience such as martyrdom or a life of sacrifice (cf. Luke 12:50). Earlier in this epistle, Paul did use "baptized" metaphorically (10:2), so it is not impossible that the Corinthians may have understood the word metaphorically at times.

The second solution resolves the problem by understanding "for" (*huper*) to mean something other than "in place of" or "on behalf of." For example, some have taken *huper* to mean "above," suggesting that some Christians were being baptized while standing over graves. A third approach is to redefine "the dead" (*ton nekron*) so that it does not refer to many who have died. Although *ton nekron* literally means "the corpses," some have taken it to mean "the bodies that will soon be dead," and others have taken it to refer to those aligned with Christ who had died.

A third solution falls under both the second and third categories, redefining both *huper* and *ton nekron* by arguing that Paul meant "regarding death" or "with reference to death."

The fourth solution changes the usual punctuation or syntax, so that "for the dead" modifies "do" rather than "baptized," or so that "for the dead" is Paul's rhetorical response to the question, "Why are people baptized?"

A different type of solution argues that the Corinthians engaged in a practice of vicarious baptism intended to benefit the dead, but that neither

Paul nor the church endorsed this practice. This view suggests that, while the practice did not bring the benefits the Corinthians thought it conveyed, the practice was not harmful and thus did not draw Paul's criticism. This view appeals in part to the fact that Paul referred to the practitioners of this rite as "they" rather than as "we" or "you." If this had been a rite he endorsed, he probably would have aligned himself with it more closely.

In any case, this verse certainly does not teach the Mormon view of baptism for the dead, by which a living person may undergo a substitutionary baptism—the benefits of which accrue to a deceased person. If this had been the Corinthians' position, Paul certainly would have refuted it vigorously.

B. Trumpet (15:52)

In the Old Testament, the trumpet frequently issued commands in battle, such as calls to assemble for war or to attack (Josh. 6:4–5; Jer. 4:19). Paul had already referred to this concept in 14:8. The trumpet also announced the anointing of kings (1 Kgs. 1:34,39), and the coming of the Lord (Exod. 19:16,19). All of these coalesce in the idea of the day of the Lord that Paul had mentioned earlier in this letter. On the day of the Lord, God will come to earth as a conquering warrior king, saving his people and defeating all his enemies. In fact, the prophets frequently spoke of a trumpet in conjunction with the day of the Lord (Joel 2:1; Zech. 9:14), and the New Testament writers echoed this idea (1 Thess. 4:16).

VII. TEACHING OUTLINE

A. INTRODUCTION

1. Lead Story: "One Thing I Know for Sure"
2. Context: Some people in the Corinthian church denied the future resurrection of believers. They thought the doctrine of the resurrection taught a morbid reanimation of corrupted corpses. By denying the resurrection of believers, they denied essential elements of the gospel: Christ's resurrection and the salvation of whole persons.
3. Transition: Many modern churches have fallen into the Corinthian error on this point. Believers must preserve the doctrine of the resurrection. We should not allow other people's poor doctrine to destroy our great hope for salvation. As Paul encouraged, we should take comfort from this doctrine and long for the day when we realize the salvation of our bodies as well as our souls.

B. COMMENTARY

1. The Reality of Christ's Resurrection (15:1–11)

a. The importance of holding to the resurrection (15:1–2)

b. The content of the resurrection (15:3–4)

c. Witnesses to the resurrection (15:5–8)

d. The preaching of the resurrection (15:9–11)

2. The Hope of Believers' Resurrection (15:12–19)

a. If there is no resurrection, then Christ has not been raised (15:12–19)

b. Preaching and faith are useless (15:14,17)

c. Christianity is a lie (15:15–16)

d. There is no hope for believers (15:18–19)

3. Christ Has Been Raised; Therefore, Believers Will Be Raised (15:20–28)

4. If There Is No Resurrection, the Christian Life Is Meaningless (15:29–34)

5. The Nature of Resurrection (15:35–58)

a. Objections to the resurrection (15:35)

b. Refutations of the objections (15:36–41)

c. Contrasts between mortal bodies and resurrected bodies (15:42–44a)

d. Jesus as the last Adam (15:44b–49)

e. Inheriting the kingdom of God (15:50–54a)

f. Christ's victory over death (15:54b–57)

g. Implication for Christian living: stand firm (15:58)

C. CONCLUSION: "WHO DID HE THINK WAS IN THE CASKET?"

VIII. ISSUES FOR DISCUSSION

1. Did Paul assume that most of the Corinthians had or had not believed the gospel? What was the gospel message Paul preached?

2. Did Paul try to prove Christ's resurrection, or did he assume that his readers accepted it? In light of this, why do you think Paul wrote this chapter?

3. What things would be true if Christ had not been raised from the dead? Do you believe Christ has been raised from the dead? Does your church teach that Christ has been raised from the dead?

4. Why is bodily resurrection important? What's wrong with the idea that believers will not have bodies in eternity? If you do not think that having a resurrected body is exciting or important, why do you think this? Why does Paul not think this?

1 Corinthians 16:1–24

Final Instructions and Closure

Quote

"*Saints* by profession are bound to maintain an holy fellowship and communion in the worship of God, and in performing such other spiritual services as tend to their mutual edification; as also in relieving each other in outward things, according to their several abilities and necessities. Which communion, as God offereth opportunity, is to be extended unto all those who, in every place, call upon the name of the Lord Jesus."

Westminster Confession of Faith

1 Corinthians 16:1–24

 IN A NUTSHELL

Paul wrapped up this letter to the Corinthians by touching on several practical matters. He also expressed his hopes for the Corinthians' continuing faithfulness to Christ.

Final Instructions
and Closure

I. INTRODUCTION

"Don't Forget . . . and Be Sure to Remember"

*H*ave you ever been about to leave a friend or loved one and found your mind racing with things to say. It often happens as you pull out of the driveway. "Don't forget . . . and remember . . . Oh yeah, be sure to . . ." Sometimes it is a hard simply to say good-bye.

That is the way Paul acted in this chapter. As he came to the end of this epistle, he had many more things to say. So he launched into some rapid-fire instructions.

II. COMMENTARY

Final Instructions and Closure

MAIN IDEA: *Having dealt with a number of crucial doctrinal and practical issues in this epistle, Paul came to some final matters. This last chapter divides into three main parts: instructions on collections, general exhortations, and final greetings.*

A Instructions on Collections (16:1–4)

SUPPORTING IDEA: *Because of a famine in Judea, churches in other areas took up collections to meet the needs of Judean Christians. Corinth was among those contributing churches. Paul took this opportunity to guide their famine relief mobilization.*

16:1. Paul began this section with a phrase he had used before: **Now about** (*peri de*). This phrase indicates that Paul replied to questions raised in a letter that the Corinthians had sent to him. They had asked about the proper procedures for **the collection for God's people** in Jerusalem.

The apostle was very practical here. He first mentioned that he had given similar directions to **the Galatian churches.** The Corinthians were not to bear a unique burden as they helped those suffering in Jerusalem. By this time famines had struck Judea, and terrible economic conditions followed. The church survived the first famine (about A.D. 46–47), having been warned of its approach by Agabus (Acts 11:28), but the next famine took its toll. As a result, Paul called on Gentile churches to remember their spiritual indebtedness to believers in Jerusalem (cf. Rom. 15:26–27).

Paul and Barnabas delivered relief to believers in Judea during the first famine (Acts 11:29–30), and Paul evidently used this method for the latter famines as well. Paul's gospel preaching often overshadowed this dimension of his ministry, but relief of the poor was an important part of his and the church's work (cf. Gal. 2:10). The church is obligated to care for poor brothers and sisters throughout the world.

16:2. Paul suggested a simple method for gathering funds. First, the Corinthians were to take a collection **on the first day of every week.** Paul mentioned the **first day** because it was the day on which early Christians gathered for worship and fellowship. This seems to have been the widespread practice of the church (Acts 20:7). Many interpreters have also drawn a connection between the **first day** and "the Lord's Day" (Rev. 1:10). This practice continues to this day as most Christians assemble for worship on the first day of each week.

Paul desired that the Corinthians offer money for the poor as a regular part of their corporate worship. Following the example of the early church, Christians throughout the centuries have included collecting alms for the poor as a regular part of their worship.

Second, Paul insisted that **each one** contribute. The apostle expected every Christian in Corinth to give to the collection. Yet, each person was not to give a specific amount, but an amount **in keeping with his income.** Paul required proportional giving. He did not state any particular amount to be given, nor did he indicate a specific percentage. The Old Testament practice of tithing (Num. 18:21–28; Mal. 3:8–10) probably lay behind the apostle's words as a basic guide. Even in the Old Testament, believers were to give according to their means rather than according to a flat rate. A similar practice should take place in the Christian church as well. Elsewhere, Paul also insisted that a heart of cheer and gladness should accompany Christian giving. To give grudgingly is not to fulfill the believer's obligation to give.

Third, the church was to be involved in **saving . . . up** the collection. Much like the storehouses of the Old Testament temple (Mal. 3:10), collections were to be taken up by the living temple of the New Testament. But the storing of these funds was for a specific purpose. When Paul came he did not want to be involved in gathering money himself. He wanted **no collections** when he arrived. Instead, he wanted to receive the money already gathered so that it could be taken quickly to Jerusalem.

16:3. Fourth, Paul was not about to assume the responsibility of transporting this money himself. He showed great practical wisdom in at least two ways. First, he knew that many accusations and temptations would come his way if he took the money himself. So he said he would **give letters of intro-**

duction to the men the Corinthians approve[d]. Paul wanted other people to carry the money. Such a courier is mentioned in 2 Corinthians 8:18–19. Paul also planned to provide letters of recommendation so the believers in Jerusalem would know it was safe to receive money from the couriers. Similar letters of recommendation are mentioned in several passages (Acts 9:2; Rom. 16:1).

Beyond this, Paul himself did not appoint people to carry the money because he wanted the Corinthians to approve of a set of couriers. The Corinthians were to choose people whom they trusted and to send their collected money through their hands. Paul was not so foolish as to insist on his own choices. He knew that trust was important in this process. Rather than assert his authority, he gave the Corinthians the responsibility of choosing their representatives. The democratic spirit of the early church is evident in this action.

16:4. Finally, Paul added that the couriers could accompany him to Jerusalem if such action appeared to be advisable when it came time to transport the collection. Paul could not anticipate the circumstances they might face upon his arrival in Corinth. So he left the matter open-ended. Once again, Paul demonstrated great practical wisdom.

🅑 General Exhortations (16:5–18)

SUPPORTING IDEA: *Paul touched briefly on a number of matters that were important to him: his own travels, Timothy, Apollos, and Stephanas.*

16:5. Paul began this section with some reflections on his travel plans. He mentioned his hope that after going through Macedonia he would be able to come to the Corinthians. These were not immediate plans but more distant plans, since for the time being he planned to remain in Ephesus.

As he mentioned in 1 Corinthians 4:18–21, Paul worried that he might meet with resistance during his visit to Corinth. He may have written 1 Corinthians in part to clear up the Corinthians' problems before his arrival so his visit would not be tumultuous. Interpreters generally agree that Paul wrote 1 Corinthians from Ephesus on the outbound leg of his third missionary journey, probably around A.D. 55 near the end of his stay in Ephesus.

The Book of Acts reveals that Paul wanted to travel from Ephesus to Jerusalem after going through Macedonia and Achaia (Acts 19:21). Corinth was located in the Roman province of Achaia. These plans may reflect Paul's intentions as stated in 1 Corinthians, since Acts 19:22 records also that Paul planned to stay in Asia (Ephesus?) a little longer, and that he dispatched Timothy and Erastus to Macedonia. Corinth was not in Macedonia, but in Achaia (immediately south of Macedonia). Thus, Timothy's trip to Macedonia made it possible that he might also visit Corinth. This compares favorably with Paul's statement, "If Timothy comes" (16:10). Paul did later travel through Macedonia into Greece, and thus perhaps to Corinth, but this trip probably took place after he wrote 2 Corinthians.

16:6. Paul also shared his need with the Corinthians. He wanted to spend **the winter** with them, allowing them to help him on his journey. The phrase **help me on my journey** translates the idea of the Greek word *propempo*, a technical term for providing aid to travelers in order to ensure safety and success. *Propempo* included provision of food, clothing, money, and traveling companions.

Paul had previously refused payment while laboring in Corinth, and this refusal had been the source of dissension among them. It is likely that Paul's detractors used his refusal to challenge his apostleship. His statement in this verse may represent a policy change toward the Corinthians, perhaps to conciliate them. Since his apostleship no longer should have been at issue, Paul welcomed their help as a practical aid to his missionary work.

16:7. Paul made certain that the Corinthians knew he had not delayed his visit because he was indifferent to their needs. On the contrary, he was waiting until he could **spend some time with** them. Of course, he qualified his plans with the recognition that he would do so only **if the Lord permit[ed]**.

16:8–9. Instead of rushing to Corinth, Paul felt it right to **stay on at Ephesus until Pentecost.** His reasoning provides a valuable lesson for those seeking to determine the will of God in a ministry situation. Paul wanted to remain in Ephesus temporarily **because a great door for effective work** had **opened** for him. In other words, Paul saw that his efforts in Ephesus were succeeding. He recognized his success as an indication that he should continue to work in Ephesus.

Beyond this, Paul also saw resistance from the world as an indication that he should stay for a while. From his point of view, believers involved in godly ministry will suffer persecution from the world (2 Tim. 3:12). Jesus taught this as well (John 15:18–20). So Paul stayed in Ephesus because there were **many who oppose[d]** him. In this, the apostle demonstrated great sensitivity to the Holy Spirit's work. He also showed himself to be flexible, ready to change his plans as the Lord directed him.

16:10. The apostle's next general remarks concerned his student and friend **Timothy.** Paul had already mentioned Timothy in 4:17. This Timothy was the same pastor and missionary to whom Paul wrote 1 and 2 Timothy. Although the precise timing is not certain, Paul did send Timothy to visit the church at Corinth (Acts 19:22).

16:11. Paul apparently feared that some within the Corinthian church might not welcome Timothy. He ordered the church to make sure that Timothy had "nothing to fear" (16:10), and to **accept him**. Some interpreters suggest Timothy's youth caused some difficulties (1 Tim. 4:12). His close association with Paul may also have biased Paul's opponents against him. Timothy was a shy person (2 Tim. 1:7), and probably was in bad health (1 Tim. 5:23). Still, Paul insisted that Timothy was doing "the work of the Lord" (16:10), and that he should be treated well.

Paul also encouraged the church to **send him on his way in peace**. Paul must have feared that some people in the Corinthian church might fail to welcome Timothy and even try to hinder his ministerial travels. For this reason, Paul added that he was **expecting him along with the brothers**.

It is difficult to know which traveling **brothers** Paul had in mind here. He expressed his respect and love for these travelers by calling them **brothers**. According to Luke, Timothy traveled with Erastus (Acts 19:22), and Paul mentioned Timothy in the company of others as well (Rom. 16:21–23). Paul may have been referring to these people or to Stephanas, Fortunatus, and Achaicus, or even to people otherwise unmentioned and unknown. In any case, Paul expected Timothy to return to him before his own departure for Corinth.

16:12. Paul's third set of general remarks began with the expression **now about**. This is the same phrase (*peri de*) that Paul used throughout this epistle to introduce his responses to specific matters raised in the Corinthians' letter to him. Paul's response concerned their mutual **brother Apollos**.

Apollos was well known in the early church for his eloquent speech (Acts 18:24–28). Paul knew Apollos to be a teacher who had watered the church that Paul himself had planted in Corinth. Some of Apollos's friends in the Corinthian church were so loyal to Apollos above all else that Paul rebuked them.

This passage does not mention what the Corinthians had asked about Apollos. Perhaps some had appealed to Paul to permit Apollos to pastor the church. Paul responded positively, in spite of the trouble caused by those who were overly loyal to Apollos, referring to him as a **brother**. Paul had even **strongly urged** Apollos to go to Corinth. He was confident that Apollos shared his views about the divisions in Corinth, and he recognized that Apollos was not the source of these divisions. Apollos was also to travel **with the brothers**. Once again, it is difficult to know precisely who these **brothers** were.

To forestall any misunderstandings, Paul stated expressly that, against Paul's urging, Apollos had been **quite unwilling to go**. Yet, Paul assured the Corinthians that Apollos would go to Corinth when he had **the opportunity**. Paul's strong urging of Apollos demonstrates that Paul understood the importance of godly church leadership.

16:13. From a logical point of view, this verse stands without much connection to its context. Paul appeared about to close the section with some final exhortations. But he decided to say more in 16:14–18. Such non-sequiturs appear in Paul's epistles from time to time (Rom. 16:1,17).

As a proleptic ending to this section, 16:13 gave five central Christian exhortations. First, Paul told the Corinthians to **be on . . . guard.** In the New Testament, this terminology frequently describes the expectation of Christ's return (Mark 13:35; 1 Thess. 5:6). Paul may have wanted the Corinthians to remain expectant of Christ's second coming. Looking vigilantly for the return of Christ implies a readiness that includes a lifestyle of holiness and service to Christ. Those who disbelieve give up hope of the return of Christ, but those who believe keep their eyes fixed on his return and live with that end in mind. On the other hand, Luke quoted Paul as using this language to exhort the Ephesian elders to guard against false teachers (Acts 20:31), and Paul himself used it to encourage alertness in prayer (Col. 4:2).

Second, Paul encouraged the Corinthians to **stand firm in the faith.** Paul frequently used this terminology to indicate the constancy with which believers should hold their commitments in the face of adversity and strife (Phil. 1:27; 4:1; 2 Thess. 2:15). The early church faced many challenges that tested believers' faithfulness to Christ. So Paul encouraged the Corinthians to persevere in their faith.

The third and fourth exhortations are closely related. Paul told the Corinthians to **be men of courage** and to **be strong.** These expressions derive from several Old Testament passages in which people were encouraged to be strong and courageous as they faced opposition (Josh. 1:6–7; 2 Sam. 10:12). God calls Christians to a way of life that incites opposition from the world. He calls his people to enter a spiritual war in which opponents seek believers' destruction and fight against believers' goals. In this hostile world, it is essential that followers of Christ be courageous and strong. Christians can do this in the face of strong opposition because their victory is sure in Christ, who has already overcome the world (John 16:33).

16:14. Fifth, Paul wanted the Corinthians to remember the importance of a theme that he had emphasized many times in this epistle: **love.** He wanted them always to show **love** in **everything.** This reminder was very important for a church riddled with strife. Paul had exalted love as the highest ideal in this epistle. He reiterated this ideal so the Corinthians would not forget it. Love for God and neighbor was to motivate and govern everything they did.

16:15. These five exhortations would have served as a well-formed ending for this section of the epistle, but apparently the mention of "love" in 16:14 brought to mind several other issues that Paul thought he should mention. Thus, he urged the church to respect the leadership of particular men.

Paul appealed to the Corinthians one last time as **brothers** because he wanted them to listen to what he had to say.

Paul first commended the **household of Stephanas**. They were among the earliest Christian converts **in Achaia**. Paul literally called them the "first-fruits." The term *firstfruits* derives from the ceremonies of the Old Testament in which the first portion of a harvest was given to God as a representation of the entire harvest to follow (Deut. 26:1–11). Paul used this metaphor to indicate not only that Stephanas and his household were the first converts, but also that they were organically united with all who were converted after them. Stephanas and all the Corinthian converts were one in Christ. Beyond this, the household of Stephanas had been **devoted . . . to the service of the saints**. The Corinthians and other believers had benefited from the faithful work of Stephanas and his family. The Corinthians owed them a great spiritual debt.

16:16. For this reason, Paul urged his readers **to submit to such as these**. Stephanas was only one of many believers who had served the church faithfully. So Paul exhorted the Corinthians to show gratitude by submitting to **everyone who join[ed] in the work and labor[ed] at it**. Leadership in the church is a difficult responsibility. Those who lead are the lowest servants of all. Their long hours of toil and sacrifice often go unrecognized. For this reason, Paul and other New Testament writers exhorted believers to encourage their leaders by honoring them (Heb. 13:17; 1 Pet. 5:5).

16:17–18. Paul added one more element to his discussion about Stephanas and his company. In 1:11 Paul had reported that some members of Chloe's household had brought informal reports about the Corinthian church. Paul's belief in the validity of these reports spurred his negative comments from time to time in this epistle. Nevertheless, this epistle also contains many words of encouragement. These positive encouragements may have come from the letter that Stephanas and his company delivered to Paul. Their report seems to have been a more complete picture. Paul **was glad** when they came **because they . . . supplied what was lacking from** the Corinthian congregation. The problems at Corinth troubled the apostle, and he grieved for the church's difficulties. Yet, the company of leaders encouraged Paul about the church in Corinth. They had **refreshed** Paul just as they encouraged the church in Corinth with positive words.

As a result, these **men deserve[d] recognition**. From Paul's special interest in the treatment of these men, it would seem that he feared the church would not receive them well. This worry may have been rooted in the church's divisions, and in Stephanas's association with Paul himself. The apostle encouraged the congregation to appreciate the ministries of these leaders. Leaders in the church can become bitter and negative because they deal constantly with problems. It is rare and precious when leaders can keep their eyes fixed on the positive work of God in the church. Paul was encouraged, and he wanted the Corinthian congregation to be encouraged as well.

C Final Greetings (16:19–24)

SUPPORTING IDEA: *Paul finally brought this letter to a close, including elements typical of his closings—greetings, blessings, and a brief note written in his own hand.*

16:19–20a. Paul mentioned a number of Christians who sent greetings to the Corinthian church in order to remind these believers that they did not stand alone against the world. Many other believers stood united with the Christians at Corinth.

First, the **churches in the province of Asia** sent **greetings**. "Asia" referred to the Roman province of Asia, which occupied the western portion of modern Turkey, including Ephesus, from which Paul wrote this letter. Paul had ministered throughout Asia. He and his disciples had established churches in Ephesus, Colosse, Laodicia, and Hierapolis.

Second, he mentioned **Aquila and Priscilla**, who also greeted the Corinthians. **Aquila** was a Jew who had lived in Rome with his wife **Priscilla**, but both had been evicted from Rome by Emperor Claudius around A.D. 49 (Acts 18:2–3). They provided lodging for Paul during his visit in Corinth, and they traveled to Ephesus where they met Apollos and instructed him in the ways of Christ (Acts 18:24–26).

Third, Paul mentioned greetings from **the church that** met **at their house.** Early Christian churches customarily met in homes. Aquila and Priscilla had house churches in Ephesus and Rome (Rom. 16:5). Nympha and Philemon also held churches in their homes (Col. 4:15; Phlm. 2).

Fourth, Paul extended the greetings of **all the brothers** in Ephesus. All the believers who were with Paul at the time extended their warm affections and respect to the believers at Corinth.

16:20b. In light of the unity of faith and affection expressed in these various greetings, Paul encouraged the Corinthians to continue the same expressions of love to one another. They were to **greet one another with a holy kiss.** The exchange of kisses among family members and beloved friends was not unusual in the Mediterranean world of Paul's day. The custom was for men to touch cheeks in greeting. The adjective "holy" makes it plain that this practice connoted nothing sexual or romantic.

16:21. In line with the spirit of affection in the preceding verses, Paul himself penned a few words, noting that he wrote **this greeting in** his **own hand.** Although he used a secretary for most of his writing, Paul characteristically added a personal touch to his letters by writing a note in his own hand (Gal. 6:11; 2 Thess. 3:17). At times, Paul wrote with his own hand to authenticate a letter. Here, however, he extended a **greeting** to show his personal affection for the Corinthian believers.

16:22. Paul placed a curse on **anyone** who did **not love the Lord.** Similarly, in Galatians 1:9 Paul cursed all who taught other gospels than the one he preached. Although Paul was convinced that most people within the Corinthian church believed the gospel, he knew that every church also contains deceivers and liars. He declared that the Lord curses even people in the church if they do not love him. The realization that such deceivers infiltrate the church caused Paul to cry out, **Come, O Lord.** He prayed that Christ would punish those who brought trouble to the church through their pretense of faith.

16:23. Paul hoped good things for the Corinthian church. So he offered a blessing over them, praying that **the grace of the Lord Jesus** would be with the Corinthians. The apostle regularly closed his letters with blessings like this. Here he expressed his hope that the Corinthians would enjoy the grace of God throughout their lives.

16:24. Paul also declared his deep affection for the Corinthian believers. He sent his **love to all of** them **in Christ Jesus.** He practiced the love to which he had exhorted the Corinthians many times in this epistle. The most important emotion believers should have for one another is love. Paul left no doubt that his affection for the Corinthians was strong and sincere. To confirm his love for them, he added **Amen,** meaning, "may it be so."

> **MAIN IDEA REVIEW:** *Having dealt with a number of crucial doctrinal and practical issues in this epistle, Paul came to some final matters. This last chapter divides into three main parts: instructions on collections, general exhortations, and final greetings.*

III. CONCLUSION

Bringing Matters to an End

In this chapter Paul brought matters to an end. He listed a number of issues he had left untouched and returned to his most important concern: love among the Corinthian believers.

PRINCIPLES

- We bear the responsibility to help other Christians who are in need.
- We bear the responsibility to support missionaries and other workers in the ministry.

- Our responsibilities as believers include encouraging one another.

APPLICATIONS

- We ought to set aside money for the poor because we welcome the opportunity to minister to others.
- We ought to offer hospitality as an opportunity to rejoice in Christian fellowship and to help our brothers and sisters.
- We ought to encourage believers at church because we desire to meet their needs.

IV. LIFE APPLICATION

Grandmother

I try to participate every year in a project known as "Angel Tree" that delivers Christmas presents from prison inmates to their children. This often takes me to some poor areas. I recall one home I visited in which a loving grandmother in her sixties cared for three grandchildren.

The grandmother was a dear Christian woman, active in her church, but she lived in abject poverty. She had no job, and she received no money from her grandchildren's father (who was in prison) or mother (who was a drug addict) to help feed the children she was raising. Because she was not the children's legal guardian, she also received no money for them from the government. Those in her church were evidently as poor as she was. She had to fish at a local pond to feed the family, and her home was in a terrible state of disrepair. Cockroaches covered the walls, floors, ceilings, and furniture. I was afraid to sit down, and I kept walking around the room to keep the bugs from crawling up my legs.

But as poor as this woman was, she gave what little she had to raising the grandchildren she loved. I, on the other hand, forgot about praying for her and her grandchildren after a couple weeks, and I never gave any money to help her.

God calls us to be like that grandmother, not to be like me. He wants the members of the Christian family to care for one another so deeply that they sacrifice to help one another. He wants us to love so much that we cannot stand to see one another suffering so that we give whatever we can to help. And he does not want us to do this just once. God calls us to a life of loving service for others.

At first it may seem difficult to apply such sections of Scripture as Paul's travel plans and greetings, but, as we look more closely, we can see that they have much to teach us. Through Paul's example as well as through his instruction, this chapter teaches us to support other believers, both materially and spiritually.

To a large degree, we modern Christians neglect the poor. Most of our churches set aside some money to help those in need, but not many of us as individuals are concerned about the needs of the poor. We leave those matters in the hands of our committees. Even then, because most Christians do not tithe, our committees have little to earmark for such charitable uses. We should follow Paul's exhortation that "each one" set aside something for the poor.

Perhaps our biggest problem is that we simply do not love people. Cold hearts indicate dead faith. Paul told us in chapter 13 that even if we give all we own to the poor, if we do not do this out of love, we gain nothing. Let us work on loving others, watching for opportunities to do good for others.

V. PRAYER

Lord Jesus, we hear the apostle Paul giving the Corinthians some important practical instructions. Help us to hear the intensity of his voice as the intensity of your voice. Make us a people who live our faith in practical ways. Amen.

VI. DEEPER DISCOVERIES

A. Collection (16:1)

God has great concern for the poor. He commanded his people to care for the poor. The New Testament church shared this concern (Acts 4:34–35; Gal. 2:10). So when famines struck Judea, the church rallied to care for the poor by taking up a collection (Acts 11:28–30; Rom. 15:26–27).

Judea and other parts of the Mediterranean world experienced famines because of flooding, drought, or other harsh weather. Famines sometimes occurred even in areas that produced good crops. Several famines plagued the Mediterranean area between A.D. 46 and 54. It was the last of these that Paul was referring to when he wrote 1 Corinthians. Although conditions in Corinth were also bad, the Corinthians must have had enough food to survive.

Still, conditions were bad enough that he encouraged the Corinthians to delay marriages due to their own "present crisis" (7:26). Paul did not expect the Corinthians to give beyond their means, but he wanted them to share what they had to provide relief for the destitute believers in Judea.

B. Paul's Travels and Letters to the Corinthians (16:5–9)

Paul planted the Corinthian church on his second missionary journey. During at least part of the eighteen months Paul spent in Corinth, Gallio was proconsul of Achaia. Gallio held this post somewhere between A.D. 51 and 53, so Paul must have been in Corinth some time during this period. Shortly after leaving Corinth, Paul apparently ended his second missionary journey by returning to Antioch.

Paul then began his third missionary journey, traveling through Galatia and Phrygia, and stopping in Ephesus. The time that elapsed between Paul's departure from Corinth during his second missionary journey and his arrival in Ephesus during his third journey is uncertain. Still, the indications are that this period was relatively short. Paul stayed in Ephesus for approximately two years and three months. Commentators generally agree that he wrote 1 Corinthians near the end of this time. By the time he wrote 2 Corinthians, he had left Ephesus and was in Macedonia. This means that he wrote 2 Corinthians probably within about three months of having left Ephesus.

C. Paul's Own Hand (16:21)

Authors in the ancient world often made use of amanuenses, secretaries who wrote down what the authors told them to write. Amanuenses sometimes had freedom to write in their own words the ideas the authors related to them, and at other times they were bound to write these things verbatim. We may be certain that New Testament authors did not send out anything the amanuenses had written without first approving it. Not only did Paul use amanuenses (Gal. 6:11; Phlm. 19), but Peter did as well (1 Pet. 5:12). Paul often chose to add a personal touch (and a mark of authenticity) by writing a few words in his own handwriting at the end of the letter.

VII. TEACHING OUTLINE

A. INTRODUCTION

1. Lead Story: "Don't Forget . . . and Be Sure to Remember"
2. Context: As Paul wrapped up his letter, he had many things on his mind. He wanted to remind the Corinthians to take up a collection for famine relief. He also wanted to send various greetings, to reaffirm his basic teachings on love, and to tell them when he might visit them. He also wanted to relay some instructions and information about various church leaders. Paul had so many things to tell them that he began listing them in rapid-fire fashion.
3. Transition: We often feel like Paul did, rushing to get final instructions to people as they leave—especially when those people are our

children or those who are taking care of our children. Even though Paul was rushing and perhaps a bit disorganized as he gave these final words, he meant them as intently as we mean our words in similar circumstances. We ought to pay close attention to them.

B. COMMENTARY

1. Instructions on Collections (16:1–4)
   - a. Purpose: relief for the church (16:1)
   - b. Guidelines for giving (16:1–2)
   - c. Delivering the collection (16:3–4)
2. General Exhortations (16:5–18)
   - a. Travel plans (16:5–9)
   - b. Timothy (16:10–11)
   - c. Apollos (16:12)
   - d. Miscellaneous exhortations (16:13–14)
   - e. Stephanas and other Corinthian leaders (16:15–18)
3. Final Greetings (16:19–24)
   - a. Greetings from other believers (16:19–20)
   - b. Paul's personal greeting (16:21–24)

C. CONCLUSION: GRANDMOTHER

VIII. ISSUES FOR DISCUSSION

1. Who was to contribute to this collection? How much were they to collect? How often? Why were the Corinthians to take up a collection?
2. Why should the church be involved in meeting the needs of others? How often should it do so? How much should Christians give for the needs of others?
3. Do you give money, food, or clothes to help people in need? Why or why not? How often do you do this? How much do you give? Do you keep the needs of others in mind continually, or do you remember them only occasionally? Does your church have any regular programs or funds to care for the needy?
4. Why should Christians show hospitality? How should Christians show hospitality? Do you volunteer your home for hospitable purposes? Why or why not? Does your church provide lodging for traveling Christians or ministers?

2 Corinthians

LETTER PROFILE

- The letter was probably written about A.D. 55–57 from Macedonia or Ephesus during Paul's third missionary journey.
- Paul wrote to the church in the city of Corinth, the capital city of the Roman province of Achaia. Paul had planted this church during his second missionary journey only a few years earlier.
- The original audience in Corinth contained members from all levels of society, but consisted mostly of people who were neither rich, wise, nor of noble birth.
- The original audience had sat under the ministry of Paul, Apollos, and Peter.
- Before the ministries of Paul, Apollos, and Peter, the Corinthian church had begun to place improper value on worldly wisdom, including probably Greek philosophy.
- After writing 1 Corinthians and before writing 2 Corinthians, Paul wrote a sorrowful letter to Corinth in which he instructed them to discipline a sinner.
- Also after writing 1 Corinthians and before writing 2 Corinthians, Paul visited Corinth for the second time, but the visit went badly.
- At the time of the writing of this letter, false apostles had influenced the Corinthian Christians and begun to turn them against Paul.
- At the time of the writing of this letter, the famine in Jerusalem continued, and many churches were contributing to the needs of the Christians in Jerusalem.
- The letter is occasional, written in response to reports Paul received about conditions in the Corinthian church.
- Paul wrote the letter to refute the false apostles, to mend his relationship with the Corinthians, to bring about repentance in the church, and to ensure the collection for the impoverished saints in Jerusalem.

- Literary form: epistle
- Doctrinal themes:
  - ➤ the nature of Christian suffering and comfort,
  - ➤ the nature, goal, and procedures of discipline and restoration,
  - ➤ the new covenant,
  - ➤ apostolic ministry and authority,
  - ➤ temporal and eternal perspectives,
  - ➤ Christian charity, and
  - ➤ self-examination in the faith.
- Practical themes:
  - ➤ the importance of reconciliation in the church,
  - ➤ discernment,
  - ➤ submission to apostolic authority,
  - ➤ the importance of church discipline,
  - ➤ ministering to the physical needs of others, and
  - ➤ the importance of repentance and restoration in the life of the church.
- Special problems:
  - ➤ Many critics have argued that 2 Corinthians was not originally a single letter.
  - ➤ Noting a sharp break in subject matter and tone between chapters 1–9 and 10–13, they have argued that 2 Corinthians was originally two separate letters.
  - ➤ Some have also argued that 6:14–7:1 was interpolated into 2:14–7:4, and then that 2:14–7:4 was interpolated into chapters 1–9.
  - ➤ Some also argue that chapters 1–7 and 8–9 were originally separate documents.
  - ➤ There is great reason, however, to believe that this letter was originally drafted as it now exists.
  - ➤ Allegedly disparate sections of the letter share common themes.
  - ➤ If these were originally separate letters, then at least some greetings and closures seem to have been discarded in forming the existing letter. This seems unlikely to have been done.
  - ➤ Most significantly, all the various tones and subjects addressed in the letter, including their various arrangements in the letter, accord with literary rhetorical norms of the first century. What looks and sounds odd to some modern commentators was not odd to the original audience.

AUTHOR PROFILE

- The apostle Paul wrote this letter.
- He was not one of the original twelve.
- He had formerly been named Saul (Acts 13:9).
- He had formerly been a zealous Pharisee (Phil. 3:5).
- He had formerly persecuted the church (Acts 8:3; Gal. 1:14,23).
- He had been converted and appointed to his apostleship by direct encounter with the risen Christ on the road to Damascus (Acts 9:3–19).
- He was one of the church's earliest missionaries, and was especially commissioned to evangelize the Gentiles (Acts 9:15; Gal. 2:9).
- He planted churches all over the Mediterranean world.
- He authored more New Testament books than any other writer: Romans, 1 and 2 Corinthians, Galatians, Ephesians, Philippians, Colossians, 1 and 2 Thessalonians, 1 and 2 Timothy, Titus, and Philemon.

2 Corinthians 1:1–2:11

Greetings and Important Explanations

I. **INTRODUCTION**
A No-Win Situation

II. **COMMENTARY**
A verse-by-verse explanation of this section.

III. **CONCLUSION**
Paul's Open Heart

An overview of the principles and applications from this section.

IV. **LIFE APPLICATION**
The Dentist

Melding the section to life.

V. **PRAYER**
Tying the section to life with God.

VI. **DEEPER DISCOVERIES**
Historical, geographical, and grammatical enrichment of the commentary.

VII. **TEACHING OUTLINE**
Suggested step-by-step group study of the section.

VIII. **ISSUES FOR DISCUSSION**
Zeroing the section in on daily life.

Quote

" *All* the instruments employed by God in the promotion of his work, have been greatly tried; their labors have been mingled with their tears; and they have not only suffered from their own personal share of human imperfection, but have found in the ignorance, the perverse dispositions, and the unholy practices of others, their sharpest sorrows. They have been grieved by foes, but more injured and vexed by pretended friends."

Jonathan Edwards

2 Corinthians 1:1–2:11

 IN A NUTSHELL

Because Paul had not visited the Corinthians when he said he would, they suspected him of duplicity. Paul defended his integrity, explaining that he had delayed his visit in order to spare them grief.

Greetings and Important Explanations

I. INTRODUCTION

A No-Win Situation

*H*ave you ever become so entangled in a relationship of misunderstanding and distrust that there was no easy way out? No matter what you did, you could not do the right thing.

It often happens in our families. We get into conflict when we fail to do our share around the house. Then when we try, we do not do it in the right way. It happens at work. We fail to anticipate the needs of one customer and get into trouble. Then we get even more grief when we do too much for the next customer. Unfortunately, the same kind of no-win situations happen even in the church.

Often what is missing from these circumstances is not performance but trust. We do not give the benefit of the doubt to others. We do not believe they have good intentions, so we condemn them, no matter what they do.

As Paul began this epistle to the Corinthians, he found himself in this kind of circumstance. He simply could not win. In the past, he had corrected serious errors in the church at Corinth, but they did not appreciate his rebukes. So, not to push too far, Paul avoided confrontation with the Corinthians, but they did not appreciate that either.

In this no-win situation, Paul had only one choice. He explained himself as best he could, appealing to the believers at Corinth to believe that everything he did was motivated by his deep love for them.

II. COMMENTARY

Greetings and Important Explanations

> **MAIN IDEA:** *Speculations had grown about why Paul had not come to Corinth sooner. Paul explained what had been happening in his life, how he had treated the Corinthians with integrity, why his plans had changed, and what his current plans were.*

𝔸 Greetings (1:1–2)

SUPPORTING IDEA: *Paul greeted the Corinthians with his desire that they might experience grace and peace.*

1:1. **Paul** identifies himself as **an apostle of Christ Jesus,** one of thirteen special emissaries whom Christ ordained as the foundation of the church (Eph. 2:20). The title "apostle" gave him authority over believers and made it clear that this epistle was more than a mere personal note. Paul's apostolic position came **by the will of God,** not by human authorization. Other apostles recognized Paul's office (Gal. 2:7–9; 2 Pet. 3:15–16), but he was appointed directly by God.

With Paul was **Timothy** their **brother,** who served the church in Corinth (Acts 18:5). Paul had sent him to Corinth earlier, but apparently Timothy had returned to Paul in the interim between this epistle and the last. The designation **our brother** expresses not only Paul's own affection for Timothy, but also the attitude he hoped the Corinthians would have.

Paul wrote **to the church of God in Corinth,** the Greek city to which 1 Corinthians was also addressed. The **church,** or entire congregation, received this letter, which was probably read aloud in church meetings. Although Paul sometimes used the term *church* to denote the universal body of Christ throughout the world, here he designated a particular local **church.** As the body of Christ, the **church** belongs only to God, and therefore is the church **of God.**

Paul was concerned mainly with the Corinthian church in this epistle, but he made it clear that his letter should be read by **all the saints throughout Achaia.** "Saint" in the Old Testament occasionally refers to priests, but in the New Testament it designates all believers (Rom. 1:7). It basically means "holy ones" or "sanctified ones." Paul did not have a special class of believers in mind. He wrote to every believer, no matter what their spiritual condition.

Achaia was the Roman designation for the southern province of Greece. The Cenchrean church was also in **Achaia** (Rom. 16:1), and Paul's words suggest that other churches also existed in the region. Corinth was the regional capital (see Acts 18:12). Paul expected this epistle to be passed among local congregations, and perhaps to be copied to or by these churches.

1:2. Paul offered one of his common benedictions as he began this letter, hoping for **grace and peace** for the Corinthians. Paul began all his canonical letters with a wish of **grace** and **peace** for his readers. No one can gain salvation except by God's **grace** or unmerited favor. Yet, here Paul did not speak of the initial grace believers receive that leads to conversion. He focused on continuing grace, the mercy from God that is necessary to complete the Christian life. New life in Christ cannot begin with grace and continue by human merit (Gal. 3:3,5).

Paul's use of "peace" derived from the frequent use of "peace" (*shalom*) in the Old Testament to mean "well-being" or "wholeness." He wanted the Corinthians not only to be redeemed from their sins, but also to receive the benefits of being in Christ. Peace with God and with other human beings is one such benefit. Both **grace and peace** come from **God our Father** and his Son, **the Lord Jesus Christ**. This formula is not trinitarian, but elsewhere similar benedictions also include the Holy Spirit (Rom. 15:13; 1 Pet. 1:1–2).

Ⓑ Paul's Ministry of Hardship (1:3–11)

SUPPORTING IDEA: *Paul had not neglected the Corinthians. In the ministry of the gospel, he had suffered in ways that benefited them and honored God.*

1:3–4. Paul began describing his hardships on a positive, exuberant note. The formula **praise be to . . . God** derived from the Old Testament (Ps. 41:13), but Paul modified it to express distinctively Christian praise. Not only is **God** praised, but he is **the God and Father of our Lord Jesus Christ**. This modification demonstrates that Paul saw Christianity as one with Old Testament religion, but not precisely the same. Christ had become the center of true belief. New Testament believers relate to God as the one who sent Christ.

Paul added that the **Father** has **compassion** and **all comfort**. This praise also derives from the Old Testament (Isa. 51:12; 66:13). **Compassion** denotes God's mercy and his concern for the plight of those who suffer. **Comfort** is what God gives to those who suffer. These terms were appropriate because Paul was about to describe his own **troubles** in suffering for the gospel.

Paul suffered and was comforted partly so he could bring **comfort** to others **in any trouble**. His suffering in ministry was an act of service to the Corinthians. Having suffered and been comforted, Paul could **comfort** others with the **comfort** he had **received from God**. Paul's use of the first person suggests that he thought primarily about himself and his company in this passage, but the principle applies to all believers. God permits his servants to suffer, and then comforts them so they may in turn comfort others.

1:5. Paul explained how he knew this principle to be true. Christians are so intimately joined with Christ that experiences **flow** from Christ, to believers, through believers, and to others. The **sufferings of Christ** extend from Christ to his followers. Believers fill up . . . Christ's afflictions because the church is his body (see Col. 1:24; cf. Phil. 3:10). This was plain enough from the hardships in Paul's own ministry. Yet, just as Christ received joy and glory in his resurrection, and sent the Holy Spirit of comfort, **comfort** also **overflows** to believers **through Christ**. In union with Christ, we face the hardships of sin and death, but we also receive compassionate encouragement from God.

1:6. Because the Corinthians benefited when the apostles were **distressed**, Paul's experiences had been the Corinthians' **comfort**. As he ministered at great personal cost, he brought **comfort and salvation** to those who heard his message. At the same time, when the apostles were **comforted** by Christ, they received the encouragement they needed to bring the Corinthians **comfort**.

Further, the **comfort** believers received from Paul's suffering **produce[d] . . . patient endurance** in the midst of their own **sufferings**. Christians must remain faithful to Christ, no matter how difficult circumstances become. **Endurance** (*hypomone*) describes how believers must continue in faithful service to the end. Yet, **endurance** will not last unless it is **patient**. Patience is the ability to wait for Christ to return and end all suffering. **Comfort** enables believers to find energy, which in turn makes them **patient** as they endure suffering.

1:7. The Corinthians faced trials, disappointments, and conflicts. But Paul believed they had saving faith in Christ and that they would endure. He hoped this because he knew the Corinthians **share[d] in** the apostles' **comfort** as well as their **sufferings**. So long as Christ comforted the Corinthians, they would be able to endure their suffering to the end.

1:8–9a. Paul continued to assure the Corinthians of his affection for them, in spite of his delayed visit, and he explained the delay. He did not want them **to be uninformed . . . about the hardships** he **suffered**. Whatever they had heard, Paul had actually been in great hardship while ministering in the Roman province of **Asia** (modern-day Turkey).

Paul's description of his sufferings revealed the depth of his heart and appealed to the Corinthians for sympathy. He had been **under great pressure**, and the problems had been **beyond** his **ability to endure**. We cannot be sure what hardships Paul had in mind, but we know he endured: riots, vicious attacks, imprisonment, and physical illness. The problems had been so great that Paul had **despaired even of life**, losing hope that he would survive. In his discouragement, he had **felt the sentence of death** in his heart, almost succumbing to defeat.

1:9b–11. Still, Paul could see a brighter side. He reflected on past events in two ways: First, God had permitted this suffering so Paul and other apostles **might not rely on [them]selves but on God**. Paul recognized the temptation to be self-reliant. Only when circumstances had exceeded his own ability had Paul learned to rely **on God**.

Paul described God as the one **who raises the dead**. He alluded to the fact that God the Father raised Christ from the dead as the firstfruits of a great resurrection. But he drew upon this truth because his sufferings in the past had brought him to feel that a sentence of death had been placed upon him. Through his trials Paul had realized that God's power to raise the dead had significance beyond Christ's resurrection and the general bodily resurrection of the last day. God was able day by day to make the power of Christ's resurrection evident in believers' lives (Phil. 3:10).

Paul next praised God's past actions. God had **delivered** Paul and those with him from **deadly peril**. This declaration follows the Old Testament form of a traditional thanksgiving hymn (Ps. 40:1–3). Paul expressed confidence that God would **deliver** him in the future. Paul stated that he and other apostles had put their **hope** in the belief that God would **continue to deliver**. **Hope** in this sense is the emotional strength to persevere in difficulty because of a heightened expectation of better things in the future.

Finally, Paul acknowledged the purpose behind his sufferings and deliverances: God's glory. Paul drew the Corinthians into his perspective by acknowledging that they would surely **help** him in the future by offering their **prayers** to God. As a result, **many** would **give thanks** to God for God's response to their prayers. Many believers would be grateful **for the gracious favor** God would grant when he answered **the prayers of many**. The Corinthians were to have a right attitude toward Paul's absence by remembering that their sympathetic prayers helped him in his suffering and glorified God.

Ⓒ Paul's Clear Conscience (1:12–14)

> **SUPPORTING IDEA:** *Paul's delay had apparently called his sincerity into doubt. Paul wanted the Corinthians to remember his integrity, and to accept his good intentions toward them, in spite of this delay.*

1:12a. Paul claimed one thing about which he had confidence. His **conscience testified** that he had ministered with **holiness and sincerity** that were **from God**. A person's conscience can condemn or justify his or her actions (Rom. 2:14–16), but that conscience cannot be the ultimate standard of judgment. Even so, in this matter Paul's conscience was clear.

Paul had ministered with **holiness** and **sincerity** everywhere. "Holiness" describes the life of a believer who remains separated from the world's corruption. "Sincerity" means "the absence of deceit and hypocrisy." These traits characterized Paul's service **in the world**. More importantly for this epistle, **holiness** and **sincerity** characterized **especially** his **relations with** the Corinthians. Unlike those who questioned his motives, he was above reproach.

1:12b. Elaborating on the integrity of his ministry, Paul asserted that he had not conducted himself **according to worldly wisdom**. In light of 1:13, this expression indicates that Paul did not use sophistry or worldly arrogance in his ministry. He did not trick or overpower anyone with the world's wisdom. Paul reaffirmed the antithesis he saw between the world's wisdom, so popular in Corinth, and his own ministry that existed **according to God's**

grace. Paul's gospel ministry rested on Christ's death and resurrection, which even the simplest minds could understand.

1:13a. To justify this statement, Paul reminded the Corinthians that he never wrote **anything** they could not **read or understand**. This statement should not be taken absolutely. Nevertheless, Paul's message was clear, compared to the sophistry and obscurity of human wisdom. Paul sought to make his teachings plain. His refusal to use pretentious, worldly wisdom demonstrated his integrity.

1:13b–14. In fact, Paul was so sincere that he had **hope**. He believed the Corinthians understood **in part** that he was a trustworthy leader. Still, he wanted them to **understand** this **fully**, so they could **boast of** Paul **just as** Paul could **boast of** them. "Boast" did not connote sinful arrogance, but appropriate confidence. Paul wanted the Corinthians to take joy and confidence in their relationship with him. He planned to **boast** of them **in the day of the Lord Jesus,** the day when Jesus would return in judgment.

🄳 Paul's Original Travel Plans (1:15–17)

SUPPORTING IDEA: *Paul continued to defend his integrity by explaining the sequence of events that led him to change his original travel plans.*

1:15. Paul had previously written that he would travel from Ephesus to Macedonia, and then to Corinth. He also had said that he might spend the winter months with the Corinthians, and that he did not want to see them simply in passing. But after writing 1 Corinthians, Paul evidently changed his mind, planning an additional visit with the Corinthians before visiting Macedonia. He felt comfortable changing his plans because his conscience was clear.

Paul stated two intentions that displayed the sincerity of his original plan. On the one hand, he had **planned to visit** the Corinthians **first**. They had been at the top of his list. On the other hand, He wanted his ministry to **benefit** them **twice**.

1:16. Paul had planned **to visit** Corinth **on** his **way to Macedonia**, returning to Corinth as he came **back . . . from Macedonia**. He hoped that after this second visit the Corinthians would **send** him on his **way to Judea** (cf. 1 Cor. 16:3–6).

1:17. Even after Paul's short visit to Corinth that had gone badly, the Corinthians expected Paul to return to Corinth after visiting Macedonia. His determination to remain in Macedonia rather than to return to Corinth caused misunderstandings between Paul and the Corinthian church. Someone had apparently accused him of duplicity. Thus, Paul asked if he had **planned** his travels **lightly** or in **a worldly manner**. Had he simply followed his own thoughts as they crossed his mind, or had he sought the will of God for his ministry? To put it another way, had Paul said **in the same breath** . . . **"Yes, yes" and "No, no."**

This last expression parallels Christ's teaching: "Let your 'Yes' be 'Yes,' and your 'No,' 'No'" (Matt. 5:37). Paul may have expressed himself in this way because his opponents accused him of violating this teaching of Jesus. After all, Paul had told them he was coming, but he did not.

E Witnesses to Paul's Integrity (1:18–22)

> **SUPPORTING IDEA:** *Paul responded to the charge that he had misled the Corinthians. He appealed to his track record, to God as witness to his integrity, and to his pure motives.*

1:18. Paul began his response to the charge of duplicity with an oath: **as surely as God is faithful.** The charges against him appeared so serious that Paul felt the need to authenticate his claims as strongly as possible. His oath before God witnessed to his truthfulness and integrity.

Paul used a type of argument common among Jewish rabbis in his day. He argued from a greater matter to a less important matter. He called the Corinthians to evaluate the accusation of duplicity in a small matter (his delayed visit) in light of his integrity in a great matter (preaching the gospel). Since he had maintained integrity in the greater matter, his integrity in the smaller matter should not have been questioned.

1:19–20. Paul supported his oath by summarizing an important feature of what **was preached among** the Corinthians. He, **Silas, and Timothy** had preached **the Son of God, Jesus Christ,** and Christ did not waver between **Yes and No.** There was no duplicity in Christ or in the message about Christ.

Paul added that in Christ his message had **always been "Yes."** Paul knew this statement was enigmatic, so he explained his meaning. **No matter how many promises God has made** throughout the history of the Bible, one thing can be relied on: **In Christ . . . they are "Yes."** Paul frequently reminded his readers of Old Testament promises God made to his people (Rom. 1:2; Eph. 2:12). He knew that immeasurable blessings had been promised to Christians as heirs of Old Testament promises. The great covenant promises throughout the Bible are all fulfilled in Christ.

Of course, the Corinthians probably had no problem with Christ's sincerity. So Paul drew a connection between himself and Christ. Since Paul represented Christ, Paul's gospel ministry could be summed up as an **"Amen" . . . spoken by** Paul **to the glory of God.** Paul's preaching affirmed the sincere affirmation of God's promises in Christ.

1:21–22. To defend his ministry further, Paul reminded the Corinthians that God himself had anointed Paul and his company to their task, guaranteeing their participation in the gospel promises. These assertions anticipated his statement in 1:23: "I call God as my witness." Though he did not use that specific language in this verse, his sentiment was the same. The evidence of God's **anoint[ing]**, **seal**, and **Spirit** proved Paul's integrity. Likewise, the same **God** made the Corinthians, Paul, and Paul's company **stand firm in Christ**, so the Corinthians stood on no more solid footing, and they could not claim superiority over Paul.

While all Christians have God's **anoint[ing]**, **seal**, and **Spirit**, just as all Christians **stand firm in Christ**, Paul applied these first three statements mainly to himself and to his company in order to defend their integrity. The logical connections among the terms **makes . . . stand firm, anointed, set . . . seal**, and **put . . . Spirit** have been widely disputed. For our purposes, we will treat each term separately.

First, God made them all **stand firm in Christ**. "Stand firm" (*bebaioo*) describes believers' faithful devotion to Christ. Instead of letting them waver or stumble, God had empowered Paul and the Corinthians to remain committed to Christ. The perseverance of those who were taught by Paul indicated God's blessing and validated Paul's ministry.

Second, God had also **anointed** Paul and his company. In the Old Testament, anointing rituals symbolized the offices of priest and sometimes prophet. These Old Testament shadows anticipated the spiritual anointing that comes on all true believers. All those who are **in Christ** (the Anointed One) are themselves **anointed** with the Holy Spirit by virtue of their union with Christ.

This anointing of the Holy Spirit involves the Spirit's indwelling presence and empowerment (cf. Eph. 3:16,20). The Spirit's anointing also empowers for special service. Paul claimed this special type of anointing in connection with his preaching (Rom. 15:18–19) and also attributed it to Timothy (2 Tim. 1:6–7). The anointing to which Paul referred was probably general (shared by all believers) because all believers also **stand firm in Christ**, and all receive God's **seal** and **Spirit**. Paul explicitly mentioned only **us** (Paul and his company) because he was in the process of defending his and their integrity. The Corinthians assumed that they had been **anointed**; Paul asserted, "So have we," proving that Paul's ministry was sincere and blessed of God.

Third, God had **set his seal of ownership** on Paul and his company, just as people in Paul's day placed their seals on objects to indicate their ownership. This sealing accompanied the reception of the Holy Spirit. That Paul and his company belonged to God was evident in the blessings God had given to them, especially the blessing of the Holy Spirit manifested in the power of the gospel.

Fourth, God **put his Spirit in** their **hearts as a deposit**. The presence of the Holy Spirit in the hearts of Paul and his company, as in the Corinthians' hearts, was a **deposit** of the eternal reward they would receive at Christ's return. This deposit **guarantee[d]** the full inheritance which was **to come.** Because the Holy Spirit is a down payment, Christians should not fear that the Holy Spirit will leave them. The Spirit of God will remain with true believers as the proof of salvation to come.

F Paul's Motivation (1:23–2:4)

> **SUPPORTING IDEA:** *Paul augmented his earlier explanation of his changed travel plans. He took a second oath, swearing that his motivations were pure.*

1:23. Paul **did not return** in order **to spare** the Corinthians. He did not state explicitly from what he hoped to spare the church at Corinth, but we can infer from the following verses that he had some harsh rebukes for them. He also mentioned in 2:1 that he had determined not to "make another painful visit" to the Corinthians.

Teaching and correction have to be timely as well as true. From Paul's perspective, the Corinthians had received enough rebukes from him for the time being. They deserved more reprimands, but the time was not appropriate. Paul avoided confrontation by delaying his planned return.

1:24. Even when Paul had corrected the Corinthians, he had not **lord[ed]** his authority **over** their **faith,** ruling over them. On the contrary, he tried to **work with** them **for their own joy.** Paul desired happiness for the Corinthians, and he knew they could **stand firm** in the blessings of Christ only **by faith.**

2:1. Returning to his main idea, Paul elaborated further on 1:23. He determined **not** to **make another painful visit.** The pain of rebuke is necessary at times in Christian relationships but not always appropriate, even when sin and error persist in the church. Paul practiced what he told the Colossians: "Let your conversation be always full of grace, seasoned with salt, so that you may know how to answer everyone" (Col. 4:6).

2:2. Not only did Paul change his plans to spare the Corinthians, but he did it also for his own sake. He feared that if he **grieved** the Corinthians further, he would have no one **left to make** him **glad.** Paul needed to be encouraged and strengthened by the church, and he depended on the Corinthians' love. He did not need grief from the Corinthians added to his other difficulties.

2:3. Paul anticipated a potential question. If he needed to be encouraged by the Corinthians, why did he write so many harsh rebukes in his letter to them? Paul responded that he **wrote** to deal with problems from a distance **so that when** he **came** he would **not be distressed** by the church at Corinth. Their proper role in Paul's life was **to make** him **rejoice.** He had written previously about problems so that his face-to-face meetings could be positive.

Once the Corinthians submitted to his written corrections, Paul **had confidence** they **would all share** his joy.

2:4. Paul insisted that he **wrote** his letter of correction **out of great distress and anguish of heart and with many tears.** He did not like rebuking the Corinthians. He grieved for the harm they did themselves. The apostle wrote about difficult things so they could **know the depth of** his **love for** them.

G A Brief Application (2:5–11)

SUPPORTING IDEA: *Paul remembered that he had dealt severely with a case of sin in the church. If Paul really cared about the Corinthians' joy, why had he judged the sinner so harshly?*

2:5. Paul explained his strong rebuke. The man had **caused grief** not to Paul, but to **all of** the church in Corinth. Paul acted firmly against this man in reaction to the widespread trouble the man had caused. Not everyone in the church had been incensed by the man's sin, so Paul qualified the scale of this congregational trouble. He did not want to **put it too severely** or to overstate the situation, so he said that all were grieved only **to some extent.**

2:6. Paul realized the situation had changed. **The punishment** or church discipline had been **inflicted . . . by the majority** of the church, and the discipline had been effective. The apostle made it plain that one purpose of church discipline is the restoration of the sinner. This purpose had been accomplished.

2:7–8. Apparently, having once decided to discipline, some people within the church were determined not to grant relief or restoration. But Paul insisted that the church **ought to forgive and comfort** the man they had disciplined. Why? Paul wanted to protect the church from too much grief. He did not want the man to **be overwhelmed by excessive sorrow.**

Sorrow should not always be avoided. In fact, it often leads to repentance. Even so, once repentance has occurred, a serious danger lurks for those who are not restored to good standing in the church: they run the risk of too much sorrow. Discouragement of this sort may actually lead the weakened believer into worse sin. **Therefore,** Paul **urge[d]** the Corinthians to **reaffirm** their **love** for the disciplined man.

2:9. To avoid any misunderstandings, Paul explained that he had instructed the church to discipline the man **to see if** the congregation **would stand the test,** if they would **be obedient in everything,** i.e., even in difficult matters. Inflicting discipline had not been easy. It was a **test** of their faithfulness to Christ and to Paul. God calls on believers to face difficult choices to prove the true character of their faith (cf. Exod. 16:4; Jas. 1:3; Rev. 2:10). The Corinthians had passed this test by disciplining the man.

2:10–11. Paul affirmed his intention to forgive the man in question. He was not waiting for the Corinthians to forgive the man before he forgave the man. He simply stated that as the Corinthians treated this man with mercy, they could be assured that he did as well. Perhaps some people in the church hesitated to lift the discipline Paul had ordered. Paul assured them that forgiveness agreed with his apostolic authority.

Paul gave two reasons for forgiving the man. First, he forgave **in the sight of Christ** (i.e., in good conscience before Christ) **for your sake** (i.e., for the benefit of the Corinthian church). He desired their benefit and joy, and so determined to restore the wayward brother.

Second, Paul forgave so that **Satan might not outwit** him (Paul), his company, and perhaps the Corinthians as well. Paul knew that Satan was clever, but he acknowledged that Satan could be resisted and outwitted by careful believers. He suspected that Satan would find opportunity in prolonged discipline to discourage the disciplined man and to harden the congregation's heart. Paul's concern regarding Satan was justified by the fact that they **were not unaware of his schemes.**

In other words, he and his company, and perhaps the Corinthian believers, had experienced enough of Satan's temptations to take notice of this possibility. Paul probably intended his forgiveness of the man to encourage the Corinthians to forgive the man, and thus to thwart Satan.

MAIN IDEA REVIEW: *Speculations had grown about why Paul had not come to Corinth sooner. He explained what had been happening in his life, how he had treated the Corinthians with integrity, why his plans had changed, and what his current plans were.*

III. CONCLUSION

Paul's Open Heart

Paul introduced this epistle by setting the record straight. His failure to visit the Corinthians as he had promised had prompted misunderstanding and accusations. Before he dealt with the difficult issues facing the Corinthians, Paul opened his heart to them. Everything he had done, both his previous corrections and his change of plans, he had done for their good. He wanted nothing more than their full joy in Christ.

PRINCIPLES

- God's grace is a higher standard than the world's wisdom.
- God's discipline is ultimately restorative.
- Suffering is a normal and necessary part of Christian life.

APPLICATIONS

- We must exercise wisdom in determining the severity and urgency of problems.
- When the church disciplines us, we should consider the charges seriously and submit to discipline, not simply adopt a defensive stance.
- When we suffer, we should not allow our personal discomfort to affect the graciousness and love that we demonstrate to others.

IV. LIFE APPLICATION

The Dentist

I have a good friend who is a dentist. He once told me: "When a patient has a toothache, I'm his best friend. But when he has no pain and I tell him we have to drill, I'm his worst enemy." Dentists inflict pain to help us avoid pain. That makes them people to avoid, but it also makes them people to whom we run for help.

Paul must have felt like a dentist as he wrote these words. He had inflicted pain on the Corinthians by correcting their misdeeds, but they hadn't liked it. Then he had avoided visiting them to keep from grieving them too much, but they hadn't liked that either. Yet, with great compassion he paused at the beginning of this epistle to reveal his heart before them. Everything he did for them—the sharp rebukes as well as sparing them more correction—was for their good. They may not have liked him. But he did everything because he loved them deeply.

This passage has many applications for us today. Observing the way Paul dealt with the Corinthians, we see many truths that helped Paul determine his course of action.

For example, Paul knew God's grace was a higher standard than the world's wisdom. When the world demands justice or discipline, grace often suggests forbearance, forgiveness, mercy, and love. While we must sometimes execute justice as the Corinthians did by disciplining a sinful brother, often we may be merciful as Paul was with the Corinthians in delaying his visit. We must exercise wisdom in determining the severity and urgency of problems.

When mature Christians criticize us or we fall under church discipline, we must not stir up trouble or assume the worst of those who have called us to account. They deserve the benefit of the doubt, and we should give serious consideration to the charges against us. Pride often leads us to defend ourselves regardless of the truth, but God's discipline is ultimately restorative.

We should submit to it for our own benefit. We should not reject a reliable dentist just because he tells us we need oral surgery.

Further, Paul's experience and testimony teach us a theology of suffering. He did not teach that Christians ought to seek out suffering. But he did teach that the Christian life involves suffering. Some teachers in the modern church would have us believe that God does not want us to suffer, and that if we suffer it is because we lack faith. Paul did not lack faith, but he experienced suffering. For Paul, suffering for Christ was an honor as well as a necessary part of Christ's redemption of his people. Suffering also strengthens believers so that we can better comfort others, and God himself promises to comfort us.

Sometimes when we suffer, even though we know that God uses it for our good, we develop impatient and irritable attitudes. We ought to follow Paul's example, not allowing our discomfort to affect the graciousness and love that we demonstrate to others. Like Paul, we must remain patient and forbearing.

V. PRAYER

Lord Jesus, we so often do not care about the joy of your people. Grant us hearts that are wise enough to avoid inflicting grief on others. Give us a firm commitment to delight in the joy of your people.

VI. DEEPER DISCOVERIES

A. Comfort (1:3–7)

Both the noun translated "comfort" (*paraklesis*) and the verb (*parakaleo*) carry many different meanings in the New Testament. In the NIV, they are often also translated "encourage(ment)" (Rom. 12:8; Phil. 2:1; Heb. 12:5). The verb frequently also appears as "urge" (Acts 27:34; 1 Tim. 1:3). In the NIV, they appear as "comfort" mainly in 2 Corinthians. Only five times outside this epistle does the NIV translate these words with the meaning "comfort" (Matt. 2:18; 5:4; Luke 6:24; 16:25; Acts 20:12).

The keys to Paul's meaning here may be found in 1:6, in which Paul wrote that comfort produced "endurance," and in 1:4, where he wrote of comforting "those in . . . trouble." He probably did not refer to comfort akin to "a pleasant and relaxed feeling." Instead, "comfort" should be understood as "consolation and encouragement" in the face of hardship, as when a person "comforts" another in the midst of loss or suffering.

B. Day of the Lord Jesus (1:14)

The Old Testament spoke of the day of the Lord as the day when God would come as a warrior king to defeat all his enemies and to bestow blessings on his people. The blessings for God's people included the restoration of the Davidic kingdom to Israel.

In the New Testament, the people of God maintained this hope in the day of the Lord, but they recognized that Jesus had been revealed as the Davidic king under whom the kingdom would be restored. As a result, they trusted that Jesus would be the divine warrior leading the heavenly troops into battle to defeat God's enemies on the day of the Lord, and that the blessings of the restored kingdom would be realized in him. The New Testament identifies Jesus as the "Lord" in the phrase, "the day of the Lord" (cf. 1 Cor. 1:8).

VII. TEACHING OUTLINE

A. INTRODUCTION

1. Lead Story: A No-Win Situation

2. Context: Paul had recently endured a painful visit to Corinth, and his relationship with the Corinthians was strained. Because he had "lost" by visiting them, he had determined not to pay them another visit. But the Corinthians had reacted negatively to his absence just as they had to his presence. It pained Paul that his relationship with the Corinthians had become so strained. To bring about healing in their relationship, Paul felt compelled to vindicate himself in their eyes, particularly with regard to his delayed visit.

3. Transition: Sometimes we find ourselves in Paul's position, and at other times we find ourselves in the position of the Corinthians. Whenever we encounter "no-win situations," especially with other Christians, we need to prevent our negative emotions from ruling the day. We must commit ourselves to loving and forgiving others and to giving them the benefit of the doubt. We may find that our dilemmas are solvable.

B. COMMENTARY

1. Greetings (1:1–2)

2. Paul's Ministry of Hardship (1:3–11)

    a. Paul and his company suffered terribly (1:4–10)

    b. They suffered so that the Corinthians would benefit (1:4–7)

        c. Their suffering increased their trust and hope in God (1:3,9–10)

        d. Their suffering increased their appreciation for the Corinthians (1:11)

3. Paul's Clear Conscience (1:12–14)
4. Paul's Original Travel Plans (1:15–17)
5. Witnesses to Paul's Integrity (1:18–22)
6. Paul's Motivation (1:23–2:4)
7. A Brief Application (2:5–2:11)

C. CONCLUSION: THE DENTIST

VIII. ISSUES FOR DISCUSSION

1. Why do believers suffer? What effect does suffering have in believers' lives?
2. What did Paul mean by the word *comfort*? Does this idea seem important to Paul in this argument? Explain your answer.
3. How effective did Paul think prayer was? How effective do you think prayer is? Does your own life reflect the importance you place on prayer?
4. How and when should church discipline be imposed? What is the church's responsibility after disciplining a person? Why? Does your church have a formal disciplinary process? If so, what is it? Have you ever seen it in action?

2 Corinthians 2:12–3:18

Commending Ourselves

"The least pain in our little finger gives us more concern and uneasiness than the destruction of millions of our fellow beings."

W i l l i a m   H a z l i t t

2 Corinthians 2:12–3:18

I N   A   N U T S H E L L

Paul related another episode from his recent experiences that led him to deal with an accusation of pride and self-centeredness. He responded that he had not exulted in his experiences for prideful reasons, but because these experiences revealed the glory of Christ.

Commending Ourselves

I. INTRODUCTION

Stop Talking About Yourself

Do you know people who cannot talk about anything but themselves? No matter what is going on in your life, they seem intent on turning conversations back to themselves.

I remember once making a pastoral visit to the hospital. The woman had been in an auto accident and was in casts practically from head to toe. She was also in a lot of pain and a bit drowsy from pain medication.

As I stood beside her bed, another church member came into the room. She was a friend of the injured woman. "Oh, sweetheart, you look just awful. I'm sure you're in a lot of pain. Why, just this morning I stubbed my little toe when I got out of bed. Can you imagine just how much that hurt? Well, it's all black and blue now; I might even lose the toenail . . . Wanna see?" At that point she took off her shoe, put her foot on the hospital bed, and began to wave it around in the injured woman's face. This woman saw her friend suffering, but still could not talk about anything but herself.

The woman in casts tried to be polite, but her visitor went on and on. After a few minutes the patient turned to me and said, "Get this self-centered person away from me!"

This is how some Corinthians were thinking about Paul. From their perspective, he seemed to talk about himself a lot. Paul answered by pointing out that he honored Christ, not himself, as he shared his experiences with them.

II. COMMENTARY

Commending Ourselves

MAIN IDEA: *Paul began to discuss more details of his ministry experiences, then turned aside to talk about how wonderfully God had provided for him. Praising God led the apostle into a lengthy explanation that he was not promoting himself, but the grace of God in Christ.*

Continuing the Explanation (2:12–13)

> **SUPPORTING IDEA:** *Paul described recent events so the Corinthians could appreciate his circumstances.*

2:12. In autobiographical style, Paul began with the fact that his commitment to preaching the **gospel** of Christ had compelled him to go to **Troas** (cf. Acts 16:9–10), a city in Asia Minor (modern Turkey) about ten miles south of Troy. Paul had been there on his second missionary journey. From there he determined to go to Macedonia, where he began churches in Philippi, Thessalonica, Berea, and perhaps Athens. Therefore, on his third missionary journey Paul's preaching was well received in the churches he had previously established in Macedonia. This is why he said that **the Lord had opened a door** for him.

An **open door** does not mean (as it often does in modern parlance) an open opportunity. Rather, the metaphor indicates that God blessed the legitimate efforts of his people with remarkable success.

2:13. In spite of his success in Troas, Paul **had no peace of mind** because his **brother Titus** had not met him there. Paul was as close as a **brother** to Titus; he even sent this particular letter to the Corinthians through Titus. But Paul's love for Titus was not the cause of his concern. He was concerned about his relationship with the Corinthians. Titus had gone to Corinth to organize the collection for poverty-stricken Jerusalem. He was to report, among other things, the feelings of the Corinthians toward Paul. Not knowing how the Corinthians felt about him, Paul bypassed Corinth and waited for Titus in **Macedonia**.

ⓑ Paul's Ministry of Triumph (2:14–17)

> **SUPPORTING IDEA:** *Paul reflected on God's goodness in his ministry despite the disappointment that took place in Troas.*

2:14a. Paul had been disappointed in Troas and Macedonia, but through it all God had been good to him. He began this acknowledgment of divine goodness with thanksgiving: **But thanks be to God.**

2:14b–16a. Paul delighted in God's care for him. He expressed this joy with the metaphor of a victory parade. Paul was convinced that God **always leads** believers **in triumphal procession in Christ.** Paul drew upon the triumphal parades that were known throughout the Roman world. Prisoners of war were marched through the streets as fragrant perfumes filled the air. At the end of each parade, many prisoners were executed. For this reason, the smells of the parade were sweet to the victors, but they were the **smell of death** to the defeated.

Paul saw several similarities between these victory parades and his own ministry. (1) He and those with him were members of the victorious army led by **Christ**, as were the rest of the apostles. (2) Their gospel preaching spread everywhere . . . the knowledge or acknowledgment of God as the victor. Similarly, Roman victory parades spread knowledge about victories and caused people to acknowledge the victors. (3) Paul said that he and the apostles were like the perfumes of the victory parades. They became to (the honor of) God like the aroma of Christ, or more specifically, like the aroma accompanying Christ's victory. Both the victors of this spiritual gospel war (those who are being saved) and the defeated (those who are perishing) smelled their aroma. (4) This aroma of Christ, however, affected each group differently. To Christ's enemies, Paul and those with him were the smell of death, but to those following Christ they were the fragrance of life.

This metaphor contrasted Christian and non-Christian reactions to evangelists. To Christians, Paul and his company presented reminders of the wonders of salvation. For non-Christians, they raised the terror of divine judgment. No one could ignore them because their fragrance was spreading throughout the world.

2:16b. As Paul contemplated his analogy between Roman victory parades and his gospel ministry, he was overwhelmed. He exclaimed, **Who is equal to such a task?** The answer he implied was that no one was worthy of playing such an important role in human history and in the kingdom of God. It was astounding that God appointed humans to this role.

2:17. Paul wanted the Corinthians to know that he did not view his ministry as an ordinary job. He did not **peddle the word of God for profit.** He distinguished himself and those who worked with him from **so many** others who had reduced their ministries to mere occupations. Unlike the gospel peddlers, Paul and his company spoke **before God with sincerity.** Paul still lingered on the accusation of insincerity and duplicity he had addressed in the preceding section. He could not have been insincere because he looked upon his ministry so highly. Instead, he served as one **sent from God,** considering his task a sacred privilege. The fact that he did not accept payment for his preaching further demonstrated his sincerity.

C Confidence from a New Covenant (3:1–6)

SUPPORTING IDEA: *Paul anticipated that his opponents might accuse him of arrogance. He asserted that he had no need to commend himself. Christ had already honored him by making him a minister of the new covenant.*

3:1a. Paul began his response to this objection with two questions to which he expected negative responses. Was he **beginning to commend** himself **again?** These words may indicate that Paul's opponents had already accused him of self-aggrandizement in his earlier visits. These people would see his joy in the ministry of the gospel as another example of his arrogance. In the verses that follow, Paul argued strongly against this accusation.

3:1b. He also asked if his credibility was so low that he and those with him needed, **like some people,** to present **letters of recommendation** to the Corinthians. Unknown Christians in the early church carried letters of recommendation to congregations that did not know them. These letters acknowledged their status in the church (Acts 18:27). Paul's letter to Philemon is to some degree such a letter. Paul wondered if he needed to present such letters as well.

3:2. In response to his own question, Paul asserted that he actually had letters of recommendation: the Corinthian Christians themselves. Their new lives in Christ proved the effectiveness and divine approval of Paul's ministry. He described them as letters **written on our hearts.** This phrase has been the subject of controversy. Some ancient texts read "your hearts." This alternate reading makes more sense with the context. If it is correct, then Paul was saying that the changes that had taken place in the hearts of the Corinthians were his letters of recommendation. These changes were on their hearts, but they were not hidden. **Everybody** was able to see these changes of the heart displayed in their lives.

3:3. The Corinthian believers showed **the result of** Paul's **ministry,** especially by the gifts of the **Spirit** in their lives. Their new lives became a **letter from Christ** validating Paul's ministry. He elaborated on this **letter from Christ** in a way that captivated his thoughts for the rest of this chapter. Their letter had been **written,** but it was not written in the normal way by men **with ink,** or **on tablets of stone,** but by **the Spirit of the Living God,** and **on tablets of human hearts.** Paul used this contrast between **ink/stone** and **Spirit/hearts** to point out an important difference between the old covenant and the new covenant.

When Paul spoke of the Holy Spirit as **the Spirit of the Living God,** he drew upon Old Testament traditions. Yahweh is called the "living God" in the Old Testament to set him apart from inanimate idols. They are powerless. But the living God can move in history and in peoples' lives. The Holy Spirit had done mighty things in the Corinthian church. The living God had been among them because of Paul's ministry.

3:4. Paul summarized 3:1–3. He had **confidence** about the commendation of his ministry. This confidence had come to him **through Christ**—through salvation that comes in Christ and through Christ's special call to Paul as an apostle. Moreover, this **confidence** was **before God.** Even though some people did not acknowledge Paul's authority, he was convinced that God did.

3:5. To make his viewpoint clear, he qualified his confidence. He was **not . . . competent in** himself, and could not **claim anything for** himself. His **competence** was **from God.** Paul's apostolic task was too great for him to perform on his own. Yet, Paul was confident in his leadership because God confirmed his efforts.

3:6. With the basis of his confidence established, Paul announced the nature of his ministry. God had **made** him **competent** in a remarkable way: he was a minister **of a new covenant**. The expression "new covenant" appears in the New Testament as a designation for the arrangements established between God and his people on the basis of Christ's death and resurrection (Luke 22:20; Heb. 8:1–13). The church derives the expression "New Testament" from this phraseology, which has its roots in Jeremiah 31:31, where the prophet described the restoration period after Israel's exile as the time of "the new covenant."

The term *new* did not mean "entirely new." It connoted "renewed" or "made anew." God promised to renew his people to fresh and sincere covenant life after the exile. Both Ezekiel and Isaiah called this post-exilic covenant a "covenant of peace" (Isa. 54:10; Ezek. 34:25; 37:26), indicating that it was based on renewed peace between God and his people.

This allusion to Jeremiah 31:31 is especially poignant because Jeremiah said that God would renew his people's hearts: "'The time is coming,' declares the LORD, 'when I will make a new covenant with the house of Israel and with the house of Judah. . . . I will put my law in their minds and write it on their hearts'" (Jer. 31:31,33b). Paul had already alluded to the idea that the Corinthians had been changed in their hearts. Following Jeremiah's imagery, he had even spoken of God writing on the heart (2 Cor. 3:2–3).

Paul distinguished between the old and the new in a different but closely related way. He declared that he did not minister a covenant **of the letter**. Instead, he proclaimed a covenant **of the Spirit**. He insisted on this distinction because **the letter kills, but the Spirit gives life**. The death brought by Moses' Law resulted from human abuse of the Law. The Law of Moses was not intended to be a way of salvation. But the early church had false teachers who insisted that the Law of Moses was designed to provide eternal life. Paul opposed these false teachers. They failed to realize that seeking righteousness by the Law was actually the way of eternal death.

Paul declared that the empowerment of the **Spirit** through the new covenant was the only way to eternal life (Gal. 6:8). The outpouring of the Spirit in the New Testament exceeded any previous display of God's saving grace. As Paul proclaimed Christ and the gospel, he announced salvation through Christ and the power of the Spirit.

Ⓓ The New Covenant Contrasted with the Old Covenant (3:7–18)

SUPPORTING IDEA: *Paul elaborated on the contrast between the old and new covenants, and on how those contrasts affected his ministry.*

3:7–11. We may summarize Paul's contrasts with the following table:

Old Covenant	New Covenant
brought death and condemnation (3:7,9)	brings righteousness (3:9)
engraved on stone (3:7)	of the Spirit, written on hearts (3:8)
fading glory (3:8,11)	more, surpassing, lasting glory (3:8,10–11)

Paul noted that Moses' covenant brought **death** and condemnation, while the covenant in Christ brought **righteousness**. This contrast should not be taken as a straightforward distinction. In Paul's perspective, the Mosaic covenant failed because of human sin (Rom. 7:9–13). Just as Jeremiah wrote, the new covenant is not like "the covenant [God] made with [Israel's] forefathers" which "they broke" (Jer. 31:32). Jesus came to fulfill the promise of Moses and the Old Testament prophets that after the exile a renewal would take place in which God would grant righteousness to his people.

Second, the Old Testament Law was originally given to guide Israel through God's grace (Exod. 34:6–7; Joel 2:12–13). Unfortunately, Israel turned from God's grace and reduced Moses' covenant to a system of works righteousness. Except for a faithful remnant, Israel reduced the Law to an external written code. By contrast, Christ and his apostles reasserted the inward, spiritual nature of obedience as Moses had originally intended (Deut. 30:1–20).

Third, Moses' covenant was glorious but fading, in that it was always intended to be preliminary to a much greater covenant. Christ and his apostles represented that greater day—the time of the new covenant whose **glory** was superior and never-ending.

These contrasts between the old and new covenants made it possible for Paul to contrast the **ministry** of one with the other. By "ministry" Paul meant the service of those who mediated the covenants to God's people. To be sure, Moses had so much **glory** as a minister of the old covenant that **the Israelites could not look steadily at his face** (cf. Exod. 34:29–30). Moses' **ministry** was **glorious**. If this had been true of a **ministry that condemn[ed]** men, the **ministry that brings righteousness** was certainly even more glorious.

Through this contrast, Paul demonstrated his earlier assertion that his competence as a minister had come from God and not from his self-aggrandizement. He was a minister of the new covenant. This made his service to God's people even more glorious than Moses' ministry.

3:12. Paul concluded that the contrasts between the old and new covenants gave him **hope** and made him **very bold**. The **hope** Paul had in mind was that Christ's covenant and its glory would last for all time and accomplish the salvation for which it was designed.

The terminology "very bold" is ambiguous. It may refer to the boldness with which Paul had just commended his own ministry. If so, Paul justified his confidence on the basis of the nature of the new covenant. It is more likely, however, that Paul introduced the theme of 3:12–18 with the word *bold:* the message of Christ is fully unveiled and freely proclaimed.

3:13. To explain his boldness, Paul asserted that he and the other apostles were **not like Moses.** Exodus 34:29–35 explains that after speaking with God, Moses' face shone with God's reflected glory. Moses left his face uncovered whenever he spoke the word of God to Israel, but otherwise he covered his face with a **veil.** Although the Old Testament does not explain it this way, Paul understood that one reason for Moses' veil was that **the radiance was fading away.** Apparently, Moses' face shone brightly for a while but then returned to normal until the next time he spoke with God. Some interpreters have suggested that Moses veiled his face to hide from the Israelites the fact that his glory faded.

3:14–15. Paul stated metaphorically that **the same veil remain[ed] when the old covenant** was **read.** When Jews in Paul's day read from the Torah, they saw glimpses of God's glory, but no more than glimpses. **Only in Christ** is the veil that obscured the glory of God on Moses' face **taken away.** Christ is the revelation of the glory of God in a much greater way than Moses ever was. Yet, because unbelieving Jews in Paul's day rejected Christ, **when Moses** was **read, a veil covere[d] their hearts.** They saw only a small bit of God's glory because the **veil** over **their hearts** also made **their minds . . . dull,** hiding the full truth from them.

3:16. By contrast, **whenever anyone turns to the Lord** in repentance and faith, his or her condition changes. Paul alluded to Exodus 34:34 which spoke of Moses removing his veil, but he shifted the language toward Christ. Those in Christ see the glory clearly because **the veil** that dulls their minds **is taken away.** Christians possess renewed hearts and minds, enabling them to see the revelation of God more fully than those under the old covenant had seen it. Many things still remain hidden (Rom. 11:33–34), but compared to its visibility under the old covenant, the glory of God is now highly visible in Christ.

3:17. Continuing to draw attention to the change that had taken place in Christ, Paul stated, **Now the Lord is the Spirit.** This sentence is difficult to interpret because it appears to assert an identity between Christ and the Holy Spirit. Such an identification would contradict the doctrine of the Trinity which states that God is one substance, but three persons. The persons of the Trinity are not identical to one another.

The context indicates that Paul used the term *Lord* here and in 3:16 to refer to Christ and that he spoke figuratively about the relationship between Christ and the Holy Spirit. He did not intend to describe an identity between Christ and the Holy Spirit. As the immediate context makes clear, Paul did not always speak literally. In the preceding three verses, he had described the related realities of Moses' veil and contemporary Jewish dullness by identifying one with the other. Thus, it is likely that when he identified Christ with **the Spirit,** he used a figure of speech (cf. Phil. 1:21).

He really meant something like "the Lord is the one who sent the Spirit" or "the Spirit is of the Lord." This is evident from 3:17b, which refers to **the Spirit of the Lord.** This second half of the verse assumes that the first half does not equate the Lord with the Spirit, but asserts a close connection between them. Paul had already drawn this connection between Christ and the Spirit a number of times in this context.

Paul explained how those who turned to Christ had the veil removed by declaring that **where the Spirit of the Lord is, there is freedom.** Paul had not yet touched on the theme of **freedom** in this context, but elsewhere in his epistles this idea is clear enough. Those who seek salvation through obedience to the Law of Moses (as many Jews did in Paul's day) are in bondage to the law and death (Rom. 6:6–22; Gal. 2:4; cf. Heb. 2:15). Those in Christ, however, are free from the dominion of sin and death (Rom. 7:6). In Christ believers are set free from sin's guilt and influence. Believers are no longer slaves to sin, incapable of resisting its influence over their behavior. Instead, they become free to withstand sin and to do good instead of evil. **Freedom** stood as one of those words that Paul used to summarize the experience of salvation in Christ.

Paul did not mean that believers were free from all obligation to obey God. Rather, for Paul **freedom** in Christ was only freedom from sin—it was not also freedom from righteousness. In fact, freedom from sin was slavery to righteousness. Only this slavery to righteousness enabled a person to serve "in the new way of the Spirit, and not in the old way of the written code" (Rom. 7:6). It is easier to understand Paul's perspective and vocabulary when one considers that he probably drew the image of **freedom** not from slaves and freemen in the Roman empire, but from Israel's freedom from their slavery in Egypt. Thus, he did not contrast slavery to another's control with freedom to be autonomous. Instead, he contrasted slavery to a sinful power that prevented proper worship with the freedom to be ruled by God—to obey him and to worship him.

3:18. Paul closed this section with a description of the new life of freedom that all believers enjoy in Christ. He declared that **we . . . with unveiled faces all reflect the Lord's glory.** By "we" Paul identified himself and those who ministered the new covenant with him, just as Moses ministered the old covenant. Of course, the same is also true for every minister of the new covenant. Ministers of the gospel of Christ **all reflect the Lord's glory.** By this Paul did not detract from his statement that all believers (not just ministers) have the veils removed from their hearts. He simply returned to his main issue: defending his own ministry and actions.

With the phrase "reflect the Lord's glory," the NIV translation becomes problematic. This phrase may also be translated as "beholding as in a mirror the glory of the Lord" (NASB). Both translations fit because they conform to the analogy set up between Moses and the ministers of the new covenant.

Moses both beheld and reflected the glory of God. Like Moses, the ministers of Christ are **being transformed into his likeness** as they are sanctified by the Spirit of God. But the transformation that takes place in followers of Christ has **ever-increasing glory**, unlike Moses' fading glory. This expanding glory **comes from the Lord, who is the Spirit.**

Once again, the language that describes the connection between the **Lord** and the **Spirit** is difficult to interpret. Literally, the Greek text reads, "the Lord Spirit." Various translations have taken different approaches to this statement, such as "the Lord, the Spirit" (NRSV) and "the Spirit of the Lord" (NKJV). Grammatically, all of these options are viable. However, their meanings are ultimately the same. We receive glory from Christ, who has sent us his Spirit.

> **MAIN IDEA REVIEW:** *Paul began to discuss more details of his ministry experiences, then turned aside to talk about how wonderfully God had provided for him. Praising God led the apostle into a lengthy explanation that he was not promoting himself, but the grace of God in Christ.*

III. CONCLUSION

The Glory of New Covenant Ministry

In this passage Paul left the path of his main story to speak about the nature of his ministry. He first affirmed the wonderful blessings God had provided him as he traveled, preaching the gospel. To defend against the accusation of self-aggrandizement, he reminded the Corinthians of the superiority of ministers of the new covenant over even Moses. The glory of the former far exceeds the glory of the latter.

PRINCIPLES

- God has appointed ministers to preach his Word and to call people to repentance and faith in Christ.
- When laypeople minister to others, they also serve the new covenant.
- God is able to use the proclamations of both trained and untrained believers to bring others to Christ.

APPLICATIONS

- Those who proclaim the gospel should do so sincerely and as ones who are accountable to the Lord.
- We should place our confidence in Christ as we minister the new covenant.

- We should be joyful and feel honored that God allows us to participate in his new covenant ministry.

IV. LIFE APPLICATION

Proud Grandparents

My friend and I stopped behind a car at a traffic signal and read its three bumper-stickers: "Grandparents—and Proud of it"; "Ask Me About My Grandchild"; and "Nothin' Better than Being a Grandfather!" My friend told me, "If I ever become a grandfather, I'll never do that. It's just not that big a deal."

Recently my friend became a grandfather. He has not put any bumper stickers on his car, but every time I see him he has only one thing on his mind: his granddaughter. He talks about her all the time. Whenever he meets people, he pulls out her picture and expects them to react with amazement at how wonderful she is.

Why do grandparents act this way? To some, it may seem that they are full of pride. Sometimes they act as if they are the only grandparents who have ever lived, or as if their grandchild is the best of all. But every grandparent knows that this is just how they express their tremendous joy. They just cannot stop talking about it. They nearly explode with excitement.

In this chapter Paul nearly exploded with excitement over the joy of his ministry. The Corinthians thought he was proud of his accomplishments, but he was actually overwhelmed with what God had done in his life. His role as a minister of the new covenant was a gracious gift from God that he did not deserve.

As a result of this call to ministry, all ministers must behave honorably and respectfully, recognizing that God has called them to administer the new covenant in Christ to his people. Gospel ministers should be respected by virtue of the glory of the new covenant. God has appointed them to preach his word and to hold his people to his covenant.

When lay believers minister to others, they also serve the new covenant and they must rely on God for their sufficiency. Ministry must flow from true love for the gospel and for others. We must conduct ourselves respectfully, without compromising the message, recognizing the great honor God bestows on us by allowing us to serve him. We may be confident that God will use our proclamations to bring people to Christ.

V. PRAYER

Lord Jesus, what a privilege it is to live in the new covenant. When we wonder if you have blessed us, help us to see that we have received a glorious faith—a treasure of glory that belongs to all who follow you. Amen.

VI. DEEPER DISCOVERIES

A. New (3:6)

Kainos, translated as "new," must be clearly distinguished from *neos,* the New Testament's other typical word for "new." *Neos* denotes that which is brand new, that which is temporally new. *Kainos,* on the other hand, indicates newness or distinctiveness in comparison with other things. It refers to nature rather than to temporality. It may also be translated with words like "different, unusual, impressive, better, improved, superior, or renewed." Paul probably intended several of these meanings, including "better," "superior" and "renewed." The new covenant is "better" because it brings righteousness and is of surpassing, lasting glory. It is "renewed" because it does not supplant the glory of the old covenant, but simply removes the veil so that that glory may be seen more clearly.

B. Glory, Glorious (3:7–11,18)

Paul's idea of "glory" is rooted in the Old Testament, as can be seen especially from his discussion of Moses and the veil. He used the word *doxa* for "glory" and "glorious." In the New Testament, which draws heavily on the Septuagint's use, its meaning differs significantly from its use in secular Greek, where *doxa* meant "opinion" or "reputation." In the Septuagint, *doxa* predominantly translated the Hebrew *kabod.*

When used of people, *kabod* had a broad range of meaning, including "portable possessions, standing/status, importance, prestige, nobility," and "inner strength." It basically referred to those things that one might possess that commanded respect from others (Gen. 31:1; Isa. 17:4).

C. The Lord Is the Spirit; the Lord, Who Is the Spirit (3:17–18)

Paul lived before the controversies surrounding the nature of God and before the church's creedal formulation of the doctrine of the Trinity (God has one substance and three persons). This does not mean that Paul was not trinitarian. But it does mean that he was not sensitive to the controversies in which the church was later to become embroiled. Had such controversy existed in his day, Paul certainly would have stated this verse differently.

One may say that Paul assumed his readers were trinitarians. He would have expected them to interpret his words consistently with the rest of the Scripture, Jesus' words, and the apostles' teachings. He certainly did not contradict Christ, who clearly distinguished himself from the Holy Spirit (Luke 12:10). Paul expected his readers to pick up on his figurative language and to understand his meaning especially through his statement: "the Spirit of the Lord" (3:17). Paul's own writings demonstrate that he also distinguished between the persons of Christ and the Holy Spirit (Eph. 1:13; Titus 3:5–6).

VII. TEACHING OUTLINE

A. INTRODUCTION

1. Lead Story: Stop Talking About Yourself
2. Context: Paul's purpose in speaking of his experiences was not for the purpose of personal promotion. Paul viewed his life as a living testimony to the transforming power and grace of God and the witness of the Corinthian believers was the result of God's Spirit working through him.
3. Transition: No witness we could ever give for Christ is as powerful or as persuasive as that of our own personal experience of what God has accomplished through our lives. When our motivation is love for others, and not pride in our own competency, Christ will be glorified.

B. COMMENTARY

1. Continuing the Explanation (2:12–13)
    a. Open door in Troas (2:12)
    b. No peace of mind (2:13)
2. Paul's Ministry of Triumph (2:14–17)
    a. Thanks to God for empowering Paul's ministry (2:14a,16b)
    b. Triumphal procession (2:14b–16a)
    c. Paul's sincerity and divine commission (2:17)
3. Confidence from a New Covenant (3:1–6)
4. The New Covenant Contrasted with the Old Covenant (3:7–18)

C. CONCLUSION: PROUD GRANDPARENTS

VIII. ISSUES FOR DISCUSSION

1. What is an "open door"? Why did Paul have no peace of mind even when God had given him an open door? Was Paul justified in leaving Troas even when he had an open door? Why or why not?
2. What does it mean to speak before God with sincerity? What does it mean to peddle the Word? When you talk about the gospel, do you think you do so with sincerity, or do you sometimes peddle?
3. What is the new covenant? How does it relate to the old covenant? How does it compare to the old covenant? Why?
4. What is the doctrine of the Trinity? Does Paul's language about the Lord and the Spirit support or oppose this doctrine? How? Does your church believe and teach the doctrine of the Trinity? Do you believe the doctrine of the Trinity? Why or why not?

2 Corinthians 4:1–18

Inside-Out Salvation

I. INTRODUCTION
Not Much to Look At

II. COMMENTARY
A verse-by-verse explanation of this section.

III. CONCLUSION
Looking Beyond Outward Circumstances

An overview of the principles and applications from this section.

IV. LIFE APPLICATION
It Will All Be Worth It in the End

Melding the section to life.

V. PRAYER
Tying the section to life with God.

VI. DEEPER DISCOVERIES
Historical, geographical, and grammatical enrichment of the commentary.

VII. TEACHING OUTLINE
Suggested step-by-step group study of the section.

VIII. ISSUES FOR DISCUSSION
Zeroing the section in on daily life.

Quote

"*K*ill us, torture us, condemn us, grind us to dust; your injustice is the proof that we are innocent. . . . The oftener we are mown down by you, the more in number we grow; the blood of Christians is seed."

Tertullian

2 Corinthians 4:1–18

IN A NUTSHELL

*P*aul continued his digression on defending and explaining his ministry. Having established the wonder of his being a minister of the new covenant, he offered a more negative portrait of his ministry, focusing on the suffering he and his company experienced for Christ's sake. Even so, Paul was confident that this suffering would lead to his own honor, to the benefit of the Corinthians, and to God's glory.

Inside-Out Salvation

I. INTRODUCTION

Not Much to Look At

*I*t was the first trip out of the inner city for most of the team. The basketball team of PS 122 was on the way to scrimmage a suburban private school. Tension filled the bus as the players stared out the windows at the rolling hills, huge houses, and lovely parks. When they pulled into the school parking lot, everyone was silent. The manicured schoolyard had as its centerpiece an Olympic-size swimming pool in front of a new gymnasium.

When the PS 122 team left the locker room for the gym floor, their hearts sank even further. The opposition team had special warm up suits, the players were all good-looking, and they smirked with superiority. PS 122 had only their playing uniforms, no fans, no band, no confidence.

In the last minutes before the game began, the coach of PS 122 called his team together. "Guys," he said, "they look good, but they *only* look good. The question today is not who looks good on the outside. The question is who's strong on the inside. We're not much to look at, but I know what's inside each one of you. Now get out there and play ball!"

In this passage the apostle Paul spoke of his life in this way. He had to admit that outwardly his ministry was not much to look at. He was like a fragile jar of clay. But something very special was on the inside of this jar of clay. Paul had been entrusted with the gospel of Christ. This treasure in his heart made it certain that Paul would be victorious over every challenge that came his way.

II. COMMENTARY

Inside-Out Salvation

> **MAIN IDEA:** *Because the Corinthians had questioned his motives and methods, Paul gave them further insight into his ministry. They needed to know that Paul's experience in ministry was a mixture of blessings from God and suffering for their sakes.*

A Serving in an Unveiled Ministry (4:1–6)

> **SUPPORTING IDEA:** *Paul stated that he expected God to triumph over Satan, re-creating people through the proclamation of the gospel, just as God had worked to re-create Paul through this same revelation.*

4:1. Paul began by drawing attention to a result of his experience as a minister of Christ. He reflected that **since** he had received **this ministry**, certain things had taken place in his life. The **ministry** to which he referred was serving in the new covenant, the glory of which exceeded that of the old covenant under Moses. Paul confessed that he felt so honored to have this place in God's purposes that he did **not lose heart** for his work as an apostle. From the verses that follow we see that to **lose heart** meant at least two things: (1) Paul did not give in to the temptation to use deceit in his ministry, and (2) he did not crumble to the pressures of persecution and hardship.

4:2. Rather than losing heart, Paul **renounced** certain behaviors that would have been inappropriate to his calling. Some of the Corinthian Christians had accused Paul of insincerity because he had not fulfilled his planned visit. Perhaps they had even asserted that Paul was a manipulative, false teacher. There are also indications that other teachers in the church, perhaps rivals of Paul, did use insincere tactics. Paul insisted that his awareness of the glorious ministry to which he had been called compelled him not to manipulate or to teach falsely.

Paul described the inappropriate practices that he resisted with three phrases. First, he said he would not resort to **secret and shameful ways.** Paul did not use underhanded tactics or methods in his ministry. Paul did not suggest there was nothing shameful in his life. He was not perfect (Gal. 5:17). Instead, he spoke of his goals and strategies in ministry. In this respect, Paul had nothing to hide. If the most secret aspects of his service to Christ were revealed, he would still have nothing of which to be ashamed. He had always ministered in holiness and sincerity, according to God's grace, and had even sworn with God as his witness that his motivations had always been pure. Paul had no skeletons in his closet.

Second, Paul insisted that he did **not use deception.** Often in the New Testament, the term translated here as "deception" (*panourgia*) denotes deplorable action or speech that tricks others. But Paul was so confident of the glory of ministering in the new covenant that he never resorted to this means of persuasion.

Third, Paul rejected the accusation that he would **distort the word of God** in his preaching and teaching. Paul's opponents could have considered any number of Paul's teachings to be distortions. For example, he rejected a legalistic outlook on the role of Old Testament law in the Christian church. In his earlier Corinthian epistle, Paul had also attacked those who relied too heavily on human wisdom. He had taught that Christians could eat meat that had been offered to idols, but also insisted that the weaknesses of others should take precedence. The natural response of Paul's opponents on these issues would have been to accuse him of distorting the Scriptures. But Paul rejected this accusation as unthinkable.

Instead, Paul took a different approach in his teaching and preaching. He presented **the truth plainly**. Paul was so convinced of this character of his ministry that he **commend[ed]** his ministry **to every man's conscience**. Paul did not fear scrutiny of his message or methods. In fact, he welcomed it so long as those who judged him did so **in the sight of God**. If his opponents sought to evaluate his ministry from good motivations rather than from evil desires, Paul was happy to receive these evaluations.

4:3. Why was Paul so open to evaluation? Some had argued that Paul's **gospel** was **veiled** because it deceived and distorted, but Paul knew otherwise. The gospel of Christ appears **veiled** only **to those who are perishing**. This precise terminology (*tois appollumenois*) also appears in 2:15, where Paul described his ministry as a fragrance of death to those who rejected Christ (see also 2 Thess. 2:10). Here he alluded to the metaphor of the Roman triumphal parade once again. How we respond to the gospel is not a matter of intellectual insight or philosophical acumen. It is a matter of spiritual condition.

4:4. Paul went on to explain in what sense the gospel he preached was veiled to unbelievers. It was not that the message itself or its true ministers hid the glory of Christ. Instead, **the god of this age has blinded the minds of unbelievers**. When the Christian message is conveyed by ministers who deceive or who rely on worldly wisdom, the gospel may be veiled. But when it is proclaimed plainly with a focus on the glory of Christ in his death and resurrection, the problem does not reside in the gospel or in its ministers. The problem is that **unbelievers . . . cannot see the light of the gospel of the glory of Christ**.

A person with such spiritual blindness cannot see the proclamation of **Christ, who is the image of God**. The **god of this age** causes this blindness. This precise expression does not appear elsewhere in the New Testament, but it certainly refers to Satan. Paul adopted the Old Testament use of the word *god* in reference to supernatural or angelic beings, not to the Lord God (cf. Ps. 82:1). This use of "god" does not assert the true divinity of the beings it identifies. Rather, it indicates that the being so identified is worshiped as if it were divine. In reality, of course, it is not the divine Creator.

Satan is known in the New Testament as the ruler of this age (John 14:30). The phrase "this age" in Paul's epistles refers to the present world of sin and death as opposed to "the age to come" that has been inaugurated in Christ's first coming (Heb. 6:5) but awaits its consummation in his return (Luke 18:30). Satan and his demons have been given a measure of dominion over the fallen world (Eph. 6:12). One of their greatest powers is the ability to deceive and blind people to spiritual truths. Paul affirmed that this was the case when unbelievers rejected the gospel of Christ.

4:5. Why was Paul so convinced that the problem with unbelievers was in them and not in his presentation of the gospel? His reason was straightforward. True ministers of the gospel **do not preach [them]selves.** They do not draw attention to their own clever or eloquent speech; they do not lord their authority over others. Instead, they draw attention to **Jesus Christ as Lord.** The true Christian gospel always focuses on Christ's honor, not on the ministers who bear the message.

Paul insisted that instead of exalting themselves in their preaching, he and other true apostles presented themselves as the Corinthians' **servants for Jesus' sake.** Paul had sacrificed much for the Corinthians and the other churches to which he preached. He had not even exercised his right to be paid for his work. He humbled himself in this way **for Jesus' sake,** so that Jesus alone would be honored.

4:6. Why did Paul lower himself and honor Christ exclusively? His reason stemmed from God's incredible act toward him. Paul described this divine act by drawing a connection between the light of creation and the light of re-creation in Christ. As the Genesis account reports, on the first day of creation, **God . . . said, "Let light shine out of darkness."** Paul did not quote the Genesis record precisely, but he paraphrased it to draw the connection to Christ. God's creative act of calling for light broke the darkness of the primordial world.

Paul's confidence that true preaching focused on the glory of Christ rather than on its ministers rested in the fact that just as God first created light, **God . . . made his light shine in** their **hearts.** When God sent Christ, he acted much as he did when he created physical light. Jesus spoke of himself as the "light of the world" (John 8:12; 9:5) and taught that his followers were also the "light of the world" (Matt. 5:14). The New Testament also describes life in Christ as walking in the light (1 John 2:8–10).

The illumination of the **hearts** of individuals is not just a mental state of enlightenment. From Paul's perspective, it is an act of re-creation. Christ's coming into the world, and the illumination of individuals to see his light, is a gracious divine act by which believers receive **the knowledge of the glory of God in the face of Christ.** When Paul came to know Christ personally on the road to Damascus (Acts 9:3), this act of God surpassed the original act of creation in its ability to reveal the glory of God.

Paul expressed this conviction to validate his claim that his preaching was about **Jesus . . . as Lord** and not about himself or some other. He was so captivated by the greatness of the revelation of Christ that he could do nothing else.

B Suffering for the Gospel (4:7–12)

SUPPORTING IDEA: *Paul stated that his weaknesses and failures existed to demonstrate God's glory, giving Paul further confidence in the gospel.*

4:7. Paul began this section with a clear thesis statement that he would develop in the verses to follow. Although Paul and other apostles were determined to serve in ministry because of the light of Christ in their hearts, they had **this treasure in jars of clay**. The image of this metaphor is twofold. On the one hand, there is **treasure**. The **treasure** represents the new covenant ministry empowered by "the light of the knowledge of the glory of God" (4:6). In Paul's day earthenware containers were used to hold many different items. Paul had in mind precious items such as silver or gold. Paul viewed the gospel and its ministry as precious cargo.

On the other hand, this priceless gospel ministry was carried about **in jars of clay**. Artifacts from Paul's day indicate that not all items were stored in earthenware containers. Boxes of gold and ivory, decorated with precious stones, were available for the wealthy. Yet, it was common for items of great value to be stored in inexpensive pots of clay.

The counterpart to the jars of clay in Paul's metaphor is the ministers themselves. Paul had in mind not only the physical body, but also the many trials and troubles that came upon him and those who ministered with him. He introduced the idea that God had placed the treasure of the gospel ministry in frail, ordinary humans. A priceless treasure was contained in common earthenware.

Paul chose this metaphor because it symbolized the reality of his ministry. He had received the incredible light of God in Christ and was commissioned to spread this gospel throughout the world on Christ's behalf. Yet, this precious treasure did not raise Paul out of ordinary human life. He still faced the weaknesses of physical trials and persecutions in this world.

What was the purpose of this design? The grand message of Christ was carried through the world by ordinary, weak human beings **to show that this all-surpassing power** was **from God and not from** the ministers. The expression **all-surpassing power** alludes to 4:6, which focused on the divine power demonstrated first at the command that light appear (Gen. 1:3), and later in the order that the light of Christ shine in the hearts of believers. God spoke and the light of creation shone; he spoke and the light of re-creation shone as well.

This power of God was also evident in the preaching of the gospel (Rom. 15:18–19). The weakness of Paul and other ministers, coupled with their refusal to use deception, could not have produced the powerful, re-creative effects that the gospel produced. God chose weak creatures to minister the gospel so that it would be all the more clear that he had accomplished the work through these ministers (2 Tim. 1:8).

The effectiveness of their ministry might have caused some people to attribute honor to the ministers themselves. But Paul insisted that the weakness of the **jars of clay** demonstrated that ministers of the gospel deserved no glory for their work. The power came through weak instruments to demonstrate that it was **from God and not from** the ministers.

4:8–10. To illustrate what he meant by treasure in jars of clay, Paul described some of the hardships he and other ministers of the gospel faced. He began with a series of examples and followed with a summary.

In a series of four pairs of terms, Paul described specific ways in which the lives of gospel ministers were like earthenware that contained treasures. The first member of each pair described the hardship they experienced as frail jars of clay. The second member indicated how God demonstrated his power (treasure) in them by sustaining them through the hardships. The following table of these pairs illustrates the apostle's perspective.

Jars of Clay	Treasure
hard pressed	not crushed
perplexed	not in despair
persecuted	not abandoned
struck down	not destroyed

The precise meaning of each term is difficult to discern. We must be careful not to tie too specific a meaning to any of these terms. Our comments will remain rather general.

Hard pressed . . . but not crushed. This first pair of terms flows from the metaphor of the jars of clay. The image is of earthenware vessels that do not break even when placed under great strain. To be **hard pressed** (*thlibo*) or "afflicted" is to be troubled from without by physical or psychological difficulties. While Paul and other ministers of the gospel endured many afflictions as did frail earthenware, they were not **crushed** (*stenochoreomai*). They were not overcome by these afflictions because they had the treasure of the gospel of Christ.

Perplexed, but not in despair. Here and in the following word pairs, Paul's choice of words began to rely more on the prior word pair (**hard pressed/crushed**) than on the original metaphor (jars of clay). He expressed himself with a wordplay: **perplexed** (*aporoumenoi*, from *aporeo*) and **despair** (*exaporoumenoi*, from *exaporeo*) are based on the same root in the Greek lanugage. The latter is more intensive. To be **perplexed** is to be in a state of confusion and discouragement because of afflictions and troubles. When used alone, **despair** (*exaporeomai*) describes well the discouragement that Paul and others felt. When contrasted with **perplexed** (*aporeo*), however, **despair** (*exaporeomai*) means something more narrow. **Despair** (*exaporeomai*) in this context means something comparable to "utter despair lacking all hope or positive counterbalance." Even though Paul and his company were deeply troubled at times, they never gave up because they had a great treasure.

Persecuted, but not abandoned. To be **persecuted** (*dioko*) is to be hunted down or chased about by others. Persecution was widespread against the early church. The persecution of the ministers of the gospel indicated how much they were earthenware jars. Yet, Paul insisted that even in persecution they were **not abandoned.** God never left them alone. He was with them in all of their persecutions (Matt. 28:20; Heb. 13:5).

Struck down, but not destroyed. When Paul spoke of being **struck down** (*kataballo*), he probably had in mind a wrestling metaphor rather than actual physical blows. A wrestler was "struck down" when he was thrown to the floor. To be thrown to the floor was a setback for a wrestler, as it was for apostles and ministers of the gospel. Yet, to be thrown down was not the same as being **destroyed** (*apollumi*) or defeated in the match. The path to victory for Paul and his company included setbacks, but they would be victorious over their foes.

After listing these four pairs of experiences, Paul summarized the experiences that he and his company endured. As jars of clay, they **always carr[ied] around in** their **body the death of Jesus.** Paul frequently mentioned that Christ's suffering and death on the cross overflowed into the life of the church (Rom. 8:17; Gal. 6:17). To **carry around** the death of Christ was to suffer repeatedly for his glory. Paul declared that these sufferings happen **always.** He and his company did not experience their union with Christ's sufferings in one act. They endured the suffering repeatedly everywhere they went.

Even so, there was a purpose to all this suffering. The goal was that **the life of Jesus** might **also be revealed in** their **body.** Paul taught throughout his epistles that the reward for those who suffered for Christ was a resurrection body for eternal life (Phil. 3:10–11). This resurrection in the future will result from our union with the resurrection of Christ (Rom. 6:5). The troubles that believers experience in this world will result in the glory of the next world.

4:11. Paul explained why his statement of 4:10 was true. He spoke of **we who are alive,** meaning the apostles and those other ministers who had not died or been killed, especially those who ministered with him. Even though they are still alive, they are **always being given over to death**. The experience of Christian ministry is constantly to go through the process of dying. For what purpose did Paul and his company suffer? **So that** Christ's **life** might **be revealed in** the **mortal body**. The corruptible, mortal human bodies of believers will enjoy the resurrection power that brought Jesus back to life. His **life** will be displayed in what God does with our **mortal body**.

4:12. Paul closed this section with a two-sided conclusion. This is one of the few times Paul clearly distinguished **we** (apostles, himself, and those in his company) from **you** (the Corinthians to whom he wrote). First, Paul drew a conclusion about himself and other Christian ministers of the gospel: **death** was **at work in** them. The meaning of this expression is clear from the context; specifically, they "are always being given over to death" (4:11). Second, Paul drew an unexpected conclusion about the Corinthians. They were not dying. Instead, **life** was **at work in** them as well.

Paul did not want the Corinthians to forget that they benefited from the sufferings of the ministers of the gospel. The pain and trials endured by Paul and others made it possible for the Corinthians to have eternal life in Christ. Those who suffered brought the gospel to the church, teaching and leading the church. The Corinthians should have realized that their new life in Christ came at the cost of suffering by those who ministered to them.

C Confidence Through the Suffering (4:13–18)

SUPPORTING IDEA: *Paul closed this section with a strong affirmation of the beliefs that served as foundation to his discussion throughout this chapter*

4:13. Why had Paul spoken of the suffering and blessing of being a minister of the gospel? How did he hold both of these themes together? To answer this question, Paul referred to Psalm 116 by quoting from one line: **I believed; therefore I have spoken**. Psalm 116 is a prayer of thanksgiving for God's deliverance from affliction. In this verse (Ps. 116:10), the Psalmist recounted how he had trusted the Lord and how he had spoken of his afflictions to the Lord. He had done so with the hope that the Lord would answer his prayer and deliver him.

Paul probably thought of this psalm because it coupled these ideas of faith with complaints of the suffering and death of God's servants. For instance, Psalm 116:3 reads, "The cords of death entangled me, the anguish of the grave came upon me; I was overcome by trouble and sorrow." Similarly, Psalm 116:15 proclaims, "Precious in the sight of the LORD is the death of his saints." Paul had just written that he had been persecuted and had despaired and that death worked in him. Still, his faith remained strong. Under these conditions, he identified with the psalmist. Thus, Paul quoted the psalmist's assertion of faith, implying that he spoke **with that same spirit of faith.** Just like the psalmist, he and his company **also believe[d] and therefore** spoke laments over their suffering as well as praise for divine deliverance.

4:14. Paul explained why he believed that even in the midst of great suffering God would deliver the ministers of the gospel. His reason began with the affirmation that God **raised the Lord Jesus from the dead.** Yet, this conviction about Jesus bore on the subject at hand only because Paul also believed that God would **also raise** him and his fellow ministers **with Jesus,** just as he would raise all believers.

Paul added another thought that expressed the greatness of his vision even further. Not only will God eventually raise ministers of the gospel with Christ; he will also **present us** (ministers of the gospel) **with you** (the Corinthians) **in his presence.** Paul hoped that God would reward him and other ministers for their suffering by resurrecting them in Christ, but he also believed they would share that resurrection life with all believers. In this way, the suffering of those who proclaim the gospel results in life for all believers.

4:15. Paul declared that the suffering of ministers, their confidence in speaking the gospel, and their future resurrection was **for** the Corinthians' **benefit.** Throughout this passage he drew attention to the fact that he and his company had suffered for the sake of the Corinthian church. He had not been insincere or duplicitous. He had not pursued worldly goals or peddled God's word for profit. And he had not acted from spite or love of power. Instead, he and his company had served faithfully, enduring hardship for the sake of the church at large and for the believers in Corinth.

But Paul knew that benefiting all believers was not the ultimate basis of his confidence in the future. Instead, he aligned his thoughts with the psalms of thanksgiving, like Psalm 116 from which he had quoted. The ultimate purpose of the apostolic ministry was that the gospel might reach **more and more people** throughout the world. These people would then **cause thanksgiving to overflow to the glory of God.**

Paul knew that God desires to be honored by people for his goodness. God's glory is the reason for all creation (Rom. 11:36). Paul used this principle to explain the suffering he and his company experienced and the future resurrection for which they and the Corinthians hoped. Paul's confidence flowed from his understanding that God purposed everything in his ministry to contribute to the **glory of God.**

4:16. In summary, Paul reaffirmed that he did **not lose heart.** As he had already illustrated so clearly, the apostle could draw a sharp distinction between what was happening to him **outwardly** and **inwardly.** In terms of his physical existence—what he called "jars of clay"—the suffering and hardship he faced as an apostle caused him to say that he was **wasting away.** This assessment of the human condition is true in a general sense for everyone.

On a physical level, we are all moving toward death. Yet, Paul had in mind not only physical suffering but hardships of every kind. In terms of the externals of his life, Paul was **wasting away.**

By contrast, **inwardly** Paul found the opposite to be true. He was **being renewed day by day.** This distinction between the outward and inward dimensions of human existence does not indicate that Paul hated his body or that he wished to escape physical existence. On the contrary, to be without one's body was to be in a state of nakedness that could be remedied only by the physical resurrection when Christ returns.

At the present time, though, a paradoxical situation exists for followers of Christ. On the one hand, they have believed the gospel and have been granted salvation. The Holy Spirit lives within believers as the "deposit guaranteeing our inheritance" (Eph. 1:14), bringing many spiritual blessings into their lives. On the other hand, they have yet to be granted full salvation, including the resurrection of their bodies at the end of the age. This is why Paul spoke of himself as decaying and being renewed at the same time. As he waited for his physical existence to be renewed at the resurrection, he took comfort and joy in the renewal of his inward person by the ministry of the Holy Spirit.

4:17. Paul had a more specific explanation of his inward renewal in mind. He found encouragement and refreshment during his sufferings by assessing them to be **light and momentary**—in other words, to be relatively insignificant by comparison with the **eternal glory that far outweighs them.** In line with the teaching of the Old and New Testaments, Paul was confident that all true believers would receive the eternal reward of glory and honor in the new heavens and new earth. The difficulties of this life are minor when compared to the wonder of our eternal salvation.

4:18a. Even so, this theological fact was of little help to Paul until he went beyond just knowing its truth. He resolved to **fix** his **eyes** on the future glory. Paul determined to focus his attention and center his hopes and priorities away from this life to the next. He insisted that he looked away from **what is seen** to **what is unseen.** We have to be careful not to confuse **seen** and **unseen** with physical and spiritual realities. The contrast is actually between the current reality of suffering and the future reality of full salvation at Christ's return. Future salvation will be physical as well as spiritual, but it is unseen because it has not yet come. By fixing his attention on the future salvation in Christ, Paul found strength in the disappointments and hardships of this life.

4:18b. Why did this concentration on the future help Paul so much? He explained that the value of this gaze into the future rests in the fact that what can be **seen** now **is temporary;** it will pass away at death and at the return of Christ. But the **unseen,** the future salvation to come at Christ's return, **is eter-**

nal. Once Christ returns in glory and brings the fullness of salvation to his people, that state of blessing will never end.

> **MAIN IDEA REVIEW:** *Because the Corinthians had questioned his motives and methods, Paul offered them further insight into his ministry. They needed to know that Paul's experience in ministry was a mixture of blessings from God and suffering for their sakes.*

III. CONCLUSION

Looking Beyond Outward Circumstances

In this passage Paul the apostle gave another important outlook on his ministry. Outwardly, his life was not much to look at. He lived with suffering and hardship throughout his Christian experience. He was not very successful in human terms. At the same time, Paul remained confident of his high calling as an apostle of Christ by looking beyond his outward circumstances to his inward renewal in Christ's blessings and the great future that would be his when Christ returned. As we face suffering for the sake of the gospel, we can take courage in the same work of Christ within us.

PRINCIPLES

- The glory that Christians will receive through the gospel is worth the suffering we endure.
- God is sovereign, having both infinite power and an ordained plan.
- New covenant ministers do not serve in their own strength. God allows undeserving people to serve him, and he gives them the abilities they need to do so.
- People do not reject the gospel because we present it poorly or because it lacks power; they reject it because Satan blinds them.

APPLICATIONS

- The knowledge of the blessings we will receive in the end times should comfort us in our present sufferings.
- Ordained ministers and laypeople who minister must rely on God's mercy for their effectiveness.
- Believers should present the truth plainly, not trusting clever speech to accomplish God's work.
- When we suffer for the gospel, we should be encouraged that our suffering honors Christ and advances the gospel.

IV. LIFE APPLICATION

It Will All Be Worth It in the End

Mothers amaze me. The pain and hardship they go through to bring a child into this world is astounding. They should be applauded for their strength and commitment. Frankly, I just do not know how they do it.

When I witnessed my daughter's birth, I gave thanks to God for two things. First, I praised him for my new baby. What a precious gift to hold in my arms! But after a moment or two, a second praise came to my lips. I thanked God for not making me a woman. Yes, that is right. After I had seen what my wife went through bringing our daughter into the world, I was grateful that I was the husband.

I have asked a number of mothers why they chose to go through the ordeal of pregnancy and delivery time and again. Many of them have told me the same thing. "I made it by telling myself over and over, 'It will all be worth it in the end.'"

In this passage Paul talked about how suffering for Christ is worth it in the end. He focused on his own ministry as an apostle, but his words teach us about all ministers of the gospel. Paul took confidence in suffering by remembering that it would all be worth it in the end; we can also find the same comfort in our own troubles.

Perhaps one of the greatest principles that Paul relied on in this passage was God's sovereignty. Paul's knowledge of God's power and plan assured him that the gospel would triumph in spite of the suffering of its ministers. The sovereignty of God led Paul to believe that the gospel would triumph over the world and that he would receive great blessings.

Paul first mentioned God's sovereignty when he said that God mercifully allows people to minister. True new covenant ministers do not serve in their own strength or knowledge. Rather, God graciously allows undeserving people to serve, and he grants them the necessary abilities to do so. This does not imply that Christians should not study God's Word, nor does it mean that ministers do not need to be qualified for their positions. It does say that we must rely on God's mercy for the effectiveness of our service to Christ.

Ministers should trust that God will accomplish his purpose through the simple, straightforward means of gospel ministry. They should not use underhanded or dubious means in their work. God's gospel has all the power necessary to bring people to faith. The same is true for all believers when they bear witness to the truth. Knowing God's power should encourage us to present our faith plainly and truthfully. We do not need to be clever or powerful for God to use us.

Sometimes when we present the gospel, our message is rejected. Paul has shown us that people do not reject our message because we present it poorly or because the gospel lacks power. They do so because Satan blinds them to the truth. In Paul's mind, this failure of the gospel to convert everyone who hears it does not call God's sovereignty into question. It proved to him—and it should prove to us—that every conversion to Christ occurs through a divine, re-creative act.

Persecution also increased Paul's confidence for two reasons. First, his suffering proved that he was not equal in his own strength to the task he had been given; therefore, any success he had showed that God was in the work. Second, the fact that Paul was not destroyed by his sufferings encouraged him that his strength came from God. Christian weakness demonstrates God's power. Suffering for the gospel honors Christ and advances the gospel and the kingdom of God.

V. PRAYER

O Lord, we give you thanks for your courage to suffer on our behalf. We also praise you for the courage you gave to so many in the past who suffered in your service. Now, O God, we cry out to you for the same courage as we face opposition and trials for the sake of the gospel. Keep us mindful of those who have gone before us. Keep our eyes fixed on the blessings that lie ahead. Amen.

VI. DEEPER DISCOVERIES

A. God (4:4)

Often in the Old Testament, and sometimes in the New Testament, the term *god* applies to a false god rather than to the Lord. This can be seen quite clearly in references to "gods" (*elohim*). There are also many references to a single "god" (*el*) that is not true God (Exod. 34:14; Ps. 81:9; Dan. 11:36). Sometimes, even the "plural" form *elohim* identifies such a false god (Deut. 4:34; 2 Kgs. 1:16).

Modern translations sometimes reflect this by substituting words other than "god" for those occurrences that do not refer to the one true deity. For example, the NASB translates Psalm 82:1: "God . . . judges in the midst of the rulers." In this verse, both "God" and "rulers" translate the same Hebrew word *elohim*. Paul followed this Old Testament precedent by using "god" to refer to a supernatural or angelic being that was not the Lord God.

B. This Age (4:4)

The term "this age" (*tou aionos toutou*) derives from a common rabbinical expression of Paul's day (*'olam hazeh*). In this use, "this age" pertains to the fallen state of the world even while it is in the process of being restored to the form it will have when the kingdom of God reaches its consummation.

The kingdom of God comes in three phases: (1) the inauguration that took place in Christ's earthly ministry and the work of the apostles; (2) the church age which continues today; and (3) the return of Christ in the consummation of the kingdom.

The "age to come" invades "this age" in the same way the kingdom of God invades the current world order. The people of "this age" oppose the kingdom (Luke 16:8) and the principles of "the age to come." Those who participate in the kingdom now, however, also participate in the age to come.

While this is not always the force of "this age," it seems to be Paul's emphasis in this section. Paul did not mean that Satan controls the world and will continue to control it until the judgment. Jesus is already reigning above those who rule in this age (Eph. 1:21). Paul's point seems to have been that Satan is the "god" of those who live according to the fallen world order—the ruler of those who live according to the principles of "this age."

C. "Let Light Shine Out of Darkness" (4:6)

By referring to Genesis 1:3, Paul did not intend only to suggest God's power. He meant to highlight God's re-creative power in salvation that continued to be a re-creative act in the New Testament as well. Jesus receives all the blessings offered to Israel in the Old Testament and shares them with those who belong to him.

VII. TEACHING OUTLINE

A. INTRODUCTION

1. Lead Story: Not Much to Look At
2. Context: Paul was not much to look at. In and of himself, he lacked the power to combat Satan and to rescue souls. He lacked the power to avoid persecution. But he recognized that God's power was sufficient to carry the day and that he would ultimately benefit from God's victory.
3. Transition: We are much like Paul—insufficient for our task and totally dependent on God. The world looms over us, bringing discouragement. But we can be confident of ultimate victory because God is our sufficiency. He is able to use the world's backlash against us to convert people and to bring glory to himself.

B. COMMENTARY

1. Serving in an Unveiled Ministry (4:1–6)
   a. Paul's confidence expressed (4:1–4)
   b. Paul's confidence was in God (4:5–6)
2. Suffering for the Gospel (4:7–12)
   a. Paul's power was from God (4:7)
   b. Paul's suffering proved that his power was from God (4:8–9)
   c. Paul's suffering revealed Jesus (4:10–11)
   d. Paul's suffering benefited the Corinthians (4:12)
3. Confidence Through the Suffering (4:13–18)
   a. Paul was confident that God would preserve him through his suffering (4:13–14)
   b. Paul was confident that his suffering would benefit the Corinthians and others (4:15a)
   c. Paul was confident that God would receive all the glory (4:15b)
4. Paul was confident of future salvation (4:16–18)

C. CONCLUSION: IT WILL ALL BE WORTH IT IN THE END

VIII. ISSUES FOR DISCUSSION

1. Why did Paul not lose heart, even though he encountered much suffering in his ministry? How did he find confidence even in the rejection of his gospel? How did he find confidence even in suffering and persecution?
2. In Paul's description of God making his light shine in believers' hearts, what is the condition of the person before God does this work? What is the condition of the person after God does this work? What role did Paul ascribe to the person who experiences this transition?
3. Why did Paul compare God making his light shine in people's hearts to the creation account of Genesis 1? How are God's actions in salvation similar to his actions in creation?
4. What is the significance of the metaphor of treasure in earthenware jars?

2 Corinthians 5:1–6:2

❧

An Urgent Ministry

❧

Quote

"At my back I always hear

Time's winged chariot hurrying near;

And yonder all before us lie

Deserts of vast eternity."

A n d r e w   M a r v e l

2 Corinthians 5:1–6:2

 I N   A   N U T S H E L L

Paul offered a final assessment of his role as a weak human being who had been called to be an apostle. Like all people, he was frail and dying, but the permanence of what lies beyond this life made his ministry of ultimate importance.

An Urgent Ministry

I. INTRODUCTION

They Thought They Were Big Stuff Too

*I*t is so easy to forget how temporary this life is. We tend to live as if nothing will ever change, as if life will keep going as it always has. We think we'll always have tomorrow. But every now and then, reality breaks through and we see our lives for what they are: a fleeting moment.

Near the Boston Commons there is a frequently visited colonial graveyard. It is a fascinating place. Many gravestones and monuments mark the sites where a number of early Americans are buried. Most of the stones are broken and turned over, even in this well-kept graveyard. Most of the names and dates are no longer legible.

I remember one day when I was overwhelmed at the neglect those graves had suffered. "Do you realize," I said to my wife, "that the people buried here looked at their lives like we look at ours? They never imagined how short and insignificant their lives would be. Most of them thought they would be remembered forever. But look at them. Their great-great-grandchildren do not even remember their names."

It's a depressing thought. Our great-great-grandchildren will probably not remember you and me. We are here today, gone tomorrow.

The Christian gospel tells us that this fleeting life on earth is not our final end. If we are in Christ, we have a glorious destiny. Our descendants may forget us in this life, but God will not forget us in the world to come. Followers of Christ receive the hope of eternal life. This future hope gives us perspective on this life and its frailties and suffering. It gives us a destiny beyond imagination that empowers us to move forward in the service of Christ.

II. COMMENTARY

An Urgent Ministry

MAIN IDEA: *As Christians, we should balance a realistic assessment of our human frailties with the honor that Christ gives us now and after death. When we do this, we will hold fast to faith in Christ and receive the salvation that God has offered in him.*

Temporary and Eternal Dwellings (5:1–5)

> **SUPPORTING IDEA:** *Paul contrasted his fragile life and glorious ministry: life in this world is like living in a tent while waiting for a house.*

5:1. The apostle began with a statement of confidence. **We know** that certain things are true. Paul had already taught these truths to the Corinthians, and he was confident they had not forgotten them.

Life in the physical body is like living in an **earthly tent** because this body is being **destroyed**. All human bodies suffer the processes of aging and death. Yet, Paul, his company, and to some extent all believers experience intensified destruction of their earthly bodies. Suffering on Christ's behalf aggravates the decay that the Fall brought upon the human race. As Paul put it in the previous chapter, we are only fragile jars made of clay.

Paul was sure that his readers knew another truth as well: all true believers **have a building from God** that will replace the **earthly tent**. The present bodies of believers are only temporary homes; we wait for a permanent house. In Paul's day people used tents while they traveled and while they were building permanent homes. Paul had in mind tents in which people lived as they waited for permanent dwellings to be built. Peter used this same metaphor (2 Pet. 1:13–14), and the Old Testament also speaks of earthly life as a tent (Isa. 38:12).

Paul described the **building from God** as an **eternal house in heaven.** His words are difficult to understand, and they have been the subject of controversy. At least two prominent outlooks have been taken. First, some interpreters think Paul spoke of believers receiving permanent heavenly bodies when they die. This understanding agrees with Paul's personal focus in this discussion. Yet, it seems unlikely because Paul taught that believers' bodily resurrection would occur at Christ's return (Phil. 3:20–21; 1 Thess. 4:15–17).

Other interpreters suggest that Paul spoke of the heavenly temple of God providing protective cover for all believers. This view appeals to the expression, **not built by human hands**, which the writer of Hebrews uses to describe the heavenly temple (Heb. 9:11). This interpretation is possible, but it is questionable.

The third and most likely possibility is that Paul referred to the future resurrected bodies of believers, focusing on the eternal state without differentiating it from the intermediate state. According to this view, Paul did not address our heavenly experience before Christ's return. Because the intermediate state is not the goal that believers are to keep in mind, it is overshadowed by the permanent state after Christ's return.

The last verse of this section (5:10) supports this third view. Paul did not direct his attention to the human condition during a long intermediate state.

Instead, he focused on the day of judgment. The contra
was between what is done "while in the body" and how v
is due." Paul referred to the individual believer's glorio
but had in view the reception of that body on the last da

5:2. Before Christ returns, believers **groan**. This t
usually referred to pain and agony. Paul had in mind the longing
ers experience when they compare their present existence with their condition when Christ returns. The suffering and pain of life in this world causes
those with hope of resurrection life to cry out for **our heavenly dwelling** (cf.
Rom. 8:23).

5:3–4. Paul explained in these verses why we groan for the heavenly
dwelling. This verse is problematic in that textual witnesses differ. But it
seems the more difficult—and thus the more likely—reading is "when we are
clothed." The basic idea is that we groan in our present condition because **we
will not be found naked** when we leave this life.

Nakedness is a metaphor for being without a body. Literal nakedness
brought shame to sinful Adam and Eve (Gen. 3:7–10). God remedied their
nakedness with clothing (Gen. 3:21), covering their shame. Clothing
remained a consistent requirement throughout the Scriptures. For this reason, Paul likened being without a body after death to the condition of nakedness. Ultimate salvation is not that disembodied souls enjoy eternal bliss in
the heavenly realms, but that they are bodily resurrected (Rom. 8:23; Heb.
6:2) and inherit the new creation (Rev. 21:1–7).

The Corinthians understood this so well that Paul did not even argue for
it. He assumed they knew the groaning of this life was a longing for glorified,
resurrected bodies to be received on the day of Christ's return. The contrast
here was not between physical and spiritual, but between present, mortal,
physical bodies and future, immortal, physical bodies.

5:5. The apostle proclaimed with great confidence, **God . . . has made us
for this very purpose.** As Genesis states, God did not design human beings
to die, but to be clothed in immortal bodies. If Adam and Eve had passed the
test of the tree of the knowledge of good and evil, they would have realized
this destiny immediately. Now, however, that destiny has been accomplished
in Christ, who has redeemed his people and secured immortal bodies for
them. These will be inherited in the future.

Paul also taught that earthly life is not devoid of God's future blessing.
Believers have already received **the Spirit** who is **a deposit, guaranteeing
what is to come** (cf. Eph. 1:13–14). He drew upon the analogy of a down
payment that guaranteed full payment in the future. The ministry of the Holy
Spirit in his life and in the life of the Corinthian church was a **deposit** or first
portion of full salvation in the future. Paul saw his life and the lives of other
believers as suffering and death as well as a grand blessing from God.

Abiding Confidence (5:6–10)

> **SUPPORTING IDEA:** *From the knowledge of the presence of the Holy Spirit, Paul encouraged confidence in future salvation.*

5:6. Paul concluded that **we are always confident.** Paul and his company knew that **as long as** they and other believers were **at home in the body,** they were **away from the Lord.** Short of leaving this life, believers must endure physical separation from God's presence. But the hardship, pain, and trials they endure will disappear when final salvation comes at Christ's return.

Paul did not mean that God was absent from the lives of believers. He had just affirmed the Holy Spirit's presence, and Jesus himself had sent the Spirit so believers would not be orphans (John 14:16–18). Yet, the Spirit's ministry represents only a small portion of what is ahead. His presence neither removes the trouble of this life nor stops the groaning. Rather, the Holy Spirit joins us in our present groaning (Rom. 8:26).

5:7. Paul explained further by characterizing the Christian life as living **by faith, not by sight.** As the writer of Hebrews put it, "Faith is being sure of what we hope for and certain of what we do not see" (Heb. 11:1). When the ultimate salvation of God's people becomes reality in the new creation, **faith** will no longer be required; all will be **sight.** But until then, **faith** that God will bring about all he has promised is required from everyone who serves Christ.

When the Corinthians examined Paul's life, they were not impressed. He did not have much to show for all his effort. He had no money, power, or possessions—but suffering and the appearance of failure. This was another reason he explained that his ministry had to be evaluated in terms of **faith** and **not by sight.**

5:8–9. Paul was **confident** that this present existence involves separation from God (5:6), but he was also **confident . . . and would** have **prefer[red]** to leave his present **body** behind in order to be **at home with the Lord.** He wanted to endure the time of separation from his final salvation and finally to be with **the Lord.** He longed for the day when sight would replace his faith. This deep desire compelled Paul toward one supreme **goal:** to honor and **please** Christ.

5:10. Why is it so important to please Christ in every way? Because Christ holds the power to grant or withhold salvation for which every believer longs. Paul wanted to please Christ because **all** will **appear before the judgment seat of Christ.** The rest of the New Testament teaches that Christ will judge all people (Acts 10:42; Rom. 2:16; 2 Tim. 4:1). Everyone **must . . . appear;** no one can avoid the judgment. Moreover, at this judgment **each one** will **receive what is due him.** The judgment will be individual, based on **the things done while in the body** (i.e., in this life). Christ will consider both **good** and **bad** that is done. Paul sought to please Christ so he would pass this judgment and receive his eternal reward.

Many interpreters think Paul's doctrine of final judgment is inconsistent with his doctrine of justification by faith alone. If salvation is a free gift by faith alone (Rom. 4:9–16; Eph. 2:8–9), then does anyone who is saved receive **what is due him?** The resolution of this tension appears later. In 13:5, for instance, Paul spoke of the Christian life as a testing period. It was a time when he and the Corinthians would prove whether they had saving faith in Christ. From Paul's perspective, no one earns or maintains salvation by works. Yet, every person will be judged according to his or her works.

This well-known adage is true of Paul's theology: "Saved by faith alone, but faith that saves is never alone." Those who have placed their faith in Christ will demonstrate their justification by living to please him.

🄲 Paul's Urgent Ministry (5:11–15)

> **SUPPORTING IDEA:** Paul had many motivations for his ministry, but he focused on the judgment of Christ that was sure to come.

5:11. Summarizing his previous remarks about judgment before Christ, Paul said he and his company knew **what it** was **to fear the Lord.** He drew upon the Old Testament expression, "the fear of the Lord." Paul apprehended what the judgment of Christ could mean for him if he were unfaithful to his calling. If he hoped to receive the reward of eternal salvation, he had to demonstrate his faith in Christ through faithfulness to Christ.

Consequently, Paul sought **to persuade men.** It is possible that he had in mind persuading people to accept his integrity, as he did throughout this letter. Yet, these words may also include his broader purpose. The apostle's responsibility was to reach the lost on behalf of Christ. He was called to take the gospel to all people. At times this task involved proclamation, but at other times it involved persuasion.

No matter what Paul's opponents in Corinth had been saying about him, the apostle was convinced that it was **plain to God** what he was. God knew his heart and understood his motivations. He hoped his ministry was **plain to** the Corinthians as well.

5:12. Paul explained he was not trying to **commend** himself or his company to them **again,** that is, as he had in earlier chapters. Instead, he was trying to give the Corinthians **an opportunity** to understand the nature of his life and ministry so they could **take pride in** him. As elsewhere in this epistle, the term *pride* (*kauchema*) did not have negative connotations of arrogance or self-conceit. It meant delight and joy in the accomplishments of a dear friend or family member. Paul considered himself the Corinthians' spiritual father and brother. He had pride in them, and he hoped they would have the same feelings about him.

Paul wanted to instill this pride in them so they would be able to **answer those who take pride in what is seen rather than in what is in the heart.** Paul's opponents had criticized the apostle's ministry by pointing to his troubles and failures. But Paul had explained these weaknesses in terms of the nature of life in this world. He had not failed. He served as all Christians should: by faith and not by sight. Paul's opponents did not consider Paul's **heart,** but he hoped the congregation would stop their attacks on him and understand his motivations.

5:13. Paul's opponents apparently also thought he was **out of** his **mind.** They may have referred to his extraordinary experiences of revelation, but the immediate context makes it more likely that they attacked the ludicrous nature of Paul's ministry and apostleship.

Paul's response revealed his deepest commitments. If there was any sense in which he was beside himself, it was not because he was not an honorable apostle; it was **for the sake of God.** Paul had committed himself totally to God's service, even to the point that he seemed to have lost his senses. If, however, he was actually in his **right mind**—doing and advising what was appropriate—it was for the Corinthians. Paul had two motivations: love for God and love for neighbor. These made him look insane at times, though in reality he was quite sane.

5:14. Paul then explained why these two motivations controlled his ministry. He began with the statement that **Christ's love compel[ed]** him. Interpreters differ over whether Paul meant the term *Christ* to be taken subjectively ("Christ's love for us") or objectively ("our love for Christ"). The grammar permits either reading. Because the following context focuses on Christ's sacrifice, it seems best to understand it to mean "Christ's love for us." Paul was compelled in ministry by the love that Christ demonstrated when he **died for all.**

Christ **died for all, and therefore all died** with him. Dying with Christ was one way Paul described conversion (Gal. 2:20). For this reason, this passage appears to teach universalism—the belief that Christ's death brought salvation to every person. But the rest of Scripture stands opposed to this interpretation. Only those who have saving faith in Christ are saved (John 3:18; 2 Thess. 2:12). The language here is similar to Romans 5:18 and 1 Corinthians 15:22. In this context, the **all** is **all** of the Corinthian Christians. It is not that Paul was assured of the salvation of each individual in the church—he plainly stated that he was not (2 Cor. 13:5). In this passage he accepted their professions of faith at face value for the purposes of his argument.

5:15. Paul's main point was that Christ died for them and they all died with him **so that those who live** through the power of his resurrection **should no longer live for themselves.** Those for whom Christ died are "bought at a price" (1 Cor. 6:20), and they no longer belong to themselves. Therefore, they are to **live . . . for him who died for them and was raised again.**

Paul ministered for the Corinthians' sake because he was compelled by the love displayed in Christ's death. He died to redeem the lost so those for whom he died might live for him. Because this was the purpose of Christ's death, it became the goal of Paul's ministry.

Ⓓ The Urgency of Reconciliation (5:16–6:2)

SUPPORTING IDEA: *Having refuted the negative views of his ministry, Paul provided a positive portrait of his apostolic work.*

5:16. Paul pointed to a change that had come over him and his company. He concluded that **from now on** something had changed. **From now on** may refer to Paul's conversion or to the death of Christ. **Now** may also identify the new era brought on by Christ's life, death, resurrection, and ascension. As Paul wrote in 2 Corinthians 6:2, "Now is the time of God's favor, now is the day of salvation." If this last understanding is correct, **from now on** would measure the time from Christ's death, and would include Paul's own experience of salvation in the new era (cf. Gal. 2:20).

The change Paul had in mind was his outlook on people. He **regard[ed] no one from a worldly point of view.** This manner of expression does not appear elsewhere in Paul, and it is difficult to know precisely what he meant. He probably meant that he was committed to viewing people in the light of their participation in Christ's death and resurrection rather than viewing them as he had before he became a Christian. **Once** he had **regarded** even **Christ** in worldly terms, failing to see the significance of Christ's death and resurrection and considering him a false teacher. But he could **do so no longer.**

5:17. Paul asserted that every person who is **in Christ**—who is joined to him in his death and resurrection—has become **a new creation.** Paul drew from Old Testament prophetic language, describing the new world that God would bring at the end of the age (Isa. 66:22). This language also appears in the New Testament (2 Pet. 3:13). "New creation" describes those who follow Christ because they have begun the transformation that will eventually lead to their full enjoyment of salvation in the new heavens and new earth. Christ's death and resurrection introduced a foretaste of that new world to come.

Paul's ministry was compelled by the display of Christ's love on the cross. Paul had been united to Christ in his death and resurrection, and thus had been inwardly renewed and regenerated. The apostle truly was a new creation. In this changed state, he began to look at people differently. Prior to coming to Christ, Paul would not have thought about the Corinthians much. He certainly would not have worked and sacrificed for the Gentiles in that church. But now the shadow of Christ's cross fell across his view every time he looked at other people. He saw believers as new creations in Christ and unbelievers as people in need of Christ. This perspective shaped his ministry.

5:18a. Paul remarked that **all this** (the changes he had just described) was **from God.** Throughout his writings Paul consistently attested that every dimension of salvation results from divine grace. He had in mind here especially the radical transformation of his outlook on other human beings that showed his transformation into a new creation. This dramatic change was a work of God in his heart.

5:18b. Paul explained the change that God had wrought in his life in terms of **reconciliation.** He repeated the Greek terms for "reconcile" and "reconciliation" (*katallasso/katallage*) five times throughout 5:18b–20, emphasizing his point. Reconciliation is the establishment of harmony and peace between enemies. Enemies are said to be reconciled when their hostility ceases and mutual love binds them together. Paul's explanation of God's re-creative activity in his life centered on this doctrine.

Paul spoke of divine reconciliation in two ways in this context. First, he stated that God had **reconciled** Paul and his company **to himself through Christ.** By his own testimony Paul had been an opponent to the ways of God. He had even persecuted the body of Christ. Yet, God established peace between himself and Paul **through** Christ. This act of divine love and grace transformed the apostle.

Second, Paul said that God **gave** him and his company **the ministry of reconciliation.** Why had his personal reconciliation changed his outlook on other human beings? It was because God had a special destiny for Paul—**the ministry of reconciliation.** A ministry (*diakonia*) is a service to others on God's behalf. God had called Paul to be an instrument of **reconciliation**; his life was devoted to making peace between God and humanity through the preaching of the gospel.

5:19. Paul continued to focus on his ministry of reconciliation by defining what he meant. First, he explained that God was reconciling the world to himself in Christ by **not counting men's sins against them.** In Paul's view, human beings had become enemies of God because they transgressed divine law (Rom. 5:10; Phil. 3:18). Men and women without Christ are hostile to the things of God and subject to his judgment (Rom. 2:16; 8:7). Reconciliation requires that God forgive people of their sins to remove this hostility.

Paul spoke of God reconciling **the world to himself** because he knew the ultimate end of God's purpose was worldwide. This passage has been used to support the false doctrine of universalism—the belief that every person will be saved from judgment. Although Paul spoke categorically of **the world**, he described this worldwide reconciliation as taking place **in Christ**. For Paul, the expression "in Christ" referred to the union that believers have with Christ in his death and resurrection as they place their faith in him. So we must understand his categorical terminology here and in similar passages in light of his clear teaching that salvation comes only to those who trust in Christ for salvation (Rom. 11:19–20; 2 Thess. 2:10–12).

Paul also wrote that **the world** would be condemned. This cannot refer to those who trust in Christ for salvation. The reconciliation of **the world** is the goal of the gospel in the sense that salvation will extend beyond the nation of Israel to all the nations of the earth. In accordance with the prophetic word of the Old Testament, the ultimate end of the gospel ministry was the reconciliation of those who are united **in Christ** from all nations of the earth.

The apostle also explained his own role in this worldwide plan. God had **committed to** Paul and his company **the message of reconciliation**. This phrase may also be translated as "the message about reconciliation," which is exactly what Paul explained this message to be. Paul went about as an apostle of Christ, proclaiming that God had provided the way of salvation through Christ. He saw himself called by God to the task of bringing to fruition God's plan to reconcile the world in Christ.

5:20a. Paul's role in the divine plan of reconciliation led him to a remarkable claim. He and his company were **Christ's ambassadors**. "Ambassadors" was a technical political term used in Paul's day that closely parallels our English word "ambassadors." An ambassador represented a nation or kingdom in communication with other nations. Paul had in mind his apostolic call to represent the kingdom of Christ to the nations of the earth. Ambassadors held positions of great honor in the ancient world because they represented the authority of the kings on whose behalf they spoke.

This was also true for Paul as the ambassador of Christ. When he spoke the message of reconciliation, it was **as though God were making his appeal through** him. Rather than speaking directly to the nations of earth, God ordained that human spokespersons would speak for him. As an apostle, Paul had authority to lead and guide the church (2 Cor. 13:3,10). Yet, this description applies to all who bear the gospel of Christ to others—even to those who do not bear apostolic authority (1 Pet. 4:11). Though we may not present the gospel as perfectly as Paul did, we do speak on God's behalf when we bring the message of grace to others. But Paul and his company were to be received as mouthpieces of God in the most authoritative sense.

5:20b–21. In these verses Paul summarized the content of the message of reconciliation. His summary includes an expression of his heart, an appeal, and an explanation.

First, Paul introduced his message in emotional terms, expressing his heart. He spoke **on Christ's behalf** because he was an ambassador. But as ordinary ambassadors often sought reconciliation between national enemies with intensity, Paul **implore[d]** others to be reconciled to God. The term *implored* (*deomai*) often connotes beseeching or begging. In imitation of the passionate ministry of Christ himself (Matt. 23:37), Paul so desired to see people come to Christ that he thought of his ministry as begging.

Paul did not actually beg people to have saving faith. He spoke metaphorically in an attempt to convey the motivations behind his ministry. Paul appealed to others for their own sake, even when he was firm or harsh. He knew the enemies of God would suffer divine wrath (Eph. 5:6; Col. 3:5–6). For this reason, his ministry was not impersonal or emotionally disconnected. He desired to see people come to Christ, as should all who minister the gospel on Christ's behalf.

Second, Paul summarized the content of his message of reconciliation in a short appeal. His practice was to tell others to **be reconciled to God.** Since Paul had to appeal to others to be reconciled, he did not believe that the work of Christ automatically reconciled every human being to God. Christ's saving work on the cross is sufficient for every human being, but it is effective only for those who believe. As the imperative (**be reconciled**, from *katallasso*) indicates, those who hear the gospel are responsible to believe in Christ in order to become reconciled to God.

Third, Paul explained that sinful people, who are the enemies of God, can be reconciled to God only through Christ and his work on behalf of the human race. Paul summarized Christ's work in two elements. On the one hand, **God made** Christ, **who had no sin, to be sin.** Paul did not mean that Christ actually became a sinner. Throughout his humiliation, Christ remained faithful and righteous. It is likely that Paul followed the Septuagint's practice of using the term *sin* (*harmartia*) as a circumlocution for "sin offering" (e.g., Num. 6:14). The New Testament frequently refers to Isaiah 53 in which the Messiah's death is declared to be "an offering for sin" (Isa. 53:10, NRSV). This language stems from the Old Testament sacrificial system and identifies the sacrifice that brought forgiveness to those for whom it was made (Lev. 4:5:5–10).

In this sense, Christ became the sin offering **for us**—for all who believe in him. In the gospel of the New Testament, salvation comes to enemies of God because Christ himself became the perfect and final substitutionary sacrifice on behalf of those who have saving faith in him.

Paul then pointed to the purpose of Christ's sacrifice. It was **so that in him we** (all who have saving faith) **might become the righteousness of God.** Note first that it is **in him** (in Christ) that reconciliation takes place. The concept of "in Christ" formed one of Paul's central teachings. To be "in Christ" was to be joined with him in his death and resurrection and thus to receive the benefits of his salvation. In this passage Paul summarized the benefits received in Christ by stating that the believer becomes **the righteousness of God.**

The precise meaning of this expression has been the source of much controversy. Paul probably intended the expression **of God** to be taken as "from God," as Romans 1:17 suggests. Yet, is this righteousness that is infused into believers as they live the Christian life (sanctification)? Or is it the righteousness that is imputed to believers when they turn in faith toward Christ (justification)? Probably Paul's emphasis is on imputed righteousness, since it was by imputation of our sin to Christ, and not by infusion, that Christ was **made . . . to be sin for us.**

Still, it is best not to divide these issues so sharply as we approach this passage. As Romans 1:17 suggests, the **righteousness from God** is by faith from first to last. Believers become the righteousness from God when they first receive the imputation of Christ's righteousness in justification, but they also receive the continuous blessing of the experience of righteousness in their lives as they grow in their sanctification (cf. Gal. 3:1–5).

6:1. Paul concluded this section by making the implications of his ministry evident. He and his company appealed to the Corinthians **as God's fellow workers.** In the preceding verses, Paul had spoken of his ministry "as though God were making his appeal" (5:20) through him and his company. The apostle and his company served alongside God as "Christ's ambassadors" (5:20). Because Paul and his company spoke the true gospel as God ambassadors, the Corinthians should have received and honored them, especially by complying with their petition that the Corinthians be reconciled to God. So Paul **urge[d]** them **not to receive God's grace in vain.**

Paul had warned the Corinthians several times not to falter in their faith. He did not believe that true believers could lose their salvation (Eph. 4:30; Phil. 1:6), but he was not convinced that everyone in the Corinthian church was a true believer. During this life, it is necessary for all who profess faith in Christ to make certain that their faith endures. Otherwise, the mercy shown to them in the preaching and reception of the word of God will be **in vain.**

6:2. To support his appeal, Paul referred to Isaiah 49:8. This prophecy focused on the restoration of God's people after the exile. God promised that he would respond to the cries of the exile, **in the time of** his **favor** and **in the day of salvation.** Paul focused attention on Isaiah's emphasis that in God's timing salvation from the judgment of exile would come.

As a result, Paul pressed the significance of this prophecy on the Corinthian situation. The days in which they lived, the days of the New Testament, were not to be ignored or taken for granted. Those days were, as our own days are, **the time of [God's] favor** and **the day of salvation.** When Christ came to earth, he began to restore God's people from exile. After Christ ascended into the heavenly places, we continue to see him fulfilling the hopes of restoration. Christ will complete his saving work when he returns in glory. In the meantime, everyone must recognize the urgency of the times in which we live.

We are in the day of great opportunity because the final saving work of God has come to earth. Yet, we are in a day of great danger because failing to receive this salvation through enduring faith will bring a severe judgment. The New Testament age is the climax of history. There will be no possibility of salvation beyond the New Testament. Paul wanted the Corinthians to prove faithful because of the critical moment in history that they occupied.

MAIN IDEA REVIEW: *Christians should balance a realistic assessment of their human frailties with the honor Christ gives them now and after death. When we do this, we will hold fast to faith in Christ and receive the salvation God has offered in him.*

III. CONCLUSION

Now Is the Day

In this section Paul focused on the weakness of his humanity. This led him also to speak of the urgency of his ministry. All of us are mortals who wait for deliverance from God. Yet, our mortality should press us toward realizing the urgency of following Christ faithfully.

PRINCIPLES

- The physical body is wasting away through the normal aging process.
- Believers will receive a glorious resurrection body when our physical bodies die.
- The Holy Spirit is a deposit on God's promise of full salvation in the future.

APPLICATIONS

- As believers, we can rest assured in God's promise of eternal life.
- We should be about the business of presenting God's good news of eternal life to others.

- Our motivation for Christian service should be the love of Christ and his sacrifice on behalf of others.

IV. LIFE APPLICATION

You'd Better Study

Many young people hate school, especially at exam time. They put off studying until the last minute. Then when exams are just a day or two away, they have to cram a whole semester's work into a short time. Students who haven't cracked a book do nothing but study.

What makes the difference? The urgency of the moment. When it seems that there is plenty of time before an exam, it is easy not to take matters seriously. But when there is little time left, most students go for the books.

In this passage Paul described the Christian life in this way. He began by discussing how he and every believer will stand before the judgment seat of Christ one day in the future. This belief gave Paul a sense of urgency in his ministry. He worked hard because he realized the New Testament church is the last stage of God's redemptive plan before the great judgment. There will be no more eras of redemptive history before the judgment of Christ. For this reason, he called the Corinthians to take his call to them seriously. They needed to make sure they were ready for the final judgment.

Paul's words in this section have many implications for Christian living today, but at least two concerns are central.

First, Paul expressed hope in the glory that he would receive one day. His life in this world was difficult, but he took hope that God would give him a new life, even a new body, in the world to come. As we look at our lives, we often find cause for disappointment. We face many troubles from the world. When we become ill, we suffer the pain and trials of our physical bodies. In the midst of this suffering, we should emulate Paul's hope in the new life we will have in Christ.

Another concern rose in Paul's mind as he wrote about the future life. He knew that before the enjoyment of eternal life would come in its fullness, every person must pass the judgment seat of Christ. We have all fallen and failed to keep the law of God. So it is urgent for us to seek reconciliation to God. There will be no opportunities for salvation beyond the offer of the gospel at this time in history. This should remove the complacency of unbelievers and bring them to faith in Christ. The urgency of the time should motivate believers to trust the message of reconciliation in the gospel. When we are tempted to turn from Christ, we should remember that the judgment day is near. This should motivate us to faithful service to the Savior.

V. PRAYER

Lord Jesus, we often fail to remember how temporary our lives are. We forget that each of us will soon face you before your throne. Grant us the mercy to be mindful of how near that time is. Give us hearts that know the urgency of bringing the gospel to others and believing it ourselves. Amen.

VI. DEEPER DISCOVERIES

A. Reconciled, Reconciliation (5:18–20)

Paul used the word group "reconcile/reconciliation" (*katallasso/katallage*) only rarely in his epistles, and no other New Testament author used these words at all. It is interesting that Paul described his entire ministry in terms of reconciliation in this passage. Fully half of the uses of these words appear in 2 Corinthians 5:18–20, with four of the five others appearing in Romans (Rom. 5:10–11; 11:15). In all uses in both Romans and 2 Corinthians, Paul spoke of God as the active agent who reconciles people to himself. Only in 1 Corinthians 7:11, where he encouraged Christian women who had left their husbands to be reconciled to them, did he use this word in reference to human relationships and refer to a human as the performer of the reconciliatory action.

The only Old Testament usage of *katallage* (Isa. 9:4–5) comes in the context of a hopeful prophecy about the Son of David who would put an end to the enmity between God's people and the Gentiles. Christ fulfilled this prophecy, and Paul wrote to the very Gentiles whom Christ reconciled. Isaiah 9:4–5 also uses *katallage* in the context of warriors throwing away their bloody clothes from battle. In this context, reconciliation appears to be the cessation of bloody hostilities, the ending of war, and uniting in common peace. It is possible that Paul had this passage in mind as he explained that Christ could end the hostility between God and sinful man. This would enable man to receive the blessings of the kingdom of the Prince of Peace rather than be slaughtered by him in his anger on the day of judgment.

B. Implore (5:20)

Deomai, translated as "implore," has a broad range of meaning. At times it carries only the force of a polite request ("please" in Acts 8:34; 21:39). At other times, it means begging, as is evident by the contexts of such passages as Luke 5:12 in which the man who begs does so while prostrating himself at the feet of Jesus, or in the case of the demoniac in Luke 8:28 who begged not to be tormented. It is also one of the normal words for "pray" (Acts 4:31; Rom. 1:10). In this passage in 2 Corinthians, it probably means "beg" or "implore." It comes in the context of Paul asking those whom he loves to find peace with God so they will not be destroyed—an urgent situation.

VII. TEACHING OUTLINE

A. INTRODUCTION

1. Lead Story: They Thought They Were Big Stuff Too
2. Context: Paul wrote to people he loved but for whom he feared. Some of them acted as if they were not accountable to God, as if they could live in their sin and not fear God's judgment. Living in a worldly way, they sought their significance in things that were destined to perish. They did not seem to realize that unless they were reconciled to God, they would not receive the blessings of resurrection and eternity in Christ.
3. Transition: Our modern churches also have people who live their lives as if they were not accountable to God. Hoping for fulfillment in this world, they do not realize that the only lasting significance is eternal life in Christ. Even some people who have a notion of true significance do not realize that their sin prevents them from receiving this blessing. We should take encouragement from Paul's confidence—but not without evaluating our hearts to make certain we trust in Christ and are reconciled to God.

B. COMMENTARY

1. Temporary and Eternal Dwellings (5:1–5)
   a. Christians await resurrected bodies (5:1)
   b. Christians long for their resurrected bodies (5:2–4)
   c. God has given the Spirit as a guarantee of the resurrection (5:5)
2. Abiding Confidence (5:6–10)
   a. Faithful confidence in the future resurrection (5:6–9)
   b. Confidence in the coming judgment (5:10)
3. Paul's Urgent Ministry (5:11–15)
   a. Coming judgment makes gospel ministry urgent (5:11)
   b. Paul's motivation: love for the Corinthians (5:12–14a)
   c. Christ's death and life can rescue man from judgment (5:14b–15).
4. The Urgency of Reconciliation (5:16–6:2)
   a. Regarding people in Christ (5:16–17)
   b. Reconciliation to God available in Christ (5:18–20a)
   c. Paul's plea that the Corinthians be reconciled to God (5:20b–6:2)

C. CONCLUSION: YOU'D BETTER STUDY

VIII. ISSUES FOR DISCUSSION

1. What did Paul describe as an earthly tent? What did he call a heavenly dwelling? What burdens accompany the earthly tent? What benefits does the heavenly dwelling have over the earthly tent?
2. What does it mean to live by faith and not by sight? What does the heavenly dwelling have to do with the judgment seat of Christ? When does that judgment occur?
3. What does it mean to fear the Lord? How can a Christian fear the Lord and be confident in the Spirit at the same time?
4. What is reconciliation? To whom or what must we be reconciled? Why is this important? What happens to people who are not reconciled? How does a person become reconciled?

2 Corinthians 6:3–7:1

Paul's Hardship and His Difficult Insistence

Quote

"*My* prayer is not that you take them out of the world

but that you protect them from the evil one."

John 17 : 15

2 Corinthians 6:3–7:1

IN A NUTSHELL

Paul prepared the Corinthians for a hard teaching by reminding them of all he had suffered on their behalf. No one could challenge his motives.

Paul's Hardship and His Difficult Insistence

I. INTRODUCTION

"Can't You See All He's Done for You?"

*W*hen someone tells us to do something that we do not want to do, it is easy to ascribe evil motives to that person. Teenagers often face this temptation. A friend of mine told me something that happened in his home recently. As his teenage daughter Kathy was leaving with some friends, he shouted from his easy chair. "Midnight, sweetheart. Don't forget your curfew."

"You're so mean," Kathy called back. "Why do you have to be so mean and strict with me?"

"It's because he loves you," Mom interjected as she came from the kitchen. "He's telling you what time to be home because he cares about you."

"That's not it," Kathy insisted. "It's just because he likes to be in control."

Mom drew Kathy into the kitchen and they sat down at the table together. "I understand that it's hard to do what Dad says," she whispered, "but you're making a big mistake if you think he is just being mean. Your dad has worked nearly every day for years and years for one main reason—you. He has put up with all kinds of problems and pain every day of the week because he cares about you. Don't forget how much he cares."

"Okay," Kathy responded. "I don't like it, but I guess you're right. I shouldn't forget the things he's done for me."

Just then the horn blew again outside and Kathy ran for the door. Before pulling the door shut behind her, she said, "Back at midnight, Dad!" She was not happy with the rule, but she could live with it by remembering that her father loved her so much.

In this passage the apostle Paul challenged the Corinthians to do something they did not like. He told them to separate themselves from the evil practices of their society. His motivations could have been questioned. "This outsider doesn't understand," they could have said. "He just wants to control us."

Anticipating these kinds of reactions, Paul introduced his instruction on separation by reminding the Corinthians of his love for them. He encouraged them not to forget how much he had done for them.

II. COMMENTARY

Paul's Hardship and His Difficult Insistence

MAIN IDEA: *Christians should remember that even the difficult requirements of Scripture grow out of Christ's love for us.*

A A Ministry Beyond Discrediting (6:3–4a)

SUPPORTING IDEA: *In defense of his ministry, Paul presented a list of hardships he had suffered which no one could dispute. His suffering testified to his credibility.*

6:3. Paul and his company had **put no stumbling block in anyone's path.** The NIV translation "stumbling block" is unfortunate because it seems to contradict Paul's insistence that the preaching of Christ's death is "a stumbling block (*skandalon*) to the Jews" (1 Cor. 1:23). The Greek expression of this verse (*proskope*) may be better translated as "cause for offense" (NASB). Paul gave no offense **in anyone's path** or "in anything." He had been careful to allow no one the right to be offended by his ministry.

The purpose of Paul's care was that his **ministry** might **not be discredited.** Paul knew that many people will distrust the truth, even the truth of the gospel, when a minister's life does not conform to that truth. Christian ministry is not just a matter of speaking the truth; it also consists of living the truth. Paul was careful not to live hypocritically.

6:4a. Paul asserted that his life was an open book. He and his company spoke **as servants of God;** their successes were services to God. They did not commend themselves self-confidently or arrogantly, yet they could categorically **commend** their actions **in every way.** Paul knew he was not. Perfection does not come to believers in this life (1 John 1:8–10). Yet, in broad terms, no major faults appeared in Paul's ministry. He had been faithful to his calling (2 Tim. 4:7).

B Paul's Exemplary Ministry (6:4b–10)

SUPPORTING IDEA: *Paul explained that he did not hesitate to commend his ministry because he and his company had ministered faithfully at great cost in many different ways.*

6:4b. Paul and his company did not have an easy ministry. At every turn they faced great difficulties. The apostle described these difficulties with ten phrases. He began with a general description of his ministry as one of **great endurance.** The Greek word for "endurance" is *hypomone,* which is often translated as "perseverance." It generally refers to facing and overcoming hardship.

What were these struggles? Three broad terms head the list: **troubles, hardships,** and **distresses.** It is difficult to know if Paul had specific experiences in mind for each of these terms—the terms are as general in Greek as they are in English. But Paul's point was clear: he had faced all kinds of difficulties in his ministry.

Troubles (*thlipsis*) is the same word Paul used to describe his "hardships . . . in the province of Asia" (1:8), as well as the **distress** in writing his sorrowful letter to the Corinthians (2:4). He also used this word to summarize the **troubles** that caused him to waste away (4:16–17).

The word translated as "hardships" (*anagke*) frequently means "compulsion" or "necessity." He may have intended to highlight difficulties that compelled certain courses of action. For example, he used it to speak of the "present crisis" in 1 Corinthians 7:26, probably a famine, that compelled a moratorium on weddings. In 2 Corinthians 12:10, however, it seems to suggest a circumstance in which personal weakness is manifested.

Distresses (*stenochoria*) appears only four times in the New Testament, and in general contexts, ranging from God's judgment against sinners (Rom. 2:9) to personal weakness (2 Cor. 12:10). These general descriptions characterize the lives of many ministers of the gospel, who must remain faithful as their lives are filled with trouble, hardship, and distress.

6:5. Paul spoke more specifically in this verse of troubles he had faced as a minister of the gospel. He had endured **beatings** (*plege*), as in Philippi (Acts 16:23) and on many other occasions (2 Cor. 11:23–25). Through *plege* and many synonymous terms, the Bible records that Paul, other apostles, and their companies underwent beatings on many occasions (Acts 5:40; 22:19), just as Jesus said would happen (Mark 13:9). Physical punishment marked their ministries, just as it had marked the ministry of Christ.

Paul also endured **imprisonments** (*phylake*). Luke records that Paul was imprisoned twice because of his gospel ministry (Acts 16:23–36; 21:30–28:31), the second time for many years.

Riots (*akatastsia*) probably refers to outbreaks of crowds against Paul. A number of such uprisings took place as he traveled (Acts 16:22; 21:35). Unbelieving Jews frequently instigated the public outbursts, which threatened the safety of the apostle and his company (Acts 9:23; 2 Cor. 11:24,26).

Paul also endured **hard work.** It is difficult to know if this terminology describes his ministry or the work he often did to support himself. The apostle not only preached and taught, but he also worked as a tentmaker (Acts 18:3; 2 Thess. 3:8).

Paul also spoke of **sleepless nights.** We do not know of specific times when Paul did not sleep, though he probably did not sleep during his "night and a day" on the open sea (he was apparently adrift in the water; 2 Cor. 11:25). It is also possible that he did not sleep when he was fleeing at night

(Acts 17:10) or when he was cold and hungry (2 Cor. 11:27). Much of his work as a tentmaker may also have been done at night (2 Thess. 3:8).

Finally, Paul asserted that he went through times of **hunger**. On a number of occasions, Paul spoke of lacking food (1 Cor 4:11; Phil. 4:12). This was not due to lack of faith or to failure to seek God's kingdom first. Rather, Paul and others suffered in the course of seeking and serving the kingdom, just as Jesus said would happen to his servants (Luke 21:12).

6:6–7a. Paul did not just put up with the troubles God brought his way. He responded with positive faithfulness, which he described in nine categories. The first eight (6:6–7a) are introduced by the preposition "in" (*en*) to indicate accompanying conditions within which he faced difficulties. The final set (6:7b) is introduced by the preposition "with" (*dia*), which often denotes the means through which something is accomplished.

Paul first said that he faced trouble **in purity**. Related forms of this term appear several other times in the New Testament. These terms describe purity of many sorts, including fidelity to Christ, sexual chastity, innocence from guilt, and honesty. Despite his hardships, Paul did not fall prey to these types of moral impurity.

He also faced difficulties in his ministry with **understanding**. This term (*gnosis*) does not refer to being sympathetic or understanding toward others. The expression is usually translated "knowledge." Paul had in mind that he never forsook the knowledge of Christ and the gospel during his ministry. In fact, Paul's knowledge of Christ allowed him to understand his afflictions as an honorable service to Christ.

Patience also characterized Paul's ministry. He was patient in circumstances (2 Tim. 3:10) and with the people to whom he ministered (Acts 20:31). Patience is the fruit of the Spirit which causes us to refrain from hasty retaliations for wrongs done against us (2 Tim. 2:24). Jesus demonstrated patience with his apostles as well as his enemies.

Paul frequently exercised much **kindness** as he spread the gospel of Christ. This term is closely associated with other concepts that suggest a pleasing, tender, and compassionate demeanor (Rom. 2:4; Col. 3:12). There were certainly times when Paul knew that kindness required harsh insistence, but even at these times his motivation was to demonstrate kindness.

Paul also insisted that his ministry was conducted **in the Holy Spirit**. He added that he also served in difficulties with a motivation of **sincere love**. The apostle considered love to be the greatest gift of the Spirit. Even so, Paul knew that it was easy to pretend to love others. So he added that his love was **sincere**. His love was not a cover for other detrimental motivations.

Truthful speech also characterized Paul's ministry. Paul frequently distinguished his preaching from others as truthful. It seems best to understand his purpose here in much the same way. He did not teach falsehoods, as tempting as they may have been at times. He taught only truth, even in difficult circumstances. Paul's reference to his preaching the truth brought to his mind the accompanying **power of God**. Paul insisted that he preached with more than human strength; his preaching was enhanced by displays of God's power.

6:7b. Paul closed this list of his positive reactions to the trials of ministry with a final qualifying remark. All he had done was **with weapons of righteousness**. The allusion to weaponry recalls the well-known passages where Paul describes the Christian life as a spiritual battle (Eph. 6:13–18). The expression **of righteousness** may be purposefully ambiguous to allow for two connotations: (1) weapons that produce righteousness and (2) weapons that derive from righteous living. Spiritual weapons are explained in more detail in Ephesians 6:13–18. Here they are spoken of as **in the right hand and in the left**, probably indicating shield (defensive) and sword (offensive).

Paul closed this section with a military metaphor to indicate the strength of his determination and the power by which he overcame the troubles of his ministry. He went into ministry as a soldier into battle, but not in his own strength. He moved forward as a soldier of righteousness in the army equipped and empowered by God himself.

6:8–9a. Paul was so positive about his reaction to ministry that we might expect him to continue in this vein. Yet, Paul closed this section by merging the themes of his list of difficulties with his list of positive responses, assessing his work realistically. Because his ministry was a mixture of difficulties and positive responses, he described it in a series of paired contrasts.

Paul began with four related sets of contrasts. Some translations render these verses as ironic statements. These translations differ only in form; the same ideas are conveyed as in the NIV. Paul's ministry was one of **glory and dishonor**, that is, **bad report and good report**. Paul's experience was similar to every person of notoriety. Some people honored him for his work, while others despised him. He was concerned especially with his treatment by the Corinthians. Some people in the church appreciated his ministry, but others slandered him.

The apostle continued to focus on how others dishonored him by saying that he and his company were **genuine, yet regarded as impostors; known, yet regarded as unknown**. In this and a number of other passages, Paul defended the sincerity of his motivations. Contrary to the accusations, he was concerned for the Corinthian church. He should not have had to defend himself in this way because he was **known** by them. Yet, despite their familiarity with the apostle, they treated him with suspicion normally reserved for a stranger.

6:9b. Paul turned next to several descriptions of his ministry from a broader perspective, moving away from things the Corinthians themselves were bringing to his life. First, he spoke of **dying** and yet living on. The record of Acts tells us that Paul came near to death many times in his service to Christ (Acts 14:19; 21:31). Many similar events besides those recorded probably happened to the apostle and his company. Yet, despite the constant experience of dying, Paul affirmed that they **live[d] on**.

Second, they were **beaten, and yet not killed**. At least two points of view may be taken toward these words. On the one hand, it is possible that the apostle alluded to Psalm 118:18. If so, **beaten** would refer to God's discipline in Paul's life. On the other hand, in light of the immediate context it seems more likely that Paul referred to the physical beatings he received at the hands of crowds and officials as he proclaimed the gospel. The apostle may also have thought of divine discipline and physical beatings as one and the same. Whatever the case, Paul reminded the Corinthians of these difficulties in his life and of how he endured them.

6:10a. Paul's final descriptions of the mixed results of his ministry stand above the others in their paradoxical nature. He pairs experiences that seem impossible to hold together. He was **sorrowful, yet always rejoicing**. Paul did not hesitate to admit that his life was full of sorrow. At the same time, Paul did not despair as he endured his sorrows. His hope in Christ caused him to be **always rejoicing** (Col. 1:24). Paul encouraged the same attitude in others as well (Rom. 5:3–5). These and similar statements do not suggest that believers should be in a constant state of rejoicing (Rom. 12:15). Yet, the lives of faithful followers of Christ will be characterized by joy as they experience God's blessing and remember his goodness even in times of sorrow.

6:10b. Paul declared that though he was **poor** he was **making many rich**. His apostolic ministry had deprived him of many economic advantages. As he traveled in the service of Christ, he depended on gifts and his avocation as a tentmaker (Phil. 4:16; 2 Thess. 3:8). This economic deprivation, however, had a positive side. Paul did not suffer poverty for poverty's sake. Through his deprivation, Paul was making others rich in the blessings of Christ. Paul spoke similarly of Christ himself in 8:9. The poverty of Christ and his apostles made it possible for the riches of the new heavens and new earth to belong to everyone who followed Christ (Gal. 3:29).

6:10c. Finally, Paul reflected in broad terms on the paradoxical character of his life, saying that he was **having nothing, and yet possessing everything**. From the preceding context, his meaning is plain. In terms of this world, Paul had practically nothing. He had lost his home, family, friends, religious standing, and livelihood. Those things of this world were of little importance to him. Even so, Paul had his eyes set on the wondrous future promised to every believer. Paul applied to himself what he had already said about other believers. He was a coheir with Christ as well (Rom. 8:17).

ⓒ An Appeal from the Heart (6:11–13)

> **SUPPORTING IDEA:** *Paul appealed to the Corinthians to open their hearts to him.*

6:11–13. Paul explained why he had described his difficult but exemplary ministry. He was appealing to their hearts, their affections for him and his company. The tenderness of this section appears in the way the apostle addressed his readers, first by name (**you, Corinthians**) and second as **my children**. He hoped the reminder of his sacrificial ministry would draw out the Corinthians' affection for him.

Paul appealed to his readers to consider **a fair exchange.** On the one hand, he and his company had just **spoken freely** without self-protection, had **opened wide** their **hearts** in full exposure of the positives and negatives of their ministry, and had not withheld their **affection** toward the Corinthians. Paul had been more than honest; he had entrusted the Corinthians with a precious gift: an honest and frank assessment of the good and bad of his life.

On the other hand, Paul felt that the Corinthians were **withholding** their affections from him and his company. They had not admitted their weaknesses as he had; they had not displayed their lives for examination as he had. So he appealed to them to **open wide** their **hearts also.**

ⓓ Admonition to Separation (6:14a)

> **SUPPORTING IDEA:** *Paul warned of the dangers of associating with the unbelieving world. He insisted that the Corinthians should reexamine their relationships with the world.*

6:14a. Paul's difficult instruction was that believers should **not be yoked together with unbelievers.** The NIV translation obscures the meaning of the original language. Paul insisted that believers should not be "unequally yoked" (NKJV) or "mismatched" (NRSV). Paul probably alluded to Deuteronomy 22:10, which prohibited the yoking together of oxen and donkeys. Like many other Mosaic laws which may seem odd to us today, this prohibition taught Israel through symbolism that they were to remain pure by separating themselves from the surrounding Gentile nations. Paul used this law in much the same way here.

It is common for Christians to apply Paul's instruction here to marriages and close business associations between believers and unbelievers. Paul taught against marrying outside the faith, and wisdom should be exercised in all business relationships. Yet, in this passage Paul focused on all associations with unbelievers that led to infidelity to Christ, particularly by involvement with pagan rituals and idol worship. Paul wanted the Corinthian believers to separate themselves from these practices.

E Justification For Separation (6:14b–18)

SUPPORTING IDEA: *Paul supported his admonition to separate by asking five rhetorical questions to which he expected the response, "nothing."*

6:14b. The first question raised the issue of what **righteousness and wickedness have in common.** Paul did not speak here of righteous and wicked people, but of **righteousness** and **wickedness** as abstract principles. He did this to make the answer to his question as obvious as possible. In abstraction, righteousness and wickedness have nothing in common.

We must be careful not to read our prejudices into Paul's words here. Although Paul spoke of believers as the "righteousness of God" (5:21) because of Christ's substitutionary death, he knew that believers did not demonstrate this righteousness in their lives in a perfect way.

6:14c. Paul's second question focused on **fellowship** between **light** and **darkness.** In Paul's writings "fellowship" (*koinonia*) frequently describes believers' spiritual union with Christ and the consequent union that believers share with one another in Christ. It is clear from this expression that Paul had in mind religious and spiritual connections between believers and unbelievers, not natural or social connections.

The New Testament frequently speaks of believers in association with the light of Christ. By contrast, unbelievers remain in the darkness of sin. Here Paul argues from an analogy in nature that just as **light** and **darkness** are opposites, so Christians and non-Christians are spiritual opposites.

6:15a. The apostle's third question concerned the absence of **harmony . . . between Christ and Belial.** As the English translation "harmony" suggests, Paul used a musical metaphor (*symphonesis*). He expected the Corinthians to remember that only cacophony occurred between believers and unbelievers in religious matters. The term **Belial** (*Beliar*) appears in a number of intertestamental writings as a personification of Satan, the chief of evil spirits. Paul spoke here of Christ and Satan as metonymies of believers and unbelievers. In principle, believers and unbelievers should have no more in common than Christ and Satan.

6:15b. Up to this point Paul had spoken abstractly and metaphorically, but here he spoke openly about **a believer** and **an unbeliever,** saying that they have no part with one another. Again, the context makes it plain that Paul had in mind the religious and spiritual incompatibility of believers and unbelievers, not normal social contacts.

6:16–18. Paul turned to speak of believers and unbelievers as **the temple of God** and **the temple of . . . idols.** This manner of speaking summed up Paul's outlooks so well that he elaborated on it for the next two verses. His lengthy attention to this matter suggests that his chief concern throughout this passage was the Corinthians' involvement in pagan idolatry.

Paul first clarified that believers **are the temple of the living God**. The Old Testament speaks of the God of Israel as **the living God** because he is active and responsive to his people. God differs dramatically from the dead idols of paganism that can do nothing. The fact that believers are the temple of **the living God** as opposed to that of idols demonstrates why believers must remain separate from the practices of idolatry.

To fill out his assertion, Paul grouped together several Old Testament passages that illustrated the intimate involvement between the living God and his people. He first alluded to Exodus 25:8 and 29:45 where God said, **I will live with them**. The living God does not remain distant from his people. He is personally present among them, thus making the people themselves the temple of God.

⬛ Final Exhortation to Holiness (7:1)

SUPPORTING IDEA: *Paul called on the Corinthians to purify themselves from all contamination.*

7:1. In light of the **promises** given to the church as the temple of God, followers of Christ have a responsibility, which Paul cast in terms of temple cleansing rituals. Paul insisted that the Corinthian believers **purify** themselves **from everything that contaminates**. The tabernacle instructions of Exodus 30:20–21 are evidently in view here. In the Old Testament, ritual washings symbolized the repentance and recommitment of worshipers. Paul applied this principle to the Christian life. Although the ritual washings themselves were not to be observed in the New Testament, the inward reality that they symbolized was to be observed.

Note that Paul mentioned **everything**. No defilement is acceptable in the Christian life, however small it may be. In fact, Paul had in mind both **body and spirit**. Paul probably mentioned the body in light of his discussion of the temptation to religious prostitution. Corinth was full of opportunities for fleshly defilement that led to the defilement of the inner person. Behavior is not just external; it corrupts the spirit of a person as well. Neither the behavior of the body nor the condition of the spirit should be overlooked by believers.

What is the goal of this cleansing through repentance and renewal? It is to perfect **holiness**. Holiness or separation from the world is a condition given to true believers when they place their faith in Christ. This holiness is the goal of daily living.

The motivation behind the pursuit of holiness is **reverence for God**. Paul reflected the Old Testament teaching that the fear of God is essential to proper living. The term *fear* (*phobos, phobeo/phobeomai*), like its Old Testament Hebrew counterpart, may have connotations of dread and repulsion, but it may also have the more positive connotations of proper respect and reverence. The latter sense is in view here.

The manifold sins of the Corinthian church made it clear that they did not recognize the danger in which they placed themselves. They needed to reconsider how the God of Scriptures is not to be ignored. They still faced the danger of proving themselves never to have been regenerated and thus headed toward the judgment of God.

> **MAIN IDEA REVIEW:** *Christians should remember that even the difficult requirements of Scripture arise from Christ's love for us.*

III. CONCLUSION

Holy People

Paul touched a sensitive issue in the Corinthian church. Through inappropriate contact with the unbelieving world, they had become defiled. He called them to separate themselves from entanglements with unbelievers by reminding them of his love and concern for them. As difficult as it may have been and as unreasonable as it may have seemed to them, he spoke for their own good. The people of God must be a holy people.

PRINCIPLES

- Christ cannot live in harmony with the world's sin.
- Paul modeled honesty and intimacy in dealing with difficult problems in the church.
- Christians are holy to God.

APPLICATIONS

- Our behavior should reflect who we are in Christ.
- Our closest unions should be with other believers, not with those who oppose the gospel.
- When we seek to help other Christians, we should be ready to open ourselves to intimate contact with them, expressing tenderness and familial warmth.

IV. LIFE APPLICATION

"Don't be Surprised If You're Shocked"

Not too many years ago, most families did not have safety covers for the electrical outlets in their homes. Parents would warn their children, "Don't touch that. It will shock you." But inevitably, it seemed that all children stuck their fingers in the electrical socket anyway. Of course, when the children came running in tears to their mothers, the mothers would often warn them, "Now do you understand why I told you not to touch it?"

Even so, some children did not learn this lesson very easily, and would return to explore the socket once again. From across the room, mom would call, "Don't be surprised if you're shocked again!" Sometimes the warning was heeded; other times it was ignored again until it was too late.

Paul warned the Corinthians in the same way. Time and again, he told them to be holy people, to be separate from the world. In this chapter he appealed to them in personal terms once again. The Corinthians were in grave danger. Their associations with unbelievers in Corinth were corrupting them. Paul warned them not to play with this danger because it could lead to judgment from God.

As followers of Christ we are often called upon to help others see difficult truths. Paul's strategy teaches us how to approach such matters. Rather than intimidating and threatening, we should be ready to open ourselves to intimate contact with those whom we seek to help. Tenderness and familial warmth establish the interpersonal trust that is so important for dealing with difficult subjects.

Finally, Paul opened his heart to the Corinthians by describing to them the paradoxes of his Christian experience. He spoke of the positive joys and pleasures of being a Christian. He also described the pain and sufferings he had experienced as well. Too many Christians today want to see their lives as either very positive or very negative. We can learn from Paul's description that we should expect both positive and negative experiences as we serve Christ. The joys of knowing Christ go along with the sorrows of living in this fallen world.

V. PRAYER

Lord Jesus, so many times we take your love as permission to compromise with the world. Give us the wisdom to know how to live in this world free of its defilement. You are our God and we revere you as the Holy One. Make us holy as well. Amen.

VI. DEEPER DISCOVERIES

A. Holy Spirit (6:6)

Interpretation would be much easier if Paul and other New Testament writers had distinguished between "the Holy Spirit" and "a holy spirit" or "a spirit of holiness" by using the definite article ("the") with the former and omitting it with the latter—but this is not what they did.

When referring to the "Holy Spirit," Paul usually left out the definite article (Rom. 5:5; 2 Tim. 1:14; Titus 3:5), though he did sometimes include it (Eph. 1:13). Also, when referring to the Holy Spirit, he sometimes called him merely the "Spirit." In these cases as well, the article is usually absent.

B. Belial (6:15)

"Belial" transliterates the Greek word *beliar,* which in turn transliterates the Hebrew *beliya'al. Beliar* appears only this one time in the New Testament, and only a few times in some texts of the Septuagint. In the Hebrew Old Testament, the term appears frequently in the construct "son(s)/daughter of Belial" (Deut. 13:14; 2 Chr. 13:7), and many other times apart from this construct (1 Sam. 25:25; Prov. 6:12). The Septuagint regularly interprets "son(s)/daughter of Belial" as identifying a scoundrel, rogue or wicked person, perhaps on the assumption that *beliya'al* is wickedness personified. Similarly, it often interprets *beliya'al* apart from this construction as wickedness itself, or as a wicked person.

In the apocryphal *Testaments of the Twelve Patriarchs,* however, it seems to be the proper name of the devil. At least portions of the *Testaments* may have been written before A.D. 135. Paul's use of *beliar* seems to accord best with the occurrences in the *Testaments,* because he contrasts *beliar* with Christ. In the other contrasts (2 Cor. 6:14b–16a), the pairs are diametrically opposed and roughly equivalent: righteousness vs. wickedness; light vs. darkness; believer vs. unbeliever; temple of God vs. idols. This seems to indicate that, since Christ is a person, *beliar* is also a person (though neither human nor divine), namely the devil.

VII. TEACHING OUTLINE

A. INTRODUCTION

1. Lead Story: "Can't You See All He's Done for You?"
2. Context: The Corinthians were involved in close associations with unbelievers that drew them into idolatrous practices. Paul loved the Corinthians, so this troubled him greatly. He challenged them to change their ways by withdrawing from pagan practices. To compel them to receive his challenge well, he began by describing his own life and ministry, explaining the hardship he suffered and the benefits he retained in the midst of hardship. He hoped to show the Corinthians that they could endure any hardship associated with forsaking idolatrous practices and still retain the benefits of Christ.
3. Transition: Modern Christians are not unlike the ancient Corinthians. We also have associations that tempt us to forsake Christ.

Like the Corinthians, we need to remember that sacrificing holiness in order to avoid hardship will not benefit us in the long run. We are holy unto God, and our lives should reflect that truth.

B. COMMENTARY
1. A Ministry Beyond Discrediting (6:3–4a)
2. Paul's Exemplary Ministry (6:4b–10)
3. An Appeal from the Heart (6:11–13)
   a. Open hearts (6:11–12)
   b. Fair exchange (6:12–13)
4. Admonition to Separation (6:14a)
5. Justification for Separation (6:14b–18)
6. Final Exhortation to Holiness (7:1)

C. CONCLUSION: "DON'T BE SURPRISED IF YOU'RE SHOCKED"

VIII. ISSUES FOR DISCUSSION

1. How many of the kinds of hardships Paul suffered have you also suffered? How is the suffering of Christians around the world today similar to Paul's hardships? Why should Christians take an interest in easing the suffering of other Christians?
2. What benefits does suffering offer? What attitudes should Christians maintain toward suffering?
3. What does it mean to be yoked together with unbelievers? Why can this be dangerous? In what ways are you yoked together with unbelievers? How do these relationships tempt you to forsake Christ?
4. What does it mean to you that God walks among you and that you belong to him?

2 Corinthians 7:2–8:9

Positive Motivations for Faithful Service

2 Corinthians 7:2–8:9

Quote

"Correction does much, but encouragement does more. Encouragement after censure is as the sun after a shower."

Johann Wolfgang von Goethe

IN A NUTSHELL

*H*aving spent most of his time dealing with negative problems in the church at Corinth, Paul began to express confidence and joy in the Corinthians to motivate them to faithful service.

Positive Motivations for Faithful Service

I. INTRODUCTION

Good Pain

*M*ost ministers are involved in hospital visitation at one time or another. This experience is deeply encouraging sometimes and at other times terribly depressing. Many pastors would agree that the most negative aspect of visiting believers in the hospital is seeing a follower of Christ in severe pain with no hope of recovery.

I remember visiting an elderly church member. She had a prognosis of full recovery, but she shared a room with a patient who was terminally ill. Both of them were obviously in pain on that day. But as I sympathized with my church member, she whispered to me, "Yes, the pain is terrible, but at least I know I'm going to be healthier after all this is over." I guess you could call that "good pain." Temporary agony that leads to the discovery and eradication of a disease is really a blessing. Without such pain, death would be inevitable.

We now come upon a portion of Paul's letter to the Corinthians in which he speaks of "good pain." Much of his communication with Corinth was negative. He inflicted pain with his sharp rebukes and warnings. But in this section he saw that the pain had brought Corinth to repentance and spiritual health.

II. COMMENTARY

Positive Motivations for Faithful Service

MAIN IDEA: *When believers repent of waywardness, they find positive motivations for obedience to Christ. Love and gratitude motivate them to express loyalty to Christ.*

A Appeal, Denial, and Affirmation (7:2–4)

SUPPORTING IDEA: *Paul appealed to the Corinthians to have affection for him, and he denied any wrongdoing that might have inhibited their affection.*

7:2. Paul asked the Corinthians to **make room for** him in their **hearts**. He did not want them to resent or reject him; he desired close fellowship with them like that between loving parents and children.

The apostle next dispelled any misgivings that may have hindered the Corinthians' love for him. In their ministry, Paul and his company had **wronged no one**, had **corrupted no one**, and had **exploited no one**. It is likely that Titus (see 7:13b–15) had reported that some in the Corinthian church had accused Paul and his company of these things in order to discredit their ministry. Paul must have feared that some people still believed these lies.

7:3. Paul shifted from the plural (**we**) to the singular (**I**) to express himself even more intimately than before as he made certain his denials were not misunderstood. He did **not say this to condemn** them. His denials were not contentious, and he intended no curse upon the church.

To clarify his motivation in denying the accusations, he reminded the Corinthians of something he **had said before**. He returned to the plural pronoun (**we**) to include his entire company in these next statements. The Corinthians had such a special place **in** their **hearts** that he and his company **would live or die with** the Corinthians. The NIV reverses the word order of the Greek text and gives the impression that Paul spoke only theoretically about what he was willing to do. Paul actually said he was ready "to die together and to live together" (NASB) with the Corinthians. This word order suggests that Paul spoke realistically of what he had already done. From his point of view, Paul was already dying as he suffered in ministry on behalf of the church. Also, he had already lived in Corinth (Acts 18:1,11). The Corinthians should have been fully aware of Paul's deep commitment to them, confident he would never abuse them.

7:4. Paul affirmed that his outlook for the majority of the church was positive: (1) he had **great confidence** in them; (2) he took **great pride** in them; and (3) he was **greatly encouraged** about them. It is unlikely that Paul approved of every Corinthian church member, especially to this degree. Yet, Titus's report (7:13b–15) led Paul to assess the congregation as a whole very positively.

Paul had **confidence** that most Corinthians were true believers who would submit to God's will; he believed they had been faithful to Christ and would certainly inherit eternal life. He had godly **pride** in their faithfulness. Just as he admitted to a holy jealousy for the Corinthians, Paul took pride as the Corinthian believers' spiritual parent. He delighted in the progress of their Christian lives. This confidence and pride caused Paul to be **greatly encouraged**. The apostle found strength from God by reflecting on what had happened in the Corinthian church.

This encouragement was precious to Paul because he continued to have many **troubles** in his ministry. Yet, he found **joy** with **no bounds** when he considered the spiritual condition of the believers in Corinth. He was beside himself with delight.

B Paul's Comfort in Macedonia (7:5–7)

> **SUPPORTING IDEA:** *Paul explained the reason for his confidence and joy. Titus had just reported to Paul that the church at Corinth had accepted Paul's instructions. This section relates the main theme of Titus's report.*

7:5. Paul had sent Titus to Corinth to deliver his earlier epistle and to collect money for believers in Jerusalem. When Paul did not find Titus in Troas, he journeyed to **Macedonia** to visit the churches at Philippi, Thessaloniaca, and Berea. Titus pursued Paul to **Macedonia** and finally brought him a report on the church at Corinth.

While Paul waited for Titus, he **had no rest.** He and his company were in turmoil, **harassed at every turn.** They faced two problems: **conflicts on the outside** and **fears within.** These **conflicts** (*mache*) were probably experienced with believers as well as unbelievers. Nearly everywhere Paul went, he faced opposition. We cannot be sure what kinds of **fears** the apostle had in mind. He could have suffered fears because of the challenges to his ministry, but it is more likely that he spoke here of his fears or doubts about the Corinthians. Paul had been concerned about how they would react to the harsh epistle that Titus delivered.

7:6. In the midst of this troubled condition, **God . . . comforted** Paul and his company **by the coming of Titus.** In a quick aside, the apostle described God as the God **who comforts the downcast.** This description of God derived from the Old Testament (1 Sam. 2:8; Isa. 49:13) describes God as one who cares for those who have been troubled by enemies. Paul recognized that Titus' good report was more than a human event. God himself had intervened to care for Paul.

7:7. Paul had feared that the Corinthians resented him because of his sharp rebukes, but Titus told Paul that the Corinthians were **longing for** him. They had **deep sorrow** over their waywardness, and were **ardent[ly] concern[ed] for** Paul. We gain a sense of how important these responses were to Paul by noting how he repeated the pronoun **your** three times in rapid succession. He was deeply moved because his desire for the Corinthians' love was fulfilled. As a result, his **joy was greater than ever.**

The Corinthians' loyalty and concern for Paul showed their acceptance of his apostolic correction as well as their loyalty to Christ. Paul delighted in the grace of God at work in the Corinthian church.

⦗C⦘ True Repentance (7:8–13a)

> **SUPPORTING IDEA:** *Paul was also confident and joyous over the Corinthians because the sorrow he had inflicted on them had brought them to repentance.*

7:8–9. Paul knew that his earlier letter delivered by Titus had **caused . . . sorrow** in the church, and Paul had mixed feelings about this. On the one hand, he did **not regret it,** but on the other hand he **did regret it.** Just as parents do not enjoy disciplining their children, Paul did not enjoy the **sorrow** he brought to the Corinthians. He did not like seeing them in pain. Yet, he knew that this sorrow was **only for a little while,** and that it had **led . . . to** their **repentance.** For this reason, he could also be **happy** that they had gone through the sorrow. Paul's goal had been to bring the Corinthians to repentance, and his strategy had worked. They had reacted **as God intended and so were not harmed in any way.**

7:10. To explain himself further, Paul contrasted two kinds of sorrow: **Godly sorrow,** which conforms to divine intent, and **worldly sorrow,** which does not.

Godly sorrow brings repentance. In this context, "sorrow" refers to regret and emotional pain, and "repentance" means a change of mind and behavior. When believers become aware of their sins, they often react with bitter sorrow. But they do not repent unless they change their lifestyles. **Godly sorrow** always leads to **repentance.** When true believers hear the rebuke of God's Word, they turn to God for cleansing and forgiveness. Thus, **Godly sorrow . . . leads to salvation and leaves no regret.**

On the surface **worldly sorrow** may look similar to **godly sorrow,** but it **brings death.** The outcome of sorrow indicates its true nature. Even unbelievers may regret sins that they have committed, but this sorrow does not bring about God-centered repentance, and thus leads to **death.**

7:11. Paul reflected further on the Corinthians' repentance by noting eight results their **godly sorrow** had **produced:** (1) **earnestness** (or sincerity); (2) **eagerness to clear yourselves** (a readiness to make amends); (3) **indignation** (repulsion from former practices); (4) **alarm** (trepidation over past sin); (5) **longing** (desire for the ways of righteousness); (6) **concern** (caring about the terrible conditions of their church); (7) **readiness to see justice done** (a commitment to doing what was right in the church); and (8) they **proved** themselves **to be innocent in this matter.**

Paul may have had in mind the case of immorality that he had addressed in 1 Corinthians 5:1–13. Although the church had hesitated at first to discipline the immoral brother, perhaps they had not failed to discipline him at the apostle's instruction. This list of evidences for repentance is to some degree tailored to the situation in Corinth. The first five or six items are easily applied to other circumstances, but the last two deal with the particular sins in the Corinthian church.

7:12. Paul explained his motivation in bringing sorrow to the Corinthians in legal terms. He had not been concerned primarily with **the one who did the wrong or** with **the injured party.** While he may have had in mind the case of incest that he had addressed, he may also have had a more generic outlook in mind. In any case, Paul had not intended to blame or defend anyone. His goal had been more positive. He had wanted the Corinthians to **see for** themselves **how devoted** they were to the ways of Christ. He had wanted them to experience the joy of seeing God at work in their lives. This divine grace displayed itself in their godly sorrow and thorough repentance.

7:13a. The positive reactions and results that God worked through the Corinthians were so dramatic that Paul could not doubt them. Upon reflection, **all this . . . encouraged** the apostle's entire company.

Ⓓ Paul's Added Encouragement (7:13b–16)

SUPPORTING IDEA: *As Paul continued to describe what had happened in Macedonia, he commended the Corinthians even further.*

7:13b. Not only had the Corinthians encouraged Paul, but they had also encouraged Titus. Paul was **delighted to see how happy Titus was.** Titus was Paul's trusted servant. Like Paul, he also suffered for the gospel. Paul was pleased by Titus's happiness. Titus had **been refreshed** by the Corinthians' reaction.

7:14. The impression the Corinthians made on Titus also delighted Paul because he had **boasted** about the Corinthians to Titus. On a number of occasions, Paul rejoiced in the work of God in the lives of others by drawing attention to their gifts and blessings. Paul had probably told Titus about the blessings of God at Corinth in a manner similar to his acclamations to the Corinthians themselves.

Because Paul had bragged to Titus about the church at Corinth, he had risked embarrassment by sending Titus to deal with troubles there. He feared that perhaps they would not respond properly to his letter and that Titus would not be impressed with the church. But the Corinthians had been filled with godly sorrow and had repented, so they had **not embarrassed** him. Thus, Paul was vindicated in his **boasting . . . to Titus.**

7:15. Paul rounded out his commendation of the Corinthians by noting that Titus and he were pleased with the church because they **were all obedient.** Paul had given many instructions in the letter that Titus delivered, and the Corinthians had obeyed in everything. It is not likely that Paul meant that every single individual complied. **All** in this context probably identified the vast majority, or the church as a whole.

Paul also remarked on the attitudes of the Corinthians toward Titus. They had not resented his presence, but had received him **with fear and trembling.** The precise meaning of this expression is not clear. The expression appears to have been quite flexible, its meaning depending on the circumstances it described. In some cases it may simply have meant intense, humble anticipation of a future task. In others it may have entailed a fear of divine judgment. The Corinthians received Paul's rebukes and warnings with humble awareness of the peril in which their sins placed them.

7:16. As a result of their compliance and emotional reaction, Paul had **complete confidence in** the Corinthians. He was sure their faith was genuine and that they could be trusted to respond appropriately to the Word of God. Although he often called the Corinthian church "brothers," Paul also expressed doubts about their eternal salvation. Still, his confidence in the church at large had increased to the point that he had **complete confidence** in them.

🄴 The Example of Macedonia (8:1–7)

SUPPORTING IDEA: *Paul turned his attention to the collection of the contribution for the poor believers in Jerusalem. Instead of rebuking and warning them, Paul emphasized positive motivations for obedience to the will of God.*

8:1. Paul encouraged the Corinthians to move forward in their renewed commitment by following the example of the Macedonians (the churches at Philippi, Thessalonica, and Berea). In a spirit of intimacy, he addressed the Corinthians as **brothers.** Paul and his company wanted the church at Corinth to be encouraged to action by **the grace that God has given the Macedonian churches.**

8:2. How did God's grace display itself in Macedonia? The churches in that region had demonstrated **rich generosity** by giving to the relief of poor believers in Jerusalem. This generosity was obviously an act of divine grace because it occurred during a time of **severe trial.** On several occasions we read about troubles suffered by the Macedonian churches (Acts 17:1–9; 2 Thess. 1:4). By comparison, the church at Corinth had probably not experienced much trouble. Even so, the Macedonians gave with **overflowing joy** even in **their extreme poverty.** Their example should motivate the Corinthians to give generously as well.

8:3–5. Paul supported his report of Macedonian generosity with his personal testimony about several details. He knew the Macedonians had given **as much as they were able.** In fact, they had given **beyond their ability.** More importantly, they had done this **entirely on their own,** without harsh rebuke or strong commands. They had even **urgently pleaded** for the privilege of giving.

In exemplary behavior, the Macedonians not only **gave themselves first to the Lord**, but also to Paul and his company **in keeping with God's will**.

8:6–7. Paul was obviously pleased with the generosity of the Macedonian believers, but he mentioned these matters primarily to motivate the Corinthians to show the same generosity. For this reason, Paul **urged Titus** to return to Corinth to complete **this act of grace on** the Corinthians' **part**. The Corinthians had already experienced many blessings from God. Paul admitted that they excelled **in faith, in speech, in knowledge**. Yet, he wanted to see them go beyond these experiences of God's grace. Out of **complete earnestness**, or full sincerity and devotion, and **love** for Paul and his company, they were also to **excel in this grace of giving**.

Paul's strategy was plain. He first affirmed that through God's grace the Corinthians excelled in many areas of Christian living. Then he encouraged them to perform with the same excellence as they collected the donation for the church in Jerusalem. He spoke of giving in this way because he desired voluntary and generous contributions. It is easy for Christian financial responsibilities to be reduced to duty, but Paul chose his words carefully to portray this matter in a positive light. He hoped the Corinthians would see the opportunity to help the Jerusalem believers as a mercy from God.

F A Test of Sincerity (8:8–9)

> **SUPPORTING IDEA:** *Paul sought generous and voluntary gifts for the poor in Jerusalem in order to test the sincerity of the Corinthian Christians.*

8:8. Paul continued positively by denying that he was **commanding** the Corinthians to give. If they responded to an order or threat from him, then their giving would be from duty and not an "act of grace" (8:6). At the same time, he admitted that his encouragement was **to test the sincerity of** their **love**. It is difficult to determine the object of this **love**. Paul may have had in mind their love for him, their love for the believers in Jerusalem, or their love for Christ. The last option seems best in light of the immediate connection in the next verse and the comparison with the Macedonians who "gave themselves first to the Lord" (8:5). Paul sought to test the depths of the Corinthians' love and to encourage them to demonstrate that love **by comparing it with the earnestness of others** (the Macedonians).

8:9. Paul supported his call for demonstrating sincere love by reminding his readers of the sacrificial love of Christ. The Corinthians knew that Christ **was rich** in his preincarnate state. As the second person of the Trinity, Christ was exalted over all before the humiliation of his incarnation (cf. Phil. 2:5–8). Despite his eternal riches, Christ **became poor** when he came into the world so believers **through his poverty might become rich**. Christ's humiliation culminated in his death on the cross, and through his death came the riches of salvation.

Believers do not become **rich** through the sacrifice of Christ in the sense that they receive physical wealth in this life. According to Paul, our true wealth is the ministry of the Holy Spirit in our lives. He is the "deposit guaranteeing our inheritance" (Eph. 1:14). Yet, as Paul told the Corinthians, in Christ all believers will inherit all the riches of the new world when Christ returns in glory.

The Corinthians were to be motivated by the example of Christ's love and generosity to give unselfishly to the poor in Jerusalem. Their response to this opportunity tested the sincerity of their love and appreciation for Christ.

> **MAIN IDEA REVIEW:** *When believers repent of waywardness, they find positive motivations for further obedience to Christ. Love and gratitude motivate them to express loyalty to Christ.*

III. CONCLUSION

Keep It Up

In this passage the apostle Paul expressed positive attitudes toward the Corinthian church. Although he sometimes wondered about the sincerity of their faith, here he affirmed his confidence in them. They had proven faithful to Paul's earlier instruction, and for this reason he commended them. He encouraged their further faithfulness motivated by gratitude and love.

PRINCIPLES

- God comforts us in our affliction, through the means of other believers.
- Sorrow is good if it leads to repentance.
- Christians have the responsibility of taking care of other Christians.

APPLICATIONS

- Christians should motivate other Christians not just with negative rebukes and warnings, but also with encouragement.
- Believers should live for Christ out of gratitude and love.
- We should repent when we are confronted with our sin.
- We should look for opportunities to help Christians who are in physical need.

IV. LIFE APPLICATION

Just One Time

Every Tuesday and Friday Ralph had to take out the garbage early in the morning before the truck arrived. "I hate doing this," he often complained to his wife. "I just can't stand to take out the trash." The complaints were so regular that they had become almost a ritual. The family expected him to grumble as he tied up the bags and dragged them out the front door.

But one morning his wife Judy was not so patient with Ralph's ritual. She blocked the front door with her foot and stared at her husband. "I wish that just one time you'd be happy to take out the garbage because you love us so much."

Judy had a point. It is one thing to do the right thing because you are threatened or under compulsion. It is quite another to do the right thing because this expresses your love for someone. When we are motivated positively by things like gratitude and love, we take pleasure even in the most trying tasks.

Paul understood this, so in this part of 2 Corinthians he shifted his focus away from negative rebukes and warnings to more positive motivations. He focused on how the Corinthian believers could live for Christ out of gratitude and love. Although Paul's words focused primarily on contributions to the poor in Jerusalem, their implications apply to all areas of life.

In the first place, Christian leaders should learn from Paul's example that correction is only one way to encourage faithfulness among Christ's followers. It is easy for Christians to fall into the habit of criticizing. Our concern for others may mutate into judgmental negativity, making us concentrate on exposing and correcting sin. When this becomes our pattern of teaching in the church, legalism soon takes root. Paul's example cautions all of us to commend those who do good as well as correct those who do evil.

Further, as the Corinthians were to follow the example of Christ and the Macedonians in giving to the poor believers in Jerusalem, modern Christians should give to poor believers. Not every poor church or poor believer needs financial assistance. Yet, some churches and believers are so poor that they cannot meet their daily needs. We may not remember them often because they are geographically distant from us (as Jerusalem was from Corinth). Still, we bear a Christian duty to help them. Our love for Christ should motivate us to give generously, knowing that our giving blesses us as well.

V. PRAYER

Lord Jesus, we are grateful that your Spirit works within us, enabling us to respond faithfully to your Word. Fill our hearts with the joy of pleasing you and the desire to do all things for your glory. Amen.

VI. DEEPER DISCOVERIES

A. Pride (7:4)

The Greek word *kauchesis*, translated as "pride," and its verbal form *kauchomai* may carry either positive or negative connotations, much like the English word "proud" (as opposed to "prideful" which is always negative). Christians should take pride in God and in his works and laws (Rom. 2:17; Gal. 6:14). They may also take pride in their own merit (Phil. 2:16) or in that of others (1 Thess. 2:19). Christians should not take pride in themselves for things for which they do not deserve credit (1 Cor. 9:16).

B. Joy (7:4)

In Paul's writings, "joy" (*chara*) appears frequently. It usually relates to the coming of the kingdom of God and the work associated with it (Phil. 2:29; 4:1; Col. 1:11; Phlm. 1:7). It is especially the feeling a person has upon receiving that for which one hoped (2 Tim. 1:4). In the continuation of the kingdom before Christ's second coming, the promised blessings are realized in part, but not in full. Christians hope for those portions that have not been realized, and they rejoice over those that have been realized.

VII. TEACHING OUTLINE

A. INTRODUCTION

1. Lead Story: Good Pain
2. Context: Paul had previously rebuked the Corinthians for their sin, and this rebuke had caused them great sorrow. But his rebuke had worked: the Corinthians had repented of their sin, and they did not hold the rebuke against Paul. The apostle was greatly encouraged by this, and he proceeded to give the Corinthians further instruction— but this time by way of encouragement rather than rebuke.
3. Transition: We also need continual instruction. Sometimes we need to be rebuked, and sometimes we need to be encouraged. Sometimes we should be the ones who do the rebuking and/or encouraging. We should understand from this passage that rebukes should bring us to repentance and that we should not resent those who care about us enough to challenge us.

B. COMMENTARY

1. Appeal, Denial, and Affirmation (7:2–4)
   a. Appeal: The Corinthians were to make room in their hearts (7:2a)
   b. Denial: Paul and his company had done no wrong (7:2b)
   c. Affirmation: Paul took confidence and pride in the Corinthians (7:3–4)
2. Paul's Comfort in Macedonia (7:5–7)
3. True Repentance (7:8–13a)
4. Paul's Added Encouragement (7:13b–16)
5. The Example of Macedonia (8:1–7)
6. A Test of Sincerity (8:8–9)

C. CONCLUSION: JUST ONE TIME

VIII. ISSUES FOR DISCUSSION

1. Describe Paul's relationship with the Corinthians on a personal level. Why had Paul been worried about this relationship? How was Paul reassured about this relationship?
2. What is the difference between godly sorrow and worldly sorrow? How can the same emotion in response to the same situation be either worldly or godly?
3. What is encouragement? Why is encouragement important? What is the relationship between the Corinthians' encouragement of Paul and Paul's encouragement of the Corinthians?
4. Why did Paul raise the example of the Macedonian churches? How would this example have made you feel if you had been a Corinthian Christian receiving this letter?

2 Corinthians 8:10–9:15

Practical Guidance for Giving

Quote

"All that we have is Thine alone, a trust,

O Lord, from Thee."

William W. How

2 Corinthians 8:10–9:15

IN A NUTSHELL

Paul had already called on the Corinthians to contribute to the relief of poor believers in Jerusalem. In this passage he explained why and how this contribution was to be made.

Practical Guidance
for Giving

I. INTRODUCTION

Never Lend Money to a Friend

*S*ome words of advice are so obviously true that you can hear them all around the world. One of these international directions is: "Never lend money to a friend." Of course, only a few people go so far as to apply this principle in literalistic fashion. But we understand the truth that lies behind it. The exchange of money is a sensitive issue. It can turn friends into enemies.

Even in the Christian community money is a touchy subject. Most pastors hate to talk about the responsibility of members to support the church. They worry over how their church members will react, and their worries are almost always right: people react negatively. Thus, church leaders must broach this subject with great care.

In this passage Paul continued to write about the Corinthians' responsibility to contribute financially to the kingdom of God. He was careful, however, to guard against misunderstandings. From his discussion of this difficult topic, we can learn much about our own responsibilities and about encouraging others in this aspect of Christian living.

II. COMMENTARY

Practical Guidance for Giving

> **MAIN IDEA:** *Paul wanted the contribution for the Christians in Jerusalem to be generous and for its collection to go smoothly. In order to ensure this, he encouraged the Corinthians to cooperate with his emissaries and to give liberally.*

A Strong Advice (8:10–15)

> **SUPPORTING IDEA:** *Although Paul did not command the Corinthians to contribute to Jerusalem, he strongly advised it. He wanted to see God's blessing come upon the Corinthians, and he knew that a generous contribution to Jerusalem would bring such blessings.*

8:10. Paul used great wisdom as he dealt with this subject. He began with a strong commendation. The Corinthian Christians **were the first**, or among the first, to begin preparations to give and expressed **the desire to do so.** At first the Corinthians were very eager to contribute to the Jerusalem church. This reaction demonstrated their commitment and desire to aid the believers who were suffering in Jerusalem.

8:11. The sequence of events behind this passage needs to be understood. After first informing the Corinthians of the need for contributions, Paul told them he would travel from Ephesus to Macedonia and then return to Corinth. After a delay, Paul visited Corinth briefly and sent a harsh letter to them through Titus. Later Titus met Paul in Macedonia with reports on the conditions at Corinth. At first the Corinthians were eager to contribute to the needs of Jerusalem believers, but troubles in the church had extinguished their eagerness. At this point Paul encouraged them to complete their commitment. Their **willingness to do it** needed to be **matched by** their **completion of it.**

As important as it was for the Corinthians to be willing to give at first, it was not enough. Recognizing the need to contribute and responding with commitments is easy. The true test is actually handing over the money. So Paul encouraged the Corinthians to fulfill their commitments.

Even so, Paul had no particular amount in mind. He left it up to the Corinthians to give **according to** their **means.** Many interpreters assume that these words reject the Old Testament practice of tithing (Deut. 12:6; Mal. 3:8–10), but this passage is not about money given to support the church. Rather, it is about charity for the poor above and beyond support for the church.

8:12. Paul justified proportional giving by appealing to a general principle: a **gift is acceptable** so long as it is **according to what one has.** Of course, Paul also accepted sacrificial giving; he praised the Macedonians for giving beyond their means. Yet, he felt free only to persuade the Corinthians to give as their means allowed. He fixed no particular amount, leaving this to their consciences.

8:13. Paul's goal justified the principle of giving according to means. He did not desire that the Corinthians be **hard pressed** while the church in Jerusalem was **relieved.** His goal was **that there might be equality.**

Care must be taken not to read too much into these words. The New Testament never indicates that all economic inequalities within the church should be eliminated. Instead, the goal of giving in the New Testament church was to insure that the basic needs of the poor were met. Even the early practice of holding everything in common (Acts 2:44–45) was designed to insure that basic needs were met in troubled times. Wealthy Christians are warned against the dangers of riches and told to be generous, but not to seek economic equality. Just as Moses instructed Israel to care for the poor (Lev.

19:9–10; Deut. 24:12–15), so the church is to care for its poor through generous contributions.

8:14–15. At least two reasons undergirded Paul's advice. First, he knew that economic situations change. **At the present time** the Corinthians were in a position to help others, but the day might come when the situation was reversed, and they would have to rely on the generosity of the church in Jerusalem.

Second, Paul appealed to a theological principle based on God's action in Israel's deliverance from Egyptian slavery. The apostle referred the Corinthians to the Septuagint translation of Exodus 16:18 which indicated that no one in Israel had **too much** or **too little.** During Israel's wilderness wanderings, God miraculously supplied each Israelite family according to their needs. Even though some **gathered much,** it did not result in an overabundance. Although others **gathered little,** it did not result in serious deprivation. This miraculous provision indicated God's desire to meet the needs of all his people.

It would have been easy for the Corinthians to think otherwise. They could have reasoned that if God had not wanted the church in Jerusalem to suffer, then he would have not permitted it. But Paul resisted this fatalistic outlook. God desired that the needs of all his people be met. Even so, God was not accomplishing his desire through miraculous distribution as in the Exodus. Rather, he called on the church to care for his people.

Ⓑ Safeguards Against Mishandling of Funds (8:16–24)

> **SUPPORTING IDEA:** *Paul explained how he intended to collect contributions from the church. His description assured the Corinthians that he was not seeking his own gain and that he would be careful with the funds.*

8:16–17. Paul mentioned that **Titus** was returning. It appears that the Corinthian church had a positive relationship with Titus. They received him well and honored him as a servant of Paul. So the apostle expressed thanks to **God** for putting affection for the Corinthians **into the heart of Titus.** Titus shared Paul's love for the church and wanted nothing but the well-being of the believers there. Paul explained by saying that Titus did more than respond to the apostle's **appeal.** He was **coming . . . with much enthusiasm and on his own initiative.** He had so much affection for the church in Corinth that he voluntarily made the arduous journey to see them again.

8:18. Paul also mentioned that the party collecting contributions would include **the brother who is praised by all the churches.** It is uncertain who this brother was. A number of suggestions have been made: Apollos, Aristarchus, Barnabas, Silas, and Timothy. Some of these candidates are more likely than others, but certain identification is not possible. Paul apparently believed that his identity would be clear enough from his reputation **for his service to the gospel.** He reminded the Corinthians of this reputation to instill confidence in this brother as a trustworthy courier.

8:19. If his reputation was not enough, Paul also noted that this unnamed person **was chosen by the churches to accompany** Paul and his company as they collected the contributions. It is not clear which churches were in view here. The apostle probably had in mind wide support for the person as indicated by "all the churches" in 8:18. The term *chosen* (*charotoneo*) probably connotes choice by an official vote or show of hands.

When Paul touched on the fact that this brother was to accompany **us** (Paul and his company) with **the offering,** he also turned to his own reliability. At first he simply mentioned that they would **administer** the offering **in order to honor the Lord himself,** not for self-aggrandizement or for their own support. They sought to **honor the Lord** whose own actions demonstrated his desire to see the poor relieved (see 8:15).

Moreover, Paul and his company went through all this trouble **to show** their **eagerness to help. Eagerness** or enthusiasm in the service of God is a consistent theme in this context. Paul spoke of himself as helping or assisting because he did not handle the money himself but aided those who had been appointed. He showed great wisdom and caution in this sensitive area.

8:20. Paul continued to explain his role as a helper or assistant by noting that he wanted **to avoid any criticism of the way** they **administer[ed] this liberal gift.** By surrounding himself with trustworthy brothers, Paul avoided the possibility that he might be accused of stealing or misappropriating funds. He expressed his enthusiasm for this role by calling the contributions **liberal.** He saw this task as important, and he demonstrated this awareness by handling the funds with care.

8:21. Paul explained what he meant by avoiding criticism. He was **taking pains** or going through much trouble **to do what** was **right.** Unlike other contexts in which he disdained the opinions of people who stood against the ways of God (e.g., 1 Cor. 4:3), Paul affirmed here an appropriate concern for the opinions of people. Much like Jesus, who "grew . . . in favor with God and men" (Luke 2:52), Paul wanted to be clear of wrongdoing **not only in the eyes of the Lord but also in the eyes of men.** In this expression Paul alluded to Proverbs 3:4. In matters of money Paul understood the wisdom of such safeguards.

8:22–23. To assure the Corinthian church, Paul mentioned several of those who were collecting funds. First was another unnamed **brother.** It would appear that the Corinthians did not know this man. He had been in Paul's company for some time because he had **often proved to** Paul and his company **in many ways that he** was **zealous.** He had **great confidence** in the Corinthians, probably because of Paul's boasting.

Second, Paul mentioned **Titus** again. This time he praised Titus by calling him his **partner and fellow worker**

Third, the apostle spoke of **our brothers.** It is not clear if he had in mind the brothers mentioned before. Some unnamed Macedonians were possibly to accompany Paul to Corinth, but this group was to precede any Macedonian's arrival. Paul may have had these men in mind here. They were **representatives** (literally "apostles" or "ones sent") **of the churches.** Moreover, their Christian lives brought **honor**, not shame, to the name of **Christ.**

8:24. On the basis of the safeguards Paul had in place for the collection, he called the Corinthians to respond appropriately. Instead of calling them to contribute, he spoke indirectly of the contributions as **proof of** their **love and the reason for** his **pride** in them. By this approach, he reminded the Corinthians of the effects of their giving. They would offer **proof** in this test and would justify Paul's boasting in them. Moreover, **the churches** in Macedonia and Jerusalem would see these qualities of the Corinthian church and would be encouraged.

Paul was practical and pastoral about this matter. Though guided by biblical principles, he was concerned with putting to rest any misgivings the Corinthians may have had. His special efforts provide guidance for all who handle money in ministry.

Service to the Churches (9:1–5)

> **SUPPORTING IDEA:** *Paul advised the Corinthians to contribute to the offering with words of confidence and positive motivation.*

9:1. The apostle began by admitting that there was **no need . . . to write . . . about this service to the saints.** The NIV omits the conjunction at the beginning of this verse. In effect, Paul supported his urging in 8:24 with his belief that the Corinthians already agreed with him. **This service** was none other than the service of contributions to the Jerusalem believers. Paul did not call the Jerusalem Christians **saints** or "holy ones" because they were special or outstanding believers. Rather, he frequently used this expression to describe "believers." Nevertheless, the name "holy ones" indicated the Christians in Jerusalem were worthy of special honor and attention from the Corinthians. They were not ordinary, but sanctified by Christ (Gal. 6:10).

9:2. Paul reaffirmed his confidence in the Corinthians' **eagerness to help.** In fact, he had been **boasting** about them not only to Titus but also to the **Macedonians.** He had even told the Macedonians that **last year** they were **ready to give.** Paul's boasting about the Corinthians had even **stirred most of** the Macedonians **to action.** Just as Paul had previously used the example of the Macedonians to inspire the Corinthians to give; he had also motivated the

Macedonians through reports about the initial enthusiasm of the Corinthians.

9:3. Paul sent Titus and others ahead to collect funds to insure that his **boasting . . . should not prove hollow.** Although at the moment Paul was confident that the Corinthians would prove faithful **in this matter**, he also knew that their attitudes could change. Paul was afraid they would not **be ready as** he had **said** they **would be** when he arrived. He sent messengers to make sure the collection was completed before he arrived.

9:4. Paul explained himself further by noting that **Macedonians** might arrive in Corinth with him. While he wrote this letter, Paul was unsure that they would actually go with him. As it turned out, Sopater from Berea and Aristarchus and Secundus from Thessalonica did go with him (Acts 20:4). If the Corinthians were **unprepared** to make their contributions, then Paul would be **ashamed of having been so confident** in them, and the Corinthians would also have cause for shame.

9:5. For this reason Paul sent **the brothers to visit . . . in advance** of his arrival. They would finalize the collection of the **generous gift . . . promised** by the Corinthians. The initial enthusiasm at Corinth must have included the promise of a large sum, and Paul wanted to insure that this promise was kept. If the **brothers** gathered the contribution before Paul and any Macedonians arrived, then the contribution would be received as a genuinely **generous gift.** If not, it might appear to be **begrudgingly given** in response to pressure from Paul.

Paul showed practical concern for the encouragement of the churches in Corinth and Macedonia. Although he was confident of the Corinthians' good intentions, he was not naïve. He took the precaution of sending messengers ahead to insure that no one would miss the opportunity for a great blessing.

𝔻 Believers Benefit from Generosity (9:6–11)

SUPPORTING IDEA: *Paul motivated his readers further by pointing to the benefits that come to those who give generously.*

9:6. The NIV translates the opening phrase *touto de* as **remember this,** but a variety of translations are possible. Literally, Paul said, "and this," which may be elliptical for something like "now consider this" or "now this is important."

The apostle began with what was probably a common agricultural proverb which taught that sowing sparingly results in a poor harvest and that generous sowing results in a plentiful harvest. It is also possible that Paul alluded to Proverbs 11:24–25; 22:9. Paul used a similar analogy in Galatians 6:7,9. This analogy encouraged generous giving. Just as farmers should not expect a large harvest unless they sow generously, so Christians should not expect many blessings from God unless they bless others in a generous way.

9:7. In light of this wise saying, Paul encouraged the Corinthians to give. As before, he did not want them to give beyond their means, and the exact amount was a matter of conscience. The reliance on inward conviction in this matter is particularly important because Paul had no directive from God. As in every ethical choice that believers must make, there comes a point when the inward conviction of the Spirit must guide specific actions. Decisions of the heart must not violate the revelation of God, but they are necessary for practical application of the principles derived from the Old and New Testaments.

Acting according to conscience was very important in this situation. Paul wanted the Corinthians to receive God's blessings in response to their generosity, but this would not occur if they gave **reluctantly or under compulsion** because **God loves a cheerful giver**. Once again, Paul relied on proverbial wisdom. This proverb probably circulated widely among Jewish rabbis and early Christian teachers because Paul used it freely as justification for his view. Paul believed that God's love extends to all who are in Christ, but he had in mind here a special affection or approval that leads to significant blessings in the life of the believer.

9:8. Knowing that God is favorably predisposed to those who give cheerfully is important because of God's ability to bless. Paul focused on God's ability, not his guarantee. **God is able** (*dunateo*), but he is free to choose whom, how, when, and to what degree he will bless. There is a sense in which every Christian has received the grace of God in Christ (Rom. 5:15), but here Paul thought of special mercy that comes to some and not to others. When God so chooses to bless, the result will be that **in all things at all times** believers will receive **all that** they **need**, and will **abound in every good work**.

Note the manner in which Paul described these abundant blessings. First, believers may be given **all that** they **need** (*autarkeia*), not all they may want (*thelo, zeloo*). God often gives believers things they desire, but Paul did not have these blessings in view here. The Corinthians faced the challenge of giving generously, which could have threatened their livelihood. Paul made it clear, however, that God (not their selfish greed) was able to supply their needs.

Second, the goal of these divine supplies is not primarily the believer's wealth or personal pleasure. God supplies so believers may **abound in every good work**—so they will be free from worry over necessities and may focus on fulfilling the commands of God.

9:9. To support his assertion that God is able to do all of these things, Paul quoted Psalm 112:9 from the Septuagint. This verse describes different characteristics of the righteous person, and verse 9 depicts him as generous to the poor. This theme fit well with Paul's emphasis on generous giving at Corinth because these contributions were destined for the poor of Jerusalem.

The second line of Psalm 112:9, "his righteousness endures forever," troubles some interpreters because similar expressions often refer to God (Ps. 111:3; Isa. 51:8). It is possible that the psalm focused on the permanence of a righteous person's actions. In other words, God will never forget or ignore a righteous man's generosity (righteousness). This interpretation fits well with Paul's purpose in this passage: encouraging the Corinthians to be generous so God would reward them. Paul's comments in the next verse support this understanding.

9:10. Paul followed his quotation from Psalm 112 with two allusions to the Old Testament. First, he referred to Isaiah 55:10, which praises God as the one who **supplies seed to the sower and bread for food.** Second, he drew from Hosea 10:12, which promises a harvest of blessing for those who sow righteousness. Paul combined these Old Testament ideas to assure the Corinthians that God would not ignore their generosity, but would **enlarge the harvest** (rewards) **of** their **righteousness.** Their righteous deeds would not be overlooked or forgotten.

9:11. Paul went on to describe what the Corinthians could expect as they contributed to the poor in Jerusalem. He first said they would **be made rich in every way.** Paul was not promising material blessings to those who give generously. He knew that faithful believers are often poor, just as the Jerusalem saints were at that time.

The key to understanding this expression is the similar language in 1 Corinthians 1:5,7, where Paul rejoiced that the Corinthians had been "enriched in every way—in all [their] speaking and in all [their] knowledge," and did "not lack any spiritual gift." The riches of the Christian life before the return of Christ are primarily the blessings of the Holy Spirit. He is the down payment on the inheritance of riches we will receive when Christ returns. When the Spirit is poured out on believers in dramatic ways, they are made rich in every way.

In this light, Paul's idea becomes clear. If the Corinthians gave generously, they could expect a dramatic enrichment of their lives by the Spirit. They would be so blessed they would be able to **be generous on every occasion**—able to meet whatever needs they encountered with the rich ministry of the Spirit.

Finally, Paul also assured the Corinthian church that he and his company would be blessed by generous giving. He pledged that **through us** (Paul and his company) the Corinthian generosity would **result in thanksgiving to God.** The apostle would praise God joyfully as he saw them fulfill this responsibility.

In these verses Paul made it clear that giving generously to the poor in Jerusalem would bring many benefits. The needs of the poor would be met. The Corinthians would be blessed, and their lives would be enriched. Paul and his company would be encouraged and thankful to God. These positive benefits were to motivate the Corinthians to fulfill their earlier commitment to giving.

E The Result: Praise of God (9:12–15)

> **SUPPORTING IDEA:** *Paul developed the theme of thanksgiving further by stating that generous contributions would result in wide-spread praise of God.*

9:12–13. The apostle began by asserting that **this service** of contributing was not only for **supplying the needs of God's people,** but also for the **over-flowing in many expressions of thanks to God,** so that **men** would **praise God.** The collection of money for Jerusalem was widespread in the church, reaching Achaia, Macedonia, and Asia Minor. As these churches heard reports of others' generosity, it surely caused much worship and praise. The goal of honoring God was supreme in Paul's perspective, and this should have been the Corinthians' goal as well.

While explaining the process by which God would be praised, Paul mentioned a number of important features of this contribution. First, by it the Corinthians would prove themselves. In 8:8 the apostle had announced that this event was a test of the Corinthians' sincerity. Here he made clear that fulfilling their promise to give would prove the true condition of their hearts. In this regard, Paul held a similar perspective to that of the apostle John, who said that love for God could not be present in a believer's life without love for other Christians (1 John 4:20).

Second, Paul described fulfilling the contribution as **obedience that** would accompany their **confession of the gospel of Christ. Confession** or profession of the gospel must be demonstrated by obedience. Paul stated this principle clearly on many occasions (Rom. 6:1; Eph. 2:8–10; 2 Thess. 1:8). In fact, he warned that flagrant disobedience would reveal the absence of saving faith (Col. 1:22–23).

By weaving these comments into his discussion, Paul reminded the Corinthians of how serious this matter was. It was a test of the obedience that must accompany saving faith in Christ.

9:14. As he ended his encouragement to the Corinthians on this matter, Paul assured them that in the **prayers** of other churches the **hearts** of those churches would **go out to** the Corinthians. **Because of the surpassing grace** that God had given them, many would pray. Other Christians would be so encouraged by God's work among the Corinthians that they would intercede on their behalf. Paul assured them of this because he understood the importance of intercessory prayer. He encouraged many churches by telling them that he prayed for them. He sought to motivate the Corinthians with thoughts of how wonderful it would be to have many Christians throughout the world praying for them.

9:15. This thought was so magnificent in Paul's outlook that it caused him to break forth in praise. He wrote, **Thanks be to God.** His heart broke out in adoration for God's **indescribable gift** which made all of this possible—the gift of salvation through Christ. He was overwhelmed by the thought of Gentiles in Corinth joining with other Gentile churches to provide for Jewish believers in Jerusalem. He overflowed with joy that all of these churches would join together in the praise of God and in prayer for one another. Paul was so ecstatic at the thought he could go no further.

> **MAIN IDEA REVIEW:** *Paul wanted the contribution for the Christians in Jerusalem to be generous and for its collection to go smoothly. In order to ensure this, he encouraged the Corinthians to cooperate with his emissaries and to give liberally.*

III. CONCLUSION

Show Your Love

Paul raised the practical issue of relief for the poor in Jerusalem. The body of Christ extended beyond the confines of the local church at Corinth, and the believers there were responsible to care for the needs of the hungry and suffering in Jerusalem. He exhorted them to use this opportunity to show their gratitude to God for his blessings and to show sincere love for their brothers and sisters in need.

PRINCIPLES

- From a pragmatic perspective, it is more effective to encourage generous charitable giving than to mandate it.
- It is our duty as Christians to help other believers.
- If our charitable giving is uncompelled and cheerful, we will be rewarded spiritually.

APPLICATIONS

- We must take realistic steps to guard against the temptation to steal or mishandle church funds.
- We must take an active part in meeting the material needs of other believers.
- Christians should give generously and freely.

IV. LIFE APPLICATION

Spoiled Brats

I was working late into the evening when an international student came into my office. "You Americans are spoiled brats!" he said angrily. I could tell he was deeply troubled, so I invited him to sit down and talk.

This dear brother had just received a letter from his family. He had been away from his home for two years to attend seminary, but he was about to graduate and return to his wife and children. That day, however, he had received a letter from his wife and father telling him to remain in the United States because the communists in surrounding villages were executing everyone who had been educated in the West. He was distraught.

"I don't think you realize how bad it is in other parts of the world," he added. "For you, it's a big problem if you can't buy a new car. It's a crisis if you can't build a big church building. But in my homeland, we are simply trying to survive. Why don't you do something to help us?"

That conversation put a real human face on something I had only known in theory. Christians throughout the world suffer because of their faith. Most of us live in comfort while they are in pain.

When Paul wrote this letter, the Corinthians were doing relatively well, living in peace and prosperity. While this prosperity was a blessing from God, it was also an opportunity for service. He encouraged them not to be spoiled brats who worried about their small needs while other Christians suffered so much.

This passage gives us many useful insights into handling money in the church today. Paul's example can help leaders use the proper cautions in this sensitive area and encourage believers to be generous in their giving.

Paul knew that even in the best circumstances practical safeguards needed to be in place to insure the orderly collection and distribution of money in the church. He set up practical safeguards against misappropriations. Christian leaders must take realistic steps to guard against the temptation to steal or mishandle money given to the church. Systems of oversight must be regulated carefully so that all may trust the process.

Paul also knew how to motivate the people to give. He did not impose a collection on the Corinthians; he urged them to complete what they had volunteered to do. Trying to force generosity will eventually lead to resistance. It is much better to encourage voluntary, heart-felt generosity. Paul also encouraged the Corinthians to consider the blessings they would receive by their generosity. As followers of Christ, we have the opportunity to receive many spiritual rewards when we give cheerfully.

The apostle also reminded the Corinthians of the ultimate reason for his request: their generosity would lead to an overflow of thanks to God from those who received. By giving to the ministry of the church, we fulfill our goal of bringing glory to God.

The financial ministry of the church is a touchy subject. It is riddled with pitfalls. By following Paul's example, we can avoid many of these difficulties as we fulfill this vital service to the body of Christ.

V. PRAYER

Lord Jesus, you have blessed us with so many wonderful gifts. Yet, we often overlook these privileges and seek more and more for ourselves. Please give us hearts that are sensitive to the needs of your people throughout the world. Call us to give of our abundance so that they may be blessed. Amen.

VI. DEEPER DISCOVERIES

A. According to Your Means (8:11) and to What One Has (8:12)

Godly generosity does not depend upon the size of the gift, but on the love and self-sacrifice that motivate it. The widow who gave "all she had to live on" to the treasury provides an interesting example of this principle. Jesus stated that the widow's offering of less than a cent surpassed the large amounts offered by the wealthy because she gave from her poverty and they from their wealth (Mark 12:41–44). In fact, her offering exceeded the offerings advised by Paul in that it cut into her ability to live. In this sense, the giving of the Macedonians was more similar to the widow's gift. While Paul recognized such giving as admirable, he evidently did not feel comfortable advising it, advising the Corinthians to give out of "plenty" (8:14).

Paul's reluctance to advise the same kind of sacrificial giving that both he and Christ praised creates an interesting tension. Does the Bible teach that Christians should give more than they are able to give? Paul's example indicates that God does not obligate Christians to give beyond their means, but that he rewards them when they do. It is tempting to think that anything we do short of the absolute best thing that we can do is sin, but Paul indicates this is not the case. Otherwise, he would have been remiss for not calling the Corinthians to give beyond their means.

B. Reap Generously (9:6); Increase Your Store of Seed (9:10); You Will Be Made Rich (9:11)

Because of common abuses of this passage, it is important to consider what it does and does not say. The passage does teach that God rewards those who give generously to other Christians in need. It also teaches that generous giving should be motivated by the desire to minister to others and that the giving itself is a ministry.

It does not teach that God will always reward giving in this way or that God is obligated to reward giving in this way. As Paul indicated in 8:14–15, even after giving generously to the Christians in Jerusalem, the Corinthians could expect lean times themselves in the future—so lean that the church in Jerusalem might be called upon to make similar donations to them. Also, the harvest from God need not be financial. It need only continue the giver's ability to minister to others ("abound in every good work," 9:8; "so that you can be generous on every occasion," 9:11).

Paul did not teach that God would reward givers whose motivation for giving was that they might reap a financial reward from God. His point was that giving motivated by love and concern for others was a righteous ministry and that those who engaged in it would be equipped to "abound in every good work" (9:8). Those people whose giving is motivated by a desire for financial gain do not give in a godly fashion motivated by love and generosity. They cannot expect any harvest, let alone a financial reward.

VII. TEACHING OUTLINE

A. INTRODUCTION
1. Lead Story: Never Lend Money to a Friend
2. Context: While many believers in Corinth and other cities lived in prosperity, the church in Jerusalem struggled to meet its daily needs. Paul was organizing a monetary donation to be delivered to Jerusalem to relieve this poverty. The Corinthians had committed to giving to this cause, so Paul encouraged them to make good on their promises.
3. Transition: Many believers around the world suffer persecution and poverty. We are responsible to help them, just as the Corinthians were responsible to help the believers in Jerusalem.

B. COMMENTARY
1. Strong Advice (8:10–15)
    a. Follow through with commitment (8:10–11)
    b. Give according to means (8:12)
    c. Equality (8:13–15)
2. Safeguards Against Mishandling of Funds (8:16–24)
    a. Trusted men (8:16–19,22–23)
    b. Take pains to do what is right (8:20–21)
    c. Prove your love to the trusted men (8:24)

3. Service to the Churches (9:1–5)
   a. Paul has boasted about the Corinthians (9:1–2)
   b. Brothers coming to make sure gift is ready (9:3–5)
4. Believers Benefit from Generosity (9:6–11)
   a. God will reward the givers (9:6,8–11)
   b. Give voluntarily and cheerfully (9:7)
5. The Result: Praise of God (9:12–15)

C. CONCLUSION: SPOILED BRATS

VIII. ISSUES FOR DISCUSSION

1. Why did Paul offer only an opinion and not a command in this section of the letter? What does this imply about Paul's authority? What does it imply about his motives?
2. Why was Paul so interested in collecting money for the saints in Jerusalem? What special connection, if any, did Paul have with Jerusalem that made this of particular personal interest to him?
3. Who was Titus? Why did Paul send Titus to help with the collection? Explain the wisdom of this decision.
4. According to Paul, what would God do to bless those Christians who gave generously to the offering? On what basis could Paul offer these blessings? Are these blessings sufficient to motivate you to give generously to Christians in need?

2 Corinthians 10:1–12:13

The Authority of a True Apostle

I. INTRODUCTION
"Who Died and Made You Boss?"

II. COMMENTARY
A verse-by-verse explanation of this section.

III. CONCLUSION
In All Matters of Faith and Life

An overview of the principles and applications from this section.

IV. LIFE APPLICATION
"I Didn't Know He Did All That"

Melding the section to life.

V. PRAYER
Tying the section to life with God.

VI. DEEPER DISCOVERIES
Historical, geographical, and grammatical enrichment of the commentary.

VII. TEACHING OUTLINE
Suggested step-by-step group study of the section.

VIII. ISSUES FOR DISCUSSION
Zeroing the section in on daily life.

2 Corinthians 10:1–12:13

Quote

"*W*hen I fight authority, authority always wins."

John Mellancamp

IN A NUTSHELL

*I*n anticipation of his upcoming visit to Corinth, Paul addressed some of the challenges raised against his authority. He defended his authority by pointing out his opponents' boasts and the legitimacy of his own ministry among the Corinthians.

The Authority of a
True Apostle

I. INTRODUCTION

"Who Died and Made You Boss?"

I was only a young child when I sat terrified in the church pew. It was a congregational meeting—a "business meeting" as they called it—and the men of the church were shouting back and forth at one another over some controversial decision that had been made. One man stood out from the rest of the congregation of several thousand. He was older and had a long, white beard. He looked just like Santa Claus, and he had always been more than kind to me. So my attention was riveted as he pointed his finger at the pastor. He stood there shouting at the top of his voice, "Who died and made you boss?"

If there is one thing that threatens the peace of every church at one time or another, it is the struggle over authority. Someone has to set the pace; someone has to take the lead. But churches often face the question of who will be "the boss."

A power struggle also took place in Corinth. In Paul's absence, opponents had resisted his authority over the congregation and asserted themselves as apostles. Paul addressed the claims of these opponents and asserted his own authority.

The modern church faces two types of problems similar to Paul's. First, we also have to endure struggles over the leadership of the church. Second, liberalism challenges the authority of the apostles and the Bible over human life.

II. COMMENTARY

The Authority of a True Apostle

MAIN IDEA: *False apostles had opposed Paul in Corinth. He hoped that by writing against these false teachers he might prevent a major conflict when he arrived.*

🅐 Bold Action to Come (10:1–11)

SUPPORTING IDEA: *False apostles had apparently accused Paul of being two-faced. He wrote to the Corinthians about this misconception.*

10:1. Paul took this issue seriously. He began with an **appeal**, saying, **I, Paul.** He used this kind of intense expression only three times in his epistles (cf. Gal. 5:2; 1 Thess. 2:18), reserving it for the most serious topics. The challenge to his apostolic authority was a grave matter. Not only was Paul personally offended, but the rejection of his authority was tantamount to a rejection of Christ.

Paul's opponents had accused him of being "**timid**" **when face to face . . . but** "**bold**" **when away.** Apparently, they asserted that he did not have a powerful enough presence to be an apostle. Paul mocked this position as incompatible with Christianity.

He **appeal[ed]** to the church **by the meekness and gentleness of Christ.** The opponents had accused Paul of being **timid** (*tapeinos*), but Paul directed the Corinthians' attention to Christ's similar qualities of **meekness** (*prautetos*) and **gentleness** (*epieikeias*). In fact, Jesus had even described himself as *tapeinos* (Matt. 11:29). By beginning this section in this way, Paul pointed to the irony of his opponents accusing him of timidity. What they saw as a liability was evidence that Paul was like Christ, and therefore substantiated the legitimacy of his apostleship.

10:2. Paul desired to remain meek toward the Corinthians. He went so far as to **beg** them not to make it necessary for him **to be bold** when he came to visit. He preferred to be gentle toward his spiritual children, and he hoped they would make this possible by not resisting his authority. Nevertheless, Paul realized he would probably have to be **bold . . . toward some people** because he did not expect everyone to accept his appeal. These people would need sharp rebuke and discipline because they evaluated Paul's leadership **by the standards of this world.** This problem loomed large in the church at Corinth. Paul had addressed it before, but apparently it was still an issue.

10:3–5. Paul responded by reminding the Corinthians that his ministry was successful warfare. He had previously described his gospel ministry as a parade of victory in war, and he used similar military analogies elsewhere as well. His apostolic effort was a war he was sure to win.

Paul admitted that he and his company **live[d] in the world,** but insisted that they did not **wage war as the world does.** They did not employ the intimidation, coercion, and violence normally associated with worldly authorities. Instead of employing **the weapons of the world,** Paul relied on **divine power.** These **weapons** appeared weak by worldly standards, but they were actually very powerful. The preaching of the cross brought great displays of God's power in the lives of believers everywhere, including Corinth.

Consequently, Paul was certain that he was on a course **to demolish** the **strongholds** or fortifications of **arguments and every pretension** that anyone set up **against the knowledge of God**. As Paul traveled the world proclaiming the gospel of Christ, he encountered pretentious disbelief supported by clever arguments and powerful personalities. But through the "weakness" of preaching Christ, Paul went about taking **captive every thought to make it obedient to Christ**.

10:6. Having established this broad portrait of his ministry, Paul addressed the Corinthian situation. As one who waged spiritual war, Paul would **be ready to punish every act of disobedience** when he arrived in Corinth. He made it clear that he would not come in gentleness toward those who opposed him. The apostle did not intend to coerce or punish his opponents. This would have been to rely on worldly weapons of war. Instead, he probably had in mind his divine power to authorize church discipline. Paul bore the responsibility to authorize the expulsion of false leaders, and he would surely do so when he arrived in Corinth. Yet, he also made it clear that he would be careful in this regard, acting boldly only **once** the Corinthians' **obedience** was **complete**.

We cannot know for certain what Paul meant by this expression. Some interpreters believe he referred to the collection for Jerusalem. Others suggest he meant the rejection of the false apostles.

Despite his pastoral strategy, Paul presented a thinly veiled threat in these words. He had determined not to ignore those who challenged his apostleship. His opponents who accused him of timidity would be shocked to see his decisive discipline.

10:7a. Having stated his intention to move decisively against his opponents, Paul declared his commitment to bold action from a different angle in 10:7–11. The sentence **you are looking only on the surface of things** may be translated in the indicative (NIV), in the imperative (NRSV), or as an interrogative (NKJV). If the second option is correct, then Paul warned the Corinthians to look beyond his opponents' superficial accusations and to evaluate the situation more carefully. If the first or third option is correct, then he exhorted the Corinthians to see what should be obvious. Whatever the case, Paul began another line of thought that would lead again to a commitment to bold action in his upcoming visit.

10:7b. What did the apostle want the Corinthians to consider? He wanted them to examine the claim made by others that they **belong[ed] to Christ** (*Christou einai*, literally "to be of Christ"). This expression may have meant more than just being a follower of Christ. In 1 Corinthians 1:12 Paul reported that one faction in the Corinthian church claimed to follow Christ, implying a special blessing or appointment by Christ or a purer faith. Yet, Paul insisted that whatever special appointment others may have had, he and his company **belong[ed] to Christ just as much.**

10:8. Of course, such a claim sounded as if Paul boasted of being above others, just as his opponents did. So he explained that if he **boast[ed]** somewhat **freely** . . . he would **not be ashamed of it.** Testing would vindicate Paul's claim to special authority but would condemn his opponents.

Paul mentioned that the special authority he received from Christ was **for building . . . up rather than pulling . . . down.** Paul had argued in his earlier epistle that all spiritual gifts were for edification. Here he affirmed this as the purpose of his apostleship. By implication, Paul's opponents used their gifts for the church's destruction. This positive service that Paul rendered to the church was one reason why he would **not be ashamed** when he visited.

10:9. The meaning of this verse is obscured by unusual Greek syntax. Different translations are possible: **I do not want to seem to be trying to frighten you with my letters.** It is likely that Paul introduced an aside here that we may paraphrase in this manner: "Now, I never intended to frighten anyone unduly with my letters, despite what others may have said about them." This understanding fits well with the verses that follow.

10:10. Paul explained that **some** said his letters were **weighty and forceful,** but they had nothing to fear because **in person he** was **unimpressive and his speaking amount[ed] to nothing.** Paul's opponents relied on their clever speech laced with human authority. They diminished any threat Paul made in writing by assuming they would outtalk him in any confrontation.

10:11. In response to this false confidence, Paul wrote that **such people** needed to understand that **what** he had been in **letters,** he would also **be . . . in actions** when he visited. Paul was confident that he would defeat his opponents.

Ⓑ Legitimate Boasting (10:12–18)

> **SUPPORTING IDEA:** *On a number of occasions in this chapter Paul responded to his opponents by boasting. He explained himself by discussing the legitimacy of his boasting.*

10:12. First, Paul mocked his opponents' tactics. He stated that he would not even **dare . . . compare** himself to his opponents according to their preferred grounds of comparison. These words must have caught the readers' attention because they sounded as if Paul had conceded his inferiority. But the sarcasm of his statement becomes evident in the next sentence. **They measure themselves by themselves,** and thereby demonstrate that **they are not wise.** That is to say, they evaluated their importance in the church by human standards alone. In modern parlance, they had become "legends in their own minds." Their self-commendation was unacceptable. At this point Paul's readers understood why he did not want to be compared to them.

10:13a–15a. By contrast, Paul said he and his company would **not boast beyond proper limits.** They would not fall into the trap of self-aggrandizement. Instead, they would **confine** their **boasting** to what **God** had established as true for them. There was nothing wrong with Paul honestly acknowledging what God had done in his life. That was both telling the truth and within **proper limits.**

Paul described the legitimate boundaries of his boasting as **the field God** had **assigned** to him and his company. Paul spoke of a **field** that God had allotted to him. Elsewhere in the New Testament, this language describes God's calling and allotment of grace to each person (Rom. 12:3; Eph. 4:7). This may have been part of Paul's meaning here. But phrases like **reaches even to you** and **we did get as far as you** indicate that Paul meant something even more specific here, something geographic.

Paul's ministry was a **field that reache[d] even to** Corinth. Paul had every right to boast about the Corinthians (7:4,11,14) because they were part of his allotment. This was not to imply that he did not share this allotment with fellow laborers, only to affirm that his ministry did include Corinth. Paul admitted that his boasting would have gone **too far** if he **had not come to** Corinth. But he **did get as far as** Corinth **with the gospel.** Paul and his company did not **go beyond . . . limits** because they did not boast **of work done by others.** Unlike his opponents' boasting, Paul's was perfectly acceptable.

10:15b–16. Paul continued defining the limits of his boasting by admitting and then qualifying his **hope** for the future. He wanted the Corinthians' **faith** to **grow** so that his **area of activity** ("sphere of action," NRSV) might **greatly expand.** That is to say, **so that** he could **preach the gospel in regions beyond** Corinth. Paul hoped that once the Corinthian church was stabilized, he and his company could use Corinth as a launching pad for more distant gospel ministry. As much as Paul traveled from place to place, his many epistles demonstrate that he knew the importance of strengthening the churches he had already established.

Paul wanted to move further into new lands because he did not want to violate the same principle by which he criticized others. He had no desire **to boast about work already done** in **territory** assigned to another. He refused to take credit for another's work.

10:17. To sum up his outlook, Paul summarized the teaching of Jeremiah 9:23–24 which warns against boasting in one's own wisdom or abilities. All boasting and confidence should be in knowing God, who is supreme. Paul summed up Jeremiah's perspective by saying that boasting should be **in the Lord.** All confidence, pride, and boasting should be in the light of what God has done. Believers often accomplish much, just as Paul had, but they should always take pleasure in these accomplishments with the awareness that they are humble servants of the Lord.

10:18. Paul explained himself pointedly as he closed this section. In an ultimate sense, we are not **approved** because we commend ourselves. Paul's opponents had a measure of approval from themselves and others, but that false approval would amount to nothing in the end. Those who follow Christ should seek to be those **whom the Lord commends.** That was Paul's desire for himself and his hope for the Corinthians.

Ⓒ Godly Jealousy (11:1–6)

SUPPORTING IDEA: *Desiring to protect the church from error, Paul continued to resist those leaders in Corinth who opposed his authority.*

11:1. Paul expressed discomfort at having to defend himself by asking his readers to **put up with a little . . . foolishness,** and by acknowledging that they had **already** been **doing that** by reading this far. Paul explained why he insisted that the Corinthians remain loyal to him: he wanted to protect them.

11:2a. Paul described his desire to protect the Corinthians from error as **a godly jealousy.** This terminology sounds like an oxymoron to most Christians today. Even in Paul's own vocabulary, "jealousy" (*zelos*) or being "jealous" (*zeloo*) is often forbidden as sin (Rom. 13:13; Gal. 5:20). But here Paul spoke of **jealousy** that was **godly** (literally "of or from God"). In fact, the Scriptures teach that even God is jealous in the sense that he desires loyalty from those who belong to him. In the preceding section, Paul had made it clear that he believed God had given him the ministry in Corinth. In this sense, Paul expressed his own desire to have an intimate relationship of loyalty between himself and the Corinthian church.

11:2b. He explained that he **promised** the church **to one husband, to Christ.** Paul constructed a complex analogy in these words. Elsewhere he declared that the church was the bride of Christ (Eph. 5:25–27), drawing on Hosea's prophecies of Israel as the bride of God (Hos. 1:1–3:5). When Paul brought the Corinthian church into relationship with Christ through the gospel, they became Christ's bride. In this passage, Paul described himself as the father who had **promised** his daughter in marriage to Christ.

One aspect of this **promise** was the presentation of the church at Corinth **as a pure virgin** to Christ, the presentation of the bride to the husband on the wedding day. The New Testament describes the day of Christ's return as a great wedding banquet (Rev. 19:7–9). Paul was jealous for the church because as their father he had promised to present the church as a pure virgin when Christ returned in glory.

11:3. As determined as he was to fulfill this promise, Paul was also **afraid** that the Corinthians might be **led astray from . . . sincere and pure devotion**

to Christ. Prior to Christ's return, the church is betrothed to him, but the possibility of infidelity and annulment still exist. Paul's responsibility was to help the church remain **sincere and pure** in its **devotion** so the marriage would eventually be consummated.

Once again, Paul drew from the prophecies of Hosea, who spoke of Israel's apostasy as sexual infidelity (Hos. 2:2–13). This analogy was appropriate in the days of Hosea because many Israelites expressed their apostasy by joining fertility rituals. In a similar way, the Corinthians were tempted by the immoral practices of Corinthian culture.

11:4. To explain why he was afraid, Paul described how the Corinthians turned from the true gospel. They had a history of accepting **easily enough** those who preached a **different Jesus**, who brought a **different spirit** or a **different gospel**. It is difficult to know exactly what Paul meant by a different **Jesus**. "Jesus" (Joshua) was a common name in Jewish communities of his day. Perhaps he meant that some preached about Jesus without accurate information about his life, death, and resurrection.

In 1 Corinthians 12:2–3 Paul described the work of the Spirit of God, indicating that only the Holy Spirit could lead a person to confess Jesus as Lord. A **different spirit**, one other than the Holy Spirit, could not lead a person to this confession. A **different gospel** would be any doctrine of salvation that was out of accord with Paul's message of justification by faith (Gal. 1:6–7). Paul wrote with godly jealousy and emphasized the fact that the Corinthians were ready to receive beliefs contrary to those that Paul had taught them. The consequences of such apostasy were severe, so he was afraid for them.

11:5. The ease with which the Corinthians turned from Paul alerted him to the reality that they considered him **inferior** to the false teachers. But he insisted that he was **not . . . in the least inferior** to them. In biting sarcasm he called these false teachers **super-apostles**. Of course, Paul did not actually consider these people his superiors, but he mocked them for their grand claims. In so doing, he rebuked the Corinthians for succumbing to their ploys.

11:6. Paul admitted that he was **not . . . a trained speaker,** implying that the so-called "super-apostles" were trained speakers. One of their favorite criticisms of Paul seems to have been that he was not very impressive in presence or speech. Even so, Paul was not an inadequate apostle because he had **knowledge** of the true gospel. Paul warned the Corinthians against the pretense that knowledge can create, but here he had in mind a positive knowledge of the truth without the associated problems. Toe to toe with these orators, Paul would fail. In many respects, his writing also lacked sophistication and talent. Yet, as a student of the Scriptures and the recipient of special revelation, Paul was no person's inferior.

The Corinthians should not have doubted Paul's insight into truth. He had **made this perfectly clear . . . in every way.** He had taught the Corinthians, written to them about complex theological issues, and led them into the mysteries of God. His great knowledge in the Christian faith that he had demonstrated time and again made up for his less impressive qualities.

𝗗 Free Service (11:7–11)

SUPPORTING IDEA: *Someone in the church had mistaken Paul's refusal to take money as an indication that he considered himself inferior to others. The "super-apostles" were well paid for their efforts, but Paul offered only free service in Corinth.*

11:7. Paul began his response to this misunderstanding with a rhetorical question. He asked if it were **sin** not to accept money. Of course, it was not. Had it been wrong for Paul **to lower** himself **in order to elevate** the Corinthians? Of course not. The opposite conclusion should have been drawn. It should have been evident that Paul chose this practice out of strength and not weakness.

11:8–9. To draw a contrast, Paul informed the Corinthians that he had **robbed other churches . . . to serve** them. The Greek term translated "robbed" (*sulao*) connotes stripping fallen enemies in battle. Paul felt as if he had imposed upon other churches in order not to take money from the Corinthian church. While he had ministered in Corinth, the churches of Macedonia had sent Paul support (Acts 18:5). From other comments he made, it would appear that economic conditions were terrible in Macedonia at the time. Corinth, however, was by comparison a busy center of international commerce. Its citizens were relatively rich. The church at Corinth had several wealthy members. Even so, when Paul had **needed something** while in Corinth, **brothers who came from Macedonia** had **supplied** his needs.

11:10. After reflecting on how his sacrifices for the Corinthians had been turned against him, Paul swore that **nobody in . . . Achaia** would **stop** his **boasting.** His upcoming visit would be confrontational, but Paul was confident that all accusations would be proven wrong. No matter what anyone said about him, Paul swore to continue defending himself.

11:11. Anticipating a negative response from his readers, Paul raised the question he expected them to ask. Did he insist on this course of action **because** he did **not love** the Corinthians? Was he causing them this pain because he was callous toward them? Not at all. In the spirit of an oath, he swore, **God knows I do!** Some in the church must have questioned whether Paul's love was genuine because he did not accept the "super-apostles" who were so important to the Corinthian believers. Paul insisted in the strongest terms that he loved the church.

E The Certain Outcome (11:12–15)

SUPPORTING IDEA: *Paul revealed his firm convictions concerning the outcome of his confrontation with those who challenged his authority.*

11:12. Paul intended to **keep on** boasting about his work in Corinth in order to discredit his opponents, who sought to be **equal with** him **in the things they boast[ed] about.** Paul had already made it clear that he did not think these men were his superiors. Now he declared his intent to **cut the ground from under** them in the confrontation soon to come.

11:13–14. Why was he so determined? Paul explained that these so-called super-apostles were actually **false apostles.** They were **deceitful** and only **masquerading as apostles of Christ.** Of course, those who followed these **false apostles** would have insisted that Paul was wrong. So he countered their anticipated objection by noting that the false apostles' deceit was **no wonder.** After all, even **Satan himself masquerades as an angel of light.**

11:15. Paul accused the false apostles of being **servants** of Satan and of imitating his tactics. They **masquerade[d] as servants of righteousness** (cf. Rev. 2:9; 3:9). The work of these false apostles led many into unrighteousness, as opposed to Paul's apostolic ministry of righteousness (see 2 Cor. 3:9).

Paul asserted that these false apostles would ultimately receive **what their actions deserve[d].** Although this statement carried serious overtones of final judgment, Paul also had in mind that these opponents would be exposed before the church and removed from their positions when he arrived. God would judge them.

F Boasting Like a Fool (11:16–21a)

SUPPORTING IDEA: *Paul prepared the way for dealing with his opponents by taking on their strategy of boasting. His words supported his own position and uncovered the true nature of his opponents' attacks.*

11:16–18. Paul began by repeating the beginning of his treatment of this subject, insisting that **no one take** him **for a fool.** Paul's earlier discussion of foolishness and wisdom demonstrated how seriously he took this charge. He did not believe himself to be a fool, but he knew that following divine wisdom made him appear foolish to many. For this reason, he asked the Corinthians to show him the same patience they would show a fool (**receive me just as you would a fool**).

Of course, Paul preferred that they not think of him as a fool. But because some did, he would take a moment to act like a fool by doing **a little boasting.** He cautioned his readers to remember that his boasting was not **as the Lord would** do, but **as a fool.** Yet, he determined that he **too** would **boast** because so many others were **boasting in the way the world does**. It was time to fight fire with fire.

11:19–20. Paul believed this tactic would succeed because he was convinced the Corinthians were undiscerning. He suggested that they were **wise**, but their so-called "wisdom" meant that they **put up with fools** and **anyone who enslave[d], . . . exploit[ed], . . .** took **advantage** of them, . . . **push[ed] himself forward, . . . or slap[ed]** them **in the face**. These descriptions sum up how Paul characterized the efforts of the false apostles. On the surface, they probably had credible ministries; they masqueraded as blessings to the church. Yet, their false teaching actually made their ministries abusive. Paul spoke this way to encourage the Corinthians to come to their senses. They had acted foolishly by accepting these false apostles as their leaders.

11:21a. By contrast, Paul and his company **were too weak for that**. They had no stomach for such deceptive activities. Paul must serve sincerely. The Corinthians would have been wise to receive him instead of the others.

Ⓖ Paul's Ethnic Qualifications (11:21b–22)

SUPPORTING IDEA: *Paul adopted the arguments of his opponents to prove that they failed to prove themselves superior even when they set their own standards. Paul compared his ethnic qualifications to those of his opponents.*

11:21b. Paul continued to speak as a fool, believing he could outstrip his opponents on their own terms. He followed the wisdom of Proverbs 26:5 and answered the fool according to his folly.

11:22. He began by saying that he had an ethnic background comparable to his opponents. He was a Hebrew—a term that distinguished him from hellenized Jews. He was an Israelite and a descendent of Abraham. As such, Paul was the heir of the grace of God promised to the patriarch Abraham. He was not adopted into Abraham's family as Gentile believers were (Eph. 2:11–19). From Paul's point of view, neither Jew nor Gentile was superior in Christ. In the outlook of his opponents, however, it seemed to matter. So Paul responded that he passed even their ethnic criterion.

Ⓗ Paul's Extraordinary Service to Christ (11:23–33)

SUPPORTING IDEA: *Paul compared his service to Christ to that of his opponents.*

11:23–27. Paul had rendered great service to Christ. His opponents must have claimed to be special **servants of Christ**, but Paul claimed to be even more of a servant than they were. He remarked that he was **out of his mind** to talk this way, but for the sake of rescuing the Corinthian church from the false apostles, he continued. Even according to the standards of these false apostles, Paul's claims exceeded any they made in this regard. The false apostles probably suffered for their convictions, but Paul suffered even more. He listed a series of events that we may categorize as external sufferings. Some of these events are corroborated in other biblical passages; others are mentioned only here:

Worked harder	Endangered by bandits
Prison more frequently	Endangered by fellow Jews
Flogged more severely	Endangered by Gentiles
Exposed to death many times	Endangered in cities
thirty-nine lashes five times	Endangered in the countryside
Beaten with rods three times	Endangered at sea
Shipwrecked three times	Endangered by false brothers
Day and night in open sea	Endured sleepless nights
Constantly moving	Endured hunger and thirst
Endangered by rivers	Endured cold and nakedness

11:28–29. In addition to these external sufferings, Paul's extraordinary service also included inward difficulties. Paul had in mind particularly the turmoil he experienced out of concern **for all the churches** as their true apostle, noting his empathy with other believers. When others were **weak**, then he was also **weak**. When they fell **into sin**, then he **inwardly burn[ed]**. The Greek term translated "burn" in this passage can refer to a number of emotions. Paul's letters to the Corinthians demonstrate the consternation he felt for the many churches to whom he ministered.

11:30–33. Closing his discussion of his extraordinary service, Paul shifted to what he must have considered more appropriate boasting. He stated that since he had to **boast**, he also wanted to **boast of the things that show[ed]** his **weakness**. Insofar as this boasting reflected his weakness, he departed from the style and standards of his opponents at this point. Yet, insofar as he continued to boast for the purpose of demonstrating his extraordinary service, in this section Paul continued to attack his opponents on their own grounds. Boasting about **weakness** suited him better because it exalted God as the source of his strength.

Paul introduced this boasting with an oath formula, acknowledging **God** as the one who **is to be praised forever**. Paul swore that **God** knew **that** he was **not lying**, and then proceeded to describe the time he barely escaped from Damascus with his life (Acts 9:23–25). This event demonstrated his devoted service to Christ, but it also made it clear that God cared for him and deserved all the praise.

⫿ Paul's Visions and Revelations (12:1–10)

SUPPORTING IDEA: *Paul compared his extraordinary experiences of visions and revelations to those of his opponents.*

12:1. Paul felt it was wise also to boast about his **visions and revelations from the Lord.** This implies that his opponents claimed special knowledge and revelations from God. Paul challenged their claims to superior apostleship by reporting his own extraordinary visions, which surpassed any the false apostles claimed.

12:2–3. From the grammar of this passage, it is difficult to know for certain if Paul spoke of himself or of someone else. At first it appears that Paul spoke of someone else: **I know a man in Christ.** It is possible that this first impression is correct. Paul may have referred to another man's heavenly experience to counter his opponents' claims to supreme revelatory experiences. In this view, his argument was that the false apostles were not superior because an even more extraordinary event happened to someone else.

But many interpreters believe that Paul referred to himself in this passage, albeit in an unusual way. In favor of this view is the fact that Paul later spoke of God keeping him humble "because of these surpassingly great revelations" (12:7) which he had. Moreover, this whole section of the letter is designed to demonstrate that the false apostles were not superior to Paul, not just that they were not superior to others. Also, this particular passage is introduced as Paul's own boasting. In this outlook, Paul spoke of himself in the third person out of modesty.

The point of the passage is clear: the false apostles have no claim to superior revelation because Paul (or another) had received such an extraordinary revelation. He had been **caught up to the third heaven.** Rabbinical sources speak of "seven heavens"; so it is difficult to know for certain the background and precise meaning of the **third heaven.** If Paul operated with a sevenfold view of heaven, he acknowledged that he had not reached what the Old Testament called "the highest heavens" (Deut. 10:14; Neh. 9:6)—the place where God dwells. Nevertheless, **third heaven** indicated that the experience was astounding. The trance was so intense that Paul did not even know if he had been **in the body.**

12:4. Paul described this level of heaven as **paradise,** the place that the dead in Christ enter (Luke 23:43). While there, Paul heard **inexpressible things,** words from angels and God that **man is not permitted to tell.** Paul's opponents probably spoke freely about their supposedly heavenly revelation, much like the apostle John was instructed to do when he received the revelation of the Apocalypse (Rev. 1:11). But Paul made the supremacy of his heavenly experience plain by saying that he was **not permitted** to convey what he heard there. By this means, Paul argued that his authority over the church at

Corinth was far beyond any authority claimed by the false apostles. His revelation was greater than any revelation his opponents had received.

12:5–6. With a touch of irony, Paul insisted that he would **not boast** of himself **except about** his **weaknesses.** He admitted that to do otherwise would still be **speaking the truth,** but he resisted exalting himself too far because he did not want anyone to **think more of** him **than** was **warranted.** Paul knew that Christians tend to exalt heroes beyond reality and that the Corinthians might go beyond what he actually said or did. So he turned quickly to speak of his weaknesses.

12:7. Paul was tempted to become **conceited** in light of his **surpassingly great revelations.** To keep that from happening, God sent him **a thorn in** his **flesh.** This expression is similar to the Old Testament terminology, "thorn in the side" in the Septuagint, where it was a metaphorical description of trouble inflicted by God. It is difficult to know precisely what the apostle had in mind. He also called it **a messenger of Satan** that brought him **torment,** but said nothing else. Endless suggestions have been made, but three proposals are feasible: (1) Paul had a physical ailment, perhaps an eye disease (cf. Gal. 4:15) or a speech impediment; (2) Paul spoke of continuing opponents in the churches; (3) Paul pointed to some troubling demonic activity, perhaps some severe temptation.

12:8–9a. Despite this uncertainty, Paul's main idea is clear. He asked God **three times** to remove this thorn from his life, but God told him that divine **grace was sufficient for** him. The tense of the expression **he said** may also be translated as "he has said," indicating that Paul saw God's statement as more than simply directed toward his situation. God wanted Paul to find comfort and security in the **grace** he had received in Christ—the same thing God desires for all believers.

In fact, in this particular case, God's denial of Paul's request turned out to be to Paul's greater good because it was to God's greater glory. God told Paul that divine **power is made perfect in weakness.** Throughout the Scripture God delights in displaying his power in situations where human strength is weak (1 Sam. 14:6–15). When God's people are weak, then God's strength becomes evident.

12:9b. As a result, Paul determined that he would **boast all the more gladly about** his **weaknesses.** He quit complaining, **so that Christ's power** might **rest on** him. The terminology translated "rest" (*episkenoo*) may be translated as "to tabernacle" or "pitch a tent." It is likely that Paul drew upon Old Testament imagery of the glory of God coming upon the tabernacle (Exod. 40:34–38). If so, he learned that taking delight in his thorn actually brought the blessings of God upon his life.

12:10. From this understanding of his weakness, Paul concluded that he would **delight in weaknesses** rather than abhor them. **Insults, hardships,**

persecutions, and **difficulties** were causes for joy because in these times of weakness, Paul was **strong** in the power of God.

ⅠⅠ A Pointed Conclusion (12:11–13)

SUPPORTING IDEA: *Paul closed his discussion of his opponents by confronting the Corinthian congregation.*

12:11–12. The apostle admitted that he had **made a fool of** himself by taking on the strategy of his opponents in boasting as he had. Yet, he insisted that the Corinthians had driven him to it. How was this so? He **ought to have been commended** by the congregation. They already knew him and his ministry. He was not **in the least inferior to the** "super-apostles" and they knew this. Of course, Paul was aware that he was **nothing** in himself, apart from the grace of God. Yet, the Corinthians should have remembered his **signs, wonders and miracles** that **mark an apostle.** Paul had performed miracles in many places as he had proclaimed the gospel of Christ, but in Corinth he had done these things **with great perseverance.** Time and again, he had demonstrated the divine authorization of his ministry before the Corinthians.

12:13. Only in one way had Paul treated the Corinthians as **inferior to the other churches.** He had **never** been **a burden to** them. With the sarcasm characteristic of this section, he noted that he had not required them to support him for his services. In reality, this was no insult at all, but an honor he bestowed on them—gracious treatment for their spiritual benefit. His only offense was to honor them more than he honored other churches. So he concluded by asking them in sarcastic fashion to **forgive** his kindness toward them.

MAIN IDEA REVIEW: *False apostles had opposed Paul in Corinth. He hoped that by writing against these false teachers he might prevent a major conflict when he arrived.*

ⅠⅠⅠ. CONCLUSION

In All Matters of Faith and Life

Throughout his epistles to the Corinthians, Paul felt the need to defend his authority as an apostle of Christ. Against the many challenges to his leadership, he insisted that his sacrificial ministry demonstrated that he was a faithful apostle and that he used his authority for the good of the church. In our day the authority of Paul and other New Testament apostles is challenged within the church, much as they were in the first century. Yet, we must listen carefully to Paul's defense of his ministry. Even when the teachings of the apostles seem difficult or even contrary to what our modern perspectives would consider true, we must receive Paul and the other apostles whose instructions are summarized in the New Testament as the unquestionable authorities in all matters of faith and life.

PRINCIPLES

- The apostles were authoritative leaders and teachers whose teaching is still binding on the church.
- There are always teachers in the church who assert false doctrines.

APPLICATIONS

- We must obey the teachings of the apostles.
- We must guard the apostles' authority in the church.
- We must be watchful for false teaching, holding everything to the standard of the apostolic word.

IV. LIFE APPLICATION

"I Didn't Know He Did All That"

I have a friend who is as ordinary as they come—a kind man, but not impressive by outward standards, not much to look at, very quiet and reserved.

One day I was sitting in a restaurant with another friend when my "ordinary" friend came in, spoke to us, and went to his own table. My friend with whom I was eating leaned over the table and whispered, "Do you know about him?"

I thought he had some juicy gossip. "No," I said, "What are you talking about?"

"He's a war hero," he replied. "In World War II he rescued about fifty marines and took a bunch of prisoners himself, single-handedly."

"Are you sure we're talking about the same man?" I asked.

"Yep, that's the one."

"Wow," I sighed. "I didn't know he did all that. I'll never look at him the same way again."

In this passage the Corinthians should have felt that way about Paul. They had been fooled by false apostles into thinking that Paul was not very impressive. After Paul revealed to them how much he had done, the Corinthian church should have been impressed. They should have rejected anyone who stood against Paul's authority.

We live in a day when nearly everyone has a problem with authority. In Western societies at large, no one wants to submit voluntarily to anyone. We obey only when we are forced to. The situation is not very different in the church. We cherish our personal freedom so much that we struggle with respecting and obeying authorities, especially when they tell us to do something that is inconvenient or uncomfortable.

This widespread disdain for authority does not extend only to authorities in our local churches like pastors, elders, and deacons. We even find ourselves questioning the authority of Christ's apostles at times. Although Christ himself ordained these men to guide the church, we sometimes have a difficult time setting aside our own traditions and opinions in submission to their authority.

In this passage Paul dealt with this tendency in the Corinthian church by reminding them of the many sacrifices he had made on their behalf. Under the influence of false apostles, they had come to believe that Paul was using his position to mislead and abuse the church. To counter this outlook, Paul reminded the Corinthians of the hardships he had faced and of the humble service he had provided them.

Paul's line of reasoning needs to be applied to the church today. Our churches are full of teachers who seek to turn believers away from the teachings of Paul and other true apostles. Sometimes they subvert apostolic authority in subtle ways, and we must be vigilant to watch for this. But many times church leaders and laypeople alike resist the authority of the apostles. They call the church to follow the ways of the world instead.

This tendency shows itself today as it did in Corinth. When the New Testament teaches a doctrine that we find difficult to believe, we reject it. In the modern world, many people reject the New Testament because it affirms the resurrection of Christ. We deplore the teachings on sexual purity and the sanctity of marriage. We hold hatred in our hearts, ignoring the apostles' instructions to the contrary. We cherish our pet sins and refuse to submit to the apostolic word.

This portion of Paul's epistle encourages us to look again at how trustworthy he and other apostles are. The apostles of Christ sacrificed their lives for the sake of the gospel. Most of them met with cruel deaths because they were faithful to Christ and his church.

As we wrestle with our attitudes toward their difficult teachings, we should always remember their sacrifices. Consider in detail the many difficulties Paul faced as he brought the gospel to the Gentile nations. Without the word of Paul and the other apostles, we would not know how to follow our Savior. They are the "foundation" of the church (Eph. 2:20) upon which we are to build our lives. They deserve our submission because Christ has ordained them and because they were so faithful to their ordination.

V. PRAYER

Lord Jesus, thank you for ordaining the word of your apostles to guide your church. Our hearts wander so easily from the truth that we need their writings to lead us in the paths of righteousness. Make us grateful for their sacrifices, and give us the wisdom to follow their teachings no matter how inconvenient or difficult they may seem. Amen.

VI. DEEPER DISCOVERIES

A. Paradise (12:4)

The Greek word *paradeisos,* translated as "paradise," appears only three times in the New Testament (Luke 23:43; 2 Cor. 12:4; Rev. 2:7). In Luke and Revelation it refers to a heavenly place where believers go when they die. In the 2 Corinthians passage, it seems to identify this same place, although Paul was allowed a vision or visit to paradise before his death.

While *paradeisos* appears many times in the Septuagint (the Greek translation of the Hebrew Old Testament), it never seems to refer to a heavenly location. Almost always it translates *gan* or *ganah,* Hebrew words for "garden." Frequently, the garden is specifically the Garden of Eden (Gen. 2:8–9; Joel 2:3). In Isaiah 51:3, it translates the Hebrew word *eden* ("Eden"), while *gan* is only implied. On two occasions, the Greek word *paradeisos* translates the Hebrew word *pardes* (Neh. 2:8; Song 4:13), both of which come from the Persian *pairi-daeza. Pardes* is fairly synonymous with *gan/ganah,* and is often translated as "orchard" or "forest."

Thus, in the Septuagint, the Greek term *paradeisos* is the common word for "garden." The Old Testament also teaches that the restoration of the kingdom of God will constitute a re-creation and restoration of the Garden of Eden for believers (Isa. 51:3). By the time of the New Testament, the restoration of the kingdom, with its newly created/re-created heaven and earth (2 Pet. 3:10–13), had come to be so identified with the restoration of the Garden of Eden that heaven itself had come to be known as "garden" or "paradise."

B. Three Times I Pleaded with the Lord (12:8)

Scripture encourages us to petition God for our needs and desires (Matt. 7:7–11), and even to ask God repeatedly when he does not answer according to our desires. For example, God blessed Jacob when Jacob refused to release the "man" he wrestled at Peniel (Gen. 32:24–30). Similarly, Paul prayed three times that the thorn would be taken from his flesh. At the same time, Scripture always assumes that faithful believers will accept clear negative responses from God and rest in the sufficiency of divine grace. They should accept his clear answers that certainly deny their requests, as when David accepted the death of his son (2 Sam. 12:22–23) or when Paul accepted God's explicit answer to him in these verses. In these examples, God did not grant David's and Paul's requests. As righteous men, David and Paul honored rather than resented God for his decisions.

VII. TEACHING OUTLINE

A. INTRODUCTION

1. Lead Story: "Who Died and Made You Boss?"

2. Context: In Corinth a power struggle was taking place between false apostles who were usurping Paul's authority and Paul himself. The false apostles stood against Paul and his teachings. Because this was so dangerous to believers, Paul defended himself and his ministry. He did this by denouncing the false apostles and defending himself.

3. Transition: In the modern church, similar attacks against apostolic authority are frequent, whether as explicit rejections of the Bible, as insidious undercutting of its teaching, or as simple rebellion against its demands. Like the Corinthians, we must recognize the importance and authority of the apostles and the Bible and then submit to them. To do otherwise is to place ourselves and our people in jeopardy of God's judgment.

B. COMMENTARY

1. Bold Action to Come (10:1–11)
2. Legitimate Boasting (10:12–18)
3. Godly Jealousy (11:1–6)
4. Free Service (11:7–11)
5. The Certain Outcome (11:12–15)
6. Boasting Like a Fool (11:16–21a)
7. Paul's Ethnic Qualifications (11:21b–22)
8. Paul's Extraordinary Service to Christ (11:23–33)
9. Paul's Visions and Revelations (12:1–10)
10. A Pointed Conclusion (12:11–13)

C. CONCLUSION: "I DIDN'T KNOW HE DID ALL THAT"

VIII. ISSUES FOR DISCUSSION

1. What kind of battle was Paul fighting in the argument of 10:1–12:10? What weapons did he use? How would you classify these weapons?
2. Describe and contrast legitimate boasting and foolish boasting and give examples of each. When is it acceptable to boast foolishly?
3. Describe Paul's tone in this section of the letter. How would you have felt if Paul had spoken to you this way? What would his words have implied to you about the nature of your faith in Christ? Would his arguments have won you over?
4. What does this passage say about authority within the church? How did Paul establish his authority in this passage? How did he use his authority in this passage?

2 Corinthians 12:14—13:14

Quote

"*Discipline is like a bridle to restrain and tame those who rage against the doctrine of Christ; or like a spur to arouse those of little inclination; and also sometime like a father's rod to chastise mildly and with the gentleness of Christ's Spirit those who have more seriously lapsed.*"

John Calvin

2 Corinthians 12:14–13:14

 I N   A   N U T S H E L L

Paul closed this epistle by reminding the Corinthians that he in-tended to visit them soon. How would the visit go? It could be a time of joy and close fellowship, or it could be a time of rebuke and discipline. It was up to the Corinthians to decide.

People Get Ready

I. INTRODUCTION

Ruining a Visit

*F*ew things ruin a family visit more than quarreling, especially during the holiday season. Christmas is one of those rare times when many of us get together with our extended families: mothers, fathers, sisters, brothers, grandparents, nephews, and nieces. We travel long distances and have every intention of sharing our love with one another. Yet, we all know that some Christmas visits end up in conflict and quarrels. Instead of enjoying the time with our family members, we end up fighting over old hurts or falling into old habits of bickering and turmoil. Parents try to control their adult children, and children act disrespectfully toward their parents. Someone is too sensitive, someone else is too distant, and everyone is on edge.

In this passage the apostle Paul told the Corinthians that he would visit them as soon as he could. He longed to fellowship with his brothers and sisters in the church, and he hoped the visit would go well. But Paul realized that it could also be a time of sadness. If the Corinthians prepared for his visit by listening to his instructions, it would be an opportunity for tenderness and affection. But if they continued to ignore his instructions, this visit would be a time of bitterness. The choice was theirs.

II. COMMENTARY

People Get Ready

> **MAIN IDEA:** *Paul encouraged the Corinthians to prepare for his upcoming visit. He wanted them to repent of their sin and to think rightly about Paul and those who would accompany him so they would be well received.*

A A Pledge of Good Intentions (12:14–18)

> **SUPPORTING IDEA:** *The false apostles apparently had warned the Corinthians that if Paul returned he would drain their financial resources. Paul pledged that he would not take money from the church at Corinth for himself.*

12:14a. Paul began by saying that he was **ready to visit . . . for a third time.** He had remained in Corinth for a year and a half during his first visit. Then he had received letters and visitors from Corinth while in Ephesus and had traveled from Ephesus to visit them a second time. As he wrote 2

Corinthians, he planned to visit again after Titus had prepared the way. He mentioned this visit again because he wanted it to be a positive experience of God's blessing.

12:14b. To head off any fears, the apostle pledged that he would **not be a burden** to the church. He had already reminded them that he had not received financial support from them previously. He wanted to assure them that he would not change this policy. Before his second visit, he had considered receiving money from the church for his mission efforts, but at this point he thought it better not to receive such help.

Paul's motives were simple but profound. He did not want the Corinthians to think their money was more important to him than they were. As he put it, **What I want is not your possessions but you.** On several occasions, Paul had expressed his desire for an intimate, trusting relationship with the church at Corinth. He wanted to experience the joy of seeing his spiritual children in harmony with one another and with him.

12:14c–15a. To explain himself, Paul appealed to the common practice of parents. **Children** do not normally provide **for their parents.** On the contrary, **parents** save and give to **their children.** Paul considered himself the father of the church at Corinth. He knew that children do at times give generously to their parents (cf. Mark 7:10–13), but this was not the primary direction of support. For this reason, Paul promised that he would **gladly spend . . . everything** he had and **expend** himself as well.

12:15b. Paul added an aside that he hoped would touch the Corinthians' hearts. He asked, **If I love you more, will you love me less?** This was the tender plea of a loving parent to his wayward children. He opened his heart to them in hopes that they would reciprocate his affection and commitment to them.

12:16. Then Paul came back to his main point. He had **not been a burden to** the Corinthians. But the apostle's opponents had filled the Corinthians' minds with false accusations. They must have argued that Paul had served without financial support in order to trick the Corinthians into remaining loyal to him.

12:17–18. To defend himself, Paul asked a question that should have settled the matter. Had he **exploit[ed]** them **through any of the men** he had **sent** to Corinth? Paul had sent **Titus** and a **brother** to them as his representatives, but they had served the church consistently with Paul's direct work. Previously, he had sent Timothy, who also had served well. By asking if Titus had exploited them, Paul challenged the Corinthians to consider that Titus had acted **in the same spirit** and followed **the same course** of selfless service as Paul had. From Paul's perspective, the answers to these questions were obvious—no one had exploited the Corinthians. There was no reason for them to question Paul's motives.

ⓑ Everything for Their Good (12:19–21)

SUPPORTING IDEA: *In the preceding chapters Paul had spent much time boasting about himself. He made sure this boasting would not be misinterpreted.*

12:19. Paul realized that the Corinthians might misunderstand his motives. He wondered if they had **been thinking all along** as he boasted that he had been **defending** himself **to** the Corinthians. It might have been easy for some of them to answer, "Yes." But the apostle wanted to make doubly clear that he felt no need to defend his own integrity or authority for his own sake. He had stooped to this strategy only for the Corinthians' **strengthening.** Paul believed that all things in the life of the Christian church should be done for edification. This was his motivation as he defended his ministry against the false apostles.

Paul's intensity at this moment is apparent. He repeated his declaration that he had been **speaking in the sight of God.** He also mentioned that he spoke as one **in Christ,** and he appealed to the Corinthians as his **dear friends.** It was important to him that they believed his selfless motivation.

12:20. Paul explained why he had gone to the extreme of boasting to edify them. He was **afraid.** He feared what he might find when he arrived on his third visit. He was afraid that he might **not find** them **as** he **want[ed]** them **to be,** and that they might **not find** him **as** they **want[ed]** him **to be.** Paul knew that if the Corinthians did not observe his instructions in this epistle, he would have to rebuke and discipline them.

Paul listed a number of things he was **afraid** he would find in the church. He had addressed some of these earlier: **quarreling, jealousy, outbursts of anger, factions, slander, gossip, arrogance, and disorder.** If these attitudes and actions continued to characterize the Corinthian church, Paul would have to deal with them in person, and he did not want to have to do that. As a wise leader, he gave the church opportunity to get itself in order before he came.

12:21. Paul was also **afraid** for himself. The sins at Corinth did not cause trouble only for the church. If they continued, then **God** would **humble** Paul himself **before** the church at Corinth. Paul considered it a humiliation to have to deal with the sins of the church another time. He wanted to take pride in his children and had boasted of them many times. Yet, if he had to rebuke them even after writing to them, his reason for boasting would be removed and he would be humiliated. He was too committed to the Corinthians to separate his feelings about himself from his feelings toward them.

Paul did not speak of this humiliation in human terms. He explained that it would come by the hand of God. Paul knew that divine grace was necessary for the Corinthians to find repentance; he understood that the success of his letters depended upon the good favor of God. He also realized that a lack of repentance in Corinth would have a divine purpose (Rom. 8:28). He did not enjoy the thought of it, but he realized that his own humiliation would be one aspect of God's purposes.

He further described his humiliation in terms of his grief. He would **be grieved** if he found **many who** had **sinned earlier and** had **not repented.** Paul desired the repentance and forgiveness of everyone who had fallen into serious sin. Just as he had rejoiced over and even advocated for the immoral brother who had repented, he would be happy if he found the church in order when He arrived. But he would be deeply grieved if he found it otherwise.

When speaking of those who had **sinned,** Paul did not have in mind the kinds of sins every Christian commits in his or her imperfection. Rather, he focused on serious violations of God's law. He was especially concerned with those who had **not repented of the impurity, sexual sin and debauchery.** The city of Corinth was known as a city of sexual immorality. The apostle realized that more than a few within the Corinthian church had fallen into these sins. But his chief concern was that they repent of these sins in which **they** had **indulged.**

C Final Warning (13:1–10)

> **SUPPORTING IDEA:** *Having raised the possibility that some in Corinth may not have repented of their serious sins before he arrived, Paul offered a forceful final warning to the church.*

13:1a. The apostle began by reminding them again that this would be his **third visit.** From the information we have in the New Testament, Paul gave more attention to the Corinthian church than to any other. He stayed there one and one-half years; he wrote to them frequently; he visited a second time; and here he told them plainly he was coming again. Paul had been patient with the Corinthians, and he had gone to great lengths to be kind to them. But his patience was waning.

13:1b. Paul told the Corinthians to prepare to face the issues he had raised with them. To begin with, he did not want to have to deal with rumors and unsubstantiated accusations. He would not listen to accusations unless they were **established by the testimony of two or three witnesses.** Paul relied on Mosaic legal procedures for this point (Deut. 19:15), applying this national policy from the Old Testament to the legal procedures to be followed in the church (cf. Matt. 18:16).

13:2. Paul's insistence on witnesses indicated his intention to deal strongly with the situation in Corinth. He had already given them a **warning** on his previous visit, and he was **repeat[ing] it** here. On his third visit, there would be no more warnings. He was **not** going to **spare those who sinned**

earlier or **any of the others.** The first group consisted of those who had fallen into the immoral practices of Corinth. **The others** of whom he spoke are more difficult to identify. Paul probably meant anyone else whom he had to discipline. If any Corinthian Christians failed to heed this warning and to repent, Paul would discipline that person when he arrived.

13:3. Impatience with the Corinthians' sin did not motivate Paul to threaten them with discipline. Rather, the Corinthians demanded **proof that Christ** was **speaking through** Paul, and the discipline was to be the **proof.** Throughout his epistles to Corinth, Paul dealt with challenges to his authority as an apostle. Some within the Corinthian church doubted Paul's authority as Christ's spokesman. They wanted to see some proof. Paul warned that the proof would come in the form of harsh discipline. We cannot be sure precisely what kind of proof Paul had in mind, though it was to be indisputable **proof** (*dokime*).

The example of Ananias and Sapphira (Acts 5:1–11) is unique in the New Testament, but it demonstrates that the apostles could exercise discipline that had physical effects. Paul instructed the discipline of the immoral man in Corinth in order that his body (*sarx*) might be destroyed, which may have physical implications. The sick and dead in Corinth who had abused their brethren at the Lord's Supper perhaps suffered similar discipline. John warned of "sin that leads to death" (1 John 5:16), which may be closely associated with the kind of radical discipline Paul had in mind here.

Through the apostle John, Jesus warned that he would revoke his blessings from rebellious churches (Rev. 2:5), and Peter warned that judgment would "begin with the family of God" (1 Pet. 4:17). At the very least, Paul must have been prepared to inflict serious spiritual discipline on the church. He believed the discipline to come would be so dramatic and supernatural that it would prove he spoke authoritatively on Christ's behalf.

13:4. To support his warning that discipline would prove Christ's authorization of his ministry, Paul reminded the Corinthians that Christ humbled himself to a shameful death (Phil. 2:8), being **crucified in weakness,** but that he also **lives by God's power.** Paul often associated divine power with the Holy Spirit (Rom. 1:4; Eph. 3:16). He also taught that God the Father raised Christ from the dead by the power of the Holy Spirit (1 Thess. 1:10).

Christ's weakness and power paralleled Paul's ministry. First, Paul and his company had been **weak.** Paul knew sufferings from persecution; he served the Corinthians at great cost and without personal profit; he even suffered the humiliation of a physical ailment by the hand of God. The apparent weakness of his ministry had led some of his opponents to defy his authority. These and other difficulties resulted from Paul's union with Christ in his suffering and death on the cross, and they were appropriate to legitimate ministry.

Second, Paul affirmed that **by God's power** he and his company would **live with** Christ **to serve** the Corinthians. Just as Christ's resurrection and ascension had demonstrated the Spirit's power, Paul's own ministry was powerful. He had been resurrected with Christ, and he had received the power of the Spirit common to all believers and peculiar to apostles.

The words **we will live with him** did not refer to the final resurrection on the day of judgment, but to Paul's third visit to Corinth. This is clear because Paul and his company were to live for the purpose of disciplining the Corinthians. This would occur when Paul visited (13:1–2). What awaited their arrival was the discipline of the Corinthians. Paul described this discipline as living with Christ **by God's power** in order to emphasize that he and his company would act as God's instruments on Christ's behalf and that the discipline would show God's power. Even harsh discipline would be for the Corinthians' benefit by leading to their eventual repentance.

13:5a. Paul wanted the Corinthians to take his third visit so seriously that he challenged them to **examine** and **test** themselves **to see whether** they were **in the faith.** Paul used the reflexive pronoun **yourselves** twice to emphasize the idea that they should start looking more at themselves than at him or others.

13:5b. To encourage them further toward self-examination, Paul asked if they did **not realize that Christ Jesus** was **in** them. Christ's Spirit at work in the believer has certain effects of sanctification and faithfulness (Gal. 5:22–23; 2 Pet. 3:18). If the Corinthians' claims to faith were true, they were united to Christ, and the Holy Spirit was making the truth of their claims evident in their lives. But if the life of any believer showed no signs of the Spirit's activity, then the Spirit was not working in him and Christ was not indwelling him. Paul had already mentioned that the Corinthians were being tested. Their response to his instructions would prove whether their faith was genuine.

13:6. Anticipating his opponents' objection, Paul assured the Corinthians that they would **discover that** Paul and his company had **not failed the test.** Paul evidently expected some people within the church to question his own Christian living. In response, he admitted that even he needed to continue demonstrating saving faith in Christ, just as the Old Testament patriarchs had to demonstrate their faith through testing (Gen. 22:1).

13:7–8. To clarify his motivations, Paul told the Corinthians that he **pray[ed] to God** that they would **not do anything wrong.** He hoped they would respond properly to his instructions. Although the Corinthians were responsible to obey and to remain faithful to Christ, Paul knew that only divine power could enable them to do so (Phil. 2:12–13).

The apostle's primary desire was not that the Corinthians would vindicate his reputation, but that they would **do what** was **right even though** in the eyes of his opponents he might **seem to have failed**. From the perspective of human wisdom so deeply cherished by many Corinthians, Paul was not very impressive, and perhaps would appear to have **failed**. He exhorted the church to conform to his instructions, despite what others said about him, so they might **do what** was **right** and pleasing to God. Paul stated that he and his company could not **do anything against the truth**. He was confident that he and his company were true believers, and therefore that they could not actually fail the test, despite what others might conclude.

13:9. Paul's ministry to the Corinthian church proved that he was not interested in preserving his reputation for his own sake. His company was likewise not interested in their own reputations. Rather, they were all **glad** when they appeared **weak** and the Corinthians **strong**. Their central **prayer** for the church at Corinth was that God would bring them to **perfection** or completion. Paul's desire was that the Corinthians would come to maturity in their service to Christ.

13:10. To close this section, Paul summarized his motivations in yet another way. He wrote **these things** when he was **absent** so that when he arrived he might **not have to be harsh**. His harshness was intended to render unnecessary any harsh **use of authority** when he visited. Paul had the power and **authority**, given to him by the **Lord**, to inflict much trouble on the church in discipline. But he knew that discipline was not the central purpose of his authority. **The Lord** had given Paul this authority **for building . . . up, not for tearing . . . down**. Insofar as discipline served to build up the church, Paul was willing to inflict it when necessary.

His primary desire, however, was to build up the church through positive means. He felt the best way to build up the church was to exhort them to repent and to discipline them only if his words failed to bring about change. Paul preferred a gentle touch, but he was ready to do whatever was necessary to rescue them from sin.

D Final Good-By (13:11–14)

SUPPORTING IDEA: *Paul closed this letter with a combination of brief exhortations, encouragements, and benedictions.*

13:11. Paul listed five exhortations, followed by a promise of divine blessing. Five imperatives introduce the exhortations.

First, the expression translated **good-by** in the NIV is often rendered "rejoice" (NASB). The latter translation is more literal, but it may be too wooden to convey Paul's meaning. The Greek expression appears to have been both a normal greeting and farewell at this point in history. If this is correct, then the NIV correctly translates it simply as **good-by**. Paul was wishing them well and expressing hope for their happiness.

Second, Paul encouraged the Corinthians to **aim for perfection.** This had already been his prayer for them in 13:9.

Third, he asked them to **listen** to his **appeal** or to "be comforted" (NASB). Paul may have been encouraging them to take comfort, as was his wish for them expressed in the letter's opening. Or he may have been reinforcing in their minds the fact that he wanted them to be swayed by his arguments.

Fourth, He exhorted them to forsake their factions and to **be of one mind,** just as he had exhorted them before.

Fifth, and similar to the exhortation to **be of one mind,** he encouraged them to **live in peace.**

If the church at Corinth heeded these encouragements, they were assured of God's blessing. God would be with them. Drawing upon Old Testament expressions, Paul assured the Corinthian church that if they conformed to his instructions, **the God of love and peace** would bless them with his presence. The expression "God of love and peace" bore a double meaning in this context. On the one hand, God delights in **love and peace** and would bless the church that was full of love and peace. **Love and peace** are blessings in and of themselves. With God's blessing the Corinthians would experience even more **love and peace** within their church.

13:12. In a manner rooted in the Jewish culture of that time, Paul encouraged the believers at Corinth to **greet one another with a holy kiss.** Even today many churches in the Middle and Far East practice light kissing on the cheek or lips among members of the same gender. To avoid erotic implications, Paul described the practice as **holy.** The kissing was that which was and is still customary among brothers and sisters in a family.

13:13. In line with his desire to see unity established in Corinth, Paul assured them that **all the saints** sent **their greetings.** The term simply means "holy ones" or "sanctified ones," and is an appropriate description of all believers (Rom. 1:7; Col. 1:2). It is not clear who Paul had in mind, but it is likely that the term *all* was intended to include all the believers in general with whom Paul associated. He wanted to assure the Corinthians of the good intentions of all churches toward their congregation.

13:14. Paul's final words to the congregation depicted his deepest desires for them. He closed with a trinitarian benediction. This is Paul's only full trinitarian benediction in all his writings. Normally, he mentioned only Christ and/or God the Father. Sometimes he mentioned none of the persons of the Godhead specifically. Only occasionally did he mention the Holy Spirit (Rom. 15:13).

The associations between the persons of the Trinity and the specific blessings are not particularly significant. Elsewhere, Paul associated **Christ** with **love** (Rom. 8:35) and **fellowship** (1 Cor. 1:9). He also set **God** alongside grace. Further, he associated the Holy Spirit with both **love** (Col. 1:8) and **grace** (i.e., *charismata* or "gifts of grace," 1 Cor. 12:4).

Paul prayed for **grace, love,** and **fellowship** with the persons of the Trinity because these blessings are so essential to the spiritual well-being of the church. Divine **grace** is the unmerited mercy of God toward his people, granting them forgiveness of sin. Divine **love** is God's affection and loyalty toward his true people that secures them in a saving relationship with him. Divine **fellowship** is the experience of the nearness of God that encourages and empowers believers in their daily walk before him.

Paul wanted all this and more for the congregation at Corinth. Despite the troubles they had given him over the years, his desire was to see them enjoy the rich blessings of God in their lives. If they would take his epistle to heart, they would surely receive those blessings.

MAIN IDEA REVIEW: *Paul encouraged the Corinthians to prepare for his upcoming visit. He wanted them to repent of their sin and to think rightly about Paul and those who would accompany him so they would be well received.*

III. CONCLUSION

Preparations

In this closing section Paul tied together many of the themes he had touched throughout this epistle, focusing especially on the significance of his upcoming visit. Paul hoped the Corinthian church would take to heart his many instructions before he arrived and that they would prepare appropriately. If they did not, he would be sure to address these matters more forcefully when he came. Paul desired God's blessing on the Corinthians, but he knew this blessing would not come apart from their submission to his apostolic instruction.

PRINCIPLES

- The longer we delay conforming our behavior and attitudes to our knowledge of Scripture, the more we risk God's discipline and judgment.
- There are always some people in the church who are not saved.
- Paul called on the Corinthians to examine themselves to see if they were in the faith.
- Salvation produces the fruit of good works.

APPLICATIONS

- Christian leaders must hold the church accountable for its profession of faith.
- We ought to repent and correct our sin when we discover it.
- If we are in serious and consistent sin, we should test ourselves to see if we are in the faith.

IV. LIFE APPLICATION

No More Time for Practice

The big day had come. Joan was waiting behind the stage to give her first piano recital. In the weeks before that day, she had practiced occasionally, but she really hadn't been very disciplined. So now that she was next, Joan was unsure of herself.

As her piano teacher walked by, Joan looked at her and complained, "I wish I could practice just one more time."

But her teacher put her hand on Joan's shoulder and said, "There's no more time for practice now, Joan. It's the moment of truth."

Lots of things in life are like this. We have opportunities to prepare for some performance or action. But eventually the time comes when there is no more time for practice. We cannot escape showing what we can or cannot do.

In these closing chapters of his epistle, Paul told the Corinthians that the time of their trial was close at hand. He had given them many opportunities to correct the problems in their personal lives and in their church. He had been patient. But the next contact they would have with him would be face-to-face. Paul had put up with their problems long enough. It was time for them to receive his instructions and to act on them. It was time to perform— no more practice.

Paul's closing words to the Corinthians have many implications for the lives of modern Christians. We do not face an imminent visit from an apostle as the Corinthians did, but we know that we should not delay responding faithfully to the Word of God. We never know when God's patience with our disloyalty may end.

V. PRAYER

Father, we know that we do not always obey you, and that we sometimes fall into serious sin. Thank you for being patient with us and for allowing us time to repent. Please forgive us for our sins, and help us repent wholeheartedly so that we can obey, adore, and praise you more. Amen.

VI. DEEPER DISCOVERIES

A. Christ Is Speaking Through Me (13:3)

In one sense, whenever a person proclaims the truth of Scripture, he or she speaks the word of God—the true word about and from God. In another sense, when one proclaims the true gospel, it may be argued that God actually speaks through that person. In this verse Paul meant that his words were actually spoken by Christ through him, but he also meant something more. Paul asserted that Christ was speaking through him in order to prove that he carried Christ's delegated authority ("he is not weak in dealing with you"). He was Christ's ambassador, Christ's representative, and as such held a position of authority.

B. Lord Jesus Christ . . . God . . . the Holy Spirit (13:14)

The doctrine of the Trinity—God exists in three persons, one essence—is not taught clearly in any single passage of Scripture. But the New Testament shows that its authors assumed the truth of this doctrine. Clearly, the Father is a distinct person from his Son Jesus Christ (Matt. 24:36), Jesus Christ is a distinct person from the Holy Spirit (John 14:26), and the Holy Spirit is a distinct person (Eph. 4:30) from the Father (Luke 11:13). Further, the Holy Spirit is divine (John 16:7), the Son Jesus Christ is divine (John 1:1; 20:28), and the Father is divine (Rom. 1:7). Moreover, there is only one God (Eph. 4:6).

VII. TEACHING OUTLINE

A. INTRODUCTION

1. Lead Story: Ruining a Visit
2. Context: Paul was ready to visit the church in Corinth, but the Corinthians had not repented of their sin. If they did not repent before he came, he would discipline them when he arrived. He hoped that by warning them of this possibility, he could inspire them to repent. If they followed his counsel and repented, their visit could be a pleasant one, and Paul could use the time to build up the church.
3. Transition: Sometimes we also find great sin in the modern church. When we do it is time to repent. Paul warned the Corinthians for two reasons: (1) God might remove blessings from the church if they failed to repent and (2) it was his job to build up the church and to encourage it to pursue further blessing from God. We face the same threats today. If we remain in our sin, God may remove blessings

from our churches, choosing instead to discipline us. If we repent, he may be pleased to bless us even more.

B. COMMENTARY

1. A Pledge of Good Intentions (12:14–18)
    a. Paul's motive: love and concern (12:14–15)
    b. Paul's record: no exploitation (12:16–18)
2. Everything for Their Good (12:19–21)
    a. Paul's intention in defending himself: strengthen the Corinthians (12:19)
    b. Reason for strengthening the Corinthians: fears they are caught in sin and may not repent (12:20–21)
3. Final Warning (13:1–10)
    a. Paul will discipline unrepentant sinners (13:1–2)
    b. Disciplining sinners will demonstrate the legitimacy of Paul's ministry (13:3–4)
    c. Testing faith (13:5–6)
    d. Prayer for the Corinthians' perfection (13:7–9)
    e. Final exhortation to repent (13:10)
4. Final Good-By (13:11–14)
    a. Exhortations (13:11–12)
    b. Encouragement (13:13)
    c. Benediction (13:14)

C. CONCLUSION: NO MORE TIME FOR PRACTICE

VIII. ISSUES FOR DISCUSSION

1. When had Paul previously visited the Corinthians? How did his previous visits with the Corinthians affect his tone and content in this section of the letter?
2. How well does the description of the Corinthian Christians' sin describe your own church and its sins? If Paul wrote to your church, what issues might he address?
3. Why did Paul give the Corinthians so many warnings? Why had he not disciplined them earlier? How often does your church deal with disciplinary matters?
4. Was Paul suggesting that the Corinthians should examine one another, or that each person should examine only himself or herself?

Glossary

apostles—Men chosen by Jesus as his official messengers; this term refers generally to his twelve disciples

baptism—The immersion or dipping of a believer in water symbolizing the complete renewal and change in the believer's life and testifying to the death, burial, and resurrection of Jesus Christ as the way of salvation

body of Christ—The church, the unity in Christ of diverse Christians

church—The community of those who believe in and follow Jesus Christ; used to designate a congregation, a denomination, or all Christians

conversion—God's act of changing a person's life in response to the person's turning to Christ in repentance and faith from some other belief or from no belief

discipline—Instruction or training used by God to train his children in righteous living

faith—Belief in and personal commitment to Jesus Christ for eternal salvation

gospel—The good news of the redeeming work of God through the life, death, and resurrection of Jesus Christ

grace—Undeserved acceptance and love received from another, especially the characteristic attitude of God in providing salvation for sinners

Holy Spirit—The third person of the Trinity; the presence of God promised by Christ and sent to his disciples at Pentecost representing God's active presence in the believer, the church, and the world

joy—The inner attitude of rejoicing in one's salvation regardless of outward circumstances

judgment—God's work at the end time involving condemnation for unbelievers and assignment of rewards for believers

Law—God's instruction to his people about how to love him and others; when used with the definite article "the," *law* may refer to the Old Testament as a whole but usually to the Pentateuch (Genesis through Deuteronomy)

love—God's essential quality that seeks the best interests of others regardless of the others' actions; love is commanded of believers

minister—The loving service of Christians to each other and to those outside the church in the name of Jesus

mission—The God-given responsibility of the church and each believer to bring God's love and the Christian gospel to all people through evangelism, education, and ministry; missions is used especially to refer to work done by Christians outside their own culture

ordinances—The two symbolic acts Jesus commanded the church to observe: the Lord's Supper and baptism; referred to by some church groups as sacraments

perseverance—The response of enduring even in the face of difficulty; Christians develop this trait by facing and overcoming hardship and adversity

reconciliation—The bringing together of alienated persons; the saving work of Christ and a ministry given believers

repentance—A change of heart and mind resulting in a turning from sin to God that allows conversion and is expressed through faith

resurrection—The raising of Jesus from the dead to eternal life; the raising of believers for eternal life with Christ; the raising of unbelievers to eternal punishment

sacrifice—According to Mosaic Law, an offering to God in repentance for sin or as an expression of thanksgiving; Christ as the ultimate sacrifice for sin

Glossary

salvation—Deliverance from trouble or evil; the process by which God redeems his creation, completed through the life, death, and resurrection of his Son Jesus Christ

sanctification—The process in salvation by which God conforms the believer's life and character to the life and character of Jesus Christ through the Holy Spirit

speaking in tongues—Use of language previously unknown to the speaker to praise God or to reveal God's message to hearers; a gift of the Holy Spirit

stewardship—Human responsibility to manage resources that God has placed in one's care

Trinity—God's revelation of himself as Father, Son, and Holy Spirit unified as one in the Godhead and yet distinct in person and function

universalism—The unbiblical belief that all people will ultimately experience salvation

Word of God—The Bible, God's inspired written revelation; God's message in oral form revealed through prophetic or angelic speakers; Jesus Christ, God's eternal Word in human flesh

Bibliography

Fee, Gordon. *The First Epistle to the Corinthians*. The New International Commentary on the New Testament. Grand Rapids: William B. Eerdmans Publishing Company, 1987.

Furnish, Victor Paul. *II Corinthians*. The Anchor Bible Commentary. Garden City: Doubleday & Company, Inc., 1984.

Grosheide, F. W. *Commentary on the First Epistle to the Corinthians*. The New International Commentary on the New Testament. Grand Rapids: Eerdmans Publishing Company, 1953.

Harris, Murray J. *2 Corinthians*. The Expositor's Bible Commentary. Grand Rapids: Zondervan Publishing House, 1976.

Hughes, Philip Edgcumbe. *Paul's Second Epistle to the Corinthians*. The New International Commentary on the New Testament. Grand Rapids: William B. Eerdmans Publishing Co., 1962.

Kistemaker, Simon J. *Exposition of the First Epistle to the Corinthians*. New Testament Commentary. Grand Rapids: Baker Books, 1993.

Kistemaker, Simon J. *Exposition of the Second Epistle to the Corinthians*. New Testament Commentary. Grand Rapids: Baker Books, 1997.

Kruse, Colin G. *The Second Epistle of Paul to the Corinthians*. The Tyndale New Testament Commentaries. Leicester: InterVarsity Press, 1987.

Mare, W. Harold. *1 Corinthians*. The Expositor's Bible Commentary. Grand Rapids: Zondervan Publishing House, 1976.

Morris, Leon. *The First Epistle of Paul to the Corinthians*. The Tyndale New Testament Commentaries. Leicester: InterVarsity Press, 1985.

Witherington, Ben, III. *Conflict & Community in Corinth*. Grand Rapids: William B. Eerdmans Publishing Co., 1995.

HOLMAN
REFERENCE

ALSO AVAILABLE:

THE HOLMAN COMMENTARIES SERIES – *Retail $19.99 ea.*

Old Testament

0-8054-9461-8	Genesis (Vol. 1)
0-8054-9462-6	Exodus, Leviticus, Numbers (Vol. 2)
0-8054-9463-4	Deuteronomy (Vol. 3)
0-8054-9464-2	Joshua (Vol. 4)
0-8054-9465-0	Judges, Ruth (Vol. 5)
0-8054-9467-7	1 & 2 Kings (Vol. 7)
0-8054-9468-5	1 & 2 Chronicles (Vol. 8)
0-8054-9469-3	Ezra, Nehemiah, Esther (Vol. 9)
0-8054-9470-7	Job (Vol. 10)
0-8054-9471-5	Psalms 1-75 (Vol. 11)
0-8054-9481-2	Psalms 76-150 (Vol. 12)
0-8054-9472-3	Proverbs (Vol. 13)
0-8054-9482-0	Ecclesiastes, Song of Songs (Vol. 14)
0-8054-9473-1	Isaiah (Vol. 15)
0-8054-9476-6	Daniel (Vol. 18)
0-8054-9477-4	Hosea, Joel, Amos, Obadiah, Jonah, Micah (Vol. 19)
0-8054-9478-2	Nahum-Malachi (Vol. 20)

New Testament

0-8054-0201-2	Matthew
0-8054-0202-0	Mark
0-8054-0203-9	Luke
0-8054-0204-7	John
0-8054-0205-5	Acts
0-8054-0206-3	Romans
0-8054-0207-1	1 & 2 Corinthians
0-8054-0208-X	Galatians-Colossians
0-8054-0209-8	1 Thessalonians-Philemon
0-8054-0211-X	Hebrews, James
0-8054-0210-1	1 & 2 Peter-Jude
0-8054-0212-8	Revelation

0-8054-2828-3   **NT Boxed Set Sale Price: $179.97** (Reg. $239.88)
(All Volumes Hardcover)

1-800-233-1123   www.broadmanholman.com